A BETTER GLOBALIZATION

Advance Praise for
A Better Globalization: Legitimacy, Governance, and Reform

"This is a thoughtful book by an experienced practitioner. Kemal Derviş' experience as a senior official at the World Bank followed by his work as a key policy maker in Turkey, and that too at a most difficult time, gives him the perspective needed to consider deep reforms in global governance and to discuss the complex politics involved in a global setting."

Montek Singh Ahluwalia
Deputy Chairman of the Planning Commission, India

"Reformers are frequently seen by decision makers as visionaries whose proposals make sense 'in theory' but never work 'in practice.' The author's proposals are both idealistic and practicable. Decision makers have no excuse. If they really feel committed to a better global governance, they cannot ignore this book by Kemal Derviş."

Giuliano Amato
Senator, Italian Senate
Former Prime Minister of Italy
Former Deputy President of the European Convention
Vice-President of the Party of European Socialists

"Kemal Derviş, who has lived and worked with international public institutions throughout his distinguished career, correctly sees global governance as the chief international problem to be solved by the coming generation. Among other proposals, his book presents one of the most imaginative solutions to the problem of reorganizing the United Nations that I have yet seen."

Francis Fukuyama
Bernard L. Schwartz Professor of International Political Economy
John Hopkins University, SAIS

"In the 21st century, international cooperation in diverse fields extending from economic matters to security issues, from environmental protection to the fight against disease is more important than ever. Using his national and international experience, Kemal Derviş addresses the key challenges of our time with imagination and determination."

Abdullah Gül
Deputy Prime Minister and Minister of Foreign Affairs of Turkey

"In the 21st century, ensuring that the benefits of globalization flow to all people will depend greatly on how well international institutions work to this end. Building on his extensive experience as Finance Minister of Turkey and from his decades of leadership at the World Bank, Kemal Derviş brings unique insight into improving the effectiveness and legitimacy of global institutions."

Paul Martin
Prime Minister of Canada

"This book is a thought-provoking contribution to the debate on globalization, the new ideological battleground of the 21st century. Striking a balance between idealism and pragmatism, Kemal Derviş makes a compelling case for building a new institutional architecture that is acceptable to advanced and developing countries alike, so that the benefits of globalization may be shared more equally. Ultimately, he demonstrates a reassuring belief in the power of good public policy to shape a better society and in the power of ideas to change the world."

George Papandreou
Former Foreign Minister of Greece
Chairman, Pan-Hellenic Socialist Party

"How can we enhance the legitimacy of globalization while rendering it more effective? Kemal Derviş weighs in on the greatest debate of our time with great authority, powerful arguments, and his characteristic humanism. Washington and Brussels better stand up and take notice!"

Dani Rodrik
Professor of International Political Economy, Harvard University

"Kemal Derviş played a critical role in his country's overcoming one of the worst economic crises of the post-war period. In this book he skillfully uses his extensive national and international experience to discuss some of the difficult global issues of our time."

Brent Scowcroft
Former US National Security Advisor
Member of the UN High Level Panel on
Threats, Challenges and Change
President of the Forum for International Policy

"For all of us who have been waiting to hear concrete proposals for introducing the missing human and social elements into the mechanical processes of globalization, this book is a most timely arrival. Derviş treats the problem in a remarkably comprehensive manner, considering the roles of all the relevant national and international actors and making suggestions for reform in each case, whether this be the United States or the United Nations."

Erdal İnönü
Former Deputy Prime Minister of Turkey
Former Chairman of the Turkish Social Democrat Party

"Kemal Derviş raises the right questions and provides excellent answers about fundamental global governance issues. If one is looking for out-of-the-box ideas on these matters, this is certainly the book to read."

Ernesto Zedillo
Former President of Mexico
Director, Yale Center for the Study of Globalization
Co-chairman, International Task Force on Global Public Goods

A BETTER GLOBALIZATION

Legitimacy, Governance, and Reform

KEMAL DERVIŞ

in cooperation with
CEREN ÖZER

CENTER FOR GLOBAL DEVELOPMENT
Washington, D.C.

A Better Globalization: Legitimacy, Governance, and Reform may be ordered from:

BROOKINGS INSTITUTION PRESS
1775 Massachusetts Avenue, N.W.
Washington, D.C. 20036
Tel.: 800/275-1447
202/797-6258
Fax: 202/797-6004
Internet: www.bibooks.edu

Library of Congress Cataloging-in-Publication data
Derviş, Kemal.
A better globalization : legitimacy, governance, and reform / Kemal Derviş in cooperation with Ceren Özer.
p.   cm.
Summary: "Discusses the two broad dimensions of the globalization debate—economic, including finance, trade, poverty, and health; and political, covering security, the fight against terrorism, and the role of international institutions—and the significance of democratic consent in the twenty-first century"—Provided by publisher.
Includes bibliographical references and index.
ISBN-13: 978-0-8157-1763-8 (pbk. : alk. paper)
ISBN-10: 0-8157-1763-6
1. Globalization. I. Özer, Ceren. II. Center for Global Development. III. Title.
JZ1318.D465 2005
337—dc22   2004029649

9 8 7 6 5 4 3 2 1

Typeset in Sabon

Composition by Cynthia Stock
Silver Spring, Maryland

Printed by R. R. Donnelley
Harrisonburg, Virginia

Don't look down on anyone,

Never break a heart,

The mystic must love all seventy-two nations.

YUNUS EMRE
*Turkish Sufi-Muslim poet and philosopher
of the thirteenth century*

Contents

Preface

Global markets require good global politics. Today we have globalization without representation—and thus without the checks and balances, the rule of law, the level playing field, and most important of all, the sense of ownership and legitimacy that democracy brings to market economies. That is the fundamental message of this new book.

From its inception, we at the Center for Global Development have been determined to deal not only with issues of efficiency and effectiveness in how the global system affects the world's poor, but with issues of fairness and legitimacy as well. This book attacks both issues squarely, calling for a re-thinking and reform of the international "governance" architecture set in stone after World War II now more than 60 years ago. In a world in which problems—of disease, drugs, and terror—have no respect for national borders, Kemal Derviş addresses what will surely emerge as a central challenge of this new century: What system of global governance would recognize the enduring importance of nation states while providing a greater sense of democratic legitimacy for the citizens of poorer and less powerful countries? Is it possible to reform the International Monetary Fund, the World Trade Organization, the United Nations, and other international institutions so that they are not only more effective but more respected and legitimate in the eyes of all the world's citizens? In a world of transnational threats, failing and undemocratic states, and limits to collective action, what does multilateralism mean in practice, both in the political and economic domains?

Kemal Derviş is an optimist. In his call for a better globalization, he invokes the example the Western liberal market democracies provide: of a synthesis between the benefits of unfettered markets and civilizing socialism. Navigating between careful realism and bold idealism, and drawing on his experience as a former senior official of the World Bank and a former minister of economy in Turkey, he formulates a vision encompassing both changes in the governance structures of the United Nations, the IMF, the World Bank, and the WTO and changes in certain of their policies and practices. Based on his experience as a member of the European Constitutional Convention, he uses the experience of Europe to argue that the 21st century requires forms of regional integration that do not compete with but are complementary to the progress of global governance.

Derviş argues that a better globalization requires change in both the political and economic domains and must start with a renewed and modernized United Nations. Within the overall and legitimizing umbrella of a modernized UN, the specialized institutions such as the World Bank, the IMF, the WTO, the UN agencies themselves, and such regional institutions as the regional development banks should preserve their operational autonomy. In the middle income countries like his own Turkey, the economic institutions should move beyond assistance for short-term stabilization efforts and develop mechanisms to bring down the excessive debt burdens inherited from the past. In the least-developed countries the rich countries should recognize the logic of a concerted big-push strategy to help these countries break out of the poverty and debt trap—a big push that will require a doubling of concessional resources but also well designed and comprehensive conditionality. Regarding trade, Derviş stresses that its tremendous potential to bring faster and more sustained growth to all countries will only be unleashed if and when the hearts and minds of people are won over to it. That requires transforming not only the WTO framework but the entire governance of the international economic system into something more responsive to people's concerns—in the rich and poor world alike. Change and adjustment need to be managed pro-actively so that losers can be compensated and overall gains realized.

The huge costs of armed conflict, the great challenges of state failure, the slow pace of international actions that would allow the world to reach the Millennium Development Goals, all point to the constraints to progress constituted by weaknesses in the global institutional framework and the need for more effective international cooperation. Burden sharing among rich countries and sustained policy and implementation reforms in the developing countries must come together within an international institutional architecture that is legitimate and effective. As recognized by the work of the High Level UN Panel appointed by Secretary-General Kofi Annan, as well as by the report prepared for the June 2003 EU summit by High Representative Xavier Solana, political and economic factors are inextricably linked in determining the extent of human security and development. If we want liberal democratic values to triumph and our security to be strengthened, we must recognize that "consent cannot stop at the borders of the nation state" (chapter 1) and that the institutional framework within which we all work on development and security must adapt to the requirements of the 21st century. The Center for Global Development is pleased to offer readers in this book a vision of a global institutional framework that is bold and deeply pragmatic, and in which our preoccupations with equity, democratic participation, and broad and sustained development progress around the world are central.

NANCY BIRDSALL
President, Center for Global Development
Washington, D.C.

Acknowledgments

I owe a huge debt of gratitude to many friends and colleagues for inspiring me and helping me complete this project. Ceren Özer, who was a researcher at the Center for Global Development and is now at the World Bank, provided invaluable support, not only doing a lot of the background research, but discussing many of the ideas. She often developed counterarguments to force us both to articulate a particular vision more clearly and helped me draft some important sections of the book. She has been a true partner throughout. Dan Robinson joined us as a summer intern in 2004 and contributed very valuable assistance in the final stages of drafting the manuscript.

The whole enterprise would not have been possible without Nancy Birdsall, president of the Center for Global Development. She provided an institutional anchor, logistic support, and much appreciated constant encouragement. She also, on several occasions, gave me challenging comments that helped me move forward. Nancy's leadership has made the Center a wonderful place to work; without my partial two summers there, I could not have written this book. Thanks are due to all the staff of CGD, and in particular

Steve Radelet, Bill Cline, Lawrence Macdonald, Kimberly Elliot, Milan Vainshaw, Jeremy Weinstein, Gunila Pettersson, Sarah Lucas, and Susan Nichols. Noora Aberman helped finalize the manuscript and coordinated the process of moving towards publication. David Einhorn improved the manuscript with careful and thoughtful editing.

While two four-week visits in the summers of 2003 and 2004 at the CGD were crucial for this project, a good part of the work was done on weekends in Istanbul and in between parliament sessions in Ankara and trips to events in Europe connected to European enlargement and Turkey's bid for membership in the Union. Banu Türk, researcher at the Forum for Economics and Foreign Policy in Istanbul, has provided and continues to provide me with enthusiastic and invaluable support. Gizem Ceylan, a student intern from Bosphorus University, helped particularly with the work on regional cooperation. I would also like to thank other staff of the FEFP as well as of the ARI movement for creating a cheerful office and pitching in when needed. Colleagues from the coordination group of the EFPF such as Sinan Ülgen, Can Buharalı, and Fuat Keyman and fellow parliamentarians such as Damla Gürel, Zülfü Livaneli, and Memduh Hacıoğlu provided very helpful comments on various issues. Faik Öztrak, my partner during crisis management time at the Turkish treasury, and Oya Ünlü Kızıl, who was my advisor and confidante first at the World Bank and then at the treasury, helped me over the years with many discussions. Thanks are also due to Osman Ulagay, himself an author of two books on global issues, for his encouragement. Bülent Eczacıbaşı and Cem Kozlu, two global Turkish business leaders with a strong social conscience, have offered good advice throughout the last two years. Yusuf Işık, my parliamentary advisor and friend of 40 years, has always been there with good ideas and warm friendship. Fırat Bayar has helped with discussions and comments.

The ideas presented owe a lot to my previous work at the World Bank and to many colleagues and friends there over the years, with the diversity of our worldviews and approaches stimulating heated debates. Special thanks for great discussions at various times are due to Masood Ahmed, Ataman Aksoy, Mahmood Ayub, Amar Bhattacharya, Ajay Chhibber, Uri Dadush, Stanley Fischer, Harinder Kohli, Caio Koch-Weser, Anne Krueger, John Page, Nicolas Stern, Joseph Stiglitz, Margret Thalwitz, Roberto Zagha, Christine Wallich, and others too numerous to name. There is one, however, no longer with us, to whom I owe a special debt, and that is Wilfried Thalwitz, boss, friend, and great world citizen. I am also very grateful to Joy Vendryes and Nathalie Tavernier for their invaluable and cheerful assistance over many years.

This book draws on the many meetings and exchanges with friends who share the hope and passion for a better globalization across the world. Many have already made critical contributions as political or intellectual leaders to greater justice and better governance. I would like to thank in particular Montek Ahluwalia, Giuliano Amato, Pervenche Beres, Matt Browne, Ozan Ceyhun, Olaf Cramme, Anthony Giddens, Elizabeth Guigou, Antonio Guterrez, Francis Fukuyama, Mary Kaldor, Maria Joao Rodriguez, Pierre Schori, Dominique Strauss Kahn, Peter Mandelson, Marcel Mersch, Moises Naím, Vural Öğer, Cem Özdemir, George Papandreou, Poul Nyrup Rasmussen, Jean Michel Severino, Gayle Smith, Bernard Soulage, Strobe Talbott, Christoph Zöpel, and Peter Westmacott. I have had excellent discussions on global and regional issues with my colleagues from the Balkan commission including Carl Bildt, François Heisbourg, Ilir Meta, as well as Sandra Breka from the Bosch Foundation, whose knowledge and enthusiasm helped us all so much. Some of the inspiration for this book comes from my earlier days working on the Balkans and from the spirit of the people of Sarajevo, a city where four great religions lived together harmoniously in a secular society before it had to go through a war imposed on it by a return to the tribalism of the past. It survived with great courage and, I hope, will soon again be a thriving European capital.

Many thanks are also due to all my colleagues on the International Task Force for Global Public Goods, in particular Sven Sandstrom, the project director, and Gareth Evans, Enrique Iglesias, and Nafis Sadik, who were also on the high level UN panel on security issues, and with whom I have had good discussions on UN reform. I am deeply grateful to Ernesto Zedillo, president of the Task Force and former president of Mexico, for his very special encouragement to be bold in my proposals, his incisive comments and the example he sets as a global intellectual and political leader. I have also benefited from careful comments by Stephanie Griffith-Jones.

Erdal has been both sympathetic and a tough critic, always there when I needed him. Erol, who almost always beats me at chess, has also been supportive, not least by reminding me that life has so many dimensions. My deep gratitude goes to Catherine, who encouraged me from the start, helped me set myself deadlines, argued endlessly with me on substance and style, and often lifted my spirits just in time with praise right after engaging in some thoughtful and difficult to counter critique. The responsibility for shortcomings remains, of course, entirely my own.

Introduction

While my generation was growing up and when we went to college in the 1960s and 1970s, intercontinental missiles were pointed at many cities of the world. Reading now about the Cuban missile crisis or the early 1970s, when fear over oil supplies triggered plans for US military intervention in the Middle East that could have possibly provoked Soviet retaliation, we realize how close the world came to nuclear holocaust during those decades. Quite paradoxically, I suspect that most of us felt "safer" in those days; we boarded aircraft without anybody searching our luggage, and we did not worry about attacks on our trains, yet the danger of massive destruction on a global scale was very real. When the Berlin Wall was removed a decade and a half ago, the imminent threat of nuclear war disappeared with it. The end of the Cold War allowed the projection of a global future of reduced conflict with heightened prospects for worldwide peace and security. Unfortunately, while we seem to have escaped, at least for now, the danger of nuclear holocaust, few would argue today that we live in a world that is secure and peaceful. Terror has replaced intercontinental missiles as a source of insecurity that we feel in our daily lives. Moreover, the threat of nuclear mass destruction may reappear in the not so distant future: the capacity to destroy is, if anything, greater today than ever before. The technology of war has become even more deadly, and, after a brief decrease in the early 1990s, worldwide expenditures on armaments have increased despite the end of Cold War rivalry. Teenagers growing up today in China, the Middle East, Europe, or the United States can communicate with each other over the Internet and share insights, hopes, and questions in a way that has truly revolutionized the world. And yet it is not clear that they have a safer future than their parents had. Far from enjoying the peace dividend that we hoped for in the early 1990s, we now feel a deep sense of insecurity as high officials declare that the worst terror is yet to come. Expenditures on armaments increase unabated while budget cuts often reduce expenditures on basic human needs. Can we not build institutions and forms of cooperation that would bring much greater safety and allow the advances of technology to go hand in hand with real security? The debate about Iraq has shown how little agreement there is on what constitutes legitimate international action in the security sphere or what can be defined as an imminent or future threat. Inevitably there will be debates over future threats, some of which will probably be much greater than the threat Iraq was purported to pose. We should prepare global governance mechanisms to deal with future crises now rather than wait until it is too late.

In the economic sphere, while there may be debate about exact numbers, the empirical evidence is quite clear: over the last two decades a greater number of people have been able to escape extreme poverty than ever before in human history. Astonishing technological breakthroughs and their implementation in an increasing number of countries and sectors have unleashed a process of transformation and growth that dwarfs the industrial revolution of the 18th and 19th centuries. China, with a current population of 1.3 billion people, has been growing on average at a rate exceeding 8 percent per year for over two decades. India, with almost as large a population, has realized growth close to 6 percent per annum since the mid-1980s. Production for the world market and productivity growth spurred by global integration of production circuits have been important sources of this growth. Productivity growth in the United States has also been at a historical high, allowing the US economy to grow at about 3 percent on average per annum over the last two decades, a remarkable performance for what is the "frontier" economy in terms of technology and know-how. Japan and some European countries have not grown much over the last fifteen years, but they maintain living standards close to or in some cases higher than those in the United States. Other developed countries, such as Spain, Ireland and Korea, have grown more rapidly than the United States.

Despite this unprecedented economic growth, there is a great deal of discontent and insecurity throughout the world. Many countries and regions seem altogether excluded from the process of global development. Africa and the Middle East have, with the exception of a few countries, essentially stagnated over the last two decades. Per capita income growth in Latin America has also been disappointingly slow, again, with some exceptions. In Europe, very high unemployment rates have destroyed the feeling of success and shared prosperity that characterized the postwar period. Even in the United States, labor-saving technical progress and global outsourcing seem to prevent GDP growth from creating much new employment in recent years, and there is a great deal of job insecurity. The same outsourcing undoubtedly contributes to growth, including employment growth, in the developing countries. Nevertheless, the conditions of that employment can be quite degrading. The *Financial Times*, hardly a radical critic of capitalist globalization, reported on research conducted by Cafod, a UK-based Catholic development charity. The research documents the harsh and often humiliating experiences of workers in emerging-market economies who make personal computers, printers, monitors, and components for the electronics industry. Young women often work illegally below the minimum wage, sometimes 16 hours a day, 7 days a week. One report describes how workers are screened to secure the most docile labor force. Psychometric tests ensure that creative and imaginative minds do not get through: candidates who drew a small unadorned stick tree were likely to be chosen while those who drew trees with big root systems, colored in the leaves, and put fruit on the branches displayed too much ambition and imagination.[1]

One can argue that at least such workers are employed and that, despite difficult and sometimes degrading conditions, they are likely to escape extreme poverty over time. There is no doubt that direct foreign investment has created many jobs and has been very beneficial to countries such as China, India, Mexico, Brazil, and many others, despite the

---

1. John Authers and Alison Maitland, "The Human Cost of the Computer Age," *Financial Times* (London), January 26, 2004, London Edition 1, p. 10.

difficult labor market conditions, particularly in the informal sectors, mentioned above. However, there are hundreds of millions of human beings in remote rural areas or urban slums who, excluded from the world economy altogether, are even worse off than the modern equivalents of the exploited labor masses of 19th century Europe.

The uncomfortable truth is that in this age of instant communication and global integration there are enormous inequalities separating human beings, with billions barely subsisting, billions working in incredibly difficult conditions, and a small elite commanding a mind-boggling degree of wealth. Perhaps such visible and extreme inequality would be more acceptable if it were not for the recurrent financial crises leading to job losses and insecurity, even in the richer countries, and the persistent extreme poverty in large parts of the world. But economic crises, a deep sense of insecurity, and extreme poverty remain defining characteristics of early 21st century globalization, threatening our confidence in the future and undermining our ability to harness knowledge and technology to create the security and prosperity we long for.

Does it really have to be this way? How can we counter the increasing threat from terror? How can preventive action be legitimate? Can we foresee and try to forestall tomorrow's biggest dangers? In the economic sphere, can we not build a process of globalization that brings about greater equality while creating wealth and eradicating poverty? Must emerging-market economies really have to experience the kinds of devastating crises we saw in Latin America, Asia, Russia, and Turkey, where real incomes often fell by 15 percent or more? How can the political and economic spheres of the "international system" interact in a more constructive manner to lead to both greater security and greater prosperity?

These are the questions, asked by many, that have led me to write this book. A great number of books on globalization and global governance have been published over the last few years. Some have become bestsellers, such as Joseph Stiglitz's *Globalization and Its Discontents,* while others have much smaller audiences; some reflect enthusiasm about globalization, such as Jagdish Bhagwati's *In Defense of Globalization* and Martin Wolf's *Why Globalization Works,* while others underline negative aspects; some are grounded in political theory and sociology, as is the work of Anthony Giddens, David Held, or Ulrich Beck, while others are more focused on economics and finance, such as the many volumes triggered by the Asian crisis. Some are written from an American perspective, such as Zbigniew Brezinski's *The Choice* or Joseph Nye's *Soft Power,* others from a more European perspective, such as Dominique Strauss-Kahn's *The Flame and the Ashes* and Jean-Francois Bayart's *The Government of the World* or Ralf Dahrendrof's *The New Beginning of History*. The growing literature reflects the need to recast much of the analysis of economic policy options and social issues into a global framework.

The objective of this book is to contribute the special perspective of someone who has acutely felt the tensions and difficulties in reconciling the new global world with national roots, the requirements of international markets with the need for political legitimacy, and policies appropriate to the global age with politics that remain very much a local affair. After teaching economics in Turkey and the United States for six years, I was active in an international institution, the World Bank, for over twenty years, learning about the world and trying to contribute to economic development, enjoying it, often frustrated by the lack of progress but sometimes hopeful about reforms, realizing again and again that technical knowledge without political legitimacy can only achieve limited results. In the spring of 2001 I was called to steer my country's economy out of one of the worst financial crises ever experienced by an emerging-market economy. This time sitting on the other side of the table, I had to negotiate with the IMF and the World Bank and try to rally the finance ministers of the G-7 countries to Turkey's support. I was then elected to the Turkish Parliament—after the worst of the crisis was over and the economy rebounded—a "global man" in national politics. The Turkish Parliament sent me to Brussels, representing the left-of-center opposition, to participate in the "Convention" on the future of Europe that was drafting a new constitution for the enlarging European Union. This was a unique experience, during which we debated the need for and the limitations of supra-national governance, the future of the nation-state, the principle of subsidiarity, the separation of Church (or Mosque) and State and the "frontiers" of Europe. I learned a lot from my colleagues there, such as Giuliano Amato, former prime minister of Italy and vice president of the Convention, and many others. This was also a period during which I became involved with progressives from around the world who were working on defining the "ideological" agenda for the first decade of our new century. I had the privilege of participating in the Global Progressive Governance network and conferences supported by the British Labour Party, the Global Progressive Forum headed by Poul Nyrup Rasmussen and his team, meetings of the club "A Gauche en Europe" organized by Dominique Strauss Kahn and his friends, the Symi Symposiums led by

George Papandreou each summer, and in other meetings and networks that were often in the context of the Socialist International led by Antonio Guterrez. I also continue to be part of and take great enjoyment in working with a Task Force on Global Public Goods headed by Ernesto Zedillo and Tidjane Thiam and a special Commission on the Future of the Balkans headed by Giuliano Amato.

The teaching of international economics, life and work in an international institution (including my last assignment at the World Bank as the vice president in charge of coordinating the global fight against poverty), the struggle to save my own "emerging-market country" from economic and financial collapse, and then work on the enlarged supra-national European Union of the 21st century, all led to a strong desire to synthesize some of the experience I gained and the thoughts I developed in a volume on global governance. As students in the late 1960s at the London School of Economics we still possessed the "modern" certainties nourished by positivist thinking and believed in nearly "linear" progress led by social engineering. More than three decades of experience with development and public policy in a world more strongly influenced by "postmodern" uncertainties and relativism has taught me to be cautious and to appreciate the fragility of human progress. I have not, however, given up my belief in the possibility of real progress, in the perfectibility of human society, and in the power of good public policy. The recent report on Europe's role in the world produced under the leadership of former prime minister Poul Nyrup Rassmussen of Denmark is entitled "The Will to Change the World." I still believe, along with the authors of that report, in the power of ideas to change the world. The world is not the happy community almost uniformly benefiting from economic growth that some enthusiasts or apologists of the current order depict. The world also remains extremely unsafe. Some of the most enthusiastic supporters of "laissez-faire" economic globalization sometimes seem to forget that political events triggered by a social crisis or war can undo decades of progress. There is indeed the need for a "will to change the world" that will translate into new policies and institutional reform.

The solution does not at all lie in a rejection of globalization or a retreat into new forms of autarchy, but in the deliberate invention and building of a new institutional setting that will *govern* the process of increasing interdependence and integration among countries, regions, and peoples of the world. Without pretending to reach their philosophical depth, the approach in this essay follows the lead of social democrat thinkers such as Karl Polanyi and Jürgen Habermas, who have emphasized the critical importance of political *institutions* and political *ideology* in shaping events, as opposed to the belief that history unfolds due to forces inherent in human society and quite beyond the control of public policy. The key problem we are facing at the beginning of the 21st century is that too many of our political ideas and institutions still reflect the post–World War II world of nation-states recovering from war and emerging from decolonization and characterized by manufacturing-dominated economic structures, while we have now entered a truly new era of global structures, service- and communication-dominated economic activity, and with it, new forms of alienation and insecurity.

The search for answers to these new challenges must acknowledge the enthusiasm and vigor of what I would like to call the "Porto Alegre Spirit." The belief in change, the refusal to conform, the revolt against injustice, the celebration of diversity and freedom, the eagerness to network globally; these are all part of that spirit that made a success of the first "alterglobalization" meeting, which took place in the Brazilian town of Porto Alegre in 2001 at the same time as the rich and powerful met in Davos. We must reach beyond protest, however, to really confront the threats and build the future while being mindful of the dangers inherent in excessive social engineering. Walden Bello, a prominent sociologist from the Philippines and an "anti-corporate globalization" activist, criticizes the idea "that the challenge is to replace the neo-liberal rules with social democratic ones," which he views "as a remnant of a techno-optimist variant of Marxism that infuses both the Social-Democratic and Leninist visions of the world, producing what Indian author Arundathi Roy calls the predilection for gigantism."[2] I think one must take this warning against positivist excess seriously in light of the failures of over-centralized models of governance practiced by the totalitarian left at the national level in the past. Surely, however, the solution cannot be a retreat into small-scale production and autarchy of the type sometimes advocated by many of the anti-globalization activists such as, for example, Martin Khor, who wants to see "Gandhi-style community based, self-reliant family units of production, trading mainly within the community and the region and only making occasional exchanges with the rest of the world, as needed."[3] The risks and new forms of dependencies created by

2. Bello (2002).

3. Martin Khor quoted in "A Better World Is Possible: Alternatives to Economic Globalization," Report of the International Forum on Globalization (2002, p. 14).

global markets are real, but we cannot undo technological progress and the growth of interdependence—nor should we want to, because there is fantastic scope in using technology and its diffusion worldwide as well as international trade to overcome poverty, disease, and human suffering and foster unprecedented prosperity. Instead of a retreat into a mythical past, we must work towards a set of practical proposals that will make the *democratic* governance of globalization possible and provide us with security and justice both in the political sphere and the economic sphere of the international system. "Embedded Liberalism"[4] must be replaced by "Embedded Globalization." There will only be progress toward such global governance if it is grounded in democratic values and practice, respectful of cultural diversity, avoidant of the dangers of gigantism and bureaucratism by leaving what can be decided locally to local levels of public policy, and able to gain the allegiance of majorities across the globe.

Achieving such global governance is, of course, a huge challenge. I have tried to address the challenge and reach a broad audience interested in a reform process based on cooperation and democratic values. The reforms must also be based on sound economics and build on what we have learned from experience. I have tried to go beyond generalities and to offer some specific proposals on both security-related and economic matters. Given that this book is an individual effort, it cannot go into quantitative detail of the kind found in some of the analysis provided by large institutions or task forces. It is only by debating specific reforms, however, that we can test general approaches and frameworks proposed in the context of globalization. Many now recognize, for example, that despite unprecedented military and economic power, the United States must seek a world order based on cooperation and legitimacy if it wants to be more secure. But what does this mean concretely in terms of reform of the United Nations, the operation of the international financial institutions, and the management of world trade? We are at the beginning of a long and difficult road, but not moving rapidly in this direction will cost us dearly. If this book succeeds in contributing some ideas on how to accelerate the movement and manages to build some bridges between those who would like to see change but worry about feasibility and those young people who dream courageously without yet having had experience with the tough process of real life reform, it will have fulfilled its aim.

---

4. Ruggie (1982) introduced the term "embedded liberalism," referring to the political and institutional context in which markets are allowed to operate and allocate resources.

1 The End and the New Beginning of History

Everything has been globalized except our consent. . . . Democracy alone has been confined to the nation state. It stands at the national border, suitcase in hand, without a passport.

GEORGE MONTBIOT
The Age of Consent, 2003

The great ideological struggle between the Soviet and Western models of society, which in essence constitutes the history of the 20th century, reached new levels of intensity only a generation ago, with fierce ideological debates raging on campuses and in election campaigns. In Vietnam and other parts of Asia, as well as in Latin America and Africa, the struggle took place on battlefields.

That "history" ended in the early 1990s, as announced ahead of time by Francis Fukuyama in his celebrated and prescient article published several months before the fall of the Berlin Wall.[1] Since then a new beginning of history has unfolded in the form of a wide-ranging and increasingly passionate debate about globalization.[2] This book is about the globalization debate. It is about the politics and the economics of globalization and the significance of democratic consent in the 21st century. The debate is ideological, in the classical 20th century sense, as illustrated by the arguments and passions unleashed by the war in Iraq or the meetings of the World Trade Organization (WTO). The "end of history" did take place in the early 1990s only to give place to a "new history." Humanity has not exhausted the great ideological debates; they are only changing in nature. The beginning of the 21st century is being shaped by a great ideological debate about the nation-state and global governance, about the

1. Fukuyama's article "The End of History" was first published in the summer 1989 issue of *The National Interest*. Fukuyama (1992) expands on the original article.
2. Ralf Dahrendorf, in his collected essays entitled *Der Wiederbeginn der Geschichte,* uses the same metaphor about a new beginning of history (Dahrendorf 2004).

legitimacy of the use of power, and about public policy at the local, regional, national, and supranational levels, all against a backdrop of huge inequalities in wealth, income, and power that divide the world.

This global debate has two broad dimensions related to economics and security. The economic discussions focus on financial volatility, world trade, the pace and quality of global growth, the distribution of income, the need to fight global poverty, and related health and environmental issues.[3] These discussions draw on economic theory and the analysis of economic institutions. Mainstream economists often use the concept of public goods at the global level to analyze the challenges facing public policy.[4] More generally, many of the books and articles dealing with the economic aspects of globalization focus on capital markets or trade and on the role of the International Monetary Fund (IMF), World Bank, and WTO.

The other major dimension of the global debate is conducted in essentially political terms, focusing on security, the fight against terrorism, the projection of US power worldwide, the role of the United Nations, and new versions of global balance-of-power analysis. Here, authors draw on political theory and history as well as international relations theory.[5] The "modern" political debate on international relations and global governance goes back to ancient Greece and Rome, with classical roots in the works of philosophers such as Thucydides *(History of the Peloponnesian War)* and Marcus Aurelius *(Meditations),* and that of great philosophers such as Dante, Hobbes, Grotius, Rousseau, Montesquieu, Kant, and Hegel, to name some of those who have been influential beyond their times. Karl Marx and Marxist theories of imperialism remain influential among writers such as Eric Hobsbawm, David Harvey, and Samir

3. See, for example, Eatwell and Taylor (2000); Rodrik (1997); Stiglitz (2001, 2003); Kenen (1994, 2001); Kuczynski and Williamson (2003); Fischer (1998, 2001, 2002, 2003); Bhagwati (2004); Wolf (2004); Stern (2002); Woods (2000, 2001); Ocampo (2000); and the Global Economic Prospects Series published by the World Bank, which contains quantitative analysis of economic globalization. For a thorough introduction to the globalization debate, see Held and McGrew (2002a, 2002b, 2003).

4. A very useful collection of essays looking at the challenge in terms of global public goods can be found in Kaul, Grunberg, and Stern (1999). See also the more recent UNDP volume entitled *Providing Global Public Goods,* edited by Inge Kaul et al. (2003).

5. A few examples are Gilpin (2001); Russet (1997); Rosenau (1992); Alger (1998); Childers (1997); Childers and Urquhart (1994); and Keohane (2002). Brzezinski (2004) focuses on the fundamental "choice" the United States faces in its foreign and security policy, but in the process offers an overall political analysis of globalization.

Amin.[6] The political part of the globalization debate thus has roots in human thought that are much more ancient than the modern economics of global public goods or international capital markets.

Anthony Giddens (1998) was quite correct when he wrote in his influential book *The Third Way: The Renewal of Social Democracy:* "The term globalization has come from nowhere to be everywhere in a period of just a decade. . . ." Indeed, it is not possible to look at the politics or the economics of the emerging world of the 21st century without making globalization a central feature of the analysis. The debate about the nature of globalization, its direction, whom it benefits, the survival of the nation-state, the "right" to intervene across borders, and other related matters has replaced the old "capitalism versus socialism" debate. The intensity of the debate and the passions around it will increase with every subsequent event that challenges us to find solutions appropriate to the realities of the 21st century, whether it is another financial crisis, an epidemic, or further acts of terror.

A point of departure for what is to follow is that it is useful to look at the economics and the politics of globalization together, as part of the overall discussion of the international system.[7] Too often, economic problems and proposed solutions are discussed without a real political context. Making progress on the globalization debate with viable proposals for change can benefit from an analysis linking the economic and political dimensions and focusing on the legitimacy of political and institutional power. This linkage is essential because without greater legitimacy at the supranational level, progress in solving global problems will be very difficult. Ideas for reform emerging from the economic debate face obstacles of an intrinsically political nature. Proposals for change in the

6. Hobsbawm (2000); Harvey (2003); and Amin (1996, 2004). In their much-publicized book *Empire* (2001), Michael Hardt and Antonio Negri use Marxist analysis and argue that as the sovereignty of nation-states erodes, a new global sovereignty, "Empire," emerges from the coalescence of "a series of national and supranational organisms united under a single logic of rule" with no clear international hierarchy.

7. Authors who linked political and economic aspects and tried to give an integrated overview include, for example, Kennedy (1993); Woods (2001); Rischard (2002); Held and Koenig-Archibugi (2003); Strauss-Kahn (2000); Cohen (2003); and Rasmussen (2003). Bhagwati (2004) and Wolf (2004) also include political aspects in their recent spiritedly argued defenses of globalization, although they remain books focused on the economics of globalization. Singer (2004) discusses globalization as a philosopher from the point of view of ethics, linking political and economic aspects. Kozlu (1999) and Ulagay (2001) provide Turkish perspectives on globalization.

economic domain cannot succeed unless they include political willingness to take steps toward greater legitimacy in the exercise of power. Concern for economic efficiency and practicality must be part of the analysis and certainly must shape the proposals for change, but the globalization debate is really about fundamental worldviews, about ideology. Conversely, the debate about security issues should take into account the economic and financial implications of the options discussed. Some of the excessive emphasis on the purely military aspects of power that prevails in some of the neoconservative thinking in the United States neglects the economic implications of the proposed security policies.

The fall of the Iron Curtain has indeed marked an important turning point and has "ended" a certain period of history, a period that has shaped the lives of all of us who experienced the 20th century. In that sense, Fukuyama's message was powerful, correct, and prescient, since his original article appeared before the fall of the Berlin Wall. The 15 years that followed that momentous event have not led us, however, to reach a relatively safe haven. After a dramatic turn, history continues to take us into uncharted waters with tremendous dangers and promises.

A Brief History of Legitimacy

From Divine Right to the Common Will

More than ever, the exercise of power requires legitimacy. The ideological triumph of liberal democracy as the model of human political organization means that everywhere the exercise of power requires the consent of those that are governed. This need for legitimacy based on consent is widely acknowledged with regard to power exercised within national borders, but the same need has emerged in international affairs. The worldwide debate over American policies and actions in Iraq has been largely concerned with their legitimacy. Among those opposing the war, practically nobody had any sympathy for Saddam Hussein. During the Vietnam War, leftists in the streets of Europe and America had carried portraits of Ho Chi Minh; there were no portraits of Saddam in the massive antiwar protests ranging from London to Rome in 2003. Most protesters would not have hesitated one second if they had been given the choice between American democracy and Middle Eastern dictatorship. The protests were not directed at the American socioeconomic model, as they had been in the 1960s, but rather at what was perceived as the illegitimate use of power projected beyond borders without some form of international sanction. In a very different context, protests against the IMF in the streets of Buenos Aires, São Paolo, Prague, and Washington have also been directed fundamentally at what people perceive, rightly or wrongly, as an illegitimate use of power; in this case financial power.

Looking at history, even the most repressive political regimes have needed some degree of legitimacy. Viotti and Kauppi (1999) define legitimacy as the implication of the existence of right: that is when a government is said to have, or to have been granted, a right to govern based on such criteria as its popular acceptance, the legal or constitutional processes that brought it to or maintain it in a position of authority, the divine right of kings, or charismatic leadership that commands a following and thus contributes to the government's popular acceptance. Plainly, legitimacy is an accepted entitlement or sanction to rule. All governments depend on some combination of coercion and consent. Without consent, it is very difficult to exercise power; as Jean-Jacques Rousseau put it in *The Social Contract*: "The strongest is never strong enough to be always the master unless he turns might into right and obedience into duty."

Throughout post-Roman history, political legitimacy was linked to and derived from the religious realm.[8] Medieval kings in Europe were religious leaders or claimed to rule in the name of the divine. Unity of the church was one of the main pillars of Charlemagne's power. The Russian tsars assumed the role of supreme heads of Orthodox Christianity, claiming the status of protector of Orthodox Christians everywhere. The blueprint for Thai state-builders was Angkor, the great Cambodian kingdom that had been at its height from the 11th to the 13th centuries. From Angkor came ideas adapted originally from Indian Brahmanical thought, particularly such concepts of society as a divinely ordained hierarchy and of *devaraj*—the ruler as an immensely potent incarnation of a Hindu deity. In the Islamic world, the *Khalif* was both supreme religious leader and head of state. He did not have a divine character, but his exercise of power derived its legitimacy from his claim to enforce divine law.

---

8. In ancient Greece and Rome, the "link to God" was more tenuous. In Greece, the ruling aristocracy derived its legitimacy from lineages, tribes, and kinship vaguely related to Greek gods. The Roman Republic was essentially a secular state. It had no constitution but functioned as a system of agreed-upon procedures developed by tradition and administered by annually elected officials answerable to the Senate. The system deteriorated by the 2nd century and Augustus transformed it into a *principate* in which legitimacy was essentially derived from the emperor's leadership and military might. It is well known, of course, that in many ways the "classical age" was a precursor of modern times.

This "link to God" was the accepted foundation of legitimacy in most parts of the world up to the French and American Revolutions. There was, of course, debate as to how this mandate should function in practice. As early as in the first half of the 14th century, Dante Alighieri argued for a kind of "secularism" in proposing a world empire where the "authority of the Empire by no means depends on the church." The church and the universal empire were to be coordinate powers, each autonomous and supreme in its respective realms. The empire was to be guided by reason and philosophy, the church by faith and theology.[9] But Dante's emperor still was to derive his legitimacy from God—what Dante emphasized was that this link should be direct and not intermediated by the church or the Pope. It was only much later in the 18th century that the thinkers of the Enlightenment such as Montesquieu and Rousseau started to delink legitimacy from the religious realm and propose that the "common will of men" exercising human reason become the source of legitimacy.[10] The radical break with the past was symbolized in its most extreme form during the French Revolution by the cult of "Goddess Reason" (*Déesse Raison*), which was not an attempt to suppress all religion, but an early effort to establish the purely secular nature of the state. In most other countries the break with the past and with the religious basis of sovereignty was not as radical as what happened in France during the revolution. Nonetheless, the French Revolution was a watershed that deeply influenced developments in the 19th and 20th centuries in Europe and throughout the world.

It is important in this context to stress that the development of "secular and democratic legitimacy" was made possible by the emergence in Europe during the 17th century of the clearly territorially defined Westphalian nation-state. During the Middle Ages, the realms of power of the Pope, the Holy Roman Emperor, feudal lords, free cities, etc. overlapped a great deal. With the end of the Thirty Years' War and the peace agreement at Westphalia in 1648, Europe entered the age of the territorially based, sovereign nation-states. The protestant reformation had a lot to do with this since it made "Christian Unity" impossible and irreversibly

9. Dante's *De Monarchia* was placed on the church's list of banned books and not removed from it until the 20th century.

10. "Law in general is human reason, inasmuch as it governs all the inhabitants of the earth; the political and civil laws of each nation ought to be only the particular cases in which human reason is applied" (Montesquieu in *The Spirit of Laws*). "Only the general will can direct the forces of the state according to the purpose for which it was instituted, which is the common good" (Rousseau in *The Social Contract*).

undermined any hope for supranational universal authority exercised by the church. Economic forces such as the development of industry and other economic activities not associated with land ownership also contributed to undermining feudalism and allowing the establishment of centralized state power, as emphasized by Marx. Once the nation-state was established, the foundation was also laid for modern democratic legitimacy based on the "will of the people" living in that nation-state, although one and a half centuries separate the Peace of Westphalia from the French and American Revolutions.

One has to be careful not to generalize too quickly from European experience and history to the entire world. Nonetheless, the ideas of the European Enlightenment enabled both the French and the American Revolutions. European ideas spread throughout the world, with colonization and postcolonial emulation of the European nation-state. Most of the new countries that emerged from decolonization tried to establish themselves "as if" they were European nation-states, admittedly with very mixed success. The idea that legitimate power had to be based on the explicit consent of citizens in a territorially defined nation-state made steady progress throughout the 19th and 20th centuries.

It is telling that in the 20th century, most repressive regimes had to keep up the pretense of elections in order to proclaim some form of legitimacy. Even in kingdoms where the sovereign's authority still derived from the religious realm, the right to exercise power had to be linked to some form of parliamentary elections to reinforce the legitimacy of these regimes. In many countries, constitutional monarchy replaced absolute monarchy and even the most totalitarian dictatorship kept the appearance of a constitution endorsed by an election. In authoritarian secular regimes or in kingdoms, some of these elections were "won" by 99 percent of the vote and nobody was really fooled; but such was the need for at least a pretense of legitimacy that even the worst tyrants could not give up an attempt to legitimize themselves through elections! It is interesting to note in this context that authoritarian regimes deriving at least part of their legitimacy from the spiritual realm have often found it easier to allow some parliamentary opposition, whereas authoritarian regimes that could not claim any religion-linked legitimacy have tended to engineer completely overwhelming electoral majorities.[11]

11. In the Soviet Union up until 1987, elections usually were held with unopposed candidates, selected by the local office of the Communist Party, receiving 99 percent of the votes. Although engineered for complete victory, elections sometimes helped citizens to

With the fall of the Berlin Wall and the collapse of communist ideology as a serious contender in the clash of ideas, the liberal democratic view of legitimacy based on free and competitive elections in the context of a nation-state has become almost universally accepted, although still not always practiced. At the core of liberal democracy is universal suffrage, which is a necessary condition for legitimacy. There are other necessary conditions, however. Legitimacy also requires a competitive political context within which the right to vote is exercised. In the Soviet and fascist systems, elections had also been held, but these elections did not take place in a free "public space" of debate. They did not involve political parties competing against each other. Legitimacy, as understood in the liberal democracies, requires not only citizens who vote, but also a process of political competition and free debate, with elections taking place in that context. This process can vary according to different constitutions and national circumstances. In democracies, the "one citizen, one vote" principle does not translate into a "the majority can do whatever it wants" situation; it is qualified and augmented by fundamental rights of the individual and of minorities, as well as by requirements for supermajorities and/or "federalist" rules often giving subnational entities special weight in the way votes translate into majorities. Despite all these qualifications, the one citizen, one vote principle is nonetheless at the core of democratic legitimacy, reflecting the essential belief that legitimacy is conferred on governments and political decisions by the sum of individual citizens exercising their right to vote. We would not call a country a democracy today if a one person, one vote electoral process were not central to its political constitution, although this basic principle can be qualified, weakened, and augmented according to various complementary rules. It took humanity roughly two centuries to reach consensus on what is an acceptable process giving rise to legitimacy of governance in a nation-state. European countries have gone furthest in codifying this

---

make their concerns public: They used furnished paper ballots to write their requests for public services! Both Mussolini and Hitler secured absolute control by intimidation and violence, yet still held elections. Mussolini abolished universal suffrage in 1928 and restricted parliamentary elections to official candidates of the fascist Grand Council. After the 1933 elections, Hitler arrested or excluded 81 communist deputies and bribed the nationalist and the center party to get the enabling bill passed that gave him unlimited power. A month later all political parties were declared illegal. In North Korea, the constitution provides for the Supreme People's Assembly, the highest organ of state power, to be elected every five years by universal suffrage. The Communist Party fields a single list of candidates who run without opposition.

consensus within the framework of the Organization for Security and Cooperation in Europe (OSCE)[12] and the Copenhagen Criteria,[13] but there is worldwide agreement on the basic concept, and even in Africa, Asia, and the Middle East, some form of democracy is increasingly becoming the only "legitimate" political model, which means that sooner rather than later the remaining authoritarian regimes will democratize or collapse. In that sense, the history of the 19th and 20th centuries has ended.

The Social-Liberal Synthesis: Ideological Foundations of Legitimacy

Before going further, I would like to argue that the success of the liberal democratic model of national governance is not just the victory of a particular model of political governance, but also reflects a much deeper ideological convergence on economic and social affairs. The history of political legitimacy is not just the history of the evolution of political constitutions and of laws regulating electoral processes. While due competitive political processes and appropriate legal arrangements, together, are necessary conditions for the sense of legitimacy that exists in well functioning democracies, there is more to legitimacy than process. If there exist, within a given society, fundamentally irreconcilable views, let us call them ideologies, on what good "outcomes" are, due democratic process is unlikely to be able to confer a widely perceived legitimacy. For Fukuyama's "end of history" to take place, the world needed an end to fundamental ideological combat.

In the Western Europe of the first half of the 20th century, for example, the gap between the ideologies of the Left and Right was so large that democratic elections failed to provide the elected majorities with a legitimacy respected by all. When there is insufficient common ideological ground regarding economic and social matters, the votes of the "others"

12. The OSCE is the largest regional security organization in the world with 55 participating states from Europe, Central Asia, and North America. It is active in early warning, conflict prevention, crisis management, and postconflict rehabilitation. The OSCE deals with a wide range of security-related issues including arms control, preventive diplomacy, confidence and security building measures, human rights, democratization, election monitoring, and economic and environmental security. All OSCE participating states have equal status, and decisions are based on consensus.

13. The Copenhagen Criteria, accepted by the European Union in a summit meeting on the process of enlargement, require that a candidate country must have achieved "stability of institutions guaranteeing democracy, the rule of law, human rights and respect for and protection of minorities" before negotiations toward full EU membership can begin. See http://europa.eu.int/comm/enlargement/intro/criteria.htm.

tend to be rejected and the functioning of democracy is endangered. Take the electoral victory of the *Front Populaire* in France in 1936. Important elements of the French Right did not at all accept the legitimacy of the outcome. This rejection explains in no small measure the nature of the Vichy regime and the degree of collaboration that was possible between elements of the French Right and Nazi Germany.[14] It is worth adding that Hitler would never have come to power in Germany had the traditional German Right not feared an "illegitimate" electoral victory of the Left. Similarly and more generally from the 1920s into the 1960s, the communist Left in Europe never really accepted the legitimacy of elected noncommunist governments because the competing worldviews of the Marxist Left and the rest of the political spectrum were just too far apart. For communists in the postwar period, noncommunist electoral victories were due to the uneven distribution of wealth and economic power and did not establish democratic legitimacy. Process alone cannot ensure a strong degree of legitimacy. For electoral outcomes to be accepted by both winners and losers, there is also need for a set of widely shared basic values that translate into agreement on the overall socioeconomic model that constitutes the framework within which political competition takes place.

In contrast to the examples referred to above, the American and German elections in the years 2000 and 2002 illustrate the existence and importance today of such common ideological ground. Albert Gore, the democratic candidate who lost the 2000 presidential election, actually got a majority of the popular vote. Nonetheless, the electoral rules as interpreted by the US Supreme Court gave the victory to George Bush. Democrats and Republicans certainly hold very different views on a multitude of issues. There is sufficient shared ideological ground in the United States, however, to make one side accept the other's victory, even when the results are very close and open to interpretation. The same can be said for today's Germany. In September 2002, the difference in the number of votes between Social Democrats and Christian Democrats was less than 8,000 votes out of a total of 48 million.[15] One may imagine what would

---

14. The Vichy Regime was the nominal French government between 1940 and 1944. The regime was only quasi-sovereign over the unoccupied zone, which comprised two-fifths of the country to the southeast. The Vichy regime was established by Henri-Philippe Petain as head of state, who suspended the Constitution of the Third Republic of 1875 and the Parliament and transferred all powers to himself. *Liberté, Egalité, Fraternité* (Freedom, Equality, Brotherhood), the French national motto, was replaced by *Travail, Famille, Patrie* (Labor, Family and Country).

have happened in Germany, France, or Italy in the 1950s if the communists had evenly split the national vote with the Gaullists or the Christian Democrats. Whatever the supreme courts or the supreme electoral commissions would have decided about such close outcomes, the loser would have challenged the legitimacy of the winner. The fact that this does not happen in Western democracies today is due not to the electoral rules as such, but to the fact that there is an underlying and agreed-upon socioeconomic framework or common ideological ground shared by the overwhelming majority of the population.

With the fall of the Berlin Wall in 1989, the common ideological ground that already existed in Western Europe, North America, and Japan acquired a more global nature. It may be appropriate to call this common ideological ground the "social-liberal synthesis," a synthesis that has gained ground throughout the 20th century and that has become universally dominant since the Soviet version of Marxism lost its claim to be a credible alternative model of society. "Liberal" is used here in the European sense and denotes a belief in markets, individual enterprise, and democracy. "Social" refers to the traditions and values of equity, solidarity, and belief in the contribution an activist public policy can make to society that has characterized the political Left. In the United States the labels are different, but the basic substance of the common ideological ground that has emerged in the second half of the 20th century is similar to what emerged in Europe, although it is fair to say that the American center is to the right of the European center. It is because of the ideological strength of the social-liberal synthesis that modern democracy can function so well at the level of the nation-state in the developed nations. In this sense, too, Fukuyama was right in proclaiming the end of history. It is useful to briefly recall how "history ended," and how the social-liberal synthesis emerged from decades of competition between the political Right and Left.

From the middle of the 19th century to the last decade of the 20th century, two powerful socioeconomic ideologies competed for preeminence and power throughout most of the world and within a very large number of individual nation-states. As Stiglitz (2001) puts it: "For almost

---

15. The Social Democrats (alone) and the Christian Democratic Union/Christian Social Union each received 38.5 percent of the total, with the Social Democrats ahead by only 8,000 votes. The Social Democrats' coalition partner, the Green Party, got 8.6 percent, and the Christian Democrats' partner, the Free Democrats (FDP), got 7.4 percent.

a hundred years, two theories had competed for the hearts and minds of people struggling to break free of poverty—one focusing on markets, and the other on government. Both of these 'modern' ideologies had their roots in the Enlightenment and in the French and American Revolutions. They were secular, focused on progress through the application of reason and science, and aimed at happiness and prosperity for all through economic progress here on earth—not in an afterlife. There was fundamental disagreement, however, on the means toward those ends."

On the Right, there was, for want of a better word, "capitalism," politically liberal or not, with a system of belief in private ownership, private entrepreneurship, and markets. On the Left there was Marxism, with rejection of private property of the means of production perceived as the source of exploitation and inequity, and the trust it placed in central planning as the best mechanism to allocate resources. It is easy, today, to forget how big the difference was between these two worldviews, particularly in the period from the 1920s to the 1970s. In the early postwar years, Oscar Lange, one of the most famous Marxist economists who also taught at the University of Chicago, proclaimed in an article entitled "The Computer and the Market" that contrary to what he himself thought in the 1930s, a socialist economy did not need markets, even for final products, because computers would allow "perfect" planning to allocate resources in a centralized fashion.[16] This view that computerized planning could solve all resource allocation problems was abandoned by most socialists in the 1970s. Nonetheless, the Left continued to believe that planning was essential to steer investment in the right direction. Leftist views were also influential in the theoretical economics literature, particularly in centers such as Cambridge, England, with many mathematical growth theorists stressing the incapacity of capital markets to steer economies on to their optimal growth paths.[17]

On the other end of the political spectrum, conservative economists in the tradition of Friedrich A. von Hayek, Ludwig von Mises, or Milton Friedman, to name three of the best known leaders of conservative thought, argued that markets, including stock markets and foreign exchange markets, would work perfectly, if only governments could

16. Oscar Lange, reprinted in Feinstein (1967). Computers could "mimic" the market and find optimal resource allocations without there being the need for "actual" markets.

17. See, for example, the works of M. Morishima and L. Pasinetti as well as other economists close to the "Cambridge School" of capital theory.

refrain from interfering with them. Monetary policy should not try to react to output or inflation indicators, but be set on automatic pilot, and stable growth would ensue. Central banks should not intervene in foreign exchange markets. "Stabilizing speculation" would ensure the smooth functioning of these markets.[18] Free markets and entrepreneurs seeking profit would ensure growth, and the fruits of growth would inevitably "trickle down" even to the poorest segments of the population. The clash between these two broad worldviews, ranging from conceptual debate to armed struggle, lasted for decades and shaped the history of the 20th century.

There is, of course, more to the history of the last two centuries than the clash between the "pure" versions of capitalism and socialism. Within the capitalist system there was a fierce struggle between the politically liberal variant and the fascist regimes of the 1930s, which ended with the decisive Allied victory in 1945. The rise of fascism itself was part of the overall dynamic referred to above. Fascism gained its initial strength from the fear of Marxism in countries such as Italy, Germany, and Spain and can only be understood within the overall context of the "clash of titans" that was the struggle between the Marxist Left and the capitalist Right.[19] It is also true that the United States, internally, was not much affected by Marxism and, therefore, Americans never fully experienced in their own political process this ideological competition the way Europe and other continents did. Americans experienced the ideological battle differently as citizens of the country that was leading one camp, with the United States in the 1950s becoming the leader of the capitalist world and one of the two key actors in the global ideological battle.

This is not the place for a detailed narrative of this struggle, which shaped modern history. It will be sufficient to remember here just how fierce the struggle was, how many millions died in the Spanish and other ideology-driven civil wars, and in wars in Korea, Vietnam, and elsewhere, and how close the world came to complete nuclear destruction during the

18. The development of "rational expectations" models in mathematical economics gave further support to ideas in the von Hayek-Friedman tradition. See, for example, V.V. Chari (1998) on Robert Lucas' contribution to modern macroeconomics.

19. "If we [National Socialists] were not, already today there would be no more bourgeoisie alive in Germany. . . . And when people cast in our teeth our intolerance, we proudly acknowledge it—yes, we have formed the inexorable decision to destroy Marxism in Germany down to its last root." Adolf Hitler's Speech to the Düsseldorf Industrial Club in 1932. Quoted in Fritz Thyssen (1941).

Cuban missile crisis.[20] In the course of this great struggle, both ideologies
and systems evolved, influenced by each other and reacting to challenge.
The United States, Western Europe, and Japan emerged victorious from
their competition with the Soviet model, but only after capitalism
adopted many "socialist" features that transformed the nature of the
advanced market economies radically from what could be observed at
the beginning of the 20th century. The average share of government in the
GDP of today's industrialized countries was below 11 percent during the
late 19th century and around 13 percent before World War I; today the
average share is around 45 percent. It stands above 50 percent in Europe
and close to 33 percent in the United States.[21] Government expenditures
had to rise to fund what is modern governance under the social-liberal
synthesis. This model of governance emerged over the course of the 20th
century with the banning of child labor, the commitment to publicly
funded universal education, the growth of progressive taxation, the development of social safety mechanisms such as unemployment insurance and
publicly funded healthcare, the commitment to take care of old people,
the increasing effectiveness of monetary and fiscal policies that counteract business cycles, and the strengthening of environmental policies and
regulations that protect public welfare.

Germany, an industrial latecomer (and where pure economic liberalism
never really became a dominant force), was perhaps the first in providing
social protection for the working class against economic insecurity. Germany's first chancellor, Otto von Bismarck, was the first statesman ever
to devise a comprehensive social insurance scheme in the late 19th century. A pragmatic leader, Bismarck was driven by the political motive of
competition with the socialists: a positive advancement of the welfare of
the masses to forestall the rise of socialism. Conservative industrialists,
such as Friedrich Harkort, Alfred Krupp, and Baron Carl Ferdinand von
Stumm, were also strong supporters of compulsory social insurance, with

20. The world came within a hairbreadth of massive nuclear strikes and counterstrikes
that would have caused the deaths of hundreds of millions of people and led to an aftermath
of economic chaos and radiology-induced illness affecting the globe. The Cuban missile crisis is the utmost example of the world coming to the brink of nuclear war. The crisis was a
major confrontation between the United States and the Soviet Union over the deployment
of Soviet IRBMs in Cuba in 1962. An American naval blockade and high alert status ensued
until the crisis was defused by the removal of the Soviet missiles and an American pledge to
dismantle IRBMs in Turkey and to never invade Cuba.

21. See Tanzi and Schuknecht (2000) for a comprehensive overview of the expansion of
the public economy. For an earlier analysis, see Cameron (1978).

similar motives. The significance of social insurance as an investment in national productivity therefore was first emphasized in Germany, but at the beginning of the 20th century the idea was gaining acceptance in other industrialized countries. Later, both Churchill and Roosevelt advocated comprehensive social insurance. In the United States, some members of Congress unsuccessfully attempted to establish unemployment payments during the 1893–94 recession as well as in 1914 and 1921. It was only in 1932 that the "Emergency Relief Act of 1932" was passed into law, supplementing local relief efforts. In 1933, Roosevelt set up the Civil Works Administration out of concern that direct relief would lead to loss of dignity among the poor. The program faced widespread opposition from the business community and was abolished the next year. In 1935, a Social Security Act was passed that included direct relief and provisions for unemployment insurance. The same year, 20 million people in the United States were already receiving relief.

In England, national health and unemployment insurance were introduced in 1911. The social insurance principle was advanced with the experience of Bismarck in mind (Bismarck had faced stiff resistance to a solely tax-based welfare system) in order not to alienate the voter base of the liberal government. Lloyd George was able to win over the opposition by offering a tripartite financing scheme from workers, employers, and taxpayers. In 1925, the Widows', Orphan's, and Old Age Contributory Pensions Act was passed. More than a decade later, William Beveridge, often considered the founder of the modern British welfare state, was asked by the government to prepare a report on how Britain should be rebuilt after the Second World War. Beveridge's report, published in 1942, recommended that the government find ways to fight the five "giant evils" of want, disease, ignorance, squalor, and idleness. Government took action by passing the Butler Act in 1944 that reformed schooling and declared commitment to full employment the same year. The Family Allowance Act was passed in 1945. Clement Attlee and the Labour Party, after defeating Winston Churchill's Conservative Party in General Elections in 1945, passed the National Insurance Act (1946), which was followed by the National Health Act (1948) providing free medical treatment for all. In Germany, the postwar economy was rebuilt as a "social market economy" by Ludwig Erhard and the Christian Democrats partly out of Christian Social convictions, and partly to take the wind out of the sails of the rival Social Democrats. In France, important social welfare legislation was passed in 1936 after the first electoral victory of the Left and was further developed during the postwar period, including by Gaullist governments to forestall and counter the Left. In the postwar period, Sweden and the other Scandinavian countries developed the social-welfare state even beyond the standards reached in the rest of Europe.

What triumphed at the end of the 20th century was not, therefore, the capitalist model of the beginning of the century. It was the synthesis that evolved between capitalism and socialism, based on private property and competitive markets as drivers of productivity growth and resource allocation, and a very large redistributive and regulatory role played by a strong state that "governs" the market mechanisms and funds public goods. Moreover, inside the private sector there is a lot of "planning" going on at the level of corporations, many of which exceed many small countries in size, whereas within the government, market principles are partially applied to improve efficiency and resource allocation. This is what can be called the social-liberal synthesis.[22]

Under the umbrella of this synthesis there is still a lively debate on details and on degree between the political Right and Left. It would be wrong to argue that the distinction between Left and Right has disappeared. Should the tax-to-GDP ratio be 2 percent higher or 2 percent lower? How long should unemployment benefits be available once a worker loses her job? To what extent is it possible to fine-tune fiscal and monetary policies to reduce the business cycle? How tightly should utilities be regulated? These are the questions that one finds in the domestic

22. Note that actual developments have been contrary to the pronouncements of purists of the Left and Right. Both von Mises and von Hayek, for example, argued that "the market economy . . . and the socialist economy preclude one another. There is no such thing as a mixture of the two systems. . . ." (von Mises, 1949); and "Both competition and central direction become poor and inefficient if they are incomplete. . . . a mixture of the two . . . will be worse than if either system had been consistently relied upon" (von Hayek, 1944, as quoted in Hodgson, 1999). For the diametrically opposite view which I believe to be correct, see, for example, Jean-Paul Fitoussi (2002, 2004), who argues that market allocation becomes acceptable only when it is tempered and circumscribed by the democratic political process intruding into the allocation process. The same point had already been developed by Ruggie (1982), who used the term "embedded liberalism" to describe what I call the "social-liberal" synthesis to stress the contribution of the socialist political family to this synthesis. Ruggie already in 1982 described how Western countries learned to reconcile the efficiency of markets with the values of social community to survive and thrive. On the political aspects of this synthesis, see the interesting collection of texts brought together by Canto-Sperber (2003). I would like to stress, however, that in this book the term "social-liberal" is used in a much broader sense than by Canto-Sperber. It encompasses all who agree like Fitoussi that socioeconomic outcomes must be determined by both markets and government action within a democratic political framework.

political debate. They are important questions and the political cleavages still remain. Within the broad framework of the social-liberal synthesis, the Left and the Right will continue to compete. American liberals are different from American conservatives. European socialists have different overall policy preferences from those of European conservatives. Tony Blair's "Third Way" Labor Party remains to the left of the post–Margaret Thatcher conservatives, just as the German Social Democrats' *Neue Mitte* remains to the left of the Christian Democrats' views. But within most nation-states' borders the basic socioeconomic "system" is no longer in question. There is agreement on seeing the government and markets as complements rather than substitutes. Conservatives may emphasize "means-testing" and time duration limits to social insurance expenditures, but the center-right does not propose to forego the social part of the social-liberal synthesis altogether; and the New Left, arguing for an enabling and ensuring state, accepts markets as the basic organizing framework for economic activity. People are no longer willing to die for the sake of nationalizing the means of production or for the sake of privatizing what is left in the hands of the state. Chancellor Schroeder has been able to govern with an 8,000 vote majority and George Bush with a minority of the popular vote because the basic socioeconomic system in their countries is not at stake. The man who used to have a high-ranking job in the KGB is president in Moscow, overseeing socioeconomic policies that are not very different in their ideological content from what we find in Berlin, Paris, Tokyo, or Madrid. Brazilian president Luiz Inácio "Lula" da Silva, who devoted his life to the struggle for socialism and whom the "markets" feared for decades, is presiding, so far successfully, over social-liberal synthesis policies. Before him, as Bhagwati (2004) points out, Fernando Henrique Cardoso, who had invented the "dependency thesis" warning against international trade in a world of unequal power, became president and implemented social-liberal reform policies that increased Brazil's integration into the world economy.[23] Prime Minister Recep Tayyip Erdogan in Turkey, coming from the tradition of political Islam, which has been distrustful of global integration, is implementing socioeconomic policies close to what one sees in non-Muslim emerging-market economies. A page of ideological history, indeed, has been turned.

---

23. Fernando H. Cardoso and Faletto Enzo's *Dependency and Development in Latin America* is one of the most important pieces of dependency literature. The book was first published in 1969 in Spanish and was published in English in 1979.

The New Beginning of History

History has not ended, however. As much as there is broad agreement on the basic socioeconomic model within which political competition takes place and policies get formulated at the level of the nation-state, fundamental disagreement and dissent exist and persist when it comes to decision making beyond the nation-state on issues that transcend national borders. There is nothing resembling the social-liberal synthesis at the international level. And yet an increasing number of problems are transnational or global in nature. These problems range from sectors such as health and the environment to the disruptions caused by excessive financial volatility and the moral challenge of extreme poverty, and extend from the threat from terror and weapons of mass destruction to the issues related to the abuse of basic human rights or the need to regulate new techniques of genetic engineering.[24] Thinking about these problems in relation, for example, to fine-tuning the domestic income tax in any single economy reminds one of an observation by Paul Krugman about the hierarchy of issues in a human being's personal life. Krugman (1997) shares with us his belief that the three most important things in a person's life are his or her career, health, and love. All three may be tremendously important, but generally difficult to change. Improvement often requires radical and sustained measures involving high upfront costs. So she or he, contemplating change on a Sunday morning, shrinks from courageous action and decides to improve the basement instead! And life for those who are unhappy but do not take action continues with dissatisfaction and a feeling of alienation at work, habits that will lead to a heart attack, and a marriage with little passion!

Something similar tends to happen in politics. The war in Iraq probably cost the US taxpayer close to $150 billion by the summer of 2004, and it cost the world economy as a whole substantial additional amounts. A crisis involving war with North Korea or a major problem with Iran could cost multiples of these amounts. Allowing a power vacuum to develop in Afghanistan, and failing to prevent the growth of a deadly terrorist network from that base, cost the United States and the world more than can easily be expressed in terms of hundreds of billions of dollars. And with each of these costs there was substantial loss of human life. Or take the examples of AIDS and Severe Acute Respiratory Syndrome

24. See Fukuyama (2002) for a broad analysis of the new challenges posed by genetics.

(SARS). For all its horror, AIDS is not easily transmittable. SARS is easily transmitted, but thankfully has a short incubation period so that it could be contained relatively easily by isolating infected persons. Suppose, on the contrary, that the incubation period of SARS had been two months rather than two weeks. SARS would have spread all over the world in a much more devastating fashion, with destructive effects on trade, tourism, and industry. The failure to rapidly report the outbreak would have cost large numbers of human lives and probably hundreds of billions of dollars in economic losses. The next disease that arises may have such features and may well constitute a much more formidable threat. Similar interdependence exists in the economic and financial sphere. Policy mistakes in one of the important countries or in a group of countries can slow down the whole world economy, creating unemployment and hardship beyond the area where the initial mistake was made. And yet, there is no framework in place, that is perceived as legitimate, to deal with these global issues. As expressed in the quote at the beginning of this chapter, democratic consent stops at the border of the nation-state.

Having an international political system in place to prevent or at least reduce the likelihood of crisis and the ensuing costs would improve the welfare of all, much more than what any individual nation can achieve by fine-tuning the income tax. It seems clear that the degree of interdependence that exists in the world of the 21st century greatly increases the scale of the damage that failure in one part of the system can inflict on all. Conversely, the benefits that can be generated by early preventive action can be immense. And yet it is extremely difficult to take preventive action. In so many fields, preventive action must be international in nature to be timely and effective. To be accepted, it must be legitimate, and it must command adhesion and respect. Unfortunately the current international institutional architecture lacks the required degree of legitimacy. It is essentially a leftover of the postwar world of the 1940s and cannot, without major reforms, help us manage the 21st century.

The new beginning of history will be driven by the debate on how to achieve this effectiveness and legitimacy in global governance. The world is in need of an extension of the social-liberal synthesis into the global sphere. Those who gathered at the World Social Forum in Porto Alegre, Brazil, in 2003 with a sense of moral outrage at the undemocratic and inequitable dimensions of the globalization process must turn their energies to finding ways of governing globalization for the benefit of the great majority, rather than trying to reject or deny an irreversible process. On the other hand, the increasingly global business and financial elites that dominate the world economy and influence political decisions must realize that the dangers of insufficient redistribution, regulation, and policy coordination are likely to lead to storms and floods where everyone will drown. How can happiness and security be ensured if hundreds of millions of people continue to live in abject poverty in an interdependent world where suffering and luxury form a dramatic contrast on television screens every night?[25] That contrast can lead some people to rationalize the most inhumane actions. How can devastating terrorism be prevented if people all over the world do not cooperate in a worldwide effort to secure peace that is perceived as fair and legitimate? Must it take a catastrophe even greater than September 11 in New York or March 11 in Madrid for humankind to really come together and face this danger? What use is it to build fences around wealth and privilege if a disease bred by poverty can travel by air, killing rich and poor alike? Has the time not come to devote some real effort and imagination to solving the big problems that threaten us rather than engaging in a continuation of the politics of the past circumscribed by irrational habits and imprisoned in a conceptual framework that is no longer relevant? History continues. If we want to survive and prosper, must we not do more than just try to fix our basement? It is appropriate to end this chapter with a quote from Oscar Wilde who defined progress as the realization of utopia:

"A map of the world that does not include utopia is not worth even glancing at for it leaves out the one country at which humanity is always landing. And when humanity lands there, it looks out, and seeing a better country, sets sail."[26]

We must indeed face the challenges of the new century by setting sail for new ideas, mindful of the dangers inherent in ideology, but understanding that new realities require new conceptual designs and new practical solutions.

---

25. Daniel Cohen (2004) makes the point that in many ways, the defining characteristic of today's globalization when compared with the globalization of the 19th century is how "visible" the contrasts are—how easily the gaps in power and wealth can be *perceived*. Brzezinski (2004, 42–43) agrees: "The contemporary world disorder stems more broadly from a new reality. The world is now awakened to the inequality in the human condition. . . . spreading literacy and especially the impact of modern communications have produced an unprecedented level of political consciousness among the masses."

26. The passage is from Oscar Wilde's essay "The Soul of Man under Socialism" (1891).

2 The International System

I am not referring to the absolute, infinite concept of universal peace and good will of which some fantasize and fanatics dream. I do not deny the value of hopes and dreams, but we merely invite discouragement and incredulity by making that our only and immediate goal.

Let us focus instead on a more practical, more attainable peace—based not on a sudden revolution in human nature but on a gradual evolution in human institutions—on a series of concrete actions and effective agreements which are in the interest of all concerned. There is no single, simple key to this peace—no grand or magic formula to be adopted by one or two powers. Genuine peace must be the product of many nations, the sum of many acts. It must be dynamic, not static, changing to meet the challenge of each new generation. For peace is a process—a way of solving problems.

With such a peace, there will still be quarrels and conflicting interest, as there are within families and nations. World peace, like community peace, does not require that each man love his neighbor—it requires only that they live together in mutual tolerance, submitting their disputes to a just and peaceful settlement.

JOHN F. KENNEDY
Commencement address at American University, June 10, 1963

The year 1945 was the end of a nightmare. Never in world history had there been a period as devastating as the years between 1914 and 1945. In the First World War, the trench warfare on the European western front and the massive casualties in Russia, Asia, and the Middle East led to tens of millions of deaths. More than 50 million people died in the Second World War. A genocide carried out with industrial efficiency exterminated close to 6 million people just because of their identity. Perhaps 20 million people died of starvation and in labor camps in Stalin's Soviet Union. Allied napalm bombing killed 30,000 civilians in Dresden in just one night. The first two atom bombs killed 150,000 Japanese. It is difficult, 60 years later, to fathom the extent of the mayhem.

The disasters of the mid–20th century were no doubt caused and magnified in part by the economic hardships experienced during the Great Depression. In the early 1930s, more than 20 percent of the US and European workforces were unemployed, with very little of the social welfare state support that was built into the advanced market economies after the Second World War. Economic cooperation between major countries was minimal. Average annual world GDP per capita growth declined from 1.3 percent over 1870–1913 to 0.9 percent during 1913–50. Growth in the volume of merchandise exports decreased from 3.4 percent to 0.9 percent in the respective periods, reflecting a significant decline in integration of the world economy through trade.[1] Economic and political problems created a vicious circle of violence and despair that imposed an almost unimaginable degree of suffering on hundreds of millions of human beings.

Against this backdrop, opinion leaders such as British economist John Maynard Keynes conceived of a new international system at the end of the Second World War, with the support of the victorious allied governments. That system included the United Nations as well as the Bretton Woods institutions. The UN charter, signed on June 26, 1945, in San Francisco at the UN Conference on International Organization, came into force on October 24 of that year. The preamble of the UN charter states:

> We, the peoples of the United Nations determined to save succeeding generations from the scourge of war, which twice in our lifetime has brought untold sorrow to mankind, and to reaffirm faith in fundamental human rights, in the dignity and worth of the human person, in the equal rights of men and women and of nations large and small, and to establish conditions under which justice and respect for the obligations arising from treaties and other sources of international law can be maintained, and to promote social progress and better standards of life in larger freedom, and for these ends to practice tolerance and live together in peace with one another as good neighbors, and to unite our strength to maintain international peace and security, and to ensure, by the acceptance of principles and the institution of methods, that armed force shall not be used, save in the common interest, and to employ international machinery for the promotion of the economic and social advancement of all peoples, have resolved to combine our efforts to accomplish these aims.

1. Maddison (2001, 126–27, tables 3-1a and 3-2a).

From its inception, the international system had the mutually comple-mentary objectives of creating structures of world security and political governance, as well as economic cooperation, that would protect the planet from World War III and promote economic reconstruction, stabil-ity, and growth. The extent of the catastrophe that the world had just endured encouraged an ambitious and far-reaching design. Many opin-ion leaders of the time thought that the United Nations should evolve toward a limited form of international governance that would prevent a return to balance-of-power politics and protect the world from nuclear holocaust. The invention of nuclear weapons and their terrifying poten-tial to destroy humankind made a world order based on the rule of law the overriding priority.

It is important to stress, however, that the limited world governance envisaged by the UN's founding fathers was firmly based on cooperation between territorially based and sovereign Westphalian nation-states. These states were the only actors on the international stage and the only entities that could claim democratic legitimacy. It was correctly foreseen that the end of colonial empires would multiply the number of these sov-ereign actors. Decolonization would not, however, change the nature of the international system based on nation-states as the legitimate entities to engage in cooperation, sign treaties, and agree to abide by certain stan-dards. The ideological atmosphere in the second half of the 1940s was broadly conducive to the "one nation-state, one vote" system that became the basic operating principle for the UN General Assembly. Thus, the period immediately following the Second World War was one of great tri-umph for nation-states. In the postwar struggle for the hearts and minds of the people of the world, both the United States and the Soviet Union stressed the right of the nations emerging from the old colonial empires to self-determination. In theory, if not in practice, the superpowers also sub-scribed to the notion of basic legal equality between nation-states.

However, the founding fathers of the postwar international system wanted to maintain the alliance against the defeated axis powers to fore-stall a resurgence of the defeated, particularly Germany, as happened in the 1930s. In addition, the design of the UN had to recognize that nation-states were very unequal in power and wealth. This led to a structure with five permanent members on the UN Security Council with veto power—the United States, the United Kingdom, France, Russia and China, often called the "Permanent Five." The permanent members, in effect, were the key victors of World War II. The veto arrangements reflected the unwillingness of the most powerful nation-states to subscribe to a system that could at times overrule them. This dual design was a hybrid between idealism and realism that was in tune with the world of the mid–20th century. The General Assembly was to be a kind of world consultative body with the individual sovereign states as equal members, and the Security Council would be the governing *directoire* managing world affairs, at least in the political and security sphere. The design was less than perfect from the start, but it was a vast improvement over what preceded it—the absence of any institutional framework whatsoever—and it marked the beginnings of institutionalized international legality in the postwar period.

In the economic sphere, freer trade and orderly cooperation were to replace the extremely harmful "beggar thy neighbor" policies of protectionism and competitive devaluations that had been responsible for much damage during the interwar years. At the domestic level, active and countercyclical monetary and fiscal policies were to prevent high levels of unemployment. At the international level, fixed exchange rates and orderly trade arrangements were to prevent attempts by individual countries to export their unemployment to others.

The key event in designing the postwar economic architecture was the Bretton Woods Conference held in New Hampshire on July 1, 1944, while war was still raging. Keynes, along with Harry Dexter White from the US Treasury, led the conference. While the United States clearly was the dominant power, Keynes' personal authority as the leading economist of his time conferred great weight to his views.

Though construction of the postwar economic and financial system began with the Bretton Woods Conference, the emergence of the environment that made it possible can be traced back to the end of the First World War. The participants at Bretton Woods were convinced that the primary cause of the Second World War had been the mismanagement of peace after the first war. The Treaty of Versailles had been a disaster, due especially to the lack of foresight in its economic provisions. Keynes, as one of the official representatives of the British Empire to the Supreme Economic Council that set out the terms of German reparations after World War I, had been outraged by the terms imposed on Germany, which betrayed a lack of understanding of international economic interdependence. He had resigned in protest and wrote his famous treatise *The Economic Consequences of the Peace* in 1919 to explain what was wrong with the terms of the peace. Many of those who were involved in designing what came to be called the Bretton Woods system thought that it would not have been possible for Hitler to rise to power had it not been for popular resentment among Germans for the terms of peace imposed on their country, along with the 1920–23 hyperinflation that effectively destroyed the politically moderate German middle class. The value of the German mark, which was 14 per US dollar at the end of the war in 1919, reached 4 trillion per US dollar on November 20, 1923. Although Germany had recovered from that collapse by the second half of the 1920s, it left deep wounds that refused to heal.

The Great Depression made it clear that, in the absence of multilateral agreements and institutions, the international economic system was in danger of creating policies that led to misery and mass unemployment. The World Economic Conference in 1931 was an unsuccessful attempt to reform the international economic order, but it did serve to inspire Keynes. Comprehensive international institution building was also advanced as a way to counter Hitler.

In 1940, the German minister of economics and president of the Reichsbank, Walter Funk, proclaimed that a "new order" was on its way that would unify Europe and its colonies under German leadership. The British government, concerned about German propaganda, asked Keynes to discredit it. Keynes' alternative vision was a completely new international system, and in 1942 the great economist and his associates in London prepared memoranda on the International Clearing Union, Plans for Relief and Reconstruction, and Commodity Buffer Stocks. These memoranda were the seeds of the Bretton Woods system.

Keynes' initial idea for the first pillar of the system, the International Clearing Union, would later become the International Monetary Fund (IMF). His bold proposals included a World Central Bank and a global currency to maintain full employment equilibrium and provide liquidity. The American side was in favor of a much smaller monetary fund with a more modest role and more emphasis on conditionality attached to the use of fund resources. While the inspiration came from Keynes, it is essentially the American vision of the IMF that eventually prevailed at Bretton Woods.

The second pillar eventually emerged as the International Bank for Reconstruction and Development, commonly known as the World Bank. The origin of the idea lies in the notion of a European Construction Fund focused on the rebuilding of Europe, but the presence of developing countries in the negotiations led to additional emphasis on the "development" function of the new institution.

The third proposed pillar, designed to help stabilize primary commodity prices and address trade issues, was the International Trade Organization (ITO). Although creation of the ITO was firmly supported at Bretton Woods, the proposal was brought to the US Congress when isolationism and anti-UN attitudes were on the rise. The effort to ratify the ITO was abandoned without even being put to a vote. Instead, the General Agreement on Trade and Tariffs (GATT) was signed in 1948. Under GATT, member nations generally agreed to accord no special trade status to any one member that was not accorded to all. GATT was a provisional legal agreement, not an international organization with permanent arrangements. It was not even close to what was envisioned by Keynes, but it did constitute a kind of third pillar concerned with trade, and eventually was transformed into today's World Trade Organization (WTO).

In many ways, this three-pillar system based on the IMF, the World Bank, and the WTO (GATT) has withstood the test of time in remarkable fashion. Today, six decades after the Bretton Woods Conference, the system still represents the core of international economic architecture.

From the beginning, the Bretton Woods institutions were created independently of the United Nations and its charter and set up with a governance that kept them out of the UN's organizational structure, even though they are, nominally, part of the UN system. The articles of agreements for the institutions were drafted in 1944 at the Bretton Woods Conference before the UN charter was approved. On December 31, 1945, governments with the required number of votes approved the Bretton Woods articles, and, after that approval, the United States called the first meeting of the Bretton Woods Governors held in Savannah, Georgia, in March 1946.

The UN institutional agreements were created by a parallel and separate process. The UN charter was approved at the San Francisco Conference in the summer of 1945 and ratified by the major powers and most other countries in November of the same year. The General Assembly and the Economic and Social Council (ECOSOC) had their first sessions in January 1946. The ECOSOC was created to coordinate the UN's economic and social programs, a number of subsidiary bodies, functional commissions, regional commissions, and specialized agencies.

The difference in the timing of the establishment of the ECOSOC and the Bretton Woods institutions made it difficult for the United Nations to firmly incorporate the latter under the UN umbrella. A letter from the ECOSOC president was sent to the Savannah conference and referred to the Bretton Woods executive directors, who were expected to meet in

May. Both the Bretton Woods articles of agreement and the UN charter required that the two institutional structures cooperate.[2] A second letter from the UN then asked the Bretton Woods institutions to negotiate a formal agreement. However, the executive directors declined the offer, saying such action would be premature. Meanwhile, UN agreements had been completed with the International Labor Organization (ILO), the United Nations Educational, Scientific, and Cultural Organization (UNESCO), and the Food and Agriculture Organization (FAO). In late June 1946, the UN secretary-general asked Bretton Woods management whether discussions with the ECOSOC negotiating committee could begin in September. But World Bank and IMF representatives—fearing that political control or influence could hurt their institutions' reputation and credit ratings on Wall Street—responded that they could not sign an agreement similar to what was put forward by the United Nations.

It is clear that achieving this degree of independence from the UN would not have been possible if this position had not had the support of the United States. The ECOSOC and the Bretton Woods institutions finally reached an agreement in 1947 that declared the Bank and the IMF as specialized UN agencies. In substance, however, this agreement was a declaration of independence that required the Bretton Woods institutions only to give "due consideration" to UN recommendations on inclusion of items in their agendas. The IMF and the World Bank maintained independent budgetary and financial arrangements. The UN connection was limited to permitting UN representatives to attend meetings of the Board of Governors, and to the Bretton Woods institutions having liaison offices at the UN headquarters and participating in some meetings.

The Political and Economic Spheres

Figures 2.1 and 2.2, adapted from Richard Falk (2002), give a summary description of the international system as it operates today, which is not very different from the way it has operated during much of the postwar

---

2. Article 5 required the World Bank to "give consideration to views and recommendation of competent international organizations." The UN charter was more specific: Article 57 requires that the "various specialized agencies, established by intergovernmental agreement . . . shall be brought into relationship with the United Nations," and that the UN "shall make recommendations for the coordination of the policies and activities of the specialized agencies." Relevant articles of the charter authorize the ECOSOC to enter into agreements and coordinate with specialized agencies, make recommendations to them and obtain regular reports from them. See Mason and Asher (1973, 55).

Figure 2.1 *The political sphere*

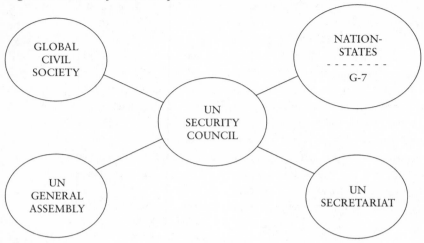

Source: Adapted from Falk (2002).

period. There is a clear distinction between the political and security sphere (Figure 2.1) and the economic and social sphere (Figure 2.2). The UN Security Council is at the center of the security sphere. The entire system has operated in an environment in which the fabric of the official international community involved two superpowers—and since the 1990s, only one superpower—alongside medium-sized and small nation-states. The UN General Assembly brings those sovereign actors together and provides a forum for debate in plenary sessions and various committees and councils, but the General Assembly has no enforcement power. The system is formally managed by the United Nations Secretariat headed by the secretary-general. Figure 2.1 also draws attention to the role of global civil society, whose importance has increased tremendously in the last 15 years, its global reach and activities greatly facilitated by the Internet.

The major difference between the architecture of the political sphere and that of the economic sphere is that the Bretton Woods institutions and the WTO—organizations that are not really part of the UN system and have distinct governance—are at the center of the institutional set-up of the economic sphere. Although many special agencies in the UN system

Figure 2.2 *The economic sphere*

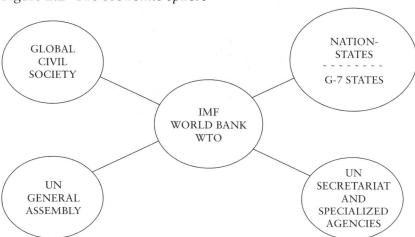

Source: Adapted from Falk (2002).

are active in the economic and social sphere—including such important entities as UNICEF, the ILO, UNESCO, the World Health Organization (WHO), the United Nations Development Program (UNDP), and the United Nations Conference on Trade and Development (UNCTAD)—these agencies are at the periphery of the institutional system, with the IMF, the World Bank, and the WTO at the center. It is through these latter institutions, or within the framework that they provide, that the most important decisions affecting economic matters are made and financial resources get allocated, with obvious consequences for social issues.

Just as in the case for the UN Security Council in the political sphere, it is the nation-states controlling and influencing the governance of these institutions that are the ultimate strategic decision makers in the economic and social sphere. The manner in which superpowers, other nation-states, and international organizations and bureaucracies interact to determine outcomes, however, is quite different in the two spheres. To move forward with reform it is important to understand the history and nature of these interactions and the situation as it exists at the beginning of the 21st century.

The Political Sphere

Although the military alliance that defeated the axis powers included the Soviet Union, within months of the final victory in 1945 the alliance ended and the world was divided into two increasingly antagonistic blocs, undermining the newly created United Nations and with it hopes for global governance based on cooperation within the legal framework of the UN system.

Cold War antagonism between the two blocs paralyzed the Security Council on many occasions. The council played virtually no role during the French and American wars in Vietnam or the Soviet invasions of Czechoslovakia and Hungary because either the US or Soviet veto could always make any such attempt futile. Between 1945 and 1975, the Soviet Union used its veto 114 times to block decisions that it perceived as working toward the objectives of the West. More than half of these vetoes concerned membership applications in the early 1950s. The United States, on the other hand, did not use its veto at all between 1946 and 1965 but used its veto 12 times between 1966 and 1975.

China was another big issue. After the Second World War, civil war erupted in China between the communists and the nationalists. The People's Republic of China was established following the victory of the communists in 1949, and the Chinese nationalists had to flee to the island of Taiwan. After 1950, the United States supported what was called the Nationalist Government on Taiwan, which continued to represent China in the Security Council. The People's Republic of China, allied with the Soviet Union, was not represented in the United Nations until 1971. The UN could respond to North Korea's invasion of South Korea in 1950 only because the Soviets had been boycotting the Security Council at that time with the objective of getting the People's Republic of China into the UN. During the 1970s and early 1980s, the Soviet Union joined newly independent countries to support self-determination for colonies, opposition to apartheid in South Africa, and the legitimization of the Palestine Liberation Organization. The United States used its veto many times to block resolutions directed at Israel.

With the fall of the Berlin Wall in 1989, the nature of the international system changed quite suddenly and dramatically. By the early 1990s, it was clear that the division of the world between the West and the Soviet bloc was over. Hope arose that a new international system based on cooperation and international legality within the framework of the United Nations could replace the balance of nuclear terror of the Cold War, during which one bloc was always able to thwart the other by using its veto in the Security Council. Moreover, the West's relations with China had already improved in the 1980s as China had increasingly opened up to the global market economy. China continued to pursue national interests that often clashed with those of the Western powers over Taiwan and other matters such as nuclear proliferation, but by the late 1970s it had given up systemic antagonism to the West and any effort to export Chinese-style communism. In fact, China's socioeconomic system evolved into a mixture of state ownership and private entrepreneurship within an overall framework close to a market economy. In the 1990s, the Soviet Union imploded and its largest successor state, the Russian Federation, also ceased to be a systemic antagonist. In fact, going much further than China, Russia gave up the communist system altogether, both economically and politically. With some oversimplification, it can be claimed that, by the end of the 20th century, the transformation of China and what had been the Soviet Union transformed the "social-liberal synthesis" referred to in chapter 1 into a global synthesis and a common ideological ground shared by a large part of humanity.

It was not unreasonable to hope, therefore, that this ideological convergence would translate itself into a UN system based on broad consensus and cooperation, ending the divisions and obstruction that had characterized previous decades. This hope was strengthened by the fact that the new international order would benefit not only from the end of the Cold War but also from national ideologies that no longer sought territorial aggrandizement through conquest. In that sense, the world at the end of the 20th century was a very different one from that at the end of the 19th century, when colonial conquest and empire building were still very much part of the national policies of the major powers.

And in fact the international system at the eve of the millennium did not just revert from the bipolar world of the Cold War back to the 19th century world of balance-of-power politics—at least not ideologically. In the 1990s, the ideology of peace was much more strongly established in the world than it had been a hundred years earlier, influenced by the success of European integration, which had a decisive impact on strengthening the ideology of peace. Germany and France, which had fought each other without mercy for 150 years, now shared important elements of sovereignty, making war between them an unthinkable prospect. This remarkable achievement has had an impact much beyond the borders of the European Union.

Despite these very positive factors, however, progress in cooperative international governance has been much more limited during the last 15 years than hoped for at the time the Berlin Wall fell. Several sources of political tension have heightened considerably and negatively affected the international system. First, the 1990s witnessed an increase in domestic strife, civil wars, and states unable to maintain even limited cohesion and domestic governance. Second, terrorism in various forms became a much larger threat with the attacks of September 11, 2001, leading to a new threshold of horror followed by numerous attacks around the world underlining the global nature of this violent scourge. Finally, the United States adopted an increasingly unilateralist approach to international affairs, at least up until the fall of 2003, when the US administration somewhat moderated its stance and decided to make a greater effort to work with the United Nations on Iraq and proceed to the extent possible with the endorsement of the UN Security Council.

An even deeper reason behind the lack of progress in developing a new world order, however, is the fact that important parts of the architecture of the international system conceived in 1945 and developed during the Cold War no longer reflect international realities at the beginning of the 21st century. This mismatch has blocked reform and led to a vicious cycle of disappointment. In fact, prospects for more cohesive and collaborative global governance within the framework of a strengthened United Nations seemed worse at the beginning of the 21st century than in the early 1990s.

Domestic Strife, Failed States, and Terror

Political scientist Robert Jackson (1990) has defined post-colonial countries that have the juridical trappings of a modern nation-state without the ability to govern as "quasi-states." In the 1990s, mainly due to the post–Cold War political vacuum, many quasi-states tumbled into further political chaos, trapped in violence and degenerating into failed states. The threat of civil war and possible disintegration looms around the world, from Haiti to Yugoslavia, Georgia, Sudan, Somalia, Congo, Liberia, Rwanda, Angola, Sierra Leone, Indonesia (East Timor, Aceh), and Sri Lanka. The degree of failure varies. When the central political authority is unable to maintain public security internally or externally, a state loses its control over the economic and political spheres—a condition described by

Zartman (1995) as "state collapse." Somalia is a telling example. In other cases, the political authority of the state is rejected by large segments of the population, as occurred in Rwanda and Yugoslavia. Failed states pose a serious challenge to the international system. Should they be allowed to fail, or should they be rescued? While concern regarding the consequences of violating sovereignty is understandable, other considerations come into play. To quote Secretary-General Kofi Annan (2000), the three functions of the UN are to serve the member states, introduce new principles in relations among states, and serve the needs and hopes of people everywhere. The third function should not be interpreted just as moral idealism, however. Failing states pose a serious challenge to the entire international system, as borders cannot contain the instability, chaos, and violence they engender. Refugees, violence, and terrorism have become major threats to international peace and stability. The events of September 11 showed what a great danger the failed state of Afghanistan posed, although in itself it seemed remote, powerless, and ever so distant from the economic and political power centers of the world.

In a broader sense as well, September 11 was a great challenge to the conventional wisdom on security and terrorism. Up until then, the world had a very state-centric view of security—it was simply difficult to imagine nonstate groups being able to acquire the means to carryout large-scale terrorist acts. There had been relatively small-scale terrorism linked to extreme nationalist movements or regional conflicts, but nothing comparable to September 11.

The newer form of terrorism, however, did not start with the September 11 attacks. The past two decades have in fact seen a marked increase in the activity of terrorist groups very different in their ideology, tactics, and organization from what can be called the classical terrorist groups. The new groups have still had political aims, but they now claim a sacred legitimacy because their war is against the "corrupt" and the "evil." Nor is the violence specifically aimed only at particular states or their representatives. Randomly chosen civilians have become targets, because the act of violence itself is an objective. Mary Kaldor (2003) uses the term "regressive globalization" to describe this type of terror movement, since these groups make extensive use of the very globalization they purport to hate.[3]

---

3. Also see Stern (2003) for an in-depth analysis of the psychological and social factors shaping terrorist actions.

According to Kaldor, these groups arise as an extreme reaction to the insecurities generated by globalization, as well as disillusions with the secular ideologies of the state. At the same time, they make use of the opportunities created by globalization—the new media, especially television and the Internet, and increased opportunities for funding from diaspora as well as from transnational criminal groups.

The challenge to deal with the new type of terrorism is exacerbated by the fact that there are millions of angry, jobless, and young potential recruits willing to kill and die in search of martyrdom—with the suicide bomber representing the ultimate phase of alienation. Beyond just declaring war on terror, the international community will have to find a more comprehensive and sophisticated way to address the broader social economic issues at hand. Means must be found to address the root causes and social dynamics underlying the problems that lead to the spread of terror. Eradicating poverty will help reduce the number of potential terrorists, but perhaps even more important is to convince potential sympathizers that the world order can evolve towards greater equity and legitimacy and that change is possible with essentially peaceful means. There will always be a small hard core of extremists that cannot be reached by reason. To contain them, majorities all over the world must be on the side of peace. This requires winning hearts and minds with arguments for justice and a roadmap towards greater participation and equity.

US Unilateralism in the Age of Interdependence

The United States has always been ambivalent about multilateral engagement, not wanting to be tied down and constrained in its ability to act. On the one hand, much of the postwar international system was designed by and functioned with US support. On the other hand, the United States has mistrusted the system and has periodically been tempted to act outside it, relying on its military and financial power alone. In the period up to the Iraq War, this temptation grew stronger. Instead of using the opportunity presented by the collapse of the Soviet Union to strengthen multilateralism and global governance, the United States has been tempted to ensure its own dominance, with some even referring to the call of "empire."[4] There have been many examples of the new, more unilateralist stance of the United States.

4. The literature on the US "empire" is quite rich. See Ikenberry (2002), Bacevich (2002), Chomsky (2003), and Johnson (2000). Ikenberry (2004) reviews five different works examining contemporary US "imperialism."

The major nuclear weapons treaties had been drawn up on the basis of a balance of forces between the United States and the Soviets. In the spring of 2002, US president George W. Bush denounced the 1972 antiballistic missile treaty (ABM), which ensured that missile defense systems would be limited to certain predetermined targets. Shortly thereafter, the number of warheads each side was allowed under the Strategic Arms Reduction Talks (START) was drastically increased.

In May 2003, the United States renounced its support for the treaty establishing the International Criminal Court (ICC) that was signed by 138 countries and ratified by 66. The countries that voted against the ICC were Libya, Iraq, China, Israel, and Qatar. Perhaps anticipating that the US Congress would not ratify the ICC treaty, President Bill Clinton noted when he signed it in 2000, that as a signatory, the United States could still negotiate the court's procedures, staffing, and budget. The Bush administration's main concern is that the treaty gives ICC judges too much power unchecked by the UN Security Council (where the United States has the veto), as well as jurisdiction over citizens of countries that have not ratified the treaty. US conservatives see the ICC as a threat to US sovereignty and freedom of action. President Bush's countermove to the ICC, the American Servicemen's Protection Act, not only bans US military aid to countries that ratified the ICC treaty, but also authorizes the president to use force to free American soldiers who might be arrested or transferred to the ICC for prosecution. The United States recently withheld military assistance from 35 democratic countries because of their resistance to bilateral immunity agreements that exempt US citizens from the first global court to try those accused of genocide, crimes against humanity, and war crimes. Also, on June 12, 2003, the Bush administration secured from the UN Security Council the renewal of a one-year exemption from ICC jurisdiction for American troops involved in UN-authorized military missions.

Although 136 countries signed and ratified the 1997 treaty banning landmines, the United States is still among the few countries that have not signed it. The Bush administration has been reviewing the country's landmine policy since 2001, but no agreement has yet been reached on how to proceed. It should be added, however, that the United States has not laid new mines and was the largest donor for the mine clearance program in 2002, contributing $76.9 million.

The United States has proposed reopening talks on the treaty banning torture, which most likely will lead to abusive states watering it down.

Then-vice president Al Gore signed the Kyoto Protocol, but the Senate voted against it and President Clinton never submitted it to Congress. The Bush administration ruled it out from the start. Over time, the Kyoto Treaty was changed to make it easier for the United States to sign—several provisions were added that addressed US sensitivities—but US opposition has not budged.

There are, undoubtedly, arguments in defense of the US position concerning each of the examples cited above. However, none can refute the clear overall picture created by the cumulative refusal to buy into strengthened global governance. The fact remains that, after the fall of the Berlin Wall, the United States could have seized the opportunity to lead an effort to build stronger international institutions adapted to the new circumstances and with the ability to enforce international law. Instead, the United States saw these circumstances as an opportunity to augment its own power and try to exercise it as a traditional nation-state and superpower. The Clinton administration had been very cautiously multilateralist. The first George W. Bush administration clearly strengthened US unilateralism, making it explicit and ideological.

Joseph Stiglitz (2003, 231), recalling the period when he was chairman of the Council of Economic Advisors under the Clinton administration, summarizes his perception of a great missed opportunity: "The disappointment in how we managed globalization was all the greater because of what might have been. The end of the Cold War meant that the United States was the sole superpower—it was the dominant military and economic power. The world was looking to America for leadership. In my judgment, leadership means that one cannot try to shape the world simply to advance one's own interests, and democratic leadership means that one advances one's viewpoint by persuasion, not by bullying, by using threats of military or economic power. We had no vision of what kind of globalized world we wanted, and we weren't sensitive enough about how what we wanted would be viewed by the rest of the world."

The failure of the international system to function in the political sphere culminated during the Iraq crisis that unfolded in 2002 and 2003. Transatlantic relations reached their lowest point in decades, and a major military intervention again took place without a UN Security Council authorization. The absence of such an authorizing resolution in Iraq was due to strong resistance by world public opinion that influenced many governments, including nonpermanent members of the Security Council such as Mexico and Chile, as well as the clear opposition of the governments of Germany, France, and Russia, which have veto powers. Nevertheless, the United States declared its intention to act as it saw fit, irrespective of the Security Council. France did the same in the opposite direction: President Jacques Chirac declared that France would veto an authorizing resolution before the weapons inspection route was exhausted even if world opinion and a majority in the Security Council shifted in favor of military intervention. Both the United States and France took a unilateralist stance, but under the present system, it could be argued that the US position was both "illegal" and unilateral, while France's position was "legal"—it does have a legal veto power—but unilateral in that France did not feel compelled to seek a majority but rather would rely on its veto. This was the position taken by Russia during the Kosovo crisis, which at the time prevented the military intervention from gaining Security Council support, despite a large majority of states favoring intervention, and which in this case and in contrast to the case of Iraq had strong public support as well.

Thus, instead of bringing about a new world order based on cooperation and a significant strengthening of the role of international law, the end of the Cold War seems to have led, instead, to a kind of disintegration of the international system, a new type of disorder where failed states, terror, and local conflict create a general sense of insecurity that the military might of the United States is unable to overcome. The enlargement of the European Union has geographically extended the area of peace and stability toward the east, but in most other parts of the globe stability has not progressed. It is becoming increasingly clear that, if new catastrophes are to be avoided, terror and conflict will have to be counteracted by powerful and decisive actions aimed at eradicating the root causes of the problems that underlie it. The experience in Iraq to date suggests that essentially unilateral US action cannot succeed. What is needed not only in Iraq but in all of the trouble spots around the globe is concerted international action, with the United States and Europe working together, backed by a strong sense of legitimacy that can mobilize the support of public opinion and civil society and attract the sympathy of developing countries. The threats emanating from the Middle East, North Korea, most of Africa, and potentially parts of Latin America and the ex-Soviet Union are real and should not be underestimated, and point to the urgent need for an international political and security system. This system cannot be what is left over from 1945, but must instead reflect today's realities and tomorrow's challenges.

The Economic Sphere

During the months leading up to the Bretton Woods Conference in 1944, Harry Dexter White from the US Treasury spent a good deal of time convincing his colleagues in the US administration as well as representatives from major US allies that the Soviet Union and other socialist countries should be included in the building and functioning of the new economic architecture. Simultaneously, he was trying to convince the Soviets that it was in their interest to join the institutions designed at the conference. The Soviets participated in the Bretton Woods Conference negotiations, but in the end decided not to ratify the agreements. The Soviets were not happy with the offer to become only the third largest shareholder after the United States and the United Kingdom, especially since they would not hold a veto power as on the UN Security Council. Moreover, Bretton Woods membership required providing specific information that was beyond what the Soviets were willing to provide. In particular, information regarding gold production and transactions was regarded by the Soviets as a national security asset. The Soviets also demanded special support for reconstruction, since they had had to shoulder a major burden of the war. While their request that reconstruction be designated as the World Bank's priority was accepted, their proposal for a 20 to 50 percent reduction of the gold portion of the subscriptions in recognition of the "home areas having suffered from enemy occupation" was refused. As a concession, the IMF set an alternative date for determining the net level of gold holdings of war-damaged states.

In addition to these important technical details, the Soviets must have felt that they had little interest in the World Bank and IMF goal to enhance private trade. Although the articles of agreement of both the IMF and the Bank prohibited taking sides on the nature of a member country's economy, both institutions worked within a capitalist paradigm. At a UN General Assembly meeting in 1947, a Soviet representative charged that the Bretton Woods institutions were " branches of Wall Street" and that the World Bank was "subordinated to political purposes which make it the instrument of one great power" (Mason and Asher 1973, 29, 46).

Despite the Soviets' concerns, many believed they would nevertheless decide to join the system by the end of the Bretton Woods negotiations. The Soviets took the draft of the agreement to study and sat on it for quite a while, sending only an observatory delegation to Savannah. The Bank and the Fund extended their deadline by six months in the hope of facilitating Soviet membership, but Cold War issues continuously increased Soviet antagonism toward the Bretton Woods sisters. The realization that these institutions would be independent from the UN further strengthened that antagonism.

The Berlin Blockade of 1948 and the communist victory in China in 1949 further restricted Bretton Woods membership. China was represented by the nationalist government on the island of Taiwan.[5] Poland, an original member, was pressured by the Soviets to withdraw from the institutions in 1950. Another original member from the communist bloc, Czechoslovakia, was asked to withdraw for not being able to provide information needed to evaluate its exchange rate policy in 1954. Socialist but relatively independent, Yugoslavia remained a member of Bretton Woods throughout the Cold War. The rest of the Soviet-dominated Eastern European countries were not members. Romania and Vietnam joined the Bretton Woods institutions in 1972 and 1975, respectively.

The fall of the Berlin Wall and the collapse of the Soviet bloc had an immediate and unifying impact on the economic and social parts of the international governance system. As was the case for the political sphere, there were high hopes in the early 1990s that the end of the Cold War would lead to much improved cooperation and a strengthening of global governance in the economic sphere. Between 1990 and 1993, 25 Eastern European and Central Asian countries became members of the World Bank and the IMF,[6] and by the turn of the century, the Bretton Woods institutions, for the first time, had become truly global institutions, with membership identical to that of the United Nations.

While the Bretton Woods Conference of July 1944 had produced the Articles of Agreement for the IMF and the agreement to create the World Bank, it took several more years to reach an international agreement on trade. The United States, the United Kingdom, and Canada had been the main actors discussing the guidelines of a new international trading system during the war years. In February 1946, the first session of the UN

5. Proper representation of China in the IMF did not occur until 1980, nine years after the United Nations' decision to recognize the People's Republic of China based in Beijing, rather than the Republic of China based in Taipei, as the government of China.

6. Bulgaria in 1990; Albania and Mongolia in 1991; Armenia, Azerbaijan, Belarus, Estonia, Georgia, Kazakhstan, Kyrgyz Republic, Latvia, Lithuania, Moldova, Russia, Turkmenistan, Ukraine, and Uzbekistan in 1992; and Bosnia-Herzegovina, Croatia, Czech Republic, Macedonia, Slovak Republic, Slovenia, Tajikistan, and Yugoslavia in 1993. Hungary and Poland had already become members in 1982 and 1986, respectively—see Boughton (2001, chapter 19) for more details on the history of their membership.

Economic and Social Council (ECOSOC) established a preparatory committee made up of 18 countries to do the groundwork. In January 1948, 23 countries signed the General Agreement on Tariffs and Trade (GATT), which did not include investment, employment, or organizational provisions. Not for another 46 years, and only after seven and a half years of Uruguay Round negotiations, was the WTO created with the full legal status of an international organization. The Uruguay Round is considered the largest and the most complex negotiation in history, with 125 countries agreeing to its terms in consensus. At present, 146 countries are members of the WTO. China became a member in December 2001, while Russia is still negotiating its accession.

Just as the convergence of UN and Bretton Woods membership and the ideological thaw of the 1990s allowed greater cooperation between the UN system and the Bretton Woods institutions, the transformation of GATT into the WTO, as well as the disappearance of the communist bloc's Council for Mutual Economic Assistance (COMECON),[7] brought trade issues and negotiations into a single and increasingly global framework.

Unfortunately, despite this progress in the international system's economic sphere, the world is still very far from a form of global economic and social governance that is considered both legitimate and effective by most citizens across the globe. Many people from São Paolo to Istanbul and from Seoul to Manila continue to view the IMF largely as a tool of rich countries and multinational businesses, rather than as an institution that works in their interest. Governments in emerging markets blame the IMF for the constraints on their budgets and for all kinds of policies and regulations, for which they refuse to take ownership. Micklethwait and Wooldridge (2003) report that during South Korea's economic crisis in 1997, a Korean television station ran a program about "IMF orphans," the program's description of children being brought up in state orphanages because their parents had either committed suicide or abandoned them in the wake of the crisis. This lack of legitimacy for the IMF is a major obstacle to successful implementation of Fund-backed economic programs, since it severely limits the domestic ownership that a program requires irrespective of its content and design.[8]

---

7. COMECON had a similar international status as the European Economic Community in design but was for countries under communist rule. Its main objective was to increase integration, mainly trade, between communist countries. After the dismantling of the Soviet Union, it was disbanded in 1991.

8. See Birdsall (2003) for a perceptive analysis of problems caused by insufficient ownership.

The challenge is not only one of perceived legitimacy, however. For a long time, the economic sphere of the international systems has suffered from massive problems of duplication between agencies, lack of coordination, and top-heavy management structures, giving rise to an image of an inefficient international bureaucracy. Much has been done over the past decade to improve coherence, coordination, and cooperation among multilateral economic organizations, as well as to make their internal functioning more efficient. James Wolfensohn, president of the World Bank Group since 1995, has made particular efforts to engage with UN agencies. There has also been substantial progress with regard to the poorest countries qualifying for international development funds within the new framework provided by the Poverty Reduction Strategy Papers launched in 1999.

Nonetheless, overall progress has been slow because of the nature of the international system, the fact that the UN agencies and the Bretton Woods sisters have divergent governance at the top, and the ongoing perception, and many would argue reality, of the Bretton Woods institutions' complete subordination to the Group of Seven (G-7). People in most countries do not accept an international economic system viewed as being run by the finance ministers and central bank governors of seven self-appointed wealthy countries that meet to decide the fate of the entire globe.

Finally, beyond process and perception is a real debate about the substance of the economic and social policies that have formed the basis of programs supported by the Bretton Woods institutions, including discussion on the theoretical foundations of IMF and World Bank policy prescriptions or policies pursued within the framework of the WTO. This debate should be conducted as part of the overall governance debate, since policy prescriptions are linked to governance. Some critics are extreme and use arguments that do not stand up to careful analysis, but others, such as highly regarded analytical economists Joseph Stiglitz and Dani Rodrik, are ideologically within the framework referred to earlier as the social-liberal synthesis. They accept the fundamental need for competitive markets, recognize the great potential benefits of free trade, and by no means advocate a return to central planning or autarchy. They stress, however, that both theory and empirical analysis show that market failure can be a serious problem, that there is nothing automatic about markets working well, and that there is scope for well-designed activist public policies much beyond what the Bretton Woods institutions have traditionally proposed, particularly during the conservative revolution of the administrations of Ronald Reagan and Margaret Thatcher. There is also a lively debate about the nature of optimal macroeconomic policies for indebted emerging-market economies and the functioning of international capital markets.

Any discussion of reforming the Bretton Woods institutions and the WTO must include not only these substantive policy issues but a focus on institutional and governance aspects as well. The chapters that follow outline the basic contours of a renewed international system in both the political and security sphere as well as the economic and social sphere. The objective is to improve both the legitimacy and the efficacy of the system. A United Nations adapted to the needs and realities of the 21st century should be the overall institutional setting for both the political and the economic sphere. Chapter 3 focuses on the political and security architecture and proposes new arrangements for the UN Security Council. The discussion of the Bretton Woods institutions in subsequent chapters focuses on economics and finance, as well as proposals for reform, while chapter 7 looks at the WTO and trade. The reforms advocated in this book for the institutional set-up as well as for the practice of policy may be considered radical, but they are quite feasible and compatible with the social and economic forces that are likely to shape the future in the medium term.

At the national level, recent decades have shown that performance is determined by the effectiveness of institutions and their interaction with cultural attitudes and economic policies. The same is true at the global level, where performance ultimately will depend on the quality of global institutions, the ideological atmosphere within which they function, and the nature of the policies that emerge from these interactions.

3 A Renewed United Nations

Excellencies, we have come to a fork in the road. This may be a moment no less decisive than 1945 itself, when the United Nations was founded.

At that time, a group of far-sighted leaders, led and inspired by President Franklin D. Roosevelt, were determined to make the second half of the twentieth century different from the first half. They saw the human race had only one world to live in, and that unless it managed its affairs prudently, all human beings may perish.

So they drew up rules to govern international behavior, and founded a network of institutions, with the United Nations at its center, in which the peoples of the world could work together for the common good.

Now we must decide whether it is possible to continue on the basis agreed then, or whether radical changes are needed.

And we must not shy away from questions about the adequacy, and effectiveness, of the rules and instruments at our disposal.

Among those instruments, none is more important than the Security Council itself.

The United Nations is by no means a perfect instrument, but it is a precious one. I urge you to seek agreement on ways of improving it.

SECRETARY-GENERAL KOFI ANNAN
Inaugural speech to the UN General Assembly, September 2003

The United Nations came into existence at the end of World War II because serious and coordinated thought had been given, with top-level political support, to a new design of the international system. Unfortunately, nothing similar happened at the end of the Cold War. A number of high-level commissions, committees, and conferences issued reports or proposals for reform around the time of the 50th anniversary of the United Nations and the Bretton Woods institutions, which happened to come about a few years after the fall of the Berlin Wall. Regarding the UN, these included the Stockholm Initiative on Global Security and Governance (1991), US Commission on Improving the Effectiveness of the

United Nations (1993), Canadian Committee for the 50th Anniversary of
the United Nations (1994), Commission on Global Governance (1995),
Independent Working Group on the Future of the UN System (1995), and
the Council on Foreign Relations Independent Task Force (1996).[1]

However, none of these initiatives reflected a systematic and holistic
effort to update the entire international architecture that involved
rethinking how to combine the political and economic spheres—this
despite the fact that the end of the Cold War was probably as dramatic an
event as the defeat of the Axis powers. The Asian financial crisis in 1997
prompted considerable discussion about a new global financial architecture that led to such innovations as the Financial Stability Forum (FSF)[2]
and encouraged closer cooperation in the financial sector between the
International Monetary Fund (IMF) and the World Bank. But these
changes were modest and not at all linked to the UN system, and so the
world entered the 21st century with an international institutional architecture in large part inherited from the immediate post–World War II era,
rather than one reflecting the needs and challenges of the new century.

The 21st century did not start peacefully—the terrorist attacks on the
United States in September 2001 signaled that the end of the East/West
divide might not necessarily bring the worldwide peace and security for
which so many had long hoped. Less than two years after September 11
came the war in Iraq and its aftermath, accompanied by worldwide
debate on the necessity, desirability, and legitimacy of such an intervention. These events have moved the question of global governance and
international legitimacy to the center of political debate throughout the
world. Again, there has been an outpouring of papers on global governance and initiatives ranging from the UN Secretary General's High Level
Panel on Global Security Threats and Reform of the International System,
to the World Commission on the Social Dimensions of Globalization
(2004), and the independent Task Force on Global Public Goods led by

1. For the UN, see also Boutros-Ghali (1992), Childers and Urquhart (1994), and South
Centre (1996). Spencer (2004) has compiled a comprehensive annotated bibliography of the
scholarship on UN reform at www.global-challenges.org/index.html. Regarding Bretton
Woods reform, see for example Kenen (1994), Bretton Woods Commission (1994), and
Haq, Jolly and Streeten (1995).

2. The FSF was established in 1999 to promote international information exchange and
cooperation in financial supervision and surveillance by bringing together senior representatives from national financial authorities, international financial institutions, international
regulatory and supervisory agencies, committees of central bank experts, and the European
Central Bank.

former Mexican president Ernesto Zedillo and Tidjane Thiam of the Ivory Coast.[3]

Yet, the international system basically continues on a business-as-usual basis, with bureaucracies pursuing their day-to-day work and protecting their privileges. There are periodic calls for change, but they do not translate into plans for action. Even the dramatic world events since 2001—which signaled more clearly than ever that the time has come to comprehensively rethink the international system—have yet to prompt significant reform.

Global Democracy and Nation-States

At a time when democracy has triumphed as the model for human political organization, it is clear that legitimacy must be part of what defines the international system. Legitimacy in our time requires a certain degree of global democracy, but at the same time realistic global governance cannot ignore existing power in economic and military relationships. Any blueprint that ignores the resources controlled by the various actors and their relative weights in the world will lead nowhere. The reform agenda, therefore, must try to balance three divergent requirements:

- more global democracy that in some fundamental sense recognizes the equal value of all human beings,
- the ability to work with existing nation-states that have legal status as sovereigns and remain fundamental units of the international system, and
- the need to take into account the divergent economic and military capabilities of these nation-states.

When trying to reconcile the fundamental value of human equality with ongoing recognition of the sovereignty of individual states and the fact that they remain the building blocks of the international system, it must be remembered that even in the context of such countries as the United States, Germany, or India and regional groupings such as the European Union, democratic legitimacy is compatible with various forms of federal structures and upper chambers that do not simply reflect the "one person, one vote" principle. What may be more difficult to accept

3. The author is a member of the task force, which is supported by several governments, led by France and Sweden.

in terms of basic legitimacy is a partial "weighting" of countries by economic and military size.[4] Nonetheless, such classification is essential for a workable system. The objective is not a world government, but rather global governance that promotes participation, uses the principle of subsidiarity, acknowledges diversity and respects the sovereignty of even the smallest states, provides global public goods, solves international problems, and reflects the basic values of human equality and dignity.

The "realists" in the international relations field tend to downplay the importance or even relevance of legitimacy as a useful concept when analyzing global issues. But their description of the international system overemphasizes the dichotomy between politics "within" states and politics "between" states. Keohane and Nye (2001, 2) describe the realist view as follows:

> It makes no more sense to ask whether an interstate organization is democratic than to ask if a broom has a nice personality. One should ask merely if the instrument works well. One might ask about the personality of the janitor handling the broom, and one might ask about democratic procedures in the states using the interstate institution. In this realist view, world politics is inherently undemocratic and there is little point in lamenting the obvious.

As Keohane and Nye point out, this "realist" distinction is overdone. While the world today is far from an ideal global political community and no true global democracy as defined in national-level terms is likely anytime soon, elements of such a global community do in fact exist, encouraged by the information revolution, increasingly integrated world markets, global nongovernmental organizations, and fundamental values with a strong worldwide following. As a result of this emerging community of values, states that do not internally function as democracies suffer from diminished legitimacy in the international arena, particularly if and when they try to weigh in on decisions affecting the international system as a whole. While such nations are still recognized as sovereign actors,

---

4. Some might argue that an important rationale for effective international institutions is to reduce the need for military power, and that military capability as a weighting factor into a voting scheme could create a perverse incentive for nations to increase military spending. However, creating effective global governance must take into account the realities of the balance of power and the enduring importance of the ability to project military power. What can be hoped for is that military power should be recognized as only one among several factors that should determine the relative weight of nations, and that it should be used to protect human security rather than in pursuit of dominance.

their influence suffers from their lack of internal democracy. Increasingly, public opinion expects that to be legitimate, principals in the international system should have a functioning democracy at home.

Another aspect of the emerging community of values that has been greatly nurtured by the practice of democracy at the national level is the intrinsic equal value of human beings wherever they are and whatever they look like. In the 21st century, the legitimacy of global governance mechanisms must somehow relate to and encompass this fundamental value. People cannot be intrinsically equal inside a given nation-state and unequal across borders. Such a dichotomy, when pushed too far, offends widely shared ethical principles. It follows that global institutions cannot just derive their legitimacy and accountability from the extent to which they "are faithful agents of democratic principals" (Keohane and Nye 2001, 2). When these institutions aggregate the will of the principals involved—that is, the nation-states—the result must be perceived as fair and acceptable to people all across the globe. At the same time, the result must also be workable in a world where nation-states retain considerable power and support from their populations. A successful recipe ultimately requires a good dose of global democratic legitimacy, a sufficient degree of realism, and the greatest possible amount of efficacy.

The Global Networks and Transnational Clubs

Some argue that in lieu of a new and overarching international governance architecture, the emerging multitude of issue-oriented networks, nongovernmental organizations, and what are sometimes called "special transnational clubs" represent a sufficient response to the challenge of global governance.[5] Prompted by a range of international issues and challenges, many international networks have formed to address a variety of specific issues such as landmines, the environment, debt relief, and infrastructure development. Reinicke (2000) calls these different policy-based groups and entities "trisectoral networks."

The International Campaign to Ban Landmines (ICBL) has brought together governments, civil society, and international institutions including the United Nations. Thanks to efforts by the ICBL, which was honored with a Nobel Prize, 120 states signed the Ottawa Treaty in 1997

---

5. Reinicke (2000), Keohane and Nye (2001), and Rischard (2002) stress the growing role of networks for global governance without arguing that they constitute a sufficient response to the governance challenge.

banning the use of landmines. Other examples abound of successful efforts by such trisectoral networks, including what was perhaps one of the most significant recent achievements regarding the environment—the signing of the Montreal Protocol to control the production of substances that are depleting the ozone layer. This initiative involved the cooperation of governments, international institutions, industry, representative organizations, and civil society.

As an advocate for canceling debt for very poor countries, the NGO Jubilee 2000 has formed an effective coalition with several governments willing to take radical steps on debt issues. Transparency International has raised the profile of efforts to fight corruption worldwide by quantifying the problem and ranking countries according to a "corruption index." Other important efforts include everything from the World Commission on Dams, a multi-actor initiative that encourages socially responsible construction, to the Roll Back Malaria Partnership and the Coalition to Stop the Use of Child Soldiers.[6]

"Clubs" are usually more official forms of international policy networks. A few examples are the Basle Club of Central Bankers, the Group of Seven (G-7) Finance Ministers, the Paris Club (a group of official creditors), and such groupings as the G-20, the G-77, the G-24, and the Nonaligned Movement in the United Nations, assembling various countries around specific agendas. Where NGO networks usually raise awareness of problems and advocate solutions, the clubs negotiate deals or lend their authority to the design of procedures such as accounting standards or banking supervision guidelines. The "Evian Approach" recently adapted by the Paris Club provides more flexibility in debt restructuring. Clubs often work well because they are self-selected and bring together members who want to cooperate. Their disadvantage, of course, is that because they are not inclusive, those that are excluded do not necessarily consider the decisions reached to be legitimate or binding.

Among these clubs, the G-7, consisting of the United States, Canada, Japan, the United Kingdom, France, Germany, and Italy, has a very special and powerful role. The role has become recognized over the last two decades, although it is resented by those who are excluded.

Networks and clubs clearly will continue to make major contributions

6. For more detail on trisectoral networks, see *Global Public Policy Project* available at www.gppi.net.

to international governance and problem solving in the years ahead—trisectoral networks, in particular, strengthen the influence of civil society on national and international decisions and often mobilize knowledge and skills more effectively than bureaucratic public organizations (Rischard 2002; Reinicke 2000). By themselves, however, these entities cannot solve more complex problems that involve long-term issues of national sovereignty or the need to legitimize important systemic decisions. No network or special club can ensure successful trade negotiations, enhance the legitimacy of the IMF, or head off a conflict or war. In order to be effective in solving some of the issue-specific problems mentioned above, networks and clubs must be embedded into an overall governance structure that is accepted as legitimate. Civil society is important and helpful in bringing attention to problems and mobilizing support and participation. Many of the actions required, however, remain in the public domain, and the role and power of nongovernmental organizations is not sufficiently comprehensive or even legitimate to substitute for real reform. Self-selected clubs can play a useful and often leading role, but almost by definition they lack legitimacy. The proposals outlined in the section that follows address the need for broader reforms directed at the overall structure within which the various elements of global governance operate, be they international organizations, special clubs or groupings of countries, or global issue networks.

An Overarching Role for the United Nations

A reformed United Nations should provide the unifying framework for global governance in both the political and economic spheres. No other overarching setting exists that is based on the reality of nation-states, but which also has accumulated the necessary experience and global legitimacy.

The importance of the United Nations was in evidence during the period leading up to the Iraq crisis and, even more so, in the period after the war. Despite all the UN's shortcomings, including serious management failures common to most large bureaucracies, and the enduring reality of politics based on military power, all actors in the Iraq drama had to take it into account. In the end, the United States acted without a clear Security Council resolution authorizing intervention, but not without first trying to secure such a resolution and not without paying a heavy political price for proceeding without UN endorsement. Public opinion across the world made the presence or absence of a Security Council resolution a litmus test for legitimacy.[7]

The UN concept has global legitimacy not only in a narrow legal sense but also in terms of the perception of a vast majority of humanity. The overall design proposed below is based, therefore, on a strong integrating role for a reformed United Nations at the top of the international system. As mentioned above, the secretary-general of the United Nations did appoint a high-level panel of eminent and experienced experts to work on UN reform and, in particular, reform of the UN Security Council. This work is under way and will no doubt come up with very important recommendations some time in late 2004. The Zedillo-Thiam–led Task Force on Global Public Goods is also looking at "security" as a global public good and will have its own proposals in early 2005. The proposals presented in this book express a long-term vision. They may have the advantage of not being constrained by the need to reach a compromise between alternative views, some reflecting national policies. They may appear as less realistic in the sense of not being so constrained. They are not supposed to be just dreams, however. They are a result of weighing the political constraints as I have experienced them personally and they also reflect many discussions, particularly with friends and colleagues involved in progressive politics across the world. I do hope that some elements of what is proposed here will turn out not to be too far removed from what emerges from the work of the formally appointed task forces. I also trust that the debate will continue for a while beyond the time the task forces make their official recommendations and before political leaders will finally take the radical steps that are needed for real reform. Moreover, reform will only be possible if global progressive forces mobilize behind a set of concrete proposals that go beyond generalities and if global civil society puts real pressure on the formal political processes to encourage far-sighted thinking and political courage.

The proposals have at their core two high-level UN governance councils—a renewed Security Council and a proposed new Economic and Social Security Council—that together would provide strategic direction and broad governance to the entire international system. They would most definitely not attempt to be a world government, but would try to

---

7. To cite just one example, the Spanish government elected in 2004 took the decision to withdraw its troops from Iraq unless the UN took overall charge. The government of the United Kingdom felt it important enough to try, however unsuccessfully, to obtain a new UN resolution that would have led Spain to stay.

reflect the global community of nations and people, serve as a source of international legality and legitimacy, and secure global participation.

The two councils would attempt to set global priorities and would make certain key decisions such as authorizing cross-border interventions, choosing the top managers of international agencies, and encouraging efficient use of resources for promoting such global "goods" as peace and financial stability and avoiding such global "bads" as armed conflict, environmental degradation, and disease. The entire world should be involved in these decisions, and all countries should be entitled to some representation. The key problem, of course, is how to organize this representation without making decisive collective action impossible.

The renovated UN Security Council would mediate in political disputes between states, fight terrorism in all its forms, promote collective security and peace, and uphold human rights and the rights of minorities. The council would set global policy on these issues and have the means to enforce it. The new UN Economic and Social Security Council, constituted at a much higher level than the current Economic and Social Council (ECOSOC), which is not much more than a debating forum, would oversee global governance in the economic and social spheres, including the environment, by serving as a coordinating and legitimizing structure for all the UN specialized agencies dealing with economic, social, and environmental matters, as well as the WTO and the Bretton Woods institutions.[8] The strengths and operational autonomy of individual agencies would be maintained, but the UN Economic and Social Security Council would provide an overall framework of legitimacy and efficiency.

The remainder of this chapter focuses on the UN Security Council, while the proposed UN Economic and Social Security Council will be discussed in the context of the chapters that follow on the Bretton Woods institutions, particularly in chapter 4. Chapter 7, which examines how the WTO could be reformed and strengthened as part of the overall international architecture, also discusses a possible oversight and coordinating role for a UN Economic and Social Security Council as regards trade, labor, and other issues. The proposals here in no way advocate absorption of the Bretton Woods institutions or the WTO into the UN administration. To be effective, these institutions should preserve their operational autonomy and continue to build on the independent professionalism

---

8. Environmental protection should be one of the key objectives of the new UN Economic and Social Security Council. One could name it Economic, Social and Environmental Security Council.

accumulated over decades. It is only their high-level governance that would become part of overall UN governance, thus benefiting from the legitimacy of a renewed United Nations.

Why propose two councils rather than just one to oversee both the political and security sphere and the economic and social sphere? The reason is because the relative importance or the most desirable "weights" of different nations or grouping of nations at the top level governance of the international system may not be the same for the different spheres. For both operational reasons (the ability to act) and because of the realities of power, military capability must be a determining factor in governance of the security domain. The situation is somewhat different, however, when it comes to economic and social matters. It would be perfectly appropriate for the weights in the top-level economic and social governance council to reflect strongly the effort of a country or a group of countries ready to spend large amounts of resources on funding global public goods. Population also should carry a larger weight in the economic and social sphere than in the security sphere.

Rather than complicating matters, differences in the relative power of countries in the different spheres could well make compromise easier. Realistically, Brazil or India, for example, might have significantly larger weights on the Economic and Social Security Council than on the Security Council.[9] In addition, at any one time, a larger number of countries could have actual seats on one of the two councils without unduly increasing the council's size. Finally, the experience and competence required in the two spheres are different, and the representatives serving on one council might well have different backgrounds than those serving on the other. For all these reasons, it may be preferable to have two councils rather than a single one that attempts to integrate across all issues. The areas of competence of each council must be clearly defined, but this need not preclude close and structured cooperation between the two. The councils could meet jointly on a periodic basis to address crosscutting areas of concern.[10] Provided the areas of competence are clearly delineated, jurisdictional disputes should be unlikely, but a dispute resolution procedure may nevertheless have to be built into the system. In the event of disagreement, the

9. See appendix B, table 1, for the country and constituency voting strengths on the proposed UN Economic and Social Security Council.

10. Alternatively, there could be two subcommittees within a council. The question would remain, however, as to whether to assign different voting weights to countries based on the subcommittee on which they serve and vote.

two councils would meet jointly, and the dispute could be resolved by a simple majority of the weighted votes of all members present from both councils. Finally, it may be important to note that a UN Economic and Social Security Council could be created as a new structure, without immediately having to implement radical change in the existing Security Council. The economic and social sphere could "lead" the security sphere.

Current Security Council

The United Nations was not the first attempt to establish a world organization responsible for international peace. The devastating effects of the First World War united internationalists such as US president Woodrow Wilson and others to propose the creation of a League of Nations to prevent future wars. The league proved to be an unsuccessful attempt to secure world peace, having failed after a decade in existence to stop the aggression of the 1930s and the world's slide into devastating war.[11]

During the Second World War, US president Franklin Roosevelt and British prime minister Winston Churchill met to draft a charter formalizing US material support for Britain. This document, called the Atlantic Charter, was to become a blueprint for the postwar period.

The initial draft included a statement that proposed the establishment of an "effective international organization," which was later revised to a "wider and permanent system of general security." The Atlantic Charter was signed on August, 14, 1941. The charter announced that the signatories sought no aggrandizement and recognized the right of all peoples to choose their own form of government and to approve any territorial changes that might affect them. It also guaranteed all nations the right to trade and to navigate anywhere in the world and called for international cooperation to promote improved labor standards, economic advancement, and social security so that "all the men in all the lands may live out their lives in freedom from fear and want."

Soon after, the United States would enter the war after the Japanese attack on Pearl Harbor in December 1941. On the first day of 1942, representatives of 26 Allied nations fighting against the Axis Powers met in Washington, D.C., to pledge their support for the Atlantic Charter

11. The league was mainly a creation of President Wilson's ideals (his famous 14 points), but Wilson's aggressive support for the league backfired in the United States. The Republicans successfully weakened Wilson when he used the league as a major issue in his democratic congressional campaign.

by signing the "Declaration by United Nations." This was the first time the term "United Nations," which was suggested by Roosevelt, was officially used.

Diplomatic interaction between the British, Soviets, and Americans, as well as US Senate approval of the initiative, opened the way to draft the constitutive texts of this new world organization. In August 1944, the United States invited the Soviets, British, and later the Chinese to Dumbarton Oaks in Washington for conversations. While there was overall agreement on the responsibilities of the Security Council, the General Assembly, and the Secretariat, veto powers in the Security Council remained to be settled after Dumbarton Oaks. The Soviets insisted on having veto power for any type of resolution. The United States wanted permanent council members to be able to veto enforcement actions, but argued that a party to a dispute should not to be able to vote on the recommendations. The veto issue was settled at the Yalta Conference in 1945, when Roosevelt, Churchill, and Joseph Stalin agreed that the permanent five members (their nations plus France and China) could veto Security Council actions, but a party to a dispute could not block discussion of an issue or attempts at peaceful settlement. The veto power of the Permanent Five was already controversial in 1945—Australia, among others, wanted to prevent use of the veto to block attempts at peaceful settlement. Stalin was determined to prevent any dilution of the veto power, and his opposition finally led the nonpermanent states to relent. After solving the veto and General Assembly membership issues,[12] the American, British, and Soviet leaders called for a United Nations Conference to be held in April 1945 in San Francisco. Two months after the conference, the UN charter was approved.

The UN charter is based on the principle of sovereign equality of members. At Dumbarton Oaks, it was agreed that all "peace-loving" states would be eligible for membership.[13] Sovereign equality meant that what mattered was the legal status of statehood regardless of size, wealth, or military power. This fundamental principle was to become the "one state, one vote" principle of the General Assembly.

---

12. The Soviets initially insisted on having 15 votes in the General Assembly, one for each Soviet republic. After President Roosevelt's counterproposal of 48 votes for each US state, the Soviets settled for three votes for Russia, Byelorussia, and the Ukraine.

13. The former Axis powers and their allies initially were denied membership, an exclusion that continued until Italy and Spain were admitted in 1955, Japan in 1956, and East and West Germany in 1973.

The General Assembly has important functions such as admitting states to UN membership, electing nonpermanent members to the Security Council and members to ECOSOC and the Trusteeship Council, appointing judges to the International Court of Justice jointly with the Security Council, and appointing the secretary-general, although the council itself must nominate the candidate. Despite these important functions, the huge disparities in the power of the 191 UN member states (as of 2002) means, and has always meant, that the General Assembly is an international body where weaker states can debate international affairs in an important official forum without having any real decision-making power.

The real power at the United Nations thus rests with the Security Council, which is responsible for maintaining international peace and security and has the authority to act on behalf of all UN members. Chapter VI of the UN charter specifies the Security Council's powers to seek a peaceful settlement of disputes and provides a wide range of techniques for investigating disputes and helping to achieve a resolution without the use of force. Chapter VII specifies the Security Council's authority to identify aggressors and to commit all UN members to take enforcement measures such as invoking economic sanctions or providing military forces for joint action. In addition, the Security Council recommends the admission of new member states, advises the General Assembly on the appointment of the secretary-general, and together with the assembly elects the judges of the International Court of Justice.

In addition to its Permanent Five members, the council has 10 nonpermanent members elected by the General Assembly for two-year, non-renewable terms, with only five new members elected each year. No country can serve successive terms as a nonpermanent member. At least four nonpermanent members must vote for a resolution to pass, a provision that allows seven nonpermanent members to block a resolution agreed to by all of the Permanent Five—something that has never happened in the history of the United Nations.

The nonpermanent membership of the Security Council was extended from six to its present 10 in 1965. Also in 1965, the General Assembly adopted a resolution allocating five seats to Africa and Asia, two to Latin America, two to Western Europe and other areas, and one to Eastern Europe. The council's presidency rotates monthly among its members.

The post–World War II division of the world into two antagonistic alliances meant that any one member of either side with veto power was easily able to bloc any attempt to obtain a binding Security Council resolution. This essentially made it impossible for the council to become the effective instrument of global governance and international legality that it was designed to be by the founding fathers.

With the collapse of the Soviet Union, the political dynamics determining Security Council behavior changed significantly, and hope emerged that with the Cold War veto standoff finally gone the council might function as originally envisioned. Since the end of the Cold War, the Security Council has indeed dealt with any number of conflicts. When Iraq invaded Kuwait in August 1990, the Security Council issued a dozen resolutions condemning the invasion and calling for international assistance to Kuwait. UN Resolution 678 authorized member states cooperating with Kuwait to use "all necessary means" to restore peace in the area. The passing of this resolution followed major US diplomatic efforts to convince the Soviets to approve the resolution. The UN-sponsored military coalition led by the United States forced an end to the Iraqi occupation and restored Kuwaiti sovereignty. The US-led coalition did not invade Iraq, staying within the limits set by the UN resolution, which did not include support for an occupation of Iraq. The first Gulf War thus seemed to signal that the Security Council might be able to deal with major threats to world peace. Unfortunately, events in the Balkans quickly changed that perception.

The Security Council became involved in the Yugoslav conflict as heavy fighting broke out in 1991 after Slovenia and Croatia declared independence from the Federal Republic of Yugoslavia, which was dominated by Serbia. The council first deferred negotiation of the ceasefire to European initiatives in line with Chapter VIII of the UN charter, which stipulates that regional organizations can resolve local disputes. But European Union diplomacy had little success. As the fighting escalated, the Security Council authorized the creation of the UN Protection Force for Yugoslavia (UNPROFOR), which initially was deployed in Croatia. Heavy fighting shifted to Bosnia-Herzegovina, and as signs of "ethnic cleansing" became more evident, UNPROFOR coordinated efforts to deliver humanitarian aid to civilians who increasingly had become targets in the conflict. The main problem facing UNPROFOR was its limited mandate, which did not authorize the use of force to stop ethnic cleansing. In fact, the presence of UNPROFOR forces without proper mandate may even have exacerbated the conflict. The Security Council could have taken more decisive action had it not been for the Russian veto threat blocking any resolution suggesting more forceful action. Learning from that experience, the United States did not wait for another deadlock at the Security Council during the Kosovo crisis and intervened without Security Council authorization, no doubt preventing massacres that might have cost tens of thousands of innocent lives, but also undermining the legal basis for the intervention. NATO also conducted air operations without Security Council authorization, although subsequent council resolutions on Kosovo *de facto* legitimized the operation *ex post*.

The threat to disable the Security Council through recourse to the veto since the end of the Cold War has not always come from the Russian Federation. The United States put the council in a difficult position by asking that immunity be granted for its soldiers from the International Criminal Court (ICC). The United States convinced the Security Council to unanimously adopt a resolution granting a 12–month immunity from the ICC to all UN peacekeeping personnel from states that are not parties to the Rome Statute.[14] In 2003, the United States pushed through another resolution extending immunity one more year by simply threatening to draw back all its forces from UN peacekeeping operations. Many nations perceived this episode as one in which the Security Council was held hostage by the United States.

The Security Council's post–Cold War problems were most clearly illustrated by the Iraq crisis of 2002–03. The United States initially seemed to have hesitated as to whether to seek a Security Council resolution at all. To some degree this was due to the fear that at least one of the Permanent Five members would exercise its veto. In the end, and with strong encouragement from British prime minister Tony Blair, the United States did try to obtain a resolution clearly authorizing the use of force, but in February 2003, Jacques Chirac announced that France would veto such a resolution as long as the UN arms inspectors had not finished their job. In the meantime, nonpermanent members, including small countries such as Cameroon and medium-sized nations such as Chile, faced intense diplomatic pressure from both the United States and France, with the latter leading the anti-intervention coalition. The fact that one country could veto the resolution, and that the United States quite clearly announced that it would act as it saw fit no matter what happened at the Security Council, underlined the reality that the UN arrangements were—and

14. The Rome Statute, which is the treaty that established the International Criminal Court, gives the ICC jurisdiction over three main classes of offenses: genocide, crimes against humanity, and war crimes.

remain—insufficient for encouraging and facilitating an effective role of the Security Council, despite the fact that the bipolar world of the Cold War has disappeared.

Reforming the Security Council

In his speech inaugurating the UN General Assembly in 2003, Secretary-General Kofi Annan recognized all that has been achieved under the UN's longstanding structure, but also acknowledged that "we must decide whether it is possible to continue on [this] basis . . . or whether radical changes are needed. . . . And we must not shy away from questions about the adequacy, and effectiveness, of the rules and instruments at our disposal. Among those instruments, none is more important than the Security Council."

For the Security Council to impart new strength and effectiveness to global governance in the political and security sphere, radical reform is needed so that council decisions be perceived to be much more legitimate than they are today, thereby commanding greater support from public opinion worldwide as well as from the community of nation-states.

Numerous global governance reform proposals have been put forth for the United Nations, but until recently the discussion concerning Security Council reform has focused on increasing the number of countries or phasing out the Permanent Five veto.[15] Larger and important countries such as India, Italy, Germany, Japan, and Brazil come to mind when one thinks about enlargement of the UN Security Council. Nigeria and South Africa are obvious sub-Saharan Africa candidates. But, then, what about Mexico as another very important Latin American country, and Egypt, a historical leader among Arab countries, or Pakistan, which claims a seat

15. A notable exception is Schwartzberg (2003), who proposed a weighted voting scheme for the General Assembly (and possibly for the Security Council) in order to reform the existing "unrealistic" one nation, one vote system and end the council veto. Schwartzberg (2004) elaborates on his earlier proposal, with greater emphasis on the Security Council. While Schwartzberg's approach is somewhat similar to that proposed in this chapter, the factors determining the weighting are different and lead to different voting strengths. Falk and Strauss (2001) have proposed a world parliament made of civil society, which in the future may be associated with the UN General Assembly. Kennedy and Russet (1995) proposed an increase in the number of both permanent and rotating members of the Security Council and a restriction of the veto to questions of war and peace, as the founders intended. For a detailed list of major proposals, see the Global Policy Forum website at www.globalpolicy.org/security/issues/debateindex.htm.

in the council as a leading "Islamic" nation, particularly if India obtains a permanent seat? While simply adding new members may be a solution that follows the path of least resistance—the old members stay and some new ones are happy to gain seats—it is unlikely to solve the fundamental problems of the Security Council. A larger and more unwieldy Security Council is unlikely to solve the underlying problem of legitimacy. Indeed, if new permanent members were given veto power, the chances of paralysis would increase further, while if they were added without veto power, a new council may be perceived as less legitimate than the old one: there would be countries of roughly equal importance as permanent members, with some having the veto power, while others would not.

Reform thus should be based on moving toward a system of weighted votes and universal participation that involves all countries, but under which the weights in the voting scheme also reflect the actual size, ability to act, and importance of the participating nation-states. Instead of individual veto rights, supermajorities would be required for the most important decisions. For cross-border military interventions, for example, the supermajority required could be four-fifths of the weighted votes. For other matters that require a majority for a binding decision, that proportion might be three-fifths.

Using these criteria, the 2003 invasion of Iraq would have required a four-fifths majority decision, while a decision on the continued application or termination of sanctions would have required a three-fifths majority. Use of military force in Bosnia, Kosovo, and Afghanistan would all have required four-fifths majorities.

In short, the ways in which the Security Council could promote peaceful means to resolve a dispute would all require three-fifths majorities. For example, appointing a UN mediator to negotiate a peaceful ending of a conflict would require three-fifths of the weighted votes, as would recommendations of new states for UN membership as well as the resolution that recognized the Iraqi Governing Council.

Currently, both military action and economic sanctions are classified under Chapter VII of the UN charter, whereas other dispute settlement techniques come under Chapter VI. One could identify decisions requiring a four-fifths majority as those coming under Chapter VII, and decisions requiring three-fifths majorities as those coming under Chapter VI. It would probably be better, however, to require a larger supermajority for actual military intervention than that required for the application of economic sanctions as suggested above.

Reform efforts should not be deterred simply because it is probably not possible to find a perfect weighting scheme for Security Council votes that all members would accept as optimal. The same could be said for any voting scheme or electoral law at a national or regional level. There are no perfect or ideal schemes, but rather schemes that are accepted and considered legitimate by large majorities of participants—which is precisely what should be the goal at the global level.

The proposal described below is based on a long-run, "steady-state" vision of the Security Council, although the exact voting strengths are based on recent data and would change over time. Transition formulas most certainly would be required—and might actually be desirable—to get the Security Council from where it is today to where it should be in the long run. Moreover, any reasonable proposal must include adjustment mechanisms that allow a given structure to evolve over time. Perhaps the most serious weakness built into the United Nations at the time of its creation was institutionalizing "ownership" of the veto power in a way that reflects the world of 1945, without any practical provision for change.

What is proposed below is a long-term vision toward which the system should progress. However difficult it may appear to realize this vision, not achieving fundamental progress toward much greater legitimacy will lead to huge problems. It is also important to add that it is informed citizens of all countries that should make the decisions on reform, not just bureaucracies that may want to perpetuate existing arrangements which provide bureaucratic advantages to a few without really being in either the national or global interest.

Under the reform arrangement, each country would be weighted by four factors reflecting relative importance in the international system: population, GDP, financial contributions to funding global goods, and military capability. The latter could ideally evolve into a proxy for potential contribution to peacekeeping. The weights would have to ascribe relative importance to these four factors. As an illustration, the weighted vote of India, W_{INDIA}, would be as follows:

$$W_{INDIA} = a_1 (P_i) + a_2 (GDP_i) + a_3 (B_i) + a_4 (M_i)$$

Here, a_1 to a_4 are agreed weights identical for all countries and adding to one; P_i is the share of India's population in the world total; GDP_i is the share of Indian GDP in the world total; B_i is the share India contributes to the global public goods budget; and M_i is India's share of global military capability. The population share is relatively straightforward to compute, although a decision would have to be taken whether residents or nationals are to enter the formula, but the other three factors involve more difficult measurement decisions.[16]

Taking for the moment nominal GDP at constant 1995 US dollars, contributions to the UN budget as a proxy for contributions to the funding of global public goods, and military spending in nominal dollars as a proxy for military capacity, and setting $a_1 = a_2 = a_3 = a_4$, India's weighted vote (W_{INDIA}) would be $W_{INDIA} = 5.162$ percent.

The voting powers that result from such a scheme must have two essential characteristics: they must appear reasonable and appeal to the public demand for legitimacy, and they must be acceptable to the nation-states that would have to agree to the reform. The process of moving toward such a reform would involve global interaction between civil society, political parties, and opinion leaders, as well as negotiations between sovereign states.

After agreement is reached on the weighting scheme and measurement issues, the question would remain as to how to organize participation on the Security Council, given that participation of all states in General Assembly style meetings would be impractical. For Security Council meetings to operate effectively and allow for discussion and debate, membership should consist of a manageable number of countries representing, at any one time, the world community. The practice of having some members as permanent and others as rotating members has advantages and could be combined with the reformed voting system. One possible compromise arrangement would have the United States, the European Union, Russia, China, India, and Japan as permanent members. Other countries

16. Any quantitative measure used in the calculation of such a weighting scheme will be somewhat controversial. For GDP, one has to decide whether to use purchasing power parity (PPP) adjusted GDP or nominal GDP. A more serious problem is military capability. Tables 3.1 and 3.2 use military expenditures as a rough measure of military capability, but a more sophisticated index of military power could be calculated by combining military spending and capitalization (a measure of spending on equipment) that reflects military power with spending on military forces capable of peacekeeping operations. Ideally, this measure over time should come to reflect the potential to contribute to peacekeeping operations—for example, the military component of the Commitment to Development Index compiled by the Center for Global Development/Foreign Policy measures the contributions of 21 wealthy countries to peacekeeping and forcible humanitarian intervention missions endorsed by international bodies. But the weights must also reflect the balance of power in the international system. In sum, careful analysis would be needed in order to establish weights that address a wide range of concerns from moral dilemmas to a realistic reflection of the power balance.

would be members of constituencies, i.e., groups of countries that would elect one or more representatives. The constituency categories would have representatives for Other Europe, Other Asia, Africa, the Arab League, and Latin America, the Caribbean, and Canada. Each of these constituencies could have up to three elected seats on the Security Council, depending on the total weight and the number of countries the constituency represents. Occupation of these seats would rotate every two years, not unlike the current practice. What would be different, however, is that each member of the Security Council so elected would "own" a share of the weighted regional vote determined by the votes received during the biannual elections in that constituency.

Table 3.1 describes a possible grouping of countries in the world by regional constituencies and the weight each country and constituency would carry in the total, using the weights and principles discussed above. The computation of the weights should be taken as broadly illustrative rather than a precise prescription. More detailed empirical work would be needed to establish precise prescriptive weights. The weights should be updated every five years to take into account changes in the underlying variables such as population and GDP. Appendix A presents a comprehensive list by country and constituency of all UN members' weights under Security Council arrangement proposed here, and weights computed based on recent data. It is important to always remember that these weights will change over time.

Table 3.1 shows that the United States and the European Union, because of their overall weight, would each have *de facto* veto power for decisions requiring a four-fifths majority. In other words, the Security Council could not sanction a cross-border military intervention if either the United States or the European Union did not agree. However, neither could individually block a decision requiring a three-fifths majority, although together they could.

Other members would have to combine to reach the blocking majority on decisions requiring a four-fifths majority. For example, even together, Russia and China could not have blocked Security Council clearance for intervention in Kosovo. They would have needed votes from other constituencies to reach a 20 percent share of the vote.[17] The developing

---

17. Kagan (2004, chapter 8) examines how Security Council action was blocked on Kosovo and compares European attitudes to US action without council authorization in Kosovo to the debate on US intervention in Iraq, again without council authorization.

Table 3.1 *Permanent and constituency member voting strengths on proposed UN Security Council*

| Countries | Factors determining voting strength (% of total)[a] | | | | Result |
	Contribution to global public goods budget	Popu-lation	GDP	Military capacity	Weighted vote
Permanent members (6 seats)					
EU and official candidates (28)[b]	0.37	0.09	0.31	0.27	26.0
United States	0.22	0.05	0.27	0.40	23.2
Japan	0.19	0.02	0.17	0.05	10.9
China	0.02	0.21	0.03	0.04	7.5
India	0.004	0.17	0.01	0.02	5.2
Russian Federation	0.01	0.02	0.01	0.02	1.6
Constituencies (8 seats)					
Other Asia (40)	0.05	0.18	0.07	0.06	9.0
Latin America, Caribbean, and Canada (35)	0.08	0.09	0.08	0.04	7.4
Arab League (21)	0.02	0.05	0.01	0.06	3.4
Africa (43)	0.005	0.10	0.01	0.01	3.2
Other Europe (19)	0.03	0.02	0.02	0.03	2.5

a. The actual weighted vote would be revisited every five years to reflect underlying changes in the determining factors.

b. Numbers in parentheses are the number of countries represented in that constituency.

Notes and sources: Contribution to global public goods budget is the member contribution to the UN regular budget for 2004. Population is that of member states in 2001, from the World Bank, *World Development Indicators,* and the CIA Factbook. GDP is that of 2001 in constant 1995 US dollars, from the World Bank, *World Development Indicators.* Military capability is based on military expenditure in 2001 in constant 1998 US dollars, from the Stockholm International Peace Research Institute (SIPRI).

countries as a group would have more than the 20 percent needed to veto decisions that require a fourth-fifths majority.

The weights in table 3.1 should not be considered only from the point of view of which action could be blocked by 20 percent of the votes. Even though the United States and European Union could individually block a decision requiring a four-fifths majority and together block a decision requiring a three-fifths majority, they could not force either type of decision without securing some form of support from elsewhere in the world.

Consider the case of the Balkan wars of the 1990s. Economic measures to be enforced by the Security Council could have been determined by a positive vote from the United States, the European Union, and Japan (23.2 + 26.0 + 10.9 = 60.1 percent). For military intervention, however, 19.9 more percentage points would have been required. These could have come, for example, from such constituency representatives as Other Asia, Latin America, and the Arab League.

Permanent Members

Although the proposed Security Council would have a mixture of permanent members and nonpermanent members representing multicountry constituencies, the actual distinction between the types of members would not be as sharp as it is today. The arrangement proposed here would assign one seat to Other Europe, two seats to Other Asia, two seats to Latin America and the Caribbean and Canada, two seats to Africa, and one seat to the Arab League. Adding these eight seats to six permanent seats would lead to a Security Council of 14 members—a manageable size that would allow for real discussion and productive meetings. Being a permanent member would of course still be desirable, but it would be less advantageous than it is now because permanent members would no longer have a right to veto just by virtue of their permanence. Some nonpermanent members representing their constituencies would have voting powers close to or even exceeding that of some of the permanent members.

In terms of permanent seats, the proposal here, because it is long term in nature, unites the 25 European Union members as of May 2004 with the three official candidate countries (Romania, Bulgaria, and Turkey) expected to become members in the near future.[18] The European Union would need an internal mechanism to determine how the EU representative would vote on the UN Security Council—one possibility would be to use the qualified majority voting (QMV) formula that is foreseen in the draft EU constitution for a range of issues, and which requires 65 percent of the EU population and 55 percent of the member states for approval of measures. The draft constitution does not, however, include foreign and security policy decisions as those to be agreed on by the QMV, retaining instead unanimity in the foreign policy and security areas. For the Security Council reform proposed here to be workable, the EU would

---

18. Alternatively, the three candidate countries could be included in Other Europe.

have to agree to use the QMV formula in the context of Security Council votes, otherwise a single member could force the union to abstain within the reformed Security Council, which would be absurd. If the European Union could not agree on at least some form of QMV for purposes of Security Council decisions, EU representation could be rearranged in a way similar to the other multicountry constituencies. However, employing the QMV model for Security Council votes would not imply the complete unification of EU countries' foreign and security policies. EU members could continue to manage their bilateral relations and defense policies individually. The only requirement would be a binding mechanism to determine a common vote on the Security Council. Some European Union countries appear already to support a limited move toward joint decision making in global governance. The Social Democrats essentially agreed in their pan-European platforms to such unification of EU representation in global institutions, and many members of the right-of-center European Popular Party share this view. There is also strong support for such "unification" of EU representation in global institutions among citizens in many EU countries.

The proposal would mean that France and the United Kingdom would lose their individual veto powers, whereas Germany would not gain that power. In terms of what might be called the "global democracy" aspect of legitimacy, it is quite clear that none of these three countries should have an individual veto power, since each has less than 1.5 percent of the world population. Their individual economic and military weights also are insufficient to justify an individual veto right.

As part of the European Union, however, it would seem entirely reasonable for them to share in the EU's veto right over decisions requiring a four-fifths majority. The EU would have to acquire legal personality as foreseen in its proposed constitution, not just in the context of the United Nations. That having been resolved, the role of Europe in a reformed United Nations would reflect the current European reality, as opposed to that of 1945.[19] It would also, incidentally, allow for a significant economy of resources for EU countries—a positive development that, unfortunately, might well face purely bureaucratic resistance.

19. Some claim it is unrealistic to ask France and the United Kingdom to give up their veto, even as part of a medium-term vision. And yet, if one were to ask any reasonable panel of experts or well-informed citizens whether the UK and France are likely to retain their vetoes, say in 2020, the answer would be no. Somehow we have to get from today to 2020!

The United States, with more than 23 percent of the overall vote under the proposed arrangement, could by itself block all decisions requiring a four-fifths majority. Given US economic and military might, any global governance system in the political and security sphere that does not give this power to the United States would be unworkable and have no chance of being accepted. In addition, the US population is much larger than that of Germany, France, and the United Kingdom combined, and is close to twice that of Japan or Russia. Thus the proposed reform would be entirely compatible with US concerns while also enabling the United States to be a global leader in an international system with greater legitimacy and that allows for real participation and common decision making. The United States would be the only individual nation-state with a veto on decisions requiring a four-fifths majority, and the US vote would be roughly equal in weight to the vote of the European Union, despite the fact that the EU population is much larger and overall European Union GDP exceeds that of the United States, because the proposal takes military capability into account.

Russia would remain a permanent member, to some degree because of its remaining military strength. It is also likely that if there is indeed continued socioeconomic stabilization, GDP will likely increase rapidly given Russia's size and natural resources—assuming the country remains socially and economically stable—increasing Russia's weight in the system. Russia does not have grounds to insist on retaining its individual veto power, however, which is a remnant of conditions in what is now a distant past. If Russia itself were to continue to have a blocking majority, legitimacy would require the same for, at the very least, China, India, Japan, and Brazil, complicating the working of the reformed council and multiplying the chances for the kind of stalemates so damaging to the UN system in the past.

Russia's voting weight in the total would likely benefit from a more comprehensive definition and measurement of military capability than the preliminary one used here, which is simply based on military expenditures. This requires a more detailed and careful quantitative analysis that is beyond the scope of this book.

China, India, and Japan are, by order of magnitude, larger players in the international system than any other individual country with the exception of the United States. Thus, they should be permanent members under the reform arrangements. However, because the proposed system would essentially rely on qualified majority voting, these countries individually would not have veto power over decisions requiring either four-fifths or three-fifths majorities. However, China's and India's respective weights would increase over time, and having India and Japan permanently join the Security Council would remedy today's unreasonable status quo and greatly enhance the council's legitimacy worldwide.

Another country with a major individual role in the international system is Brazil, which conceivably could be included as a permanent member. However, Brazil's individual weight, 2.17, is much smaller than the weights of what would be the two new permanent council members, Japan and India. Instead, Brazil would play a leading role in the Latin American constituency, as explained below.

Constituencies and Nonpermanent Members

In addition to the six permanent members discussed above, the new Security Council would have eight nonpermanent members representing various, essentially regional, constituencies. Other Europe would have one seat, Other Asia two, Latin America and the Caribbean and Canada two, the Arab League one, and Africa two. The computed weights, not the number of seats, would determine voting power—in other words, under the proposed arrangement it is the weights that are more fundamental to the nature of governance than the number of seats.

Nonetheless, the number of seats would also have some importance, since, irrespective of their voting power, countries would want to participate in Security Council meetings. Take, for example, Other Asia, including such countries as Indonesia, Thailand, Malaysia, Australia, and New Zealand, as well as small states like Vanuatu and Brunei. These countries would form a regional constituency and elect two representatives every two years to sit on the Security Council. These two nonpermanent members would each own a share of the regional vote, which could be determined by the amount of support they obtained during constituency elections. Let us assume, as an example, that Thailand, Indonesia, and New Zealand put forward their candidatures for nonpermanent seats for a given two-year period. Let us further assume that in the ensuing constituency election, Thailand gets 30, Indonesia 50, and New Zealand 20 percent of the weighted votes. As a result, Indonesia and Thailand would become nonpermanent members for the next two years.

To how much of the regional vote should they be entitled? The most reasonable of various formulas that might be considered would be one where Indonesia gets 62.5 percent of the regional weighted vote, and Thailand 37.5 percent, reflecting their relative success in the constituency vote, with the votes that went to New Zealand distributed proportionally to that success. This is a formula often used in national elections when there are threshold levels that parties must reach to enter parliaments. The votes that went to parties that did not reach these thresholds get distributed to those parties that made it past the post. In principle, each constituency could decide what rules it would want to use, including whether or not countries could be reelected for more than one term, or particular rotation arrangements. The details matter less than respect for the overarching principles as well as for giving some allowance for rules and arrangements that best suit the specific circumstances of particular constituencies.

The result of the proposed arrangement would be a Security Council with six permanent and eight nonpermanent members, but one where all countries of the world would be represented. The council would meet at the head of state or government level at least once a year, perhaps during the September meetings of the United Nations in New York.[20] The other meetings would continue to be held in New York with the participation of the "permanent representatives" (ambassadors) to the UN. It may be desirable, however, to introduce specific internationally accepted criteria for membership on the UN Security Council in terms of career experiences, seniority, etc. The total number of 14 members would allow for efficient and productive meetings. The UN Security Council would have wide-ranging powers to set up particular subcommittees, to open certain meetings to civil society and the press, to hold entirely closed meetings, and to raise funds for security-related purposes.

A new UN Security Council along the lines proposed above would represent a quantum leap in terms of the council's legitimacy worldwide and would open the way for a more powerful global governance mechanism in the security and political sphere. Growing to some degree out of existing arrangements, the proposed scheme would preserve a certain amount of continuity, yet reflect the world of the 21st century and the challenges faced today rather than those faced almost 60 years ago in what was a very different world.

20. Note that there is no such meeting for the current UN Security Council.

Weighting Quality of Democracy

Some object to a strengthened role for the United Nations because of the uneven quality of the democracy that is practiced by member countries. In fact, while liberal democracy based on free and competitive elections has spread worldwide in unprecedented fashion over the last few decades, many countries still cannot be said to practice democracy in a manner accepted by most nations in today's world. Robert Kagan has argued that NATO would be a better instrument than the UN for collective action because NATO is an alliance of liberal democracies without undemocratic members ("A Tougher War for the US Is One of Legitimacy," *The New York Times,* January 24, 2004).

There is no doubt that the international system should evolve in a direction where the quality of domestic democracy becomes very important in determining a sovereign country's legitimacy as an international actor. However, the weight of history has to be overcome before a simple link between domestic democracy and international legitimacy can be firmly and simply established. First is the lingering memory of colonialism, when advanced democracies subjugated other countries and peoples and totally ignored the democratic aspirations of the conquered populations. Second, even as colonialism came to a close, the advanced democracies continued not only to condone but also sometimes to actively support undemocratic regimes across the world. Salvador Allende was the democratically elected president of Chile when he was assassinated in a CIA-backed coup in 1973—a particularly blatant example, but by no means the only one. So it seems premature today for the leading nations of the world to require flawless internal democracy from countries where not so long ago they themselves had undermined democratic development. With time, the situation may change, particularly if the advanced democracies consistently withdraw support from undemocratic regimes and work for more democracy within the international system as such. It is inconsistent, after all, to stress the liberal-democratic principle of equality and freedom and at the same time narrowly defend realistic-nationalistic principles in international affairs. Liberal democracy implies a system of values that extends beyond one's borders, and only consistent practice of these principles in international affairs will allow for the emergence of an ideological and historical basis upon which to hold every country strictly to democratic standards before allowing it to participate in international decision making. In the long run, those standards could become an important factor in determining a sovereign country's weight in international decision making. But this is likely to be a gradual process during which time a strongly shared set of international values, applied consistently and transparently, gradually replace the memories of colonialism and the Cold War.

Appendix A, table 2, outlines a variant of the proposed weighting system for the new Security Council that would employ the Freedom House Index to measure domestic freedoms as one of the weighting factors.[21] An alternative approach would be to move toward a system which sets certain basic democratic standards that would have to be met in order for a country to qualify for membership in international institutions, not unlike what the European Union requires of countries that want to join the union.

Transition Phase

The reforms necessary to put in place a reasonable and balanced alternative to the current but outdated UN Security Council arrangement would require a transition phase during which the existing Permanent Five nations would retain some of their special status, perhaps in the form of greater voting weight than the formula that represents the ultimate reform objective. Current permanent council members could, for example, retain their individual veto power for a period of years while the new system would be phased in. The existing veto power could remain "superimposed" on the new weighted voting scheme for a number of years, perhaps a decade. The existing Permanent Five might also agree to restrict the use of their vetoes to a narrower range of decisions. Reform may in fact be easier to achieve if the old Permanent Five have a strong say in exactly how the weights proposed above would be computed. In addition, it might be reasonable for each of those nations to get an upfront 2 percentage point allocation in voting strength—in addition to the weight derived from the four-factor formula—for a longer transition period of, say, 20 years. In other words, the whole world, including the current

---

21. Appendix A, table 2, focuses on the political rights element of the Freedom House Index, which measures countries using a scale from 1 to 7 (the higher the number, the more antidemocratic the regime). According to the index, the advanced Western democracies and Japan get a 1, China a 7, India a 2, and Russia a 5. For the appendix, the scale was linearly transformed to a 1.5–0.5 point scale (half being worst), and the existing weighted votes were multiplied by the transformed Freedom House Index. Later these weights were scaled so that the total of all countries' weights would add up to 100 percent. Table 2 in the appendix was prepared following a suggestion of Francis Fukuyama.

Table 3.2 *Permanent and constituency member voting strengths in transition phase of proposed UN Security Council*

| Countries | Factors determining transition period voting strength[a] (% of total) | | | | Result |
	Contribution to global public goods budget	Population	GDP	Military capacity	Weighted vote
Permanent members (6 seats)					
EU and official candidates (28)[b]	0.37	0.09	0.31	0.27	27.4
United States	0.22	0.05	0.27	0.40	22.9
Japan	0.19	0.02	0.17	0.05	9.8
China	0.02	0.21	0.03	0.04	8.8
India	0.004	0.17	0.01	0.02	4.6
Russian Federation	0.01	0.02	0.01	0.02	3.4
Constituencies (8 seats)					
Other Asia (40)	0.05	0.18	0.07	0.06	8.1
Latin America, Caribbean, and Canada (35)	0.08	0.09	0.08	0.04	6.7
Arab League (21)	0.02	0.05	0.01	0.06	3.1
Africa (43)	0.005	0.10	0.01	0.01	2.9
Other Europe (19)	0.03	0.02	0.02	0.03	2.3

a. The actual weighted vote would be revisited every five years to reflect underlying changes in the determining factors.

b. Numbers in parentheses are the number of countries represented in that constituency.

Notes and sources: Contribution to global public goods budget is the member contribution to the UN regular budget for 2004. Population is that of member states in 2001, from the World Bank, *World Development Indicators,* and the CIA Factbook. GDP is in constant 1995 US dollars, from the World Bank, *World Development Indicators.* Military capability is based on military expenditure in constant 1998 US dollars, from the Stockholm International Peace Research Institute (SIPRI).

Permanent Five, would share 90 percent of the total votes according to the proposed formula, and the Permanent Five would get an additional equal allocation of the remaining 10 percent in recognition of their previous status. Table 3.2 shows what Security Council voting strength would look like at the beginning of the 20-year transition period.[22]

22. See appendix A, table 3, for country-by-country voting strengths on the proposed Security Council at the beginning of the 20-year transition period.

As discussed earlier, the EU countries would have to resolve among themselves how to organize their shared Security Council vote both in the transition phase and in the longer term. The transition arrangement would be particularly important for the Russian Federation, where current GDP may be unnaturally low because of the country's difficult transition from communism. Since the voting weights in the base formula would be revised every five years to reflect changes in the four factors determining voting weight, it is likely that the Russian Federation would increase its basic weight over the 20-year transition period. That transition thus would recognize Russia's special circumstances and work toward an equitable outcome for that nation.

The type of UN reform discussed in this chapter will be difficult to achieve politically even with a transition phase. The governance of reform must be accompanied by serious internal management reforms. Maintaining the current status quo will also be very difficult, however, because it is blatantly unfair and does not work. For all those who do believe that very worrisome security problems are awaiting the world as a whole, reform is in fact unavoidable. The world must face up to the need for a serious reform of global security arrangements. The proposals outlined above reflect arrangements that could work and may become acceptable, given some transition measures. No doubt other, somewhat different proposals could also constitute substantial progress. What is certain is that the Permanent Five cannot simply pretend that the veto they gave themselves will be accepted forever in its current form. One cannot set up an organization or a structure of governance at some point in history and expect that it remain unchanged forever. Insisting on the status quo is equivalent to undermining the United Nations as an instrument of global governance and peace. The security of all, including the security of Permanent Five citizens, depends on a strong and legitimate UN Security Council, able to enforce international law and champion the peaceful resolution of disputes. The concluding chapter of this book attempts to outline the political dynamics that could lead to UN reform of the type presented above.

Global Economic Governance and a New UN Economic and Social Security Council

To master globalization, we have to answer three basic questions. What institutional architecture do we need for international governance? How can we achieve legitimacy in the decision making? How can we arbitrate between domains?
DOMINIQUE STRAUSS-KAHN, FRENCH STATESMAN
La Flamme et la Cendre, 2002, p. 155.

Looking back at the six decades since John Maynard Keynes and Harry Dexter White launched the Bretton Woods institutions at the heart of global economic governance, one must recognize that the original design has proved remarkably durable. The International Monetary Fund (IMF) and the World Bank have remained active, relevant, and important to the global economy since their conception. Both have been controversial institutions, and their activities have been more criticized than praised, but they have not been irrelevant. The basic nature of the original design was more flexible, and has allowed for adjustments more easily, than has been the case for the United Nations Security Council. Decisions taken by the Executive Boards of the Bretton Woods institutions have affected economic, social, and political life in a vast number of countries. The Board of Governors meetings in the fall of each year, as well as the more restricted meetings that take place each spring, have always been important occasions and have often led to decisions that would affect the lives of billions.

The Bretton Woods Sisters: The Need for Renewed Legitimacy and Leadership

Continuity and a Central Role

A review of the last few decades shows that the Bretton Woods institutions adopted a number of highly significant and innovative policies. The setting up of the International Development Association (IDA), special drawing rights (SDRs), the Brady Plan, and the Heavily Indebted Poor Countries (HIPC) and Poverty Reduction Strategy Papers (PRSP) initiatives come to mind. These initiatives show that the Bretton Woods institutions are less likely to be deadlocked over important decisions than the UN Security Council, which often finds itself unable to act due to permanent member vetoes, as discussed in previous chapters.

The IDA was not part of the original design of the World Bank Group. The initial years of the World Bank were mainly devoted to helping Europe recover from World War II by extending long-term reconstruction loans. As Europe recovered, World Bank resources became more available to the developing countries. Yet many of these countries did not have the capacity to service the loans on the nonconcessional terms offered by the Bank. At the initiative of the United States, a group of Bank members came together to set up what was to become the IDA with the capacity to extend concessional loans to countries below a minimum level of per capita income. The IDA's Articles of Agreement went into effect in 1960, and the first loans were approved in 1961.

A second example of innovation within the Bretton Woods framework was the creation of special drawing rights. The IMF initially created SDRs to support the Bretton Woods fixed exchange rate regime in 1969.[1] The supply of international reserves, US dollars, and gold was not keeping up with the expansion of the world economy. SDRs were issued as a world reserve currency with the hope that they would supply the required liquidity. The problem was not just one of liquidity, however, and the creation of SDRs did not, in fact, prevent the collapse of the "dollar standard," the

---

1. The creation of SDRs was a response to what was also called the "Triffin dilemma," named after the famous international economist Robert Triffin and based on his testimony before the US Congress in 1960. The dilemma arose because the dollar was the only currency countries wanted to keep as a reserve currency, and, therefore, the US payments deficit needed to increase in order for international reserves to increase. But the US deficits undermined the credibility of the dollar's gold convertibility and hence weakened confidence in the international monetary system. The Bretton Woods exchange rate regime was an adjustable peg and a gold exchange standard. The US dollar had a central role in this system. IMF members kept their exchange rates fixed within a narrow band by buying and selling US dollars. In return, the dollar was convertible into gold for official currency holders. The United States was expected to sell or buy gold for $35 per ounce. The "Triffin dilemma" was not an issue until the end of the 1950s. As European and Japanese economies recovered from the war and progressively improved their balance of payments positions, their dollar holdings grew. The increase of US gold reserves was not keeping up with the increase in the cumulative dollar holdings of other countries, casting doubt on the value of the dollar in terms of gold.

system whereby exchange rates were fixed with respect to the dollar, which in turn was convertible into gold at a fixed price. Nonetheless, SDRs did become an international unit of account and still have the potential to play a larger role. Initially defined in terms of the dollar, the value of SDRs was redefined after the collapse of the dollar standard as that of a basket of currencies in fixed proportions (the euro, the yen, pound sterling, and the dollar). SDRs were allocated to member countries in proportion to their IMF quotas. The first allocation (SDR 9.3 billion) was distributed in 1970–72, and the second (SDR 12.1 billion) in 1979–81 at the height of the second oil crisis. Throughout the 1980s, countries holding close to two-thirds of the votes in the Executive Board favored making further allocations, but support continually fell short of the required 85 percent (Boughton 2001, 945).

In 2003, 126 members that make up 76 percent of the total voting power accepted an amendment for a special one-time allocation of SDRs to enable all members of the IMF to participate in the SDR system (one-fifth of the members joined the Fund subsequent to the 1981 allocation). But this "majority" was still short of the required 85 percent super-majority.

Another "innovation" related to the 1980s debt crisis. The recycling of petrol dollars by commercial banks, which lent the resources coming from the oil-rich countries to a number of middle-income countries, followed by a domestic rise in US and world interest rates, had caused a massive debt servicing problem for many countries, particularly in Latin America. In the early 1980s, there was an urgent need for a new debt strategy. US Treasury Secretary Nicholas Brady and his deputy, David C. Mulford, who drafted the new debt relief plan, were aware that a radical approach was needed to deal with the debt problem. Brady's proposed debt relief plan, to be implemented within the framework of Bretton Woods–supported economic programs, included five novel elements. First, commercial banks would agree to a "general waiver of the sharing and negative pledge clauses for each performing debtor" to enable individual banks to "negotiate debt or debt service reduction operations." Hence, small creditor banks could not block agreements and cause endless negotiations. Second, the IMF and the World Bank would dedicate a portion of loans to qualified countries "to finance specific debt reduction plans." For the Fund, this proposal was to become known as the provision of "set-asides" and primarily used to help countries buy back their commercial bank debts at a discount. Third, the Bretton Woods institutions would "offer new, additional financial support to collateralize a portion of interest payments for debt or debt service reduction transactions," a suggestion that would become known as "augmentation." Fourth, Brady signaled a shift in the US position toward favoring an increase in Fund quotas to support the provision of resources for the new debt strategy. Fifth, he called upon the IMF to reconsider the policy of requiring firm financing assurances to be in place before approving a stand-by. The banks and the country should negotiate the type of financing needed, and if arrears accumulated while those negotiations proceeded, the Fund should not let that problem prevent it from approving a financial arrangement.[2] The plan was soon accepted in a regularly scheduled Group of Seven (G-7) meeting after the United States agreed to limit the proposal for the additional use of the IMF resources to the support of reduction in the debt that reflected accumulated interest only, rather than interest and principal. After the G-7 endorsement, the Interim Committee[3] formally endorsed the Brady Plan and requested that the IMF Executive Board consider the matter urgently. The Executive Board members were concerned with the specifics of the Fund's involvement in four areas: magnitude and treatment of additional access to Fund resources; the handling of set-asides; eligibility of countries for the plan; and modifications to the policy on financing assurances. The Executive Board spent four days negotiating the details. Germany and the United Kingdom, backed by some other European countries, sought to limit the degree to which the Fund would modify its procedures and intensify its involvement in the debt strategy; the United States, backed by other industrial and most developing countries and by the managing director, sought to retain as much as possible of the original proposals. In the end, the Brady Plan was adapted in a form quite close to the original.

A more recent example of significant innovation by the Bretton Woods institutions has been the launching of the Heavily Indebted Poor Countries initiative, accompanied by the Poverty Reduction Strategy Papers. Economic performance in the poorer developing countries declined

2. The five elements of the Brady Proposal are taken directly from Boughton (2001, 493).

3. The Interim Committee was transformed into the International Monetary and Financial Committee (IMFC) in 1999. The IMFC has 24 members who are IMF governors (generally ministers of finance or central bank governors). The membership reflects the composition of the IMF's Executive Board. Each member country that appoints, and each group of member countries that elects, an executive director appoints a member of the IMFC. A number of international institutions, including the World Bank, participate as observers in IMFC meetings.

significantly in the 1980s and early 1990s. The total foreign public debt burden of these countries reached proportions that were clearly unsustainable. Moreover, a significant fraction of this debt was debt owed to the Bretton Woods institutions and the regional development institutions. These institutions shared with Bretton Woods a basic policy of not rescheduling or reducing debt owed to them, a principle that had been adhered to with only minor exceptions and that protects the credit rating of the Bretton Woods institutions and regional banks, allowing them in turn to extend credit on relatively favorable terms or, in the case of IDA funds, to extend new IDA credit.

By the mid-1990s, it had become clear, however, that many of the poorest countries were caught in a debt trap that made further growth impossible and the debt unsustainable. What was needed was a concerted effort by all creditors aimed not just at rescheduling but also at actually reducing the debt burden of these countries. A group of nongovernmental organizations had started an effective campaign for such debt relief, which gathered increasing momentum. In response to these developments, the World Bank and the IMF jointly launched the HIPC initiative in 1996, agreeing to reduce the debt owed to them alongside other public debt provided certain conditions were met by the countries concerned. This was a radical but necessary departure from previous practice. Debt reduction would be conditional on countries preparing and committing themselves to poverty reduction strategies summarized by the countries themselves in strategy documents that would have to be approved by the Bretton Woods institutions.

The degree of success of this initiative will be discussed later in this book. What needs to be underlined at this stage is that the Bretton Woods institutions were able to change course and innovate in the face of changing needs and the pressure of public opinion, as had previously been the case with creation of the IDA, issuance of SDRs, and implementation of the Brady Plan. None of these innovations has led to a pure success story, but all constituted responses to new demands emanating from the world economy and showed how the Bretton Woods institutions could evolve over time given the right impulses from their leadership and shareholders, as well as public opinion.

What have been some of the key factors explaining this continuity and endurance?

First, the fact that the Soviets and their allies opted out of the Bretton Woods system in 1946 meant that the deep fault line at the United Nations during the Cold War was absent at the IMF and the World Bank.

The Soviets and their allies were simply not present, and decision making was therefore much easier. There were differences of view but no ideological clash inside the Bretton Woods institutions. It was only after the collapse of communism, when the social-liberal synthesis had become dominant and history had "ended" in the sense described in chapter 1, that the successor states of the Soviet Union and the ex-communist Eastern European countries joined the IMF and the World Bank.

A second important factor that facilitated decision making is the system of governance based on constituencies and weighted voting. The essential design of the Bretton Woods governance system has worked reasonably well for decades because it has allowed participation by all, even the small countries, and has not explicitly endowed the richest countries with a different status (as has been the case in the UN) while at the same time reflecting the reality of their power and wealth in their shares in the overall vote. The system has progressively lost legitimacy, as will be argued in detail below, but its flexibility has allowed it to accommodate change. Moreover, the absence of veto power for individual shareholders, except in votes where an 85 percent majority is required, has allowed decisions to be taken that have sometimes even overruled the largest shareholder.

The governance structures of the World Bank and the IMF are very similar. The World Bank is run like a cooperative, with its member countries as shareholders. A country's number of shares is based roughly on the size of its economy. The United States is the largest single shareholder, with more than 16 percent of the total votes, followed by Japan, Germany, the United Kingdom, and France.[4] The Executive Board is responsible for conducting day-to-day business and is composed of 24 directors, appointed or elected by member countries or by groups of countries, and the president, who serves as its chairman. The five major shareholders each appoint an executive director. Currently, Saudi Arabia, China, and Russia also choose their own executive directors.[5] The rest of the members group themselves into constituencies, and each constituency elects its own executive director. Regular elections of executive directors are held every two years, normally in connection with the Bank's annual

4. See appendix B, table 1, for voting strengths of each member country. Distribution of voting shares is almost the same for the IMF.

5. Certain member countries, such as Italy and Canada, have more or equal voting power as compared to Saudi Arabia, China, and Russia but are represented as part of a constituency.

meetings. Increases in the number of elected executive directors require a decision of the Board of Governors by an 80 percent majority of the total voting power. In 1992, after a large number of new members joined the Bank following the fall of the Berlin Wall, the number of elected executive directors increased from 17 to 19. The two new seats—Russia and a new group around Switzerland—brought the total number of executive directors to its present level of 24. The Bank's president is, by unwritten agreement, a national of the largest shareholder, the United States. Elected for a five-year renewable term, the president of the World Bank chairs meetings of the Board of Executive Directors and is responsible for overall management of the Bank.

Similarly, each IMF member country is assigned a quota, which is the country's participation in the capital of the Fund. These quotas determine member countries' voting power. The original formula used for the calculation of the quotas included national income, reserves, external trade, and export fluctuations. The quota formula was revised in the 1960s such that national income gained greater weight in the formula for most industrial and other large countries, while current payments and the variability of current receipts became important components for small economies with high shares of foreign trade to their GDP and for most developing countries. Since the early 1980s, the variables in the quota formula have included GNP, official reserves, current external payments and receipts, the variability of current receipts, and the ratio of current receipts to GNP.

All powers of the IMF are vested in the Board of Governors, which in 2003 had 184 members. Each member appoints a governor who is usually the minister of finance or the governor of the Central Bank. The Board of Governors delegates most of its powers to a full-time Executive Board, housed in the buildings of the IMF, which is responsible for the general operation of the IMF, excluding matters clearly reserved for the Board of Governors by the Articles of Agreement as being of a fundamental or political nature, or that may have a profound economic impact, such as the power to admit new members, require a member to withdraw, revise quota distributions, allocate or cancel SDRs, and change the number of executive directors to be elected. The IMF Executive Board is elected in the same way as the World Bank's, and the constituency groupings are the same. The Executive Board elects the managing director, who, by unwritten rule, has had to be a Western European. Most of the actual policymaking is done at the level of the Executive Board, which is also quite influential through the recommendations it makes to the Board of Governors. Although ordinary decisions require just a simple majority, certain decisions require a 70 or 85 percent majority to be adopted by the IMF. The original Articles of Agreement specified only nine categories of decisions that needed special majorities, but over the years the number of categories has risen to 50.[6]

A third and very important factor that has sustained the relevance of the Bretton Woods institutions is that these institutions have had *serious resources* committed to them, both in terms of their administrative budgets (the quality and number of staff) and the funds they can make available to borrowing members. In other words, they have intellectual and financial clout. The fact that these institutions have such resources is not unrelated to the existence of broad ideological consensus and the functioning of the governance system referred to above.

A few figures serve to give an idea of the scale of these institutions. The World Bank has around 7,000 employees in Washington and over 3,000 employees in the country offices. The annual net income of the Bank exceeded $1 billion for more than 15 years. The administrative budget for fiscal 2002 was over $1.589 billion, net of reimbursements, and included $176.9 million for the Development Grant Facility, a special fund that extends small grants rather than loans. In the same year, the IMF had approximately 2,700 employees from 141 countries. Its total quotas amount to $299 billion and loans outstanding were $107 billion to 56 countries, of which 38 were on concessional terms as of the summer of 2003. The administrative budget of the IMF for 2002 was $695.4 million.

It is useful to stress, however, that the Bretton Woods institutions remain mid-size bureaucracies when compared to the large private banks. For example, Citigroup Inc., the world's largest bank measured by assets, has around 275,000 employees spread across more than 100 countries, and its total assets were $1.32 trillion as of March 2004. The operating expenses of Citigroup in 2002 were $37.3 billion, more than 20 times the operating expenses of the World Bank.

The Challenge of Legitimacy

Despite the central role the Bretton Woods institutions have played in the world economy throughout the post–World War II period, and the

---

6. This section on IMF governance is based on Van Houten (2002), who provides a very useful up-to-date overview.

resilience and capacity to adapt they have shown as circumstances have changed, they have never been able to overcome fundamental doubts about the legitimacy of their role and the impartiality of their advice. With respect to the perception of the Bretton Woods institutions, it is useful to divide the world into four broad categories of countries: the borrowing countries, the European Union, Japan, and the United States. In the borrowing developing countries of Asia, Latin America, Africa, the Middle East, and southeastern Europe, the public perceives the Bretton Woods institutions as belonging to and furthering the interests of the rich countries. They are also perceived as entirely "external" forces, despite the fact that the borrowing countries as a group actually "own" more than 38 percent of the shares of these institutions, as described above.[7] In opinion polls taken throughout the borrowing countries, the share of individuals with a positive view of the Bretton Woods institutions is quite low. In many countries with active IMF programs, that percentage falls to the 10 to 15 percent range.

There is a small but consistent difference between the World Bank and the IMF, with the former viewed more positively in many countries. But even the World Bank alone does not even get close to a 40 percent "approval rating," despite important public relations efforts over the last decade and a substantial opening to dialogue with civil society and the press. In Europe, the Bretton Woods institutions are viewed critically for somewhat different reasons than in the borrowing countries. Europeans tend to view the Bretton Woods institutions as "American," despite the fact that the 25 nations of the European Union have almost twice the voting strength of the United States on the boards of these institutions, and the fact that, while the president of the World Bank has always been an American, the managing director of the IMF has always been a European! Left-leaning Europeans perceive the Bretton Woods institutions as furthering the interests of high international finance and multinational corporations rather than the interests of ordinary citizens. The populist right has an equally negative perception, viewing the Bretton Woods institutions as imposing an American-led and at the same time cosmopolitan world order on nation-states that are trying to resist globalization and preserve national identity and tradition. The situation is not very different in Japan, with most Japanese having perceptions similar to those of

7. The voting share of developing country borrowers in the IMF is 38 percent, and in the World Bank it is 38.8 percent (Birdsall 2003, table 1). Also, see appendix B, table 1, for individual country shares in the World Bank.

Europeans, although official Japanese policy has generally been very supportive of the Bretton Woods institutions. Finally, even in the United States, which is perceived by the rest of the world as dominating the Bretton Woods institutions, the public is not very sympathetic either! The IMF and the World Bank are perceived by most Americans as using US money to subsidize the rest of the world, and as large bureaucracies beyond the control of US authorities.

Gallup International's 2002 Voice of People Survey interviewed 36,000 people across 47 countries from six continents statistically representing 1.4 billion people. Almost half of the respondents did not trust the Bretton Woods institutions (or the World Trade Organization—WTO) to operate in society's best interests. Interestingly, the WTO, the target of the most aggressive antiglobalization demonstrations, was perceived slightly more favorably. In 2002, Latinobarometro respondents in Latin America gave the poorest evaluation among international institutions to the IMF with a 5.10 score on a 0 to 10 scale. The best performing institution was the United Nations, with a score of 6.86. When results are broken down to the country level, the most discontented nations are also the ones that had the most significant IMF interventions, such as Argentina (2.16) and Brazil (3.98). In a similar fashion, Afrobarometer asked respondents to evaluate international institutions using a scale of 0 to 10. In Africa, half of the respondents had never heard of the institutions they were asked to evaluate, a list that included the UN, the Bretton Woods institutions, the EU, and a few other regional organizations. But among the remaining half who had some knowledge of these institutions, the World Bank and the IMF fared better, scoring 6.78 and 6.40, respectively, only a little below the UN. The Global Poll Multinational Survey of Opinion Leaders commissioned by the World Bank in 2002 found that more than half of the respondents in sub-Saharan Africa, South Asia, the Middle East and North Africa, and Latin America believe that economic reforms recommended by the World Bank hurt the poor more than they help them.

An optimist might say that this almost universal lack of popularity is a good thing and argue that it shows that the Bretton Woods institutions are steering a middle course, striking difficult compromises between divergent interests. The optimist will suggest that it is their very impartiality and pursuit of "economic virtue" by the Bretton Woods institutions that gets them such low approval ratings! The Americans, Europeans, and Japanese are unhappy because the Bretton Woods institutions refuse to be totally subservient to their respective interests, and people in the developing countries are unhappy because there is too much influence by the rich countries and too much conditionality linked to repayment capacity. If the Bretton Woods institutions tried to make developing country citizens too happy, their resources coming mostly from the rich countries would quickly dry up, and not necessarily be used effectively by borrowing countries. If, on the other hand, they tried to make Americans, Japanese, or Europeans too happy, they would be criticized even more for furthering the interests of one of these powers at the expense of the others, and for even greater "technocratic harshness" towards the populations of developing countries.

There is something to this optimist's argument. International institutions have to be "honest" brokers between often antagonistic parties and therefore keep a certain distance from any of the parties concerned. This will not make them wildly popular anywhere. One cannot let matters rest at this, however. The United Nations, for example, has a much higher approval rating than the Bretton Woods institutions everywhere in the world except perhaps recently in the United States,[8] despite the fact that it faces similar trade-offs and constraints. The approval and support enjoyed by the various specialized agencies such as the World Health Organization (WHO), International Labor Organization (ILO), or organizations such as the United Nations Educational, Scientific and Cultural Organization (UNESCO) is even stronger.

A very interesting result from a survey recently taken in Turkey is intriguing and revealing of the general problem: only 12 percent of Turks have a positive view of the IMF (19 percent for the World Bank) compared to almost 50 percent with a positive view of the European Union.[9] This despite the widespread perception that the EU has unfairly favored the Greek side on Cyprus and despite doubts among a majority of Turks until recently about the EU's willingness to accept Turkey as a member. It is also worth stressing that Turkey has been a member of the Bretton Woods institutions for more than five decades and is represented on the Executive Boards, whereas it is not a member of the EU and, so far at least, has zero say in EU governance. Moreover, the EU has provided very few financial resources to Turkey, whereas the Bretton Woods institutions provided close to $30 billion in reasonably favorably priced credits over 2000–03! Such survey results illustrate the deep-seated problem of

8. Note that the widespread perception that the UN has had no support among US citizens is not correct. See Brzezinski (2004) and Nye (2004) on this point.

9. Strateji-Gfh poll, October 2003, Istanbul.

legitimacy faced by the Bretton Woods institutions that undermines their effectiveness and limits the benefits they bring to the world economy.

Governance and Legitimacy

A fundamental set of reasons explaining why the Bretton Woods institutions have such a serious problem with legitimacy relates to their governance, both in terms of the actual articles of agreement and more informal *de facto* arrangements. By informal agreement, the president of the World Bank has always been an American citizen nominated by the US presidents, and the managing director of the IMF a European nominated by a complex and not very transparent process in Europe. These two individuals have great personal internal power over their organizations. The fact that these appointments are purely discretionary political appointments, with the nominations taking place behind closed doors in the rich countries and excluding everyone outside Europe and the United States, certainly does not add a sense of worldwide legitimacy to Bretton Woods governance.[10]

Another important factor is the location of the Bretton Woods institutions in Washington, a five-minute walk from the White House and the US Treasury and State Department. This enhances the view of these institutions as "American" institutions. There is indeed little doubt that the involvement of the US government, and in particular the US Treasury, in week-to-week operations of the Bretton Woods institutions goes much beyond what the 17 percent voting power of the United States would

10. Kahler (2001) argues that the strength of the nationality principle cannot be explained by calculations that common nationality will serve as a conduit for influence between a government and the head of the organization. He believes that the main reason for persistent attachment to this principle (by the United States and the Europeans) lies in domestic politics: patronage, a symbol of international influence for the country to its domestic audience, and national status. Among the Bretton Woods insiders Kahler interviewed for his 2001 book entitled *Leadership Selection in the Major Multilaterals,* a surprising number suggested that this US-European convention was crumbling. But the potential demise of the current convention does not guarantee more legitimacy if selection of Bretton Woods leadership is then solely made by G-7 countries. Moreover, some argue that effective leadership requires a managing director or a president from a creditor country. In an interview with Kahler, former IMF managing director Jacques de Larosiere said that if he had been from an emerging-market country during the 1980s debt crisis, his ability to deal with that crisis on behalf of the IMF membership might have been impaired. Larosiere claimed that his longstanding relations with other G-7 finance ministers and central bank governors provided a reservoir of trust that could be relied upon to deal with financial crises. Others would argue that while a career that inspires trust is essential, the job should be open to all who have had such a career, irrespective of nationality.

suggest, and that it is qualitatively different in intensity from the involvement of any other country. This is indeed partly due to proximity. It has always been very easy for a Bretton Woods official to meet over lunch with an official from the US Treasury. There are no time zone problems and it is easy to talk over the phone, sometimes several times a day. Quite naturally, personal friendships can develop more easily than with colleagues in Paris, Tokyo, or Delhi. Modern communications technology has no doubt reduced the importance of the proximity factor, but it does not abolish the role of location. Personal contact remains important, despite e-mail and the reduced cost of phone calls. It still takes about eight hours to cross the Atlantic and 11 hours to fly from Washington to Tokyo.[11]

Another dimension of the problem relates to the fact that although there may be "groupings" on the board, countries tend to act individually, leaving the United States with its close to 17 percent share of the vote as, by far, the single most important player. In particular, the EU does not really exist as a cohesive actor on the boards of the Bretton Woods institutions. There are executive directors for Germany, Great Britain, France, and so on, but no European executive director who would compete in voting power with the US executive director. This reinforces the image of the Bretton Woods institutions as American-run institutions.

Then there is language and education. English is, of course, the working language of the Bretton Woods institutions, and no one without a very strong command of English can hope to rise in the ranks of the organizations, even if he or she were to speak several other languages perfectly. The overwhelming majority of the highly qualified staff of these institutions have an Anglo-Saxon university education and, particularly at the IMF, a large majority are economists. The language factor should not be stressed as only negative. It contributes to greater speed, effectiveness, and cohesion. But it does also further strengthen the "American" image of the institutions.

Alongside these factors related to location, education, and culture is the very important role played by the G-7 countries in the governance of the Bretton Woods institutions. Starting in the 1970s and increasingly thereafter, the G-7 have organized themselves to be the real governing *directoire* of the economic and financial sphere of the international

11. The United States was determined to have the Bretton Woods institutions located in Washington and pushed hard to achieve that during the Bretton Woods negotiations.

system. It is at G-7 summits that policy directions are set and that new initiatives are taken, endorsed, or blocked. In fact, the influence of the G-7 goes way beyond the setting of strategy at summit meetings. Through regular contacts of G-7 "deputies"—as the deputy undersecretaries for international affairs in the treasury ministries are called—the G-7 strongly influence the operational management of the Bretton Woods institutions, thereby sidelining the much more "global" Executive Boards and crossing the line between *governance* and the *management* of day-to-day operations. G-7 deputies often organize conference calls during which they try to reach consensus on country and policy matters, even though time zone problems may lead to sleep deprivation! If consensus is reached during those conference calls, Bretton Woods management and staff are informed, and it becomes practically impossible for staff to act in a way that is different from the direction set by the G-7. Needless to say, the subsequent Executive Board meetings become pure formalities.

Another important factor that one must add in this context is the overwhelming weight carried by treasuries and central banks in the activities of the G-7 with respect to the Bretton Woods institutions, as well as the importance of these economic institutions worldwide in influencing the boards more generally. As seen by critics, given the close working relationship and professional links that treasuries and central banks have with the private *financial* sector, the governance of the Bretton Woods institutions is dominated not only by the G-7 governments, but also more generally by the financial world and the world outlook of financiers, unencumbered by the likes of ministers of education or transport!

All the factors mentioned above coalesce to create the prevalent view of the Bretton Woods institutions as rich country institutions, strongly influenced by financial sector interests within the rich countries and with the US Treasury playing a leadership role.[12]

How closely these views reflect reality is arguable. The management and staff of the Bretton Woods institutions have, in fact, a great deal more autonomy than most outsiders believe. A lot depends on the top management. Institutional leaders with personal stature and charisma can develop and defend independent positions, *particularly if there are differences of opinion among the G-7*, creating room to maneuver.[13] Moreover, a great

12. See Woods (2003); Woods and Narlikar (2001); Birdsall (2003); and Buira (2003a) for discussion.

13. See Mallaby (2004) for an account of how the World Bank has functioned over the last 10 years. There are some vivid examples in this account of management and staff taking the initiative and acting quite independently.

number of the staff of the institutions have a sense of mission with respect to development and international cooperation, making them a large and fairly cohesive group of people, many with common values dedicated to global public service. There have also been G-7 and other wealthy country officials who have used their influence with great vision and courage to further the goal of global development and poverty reduction, rather than pursue narrow national interests. Among many examples, the ones that I recall most vividly are British chancellor of the Exchequer Gordon Brown's strong support for poor country debt reduction in the late 1990s, as well as his more recent initiatives to generate greater upfront resources allocated to development, and the remarkable efforts by the British, Scandinavian, Dutch, and German development ministers in support of resource mobilization for poverty reduction since the mid–1990s.[14] This is definitely part of the story that should not be ignored. Unfortunately, these positive examples have not been sufficient to generate a perception around the world of the Bretton Woods institutions as positive and legitimate. Episodes such as the various bailouts of Russia in the mid–1990s, despite obvious and serious governance problems and massive capital flight and profiteering at that time, or the Bretton Woods institutions' continued support for the Argentine Currency Board when it had clearly become unsustainable, are examples critics often use to vindicate their negative assessment. It is important to stress that during both these episodes, the Bretton Woods decisions were determined by G-7 pressure and *not* by the professional judgment of the staff working on Russia and Argentina or by a consensus among a wide range of shareholders.

Policy Prescriptions and Legitimacy

The nature of the governance of the Bretton Woods institutions is important both because of its impact on how Bretton Woods policies are *perceived,* as well as the *actual nature* of these policies. Perception is important in itself, because if policy prescriptions are perceived as being driven by illegitimate "foreign" interests, it is impossible to build a sense of

---

14. Many in the international community, developing countries, and civil society recognize the hard work of four women development ministers from Europe who founded the Utstein Group. The women are Clare Short, former secretary of state for international development of the United Kingdom; Eveline Herfkens, former minister for development cooperation of the Netherlands; Hilde F. Johnson, minister for international development of Norway; and Heidemarie Wieczorek-Zeul, federal minister for economic cooperation and development of Germany. The Utstein Group is organized around the principle that coherence in wealthy nation' polices—such as trade, anticorruption, conflict management, and foreign aid—is critical for support of development in poor countries.

domestic *ownership* to support these policies. Without sufficient ownership there is always the danger of policy reversal, and reforms that are
otherwise quite justified will suffer from being viewed as imposed from
abroad.

True stories from Turkey and Morocco will illustrate the point. During
2001, Turkey had implemented far-reaching reforms in agricultural support policies as part of the overall economic program supported by the
IMF and the World Bank. The old system of *price* supports to many crops
was replaced by a system of *income* support to farmers, capped by an
upper limit in terms of land worked on. The reform was designed in line
with international best practices and had the objective of bringing domestic prices closer to world prices, shifting resources into activities where
Turkey had greater comparative advantage, as well as targeting government support to the poorer farmers. The design was correct and supported by Turkish economists with an understanding of agricultural
issues, although implementation was difficult because of administrative
problems in ensuring that the new income support actually reached the
intended beneficiaries. Moreover, the issue of comparative advantage is
not a simple one given the role rich country agricultural subsidies play in
distorting world prices. Nonetheless, the reform was a good and necessary one, supported by reform-minded experts inside the Turkish Treasury and Agriculture Ministries.

Two separate events happened in early 2003. A newly formed government had trouble getting to closure with the IMF on budget measures
needed to achieve the budget targets for the year, and Turkey hesitated
about joining the US-led coalition that was preparing to intervene in Iraq.
In order to come to closure with the IMF on the budget, the government
drastically reduced the amount of expenditures originally earmarked for
the direct income support to farmers. The IMF accepted the government's
proposal. The World Bank's resident country director, however, strongly
and publicly objected to this budget cut, arguing, quite correctly, that it
would completely undermine the agricultural reforms and break a clear
promise that had been made to poor farmers. The World Bank country
director was quite right on the substance of the matter. The budget targets
could and should have been met by other revenue or expenditure measures, rather than by undermining the difficult but essential agricultural
reform process and openly breaking a promise to poor farmers that had
been endorsed by the Bretton Woods institutions. Unfortunately, the
World Bank's support for a subsidy directed at poor farmers did not "fit"

its image as one of the Bretton Woods sisters subservient to financial sector and rich country interests. So, some in the press found an interesting explanation for the dispute between the IMF and the World Bank. Several columnists developed a conspiracy theory according to which the IMF's *European* managing director wanted to make sure IMF financial support got disbursed so that Turkey would be less dependent on possible US financial contributions that were being promised in exchange for Turkish support in Iraq. The World Bank's *American* president, on the contrary, wanted to undermine the budget compromise reached between the government and the IMF and thereby delay Bretton Woods financial support in order to maximize American leverage over Turkey at a critical time! Instead of arguing about the merits of agricultural policies and their links to fiscal policy, the public was encouraged to speculate about what influence the US-European (Franco-German) disagreement over Iraq had on the Bretton Woods institutions' behavior towards Turkey.

Another rather funny example I experienced took place in Morocco. In 1987, the new World Bank president, Barber Conable, a jovial, very well meaning ex-congressman from upstate New York, was on his first visit to Morocco. One of the hot topics to be discussed during that visit was a new large dam that the Moroccans were hoping to build with the support of a French-led financial consortium. The staff of the World Bank working on Morocco was doubtful about the project, given Morocco's already high level of indebtedness at the time, as well as environmental concerns that were negatively affecting support for these kinds of projects worldwide. King Hassan II received President Conable with great formality in his palace in Rabat. After a few brief welcoming remarks the king opened the meeting, in French, by asking President Conable why he had let the Soviets into the Middle East, creating so many problems everywhere. Having volunteered to be the interpreter, I had to translate the question into English and was quite puzzled at first, wondering what Hassan II had in mind. I could not see how or when Barber Conable had in any way helped to enhance Soviet influence in the Middle East. I was in the middle of translating the king's words when I remembered the Aswan Dam! Yes indeed, in the mid-1950s, World Bank management, under the strong influence of the British, French, and US governments, had refused to finance the Aswan Dam, leading Nasser's Egypt to accept a Soviet offer to finance and build that dam, thus, in King Hassan's words, "letting the Soviets into the Middle East"! After I explained the reasons for the king's remark, Barber Conable assured Hassan II that he had had nothing to do whatsoever with that decision made three decades earlier and the conversation turned to other matters. Mr. Conable did not argue about the new dam Morocco wanted to build, and Hassan II had thus skillfully achieved his objective of making the World Bank president feel guilty about the way the institution had allowed itself to be pressured in the past by some of its large shareholders!

These examples are not uniquely Turkish or Moroccan. Similar episodes have been reported from throughout the world. They all illustrate how suspicions about Bretton Woods governance infect the necessary debate about economic policies and reforms. Instead of arguing about the nature of economic and social policies, people argue about the possible *motives* of World Bank and IMF management and staff, as well as about various foreign plots behind the given policy advice. This is not at all helpful for a healthy and professional policy debate, which is so necessary to the formulation and design of policy reforms.

"Washington Consensus" or "Washington Contentious"

As described above, *perceptions* of how the Bretton Woods institutions are governed are inextricably intertwined with the debate on the actual *content* of the economic policies advocated by these institutions. This explains why the term "Washington consensus" has had such great resonance. John Williamson originally coined the term "to refer to the lowest common denominator of policy advice being addressed by the Washington-based institutions to Latin American countries as of 1989."[15] For Williamson, the Washington institutions included the IMF, the World Bank, the Inter-American Development Bank (IDB), and the US Treasury, and the consensus he referred to did summarize accurately the essence of the policy advice given by the Bretton Woods institutions with general support from not only the US Treasury but also from other major shareholders. The message that these policies originated in *Washington* helped make the term "Washington consensus," in the eyes of much of the global public, synonymous with the neoliberal policies pushed by US interests.[16]

---

15. Williamson (2000) is cited here. Williamson (1990) is the original article where the "Washington consensus" concept first appeared.

16. Williamson's original "Washington consensus" policies were fiscal discipline; a redirection of public expenditure priorities toward activities offering both high economic returns and the potential to improve income distribution, such as primary health care, primary education, and infrastructure; tax reform to lower marginal rates and broaden the tax base; financial liberalization, the ultimate objective being market-determined interest rates; a competitive exchange rate; trade liberalization; the abolition of barriers impeding the

While this focus on political motivations persists among some critics of the Bretton Woods institutions as well as in the press, there have also been further analytical work and publications by economists focusing on the economic merit and results of the policies pursued.

Williamson himself, with Pedro Pablo Kuczynski, edited a book in 2003 entitled *After the Washington Consensus,* which takes a careful look at what did not go right in Latin America in the 1990s and revisits the substance of the Washington consensus recommendations. The authors generally emphasize the need for "crisis-proofing" economies, particularly by staying away from fixed exchange rate policies; the need for more countercyclical fiscal policies; and, very important, the need for second-generation reforms emphasizing better income distribution. Moisés Naím, the editor of *Foreign Policy* magazine, has argued that no consensus actually exists and emphasizes that economists are divided over issues such as the causes of the East Asian crisis, the need for an international financial architecture, and the effectiveness of "open" trade policies, reflecting more of a "Washington confusion" than consensus (Naím 2000). Rodrik (2000) augments the original 10 points with an additional 10, summarizing what he interprets to be the consensus as of 1999.[17] One concrete policy proposal for "augmentation" has been put forward by Birdsall and de la Torre (2001), who focus on 10 "Washington contentious" reforms that would improve equity without reducing growth.[18] Much of this debate is conducted in "reformist" terms, accepting the basic framework of the social-liberal synthesis and the basic architecture of the international system.

There are also more extreme critics who argue for much more radical changes in policies and architecture, including those who want to abolish the Bretton Woods institutions altogether.[19] Activist movements in favor of

entry of foreign direct investment; privatization of state-owned enterprises; deregulation in order to ease entry by new firms into the market and increase competition; and secure property rights. There is a mistaken view that the consensus included capital account liberalization and single-minded minimization of the role of state.

17. The additional 10 points cited by Rodrik (2000) are legal/political reform; regulatory institutions; anticorruption; labor market flexibility; WTO agreements; financial codes and standards; "prudent" capital account opening; nonintermediate exchange rate regimes; social safety nets; and poverty reduction.

18. See also Stiglitz (2001). For a recent and comprehensive analysis, including "reformist" proposals for change in both governance and policies, see Griffith-Jones and Ocampo (2004).

19. See Ziegler (2003); Green (2003); Harvey (2003); Khor (2002); and the report of the International Forum on Globalization (2002).

abolishing the Bretton Woods institutions such as the "Global Exchange" and the "50 Years Is Enough" groups accuse these institutions of causing widespread poverty, inequality, and suffering by ensuring open market access for corporations while cutting basic spending on education, health care, and production credits to poor farmers. The "50 Years Is Enough" group goes one step further and calls for a "Truth Commission" to investigate the Bretton Woods institutions and demands that they pay reparations for structural adjustment and social and ecological devastation.

Critics of the World Bank and the IMF are not just those to the left of the political spectrum. The US Congress created the Meltzer Commission in 1998 in the context of an $18 billion increase in the US capital contribution to the IMF. Led by conservative economist Alan Meltzer, who in a 1998 Brookings conference called for the abolition of the IMF, the commission's duty was to assess the mission and performance of the World Bank and the IMF. The outcome of the commission's work, published in 2000, concluded that the World Bank had become irrelevant to poverty reduction and that the IMF had become more of a problem than a solution. The report emphasized the danger of moral hazard due to IMF lending and argued for a drastic reduction of the IMF's policy role.[20]

In the face of such often extreme criticism coming from both the right end the left of the political-ideological spectrum, the Bretton Woods institutions are trying to chart their course for the coming years, subject to many external pressures and in the context of a governance regime that needs reform. The Bretton Woods institutions continue to have a very important role in both the emerging-market economies and in the poorer developing countries. To play that role effectively, they must be able to deal with the root of the problems, not just the superficial symptoms. In doing so they must be supported by a renewed, more legitimate governance framework that promotes in-depth solutions and allows their implementation with much greater domestic "ownership" and backing from public opinion, both local and international.

Reforming Bretton Woods governance must go hand-in-hand with reforming important parts of the strategies and policies supported and pursued by these institutions. Governance reform will encourage courageous thinking and initiative among the staff of these institutions, which has often been frustrated by the conservative bias of existing governance structures, and will allow much greater substantive give-and-take

20. The Meltzer Commission's report is available at www.house.gov/jec/imf/meltzer.htm.

between these institutions and civil society, as well as dialogue with parliamentarians and activists from the developing world. Over the last decade, Bretton Woods management has made an effort to open the institutions to dialogue and criticism. There is widespread conviction, however, that the decision-making process remains remote from this more open debate. If reformed governance were to succeed in conferring much greater legitimacy on the Bretton Woods institutions, allowing people throughout the world to feel that these institutions are indeed *their* institutions, reform policies pursued in developing and emerging-market economies could enjoy real domestic support *even if* they are implemented as part of Bretton Woods–financed economic programs. This would greatly increase the long-term effectiveness of these reforms and programs and thereby be good for both "creditors" and "borrowers," "donors" and aid "recipients."

A great deal of effort has gone into improving the policy advice and the quality of the conditionality in Bretton Woods–supported programs, but some of the most difficult issues remain unresolved. At the root of the problem one often finds a schizophrenic attitude toward conditionality. Nowhere is this more obvious than in some of the more radical critiques of the Bretton Woods institutions. These critics argue against conditionality as an unacceptable way to "subordinate" the developing countries to the will of the G-7-led Bretton Woods institutions. The same critics will also, however, often criticize Bretton Woods for not imposing *enough* conditionality when it comes to democracy and good governance. The quote below from Walden Bello (2002), a prominent sociologist from the Philippines and a leading critic associated with the International Forum on Globalization, illustrates the point:

> [T]he claim that the Bank was concerned about good governance was contradicted by the exposure of its profound involvement with the Suharto regime in Indonesia, to which it funneled over $30 billion in 30 years. According to several reports, including a World Bank internal report that came out in 1999, the Bank tolerated corruption, accorded false status to false government statistics, legitimized the dictatorship by passing it off as a model for other countries, and was complacent about the state of human rights and the monopolistic control of the economy.

The critics fundamentally disapprove of the Bretton Woods institutions' practice of attaching conditions to loans as infringing on the sovereignty of the borrowing countries. The problem is that one cannot be against conditionality in the economic domain because it infringes on sovereignty and, *at the same time*, argue that the Bretton Woods institutions should impose tough social and political conditions on the borrowing countries. Such contradictions have been very evident in the debate about the Poverty Reduction Strategy Papers in low-income countries. At the center of these difficulties lies the problem of legitimacy. If the governance of these institutions were considered *more legitimate*, conditionality would become *more acceptable* and the debate could focus, in a much healthier way, on the nature of policies and conditionalities without always being hijacked by apprehension about motives and intentions.

That is why the reform of *policies* must be linked to the reform of *governance* and vice versa. Courageous policy reforms are needed to solve the systemic problems that threaten global economic development: the *debt trap* of the *emerging-market economies* and the *state failure* and danger of *exclusion* from the global development process of many of the *poorest countries*. The necessary policy reforms can only be implemented with accompanying governance reforms, however, because otherwise, lack of sufficient legitimacy will hamper both the design and implementation of the most effective policies.

Real progress in the direction of much greater effectiveness for the Bretton Woods institutions will be possible with courageous governance reforms that meet the challenge of legitimacy and succeed in changing the perception of these institutions. The world of the 21st century needs these institutions more than ever. They have accumulated very valuable experience. They have financial and human resources that can be leveraged even further. They are instruments of public policy on a global scale in a world where global issues require global policies. They can be used to stabilize the world economy and counteract the tendency of financial markets to exhibit herd-like behavior. They can be instrumental in ensuring that global standards and policies reflect the needs and aspirations of all. Despite considerable efforts, however, these institutions have been unable to establish sufficient trust and gain the support of the billions of people they are trying to serve. East Asian countries are building huge amounts of foreign exchange reserves with the hope that these reserves will protect them from ever again requesting IMF assistance. In Latin America, there is widespread disillusion with the "Washington consensus," which is identified with the Bretton Woods institutions and the US Treasury working closely together. In Africa, the situation is similar, despite the Poverty

Reduction Strategy Papers, the Heavily Indebted Poor Countries initiative, and the very substantial amount of resources Africa receives from the Bretton Woods institutions on concessional terms. Even sensible economic programs become impossible to "market" to public opinion when they acquire the label of "IMF programs."

For all this to change, the governance of the Bretton Woods institutions and of the international economic system as a whole must be allowed to change. Governance arrangements should meet the challenge of legitimacy and conform to a much greater extent than today to norms that the billions of people they serve will accept as fair. Of course, as is the case for UN Security Council reform, the change in governance cannot simply ignore the power balance that exists in the world. New governance arrangements must reflect a reasonable compromise between those who provide the lion's share of resources to the system and those who are on the receiving end of these resources. It is not only public opinion in the developing countries that must support the Bretton Woods institutions and the WTO, but also public opinion in Europe, North America, and Japan.

The need for reforms that would broaden the top governance of the international economic system beyond its current, essentially G-7-driven, architecture is actually widely acknowledged. The G-7 themselves have started inviting selected other countries to their meetings. Russia now is a regular guest invited to participate in some of the summit sessions, and the G-7 become the G-8 when it participates. While the G-7 reserve some meeting time to themselves as a group, they now regularly invite several developing countries to parts of the summit meetings. Another more regular "broadening" exercise has been taking place through the G-20, a "club" in which a dozen of the most important developing countries join the G-7 and the EU for semi-annual meetings as well as follow-up work in between meetings. The G-20 include Argentina, Australia, Brazil, China, India, Indonesia, Korea, Mexico, Russia, Saudi Arabia, South Africa, and Turkey, in addition to the G-7 and a representative of the EU. Together the member countries represent around 90 percent of global gross national product, 80 percent of world trade (including EU intra-trade), and two-thirds of the world's population. This is clearly a much more inclusive club than the G-7. The problem is that neither the broadened summit meetings nor even the more structured G-20 meetings have real decision power. These are forums for discussion and, in the case of the G-20, for some very good follow-up work, but they do not substantially affect the governance system. Moreover, even the G-20 somewhat arbitrarily exclude a large number of countries without any real justification beyond practicality. The G-20 have been a very useful step forward and they should no doubt continue the work they have started, but more is needed in terms of overall governance reforms.

A United Nations Economic and Social Security Council

A radical but desirable step would be to make the top governance of the Bretton Woods institutions and other global economic institutions part of the overall framework of a reformed and renewed United Nations. The system of constituencies and weighted voting has worked well for the Bretton Woods institutions, allowing a considerable amount of adaptation and flexibility. Without destroying the positive features of the existing system that, on the whole, has served them well, it is desirable, however, to bring the Bretton Woods institutions under the broad, legitimizing umbrella of the United Nations.

The best way to achieve this would be through the creation of a new United Nations Economic and Social Security Council (UNESC) similar to the renewed UN Security Council but responsible for the economic and social sphere of the international system.[21] The new UNESC would be constituted at a much higher level than the existing ECOSOC, with a much stronger mandate. It would be a "twin" of the UN Security Council. The UNESC would function with a system of weighted votes and constituencies similar to that of the UN Security Council, the only difference being that *"military capability" would not enter into the formula* determining the voting strength of a country. Thus voting strength would be determined by a country's share in world population, GDP, and contributions to the UN global goods budget. India's weighted vote would thus be:

$$Z_{INDIA} = b_1 (P_i) + b_2 (GDP_i) + b_3 (B_i),$$

---

21. Proposals along this line have been made, notably by the Rasmussen Report (2003). A similar recommendation can also be found in the final report of the Commission on Global Governance entitled *Our Global Neighborhood* (1995). The commission's proposal was later endorsed by the Panel on Financing for Development led by former Mexican president Ernesto Zedillo. Joseph Stiglitz also has supported such a UNESC in various speeches and articles.

Table 4.1 *Voting strengths on the proposed UN Economic and Social Council*

Countries	Factors determining voting strength (percent of total)			Result
	Contribution to global public goods	Popu- lation	GDP	Weighted vote
Permanent members (6 seats)				
EU and official candidates (28)[a]	0.37	0.09	0.31	25.7
United States	0.22	0.05	0.27	17.8
Japan	0.19	0.02	0.17	12.8
China	0.02	0.21	0.03	8.7
India	0.004	0.17	0.01	6.3
Russian Federation	0.01	0.02	0.01	1.5
Constituencies (8 seats)				
Other Asia (40)	0.05	0.18	0.07	9.9
Latin America, Caribbean, and Canada (35)	0.08	0.09	0.08	8.5
Africa (43)	0.005	0.10	0.01	4.0
Arab League (21)	0.02	0.05	0.01	2.6
Other Europe (19)	0.03	0.02	0.02	2.2

a. The numbers in parentheses represent the number of countries in that constituency.

where $b_1 + b_2 + b_3 = 1$ and P_i, GDP_i and B_i are the shares mentioned above. The weights attributed to each of the variables can all be equal, as was proposed for the UN Security Council, or they can be different. If they were equal, India's weighted vote in the UNESC, ZINDIA above, would be 6.28 percent, compared to India's 5.162 percent voting strength in the renewed UN Security Council as described in chapter 3. Table 4.1 describes the voting strength of the various constituencies in the UNESC, using equal weights for population, GDP, and contributions to the UN budget, and can be compared to tables 3.1 and 3.2 describing voting strengths in the UN Security Council in chapter 3.

If the UNESC proposal were adopted, how could it fit in with the existing Board of Governors of the Bretton Woods institutions as well as the existing Executive Boards? What exactly would the UNESC do? At what level would it function? These questions have so far not been sufficiently addressed in the proposals to create a UNESC. To make progress in this direction one must provide explicit and practical suggestions that go beyond the general idea of an Economic and Social Security Council.

As proposed for the renewed UN Security Council in chapter 3, the UNESC would function at two levels. It would normally meet at the level of *heads of government* once a year during the annual meetings of the United Nations in New York in September. Principals here would be the *same* as those in the heads of government level meeting of the UN Security Council. In addition, every second year, at the General Assembly meeting, the world community would elect the UNESC for a two-year period in exactly the same way it elects the UN Security Council, but with the different voting strengths as described above. The UNESC would thus consist of 14 council members who would meet very regularly and would be assisted by a small staff. These 14 council members would have to satisfy certain criteria in terms of experience with designing and implementing economic and social policies at the national, regional, or global level. These criteria should be explicit and binding. One difference between the new UNESC and the UN Security Council is that the council members would not be the ambassadors of these countries to the United Nations. It would be important that the new structure cut across existing bureaucracies, be they foreign ministries or treasury departments. The council members would be senior officials with distinguished careers in the economic and social sphere. Council members would be expected to have had ministerial experience in their countries or be top business, civil society, or academic leaders still active in their fields and enjoying strong national and international recognition. When the UNESC meets, what the world should see is a diverse group of men and women with the prestige, skills, and dynamism to act as global leaders in the economic and social domain.

The UNESC would be the governance umbrella for *all* specialized economic and social agencies currently in the UN system, such as the ILO, the UN Development Program (UNDP), the UN Conference on Trade and Development (UNCTAD), etc., as well as the Bretton Woods institutions and the WTO. The job of the UNESC would be to provide an overall framework of coherence and efficiency to international institutions and cooperation in the economic and social sphere. It could and should play a crucial role in putting together the global package needed to augment the resources that can be mobilized for development. The UNESC would elaborate guidelines to avoid duplication, work on long-term reform and cooperation strategies, evaluate the effectiveness of all institutions and their programs, conduct some comparative research focused on effectiveness, and be accessible to civil society networks and their criticisms and proposals for changing the policies and practices of the various institutions. It would also, and this is crucial, *appoint all heads of institutions* with the help of transparent search procedures and criteria, which would include professional qualification and experience, a track record of leadership and good management, and overall gender, race, and geographical balance in the top management of international institutions. The *de facto* requirement that the head of a particular institution should come from a particular country would no longer apply. All positions would be open to talent from across the world subject to tough criteria known to all and subject, of course, to the ability to get elected by a UNESC in which the "big players" would still retain a dominant vote. The UNESC would not just reflect the world of finance but would represent the world as a whole: officials with experience in agriculture, the environment, or education would be as qualified and relevant to become council members as former ministers of finance or leaders in the financial sector. Given that the Bretton Woods institutions and the UN Security Council are headquartered in the United States, it may be desirable for the UNESC to have its permanent seat somewhere else—for example in Geneva, which is already the seat of important agencies and institutions such as the WTO, the ILO, UNCTAD, the WHO, and others, or perhaps in an Asian city where there are other international institutions and to which there is easy access. (Shanghai, Singapore, Manila, or Kuala Lumpur come to mind.) On the other hand, there would be advantages of having the UNESC also headquartered in New York, close to the UN Security Council. Periodically, the two Security Councils should have joint meetings on issues with overlapping security and economic dimensions, as already mentioned in chapter 3. Subcommittees with representatives from both councils may have to be created, and geographical proximity may be a facilitating factor.

What is proposed here is a UNESC that acts as a strategic board for the entire international system in the economic and social sphere, and a UNESC that has the very important function of appointing heads of agencies and which also reviews performance, promotes cooperation, evaluates effectiveness, and supports research on effectiveness. It would do so very independently of any one agency and reflect the hopes, aspirations, and concerns of humankind as a whole rather than of any one particular group or set of interests. It would be a source of strengthened legitimacy for all institutions, particularly the Bretton Woods institutions. The UNESC would *not interfere*, however, in the workings of the institutions themselves. Having appointed the chief executives, the UNESC would not go beyond providing strategic guidance, promoting communication and public discussion, and evaluating performance. The UNESC would not have any executive function at all. It may be useful to discuss how this could work, for example, in the case of the Bretton Woods institutions and the ILO.

In the case of the Bretton Woods institutions, what would change would be the appointment procedure of the chief executives and the shifting of some of the external evaluation function to the UNESC. Beyond that, the UNESC would be able to suggest and analyze, but would have no decision-making role. The Board of Governors of the IMF and the World Bank would continue to exist and function, although there should be some changes in the voting weights of the Bretton Woods Executive Boards themselves, reflecting current economic and demographic realities and giving greater weight to the developing countries.[22] It is not necessary, however, to have the same voting weights for the Executive Boards of the Bretton Woods institutions as for the UNESC, and it may also not be necessary to harmonize the weight in formulas and country groupings. Appendix B, table 1, compares voting strength under the existing Bretton Woods system and the proposed UNESC system. Some of the differences are significant. In the proposed UNESC, there is a significant and desirable increase in the voting strength of the developing countries as a whole. Some movement in that direction is also very desirable for the boards of the IMF and the World Bank, although it need not be in the same magnitude. EU countries are clearly overrepresented there, and eventually a move towards joint EU representation could also be the occasion to correct the anomaly that inter-EU trade counts as international trade in the Bretton Woods weighting formulas. This would allow some redistribution of voting power to the developing countries on the Bretton Woods boards themselves.

The International Monetary and Finance Committee and the Development Committee, which are the high-level policy committees of the Bretton Woods institutions, could continue to meet semi-annually with the addition of the current chair of the UNESC participating in the meetings.

---

22. See Woods and Narlikar (2001) and Buira (2003a and 2003b) for in-depth discussion of the composition of the Bretton Woods boards.

The Executive Boards would continue to oversee the day-to-day operations of the Bretton Woods institutions and approve many of the management decisions. These boards would continue to reflect the world of central banks and treasury departments, with the usual addition of development ministries for the board of the World Bank, because these departments control the resources and formulate the monetary and fiscal policies. Many of these policies may need to change or evolve, but it would not be feasible or appropriate to separate the Bretton Woods institutions from the departments that deal most closely with financial and fiscal issues in the home countries. The results of these policies and the performance in implementing them would be evaluated, however, by the UNESC in a truly independent and arm's-length manner and with a broader and more interdisciplinary spirit. Moreover, having been appointed by the UNESC, the chief executives are likely to show sensitivity to broad strategic UNESC guidance and suggestions.

Taking the International Labor Organization as another example, creation of the UNESC would not affect the internal governance mechanism of this agency, except, again, for the selection of the agency head and the addition of the arm's-length evaluation process by the UNESC. [23] The director-general of the ILO would be appointed through the same transparent process as all other heads of agencies. Without interfering in the

---

23. The ILO has three main bodies, all of which encompass the unique feature of the organization, which is its tripartite structure (government, employers, workers). The member states of the ILO meet at the International Labor Conference every year, and each member state is represented by two government delegates, an employer delegate, and a worker delegate who are accompanied by technical advisors. It is generally the cabinet ministers responsible for labor affairs in their own countries who head the delegations, take the floor, and present their governments' points of view. The governing body is the executive council of the ILO and meets three times a year to take decisions on ILO policy. It establishes the program and the budget, which it then submits to the conference for adoption. It also elects the director-general. It is composed of 28 government members, 14 employer members, and 14 worker members. Ten of the government seats are permanently held by states of chief industrial importance. Representatives of other member countries are elected at the conference every three years, taking into account geographical distribution. The employers and workers elect their own representatives, respectively. The International Labor Office is the permanent secretariat of the ILO and the focal point for the overall activities that it prepares under the scrutiny of the governing body and under the leadership of a director-general, who is elected for a five-year renewable term. The office employs some 1,900 officials of over 110 nationalities at the Geneva headquarters and in 40 field offices around the world. In addition, some 600 experts undertake missions in all regions of the world under the program of technical cooperation. The office also constitutes a research and documentation centre and a printing house, issuing a broad range of specialized studies, reports, and periodicals.

day-to-day management and functioning of the ILO, the UNESC could, however, suggest new directions for the agency's work program and look into coordination problems and coherence between the work of the ILO and other agencies, notably the WTO. There has been a great deal of debate, for example, on labor standards, including child labor, and in particular on whether or not to link the issue of labor standards to trade and market access negotiations under the WTO. There is also the overlap between international practice and law regarding refugees, which comes under the jurisdiction of the United Nations High Commissioner for Refugees (UNHCR), policies with regard to migration, which currently are not the responsibility of any UN agency in particular, and policies with regard to workers' rights, which are directly in the ILO's domain. The UNESC would and could clarify responsibilities in these areas by suggesting, for example, to put the ILO rather than the WTO clearly in charge of dealing with labor standards, if that is what the majority weighted vote at the UNESC indicates. It could also augment the domain of responsibility of the ILO by giving it a mandate to oversee cross-border migration issues, including migrant rights as well as international cooperation to prevent illegal migration.

Another major function of the UNESC would be to help raise the resources needed for the better functioning of the international system in the economic sphere. At the Millennium Summit of the United Nations in 2000, the international community adopted the Millennium Development Goals (MDGs). World leaders set specific targets to reduce poverty, disease, hunger, and illiteracy, improve the environment, and promote the rights and participation of women by 2015. The International Conference on Financing for Development, held in Monterrey, Mexico, in 2002, made recommendations on how to achieve the MDGs based on a report prepared under the leadership of Ernesto Zedillo, former president of Mexico (known as the Zedillo Report).[24] The consensus in Monterrey was that about $50 billion in additional resources was needed annually for the MDGs to be met.

Since then, many proposals on how to increase the resources devoted to development have been put forward, ranging from simply increasing the development assistance budgets of the rich countries to ideas about the introduction of international forms of taxation (on carbon emissions,

---

24. The Zedillo Report is available at www.un.org/reports/financing/.

arms, currency transactions), and including a revival of the older idea of channeling SDR allocations to development and other forms of financial engineering. While there has been a lot of debate, actual progress with any of these ideas has been very slow, and the world is far from raising the additional $50 billion a year needed for the MDGs. The proposed UNESC could take a leadership and coordinating role in designing institutional and policy innovations to help raise resources for global development, put some order into all the competing initiatives and proposals, and ensure the required institutional linkages.

The reform proposed here for the governance of the economic and social sphere of the international system does have the merit that it could be implemented without major disruption to existing institutional arrangements and administrative budgets. This is an advantage, of course, since any major disruption would be a formidable obstacle to reform, whatever the merits the reform may have in the long run. Despite the *relative* modesty of the proposal in terms of institutional arrangements, it could bring much greater legitimacy to governance of the international system in the economic and social sphere. The Bretton Woods institutions and the WTO would no longer be totally outside the UN system, and they would benefit from the legitimacy of the United Nations. The fact that the managing director of the IMF and the president of the World Bank would be appointed by the UNESC alongside all other agency heads through a tough and transparent procedure open to talent worldwide would confer tremendous *legitimate* strength to these top managers of the international system. The evaluation and research support role of the UNESC would be perceived as more objective and impartial with respect to the various institutions, and therefore more credible than current evaluation procedures still tied to the institutions themselves. The UNESC would also be able to provide much needed impetus to coordination between various agencies, streamlining and promoting coherence and efficiency in the use of resources. The UNESC could act as a facilitator and, at times, as a regulator for civil society activism in the economic and financial sphere. The UNESC could play a leading role in promoting resource mobilization for development. The donor nations would retain sufficient control over resource amounts and use through their weight in both the new UNESC and on the Executive Boards of the Bretton Woods institutions to make the proposal politically reasonable and feasible. At the same time, directly and indirectly, global democracy would have made a big step forward and people across the world could start perceiving not only the various existing UN agencies but also the Bretton Woods institutions as *their* institutions rather than simply the instruments of the G-7 (or the G-1, as the United States is sometimes called!). This would greatly strengthen the effectiveness of these crucial institutions—and their effectiveness is needed more than ever for the overall good performance of the world economy and for achieving a better globalization.

5 | Enabling Stable Growth in the Emerging-market Economies

Roughly once a year—if history is any guide—the managing director of the International Monetary Fund (IMF), the US treasury secretary, and in some cases the finance ministers of other Group of Seven (G-7) countries get a phone call from the finance minister of a large emerging-market economy. The precise details of each conversation differ, but the core does not. The emerging-market economy's finance minister indicates that the country is rapidly running out of foreign reserves, that it has lost access to international capital markets, and that it has perhaps even lost the confidence of its own citizens.

NOURIEL ROUBINI AND BRAD SETSER
Bailouts or Bail-ins? Responding to Financial Crises in Emerging Economies,
2004, p. 1.

Record low international interest rates in the 2002–04 period have made the phone calls referred to in the above quote less frequent. With nominal base interest rates in the United States, Europe, and Japan in the 0 to 3 percent range and real interest rates close to zero, it has been easier for emerging-market economies to service their debt, even allowing for large sovereign risk spreads. The debt burdens of many emerging-market economies remain very heavy, however, and most observers agree that if and when interest rates rise again in the richer countries, the phone calls will again have to be answered. The interaction of volatile international capital markets with large accumulated stocks of debt have created chronic macroeconomic vulnerability in a whole class of emerging-market economies, constraining their growth, reducing their capacity to fight poverty, and, at times, constituting a systemic threat to the entire world economy.

It is now again increasingly recognized, not only by left-wing critics but also by mainstream economists, that capital markets are not the incredibly efficient processors of information that market fundamentalists would have us believe. Instead, capital markets display substantial amounts of herd behavior leading to what no less an authority than Alan Greenspan, in a now much-quoted speech on December 5, 1996, called "irrational exuberance."[1] Sometimes, of course, irrational exuberance becomes "irrational panic." Financial markets surge and collapse, often without any discernible change in the "fundamental" economic environment. Eminent economists such as Charles Kindleberger, one of the top international economists of the last 50 years, and Robert Shiller of the younger generation, who is a professor at Yale University and winner of the 1996 Paul A. Samuelson award, have described market volatility, panics, manias, and irrational exuberance in financial markets.[2]

These books tell the stories of speculative bubbles, market panics, and Ponzi schemes, from the famous Tulipmania of 17th-century Holland to the dotcom bubble of the late 1990s. Their analysis of financial markets shows that reality is much more complex than that suggested by simplistic versions of efficient markets theory. First, it is not true that most actors in financial markets simply behave by rationally evaluating "objective" information about underlying economic and financial variables as it becomes available. It is not so much that people behave in an irrational way, although there are historical examples of outright irrational behavior in financial markets. The problem is more that individually rational behavior does not lead to the efficient market model. In the words of Robert Shiller (2000), "Even completely rational people can participate in herd behavior when they take into account the judgments of others, even if they *know* (emphasis added) that everyone else is behaving in a herd-like manner. This behavior, although individually rational, produces group behavior that is, in a well defined sense, irrational."

This type of irrationality is due to what the technical literature calls "information cascades." Shiller (2000, 152) uses a simple story to make his point:

"Suppose two restaurants open next door to each other. Each potential customer must choose between the two. Would-be customers may be able to make some judgments about the quality of each of the restaurants

---

1. Remarks by Chairman Alan Greenspan at the annual dinner and Francis Boyer Lecture of The American Enterprise Institute for Public Policy Research, Washington, DC. Available at www.federalreserve.gov/boarddocs/speeches/1996/19961205.htm
2. Kindleberger (2001) and Shiller (2000, 2003). See also Eatwell and Taylor (2000). For an analysis stressing the potential of capital markets to create and spread prosperity, see Rajan and Zingales (2003). This book also, however, stresses the need for good regulation and supervision.

when viewing it through the front window, but such judgments will not be very accurate. The first customer who arrives must choose based only on viewing the two empty restaurants and makes a choice. However, the next potential customer can rely not only on his or her own information, based on the appearance of the restaurants, but also—by seeing the first customer eating in one or the other of the restaurants—information about the choice made by the first customer. If the second customer chooses to go to the same restaurant as the first, the third customer will see two people eating in that restaurant. The end result may be that all customers may wind up eating at the same restaurant—and it could well be the poorer restaurant, since there was no real consideration of the combined evidence inherent in all their observations about the two restaurants."

This story illustrates how herd behavior can lead perfectly rational actors astray. Instead of investors independently assessing the true value of the market and then "casting their vote," they choose not to "waste their time" in exercising their independent judgment about the market and, instead, follow the herd. There are numerous studies in psychology that document this type of behavior. People will tend to "agree" with the majority, even in cases where they have different priors.[3] This type of herd behavior is due to the absence of information about true value or to the willingness of individuals to agree with the majority, even if that means going against their own initial feelings at times.

There is also a different type of herd behavior, however. In the example of the two restaurants, people would not go to the first restaurant if they *knew* that the food was better at an equal price in the second restaurant.

---

3. Psychologist Solomon Asch, in an experiment to show the power of social pressure on individual judgment, placed his subject in a group of seven to nine people. Asch had coached the rest of the group, but the subject did not know that. The group was asked to answer 12 questions about the lengths of line segments shown to them on cards. Asch's confederates deliberately gave wrong answers to seven of the 12 questions. A third of the time the subject gave the same wrong answers as had been given by the confederates. Asch interpreted his results as due to social pressure. Later, psychologists Morton Deutsch and Harold Gerard reported a variant of Asch's experiment in which the subjects were told that they had been placed anonymously into a group of people that they never saw, would never see, and whose answers the subject could observe only indirectly through an electronic signal (in fact there was no such group). Subjects would give their answers by pressing a button, unobserved by others, and therefore would not need to face the group. And yet the subjects gave nearly as many wrong answers as in Asch's experiment. Deutsch and Gerard concluded that the wrong answers had been given in large part because people simply thought that all other people could not be wrong. See Shiller (2000, 149–50).

There are many situations, however, where people *know* that "values are exaggerated" and buy nonetheless, believing, often correctly, that others will *follow* and hoping they can be the first to exit once the bubble bursts. It is this kind of behavior that again and again has led to the success of Ponzi schemes.[4] The essence of a Ponzi scheme is that those who set it up pay out very high returns to the initial investors, not by making an actual profit from an economic activity but by using the money of subsequent investors to pay the returns to the initial investors. A fairly recent and dramatic example took place in Albania in the mid-1990s, when a small number of so-called new investment banks were able to attract more than 30 percent of total national income by promising huge monthly returns (often 20 percent or more) to the investors. When the schemes collapsed less than two years after their emergence, the country went into civil war–like disorder. Similar if somewhat less dramatic episodes occurred throughout Eastern Europe in the years of transition to market economy. It is often the case in these episodes that valuations become so ridiculously high that few people believe they reflect real underlying profit opportunities due to actual economic activity. People continue to buy, however, believing that others will also continue to buy and bid up prices further, all the while readying to be the first to exit at signs of trouble. In situations like this, when trouble starts, there is no orderly exit but a stampede, since the only reason people were in the market was that they believed others were still about to enter. When that belief vanishes, the collapse is usually immediate.

Many episodes of financial market frenzy are not *pure* Ponzi schemes, in that there is some underlying real economic activity and perhaps there are even real profits! Nonetheless, prices are bid up, not so much because of expectations based on careful evaluation of potential profits, but because of herd-like behavior, with individuals following the herd either because they believe the majority must be right (the restaurant example)

4. The US Securities and Exchange Commission summarizes Ponzi schemes as a "type of illegal pyramid scheme named for Charles Ponzi, who duped thousands of New England residents into investing in a postage stamp speculation scheme back in the 1920s." Ponzi thought he could take advantage of differences between US and foreign currencies used to buy and sell international mail coupons. He told investors that he could provide a 40 percent return in just 90 days compared with 5 percent for bank savings accounts. Ponzi was deluged with funds from investors, taking in $1 million during one three-hour period—and this was 1921! Though a few early investors were paid off to make the scheme look legitimate, an investigation found that Ponzi had only purchased about $30 worth of the international mail coupons. Decades later, the Ponzi scheme continues to work on the "rob-Peter-to-pay-Paul" principle, as money from new investors is used to pay off earlier investors until the whole scheme collapses.

or because they believe that others will continue to be "buyers" for a while and that they can always jump away ahead of others. It is a combination of these and some other factors that caused the stock market bubble of the late 1990s. Take the comparison, for example, between the well-established Toys 'R Us retail company and the upstart eToys firm established in 1997, which Shiller also mentions. Shortly after an initial public offering, eToys stock value soared to $8 billion compared to the value of $6 billion of Toys 'R Us. This at a time when eToys had sales of only $30 million, compared to $11.2 billion for Toys 'R Us, and "profits" of *negative* $28.6 million, compared to positive profits of $376 million for the established company! Stories like this can be multiplied, and they led to a huge surge in stock market indices followed by a serious and inevitable retrenchment in 2000.[5]

Foreign exchange markets exhibit elements of the same type of behavior. They cannot, of course, be compared to pure Ponzi schemes, since the value of the currency of a nation always reflects real economic conditions in that country. It is clear, however, that herd behavior is prevalent also in foreign exchange markets. The story of the exchange rate between the dollar and the euro is quite telling in that respect. When the euro was launched in January 1997 at an initial exchange rate of 1.15 dollars to the euro, the most prestigious investment banks, such as Goldman Sachs, predicted publicly that the exchange rate would quickly reach 1.25 dollars to one euro! Instead, the euro quickly retreated and fell to as low as 0.823 dollars to one euro in 2001. Then, starting in 2002, the trend reversed, and on December 31, 2003, the euro surged to the 1.25 dollar exchange rate predicted by the investment banks for 1997! Some may argue that this 30 percent drop in the dollar with respect to the euro in a period of two years reflects changed fundamentals, such as the large increase in the US budget deficit, and they are surely partly right. It is very hard, however, to explain the magnitude and timing of the change by new information about fundamentals. Already in the late 1990s many market players were arguing that the dollar had to fall, citing the huge cumulative current account deficits in the US balance of payments. Nonetheless, market players did not move for a long time and then started to move very rapidly, not because some new important information became suddenly available, but because of strong elements of herd behavior.

5. The Dow Jones Industrial Average tripled from 1994 to 2000, which meant a total increase in stock market prices of over 200 percent. The NASDAQ stock price index is used mainly to track technology stocks. NASDAQ tripled its value from 1997 to 2000.

The same kind of destabilizing, speculative herd behavior has been prevalent with respect to financial investments in emerging markets. These "surges and droughts" have been documented in many studies, including those in a recent book edited by Ffrench-Davis and Griffith-Jones (2003). The magnitude and speed of the swings are such that it is not possible to view them as caused by new information about fundamentals becoming available to market participants.

In 1997–98, overborrowing combined with rigid exchange rate regimes caused disastrous financial crises in Asian countries. Perceived by foreign investors as safe and very profitable outlets for lending, Asian countries had taken advantage of low interest rates; many over-invested in oversensitive export industries and the construction sector. But their basic fundamentals were strong, with high saving rates and relatively sound policies. The Asian crisis started in Thailand and spread to Korea, Indonesia, Malaysia, and the Philippines. Thailand had experienced capital inflows as early as the 1990s. From 1989 to 1994, foreign exchange reserves rose from $9.5 billion to $28.9 billion, despite large current account deficits, because capital inflows more than compensated for these deficits. Capital inflows peaked in 1995, when net non-FDI capital inflows reached a staggering 12.6 percent of GDP, and remained at high levels in 1996. Inflows were channeled into the economy mainly as credit to domestic borrowers. Equity prices fell sharply in 1996, and this meant serious trouble, as large amounts of lending by Thai banks and financial companies were secured by real estate. When a worldwide downturn in the demand for key Thai exports combined with these financial sector problems, pressure built up in May 1997 on the Thai baht. By 1997, non-FDI net capital outflows were 14.9 percent of GDP. By July, Thailand's reserves were depleted and the Thai authorities were forced to let the currency float.

The events leading to the Turkish crisis of 2001 include a similar story of "surge and drought." At the beginning of 2000, Turkey embarked on a new IMF-supported program featuring a preannounced crawling peg exchange rate regime that would give way to a more flexible "widening band" regime after 18 months. The objective was to defeat chronically high inflation, which had averaged close to 70 percent in the 1990s, and to regain debt sustainability that was threatened by the very high real interest rates that had prevailed for years. The program got off to a good start, as markets "believed" the preannounced path of the nominal exchange rate would be followed, at least for a while. With risk premia declining, short-term capital flowed into Turkey, taking advantage of the large exchange rate depreciation-adjusted interest rate differentials. The current account deficit widened dramatically by the summer of 2000 without much worry in the financial markets, for inflation was indeed declining rapidly, although not rapidly enough to avoid a significant appreciation of the real exchange rate. The Turkish economy could possibly have digested the real appreciation, at least during the 18-month period for which the exchange rate path was to remain rigid and preannounced, had it not been for serious weaknesses in the banking system translating into large contingent liabilities for the government. The combination of the large current account deficit and the underlying fiscal weakness led to attacks on the Turkish lira first in November 2000 and then again in February 2001. Just as some Asian countries had to give in to overwhelming market pressure, Turkey too had to abandon the exchange rate regime and let the lira float, leading to a massive devaluation in the early spring of 2001. Private short-term capital that had provided an inflow of about 5 percent of GDP in 2000 changed direction, with outflows totaling about 7 percent of GDP in 2001!

At a meeting with the Latin American Central Bank and Finance Ministry Network at the Inter-American Development Bank in 2001, Stanley Fischer, then first deputy managing director of the IMF, evaluated the problem of excessive volatility in capital markets with the following words:

> The spread of financial crises is far from random: contagion tends to hit weaker economies more quickly and more forcefully than strong ones. But even so, it is hard to believe that the speed and severity with which crises spread can be justified entirely by economic fundamentals. The contagion in Latin America from Russia's financial crisis in August 1998 is a case in point. One reason to take excess contagion seriously is that an investor panic can itself push an economy from a good to a bad equilibrium: when a country's policies and institutions are subjected to pressure from a reversal of capital inflows, they may crack, appearing in retrospect to justify the reversal of flows that caused the crisis to begin with.[6]

---

6. Fischer is here referring to the possible existence of multiple equilibria in general equilibrium models. The Asian crisis has led to a renewed interest in general equilibrium models where there can be "jumps" between "good" and "bad" equilibria, triggered by a change in expectations or speculative attacks. See, for example, Krugman (1996), Radelet and Sachs (1998), and Arifovic and Masson (2000) among many technical articles on the subject.

The preceding discussion of financial market imperfections and failures should not be taken to imply that it is possible or desirable to retreat from these markets or that they do not also bring benefits in terms of broadening and deepening global investment opportunities. Moreover, there are signs that market analysts have become more sophisticated and that liability positions of emerging-market countries have become more transparent. This may in the future lead to greater differentiation by country and less herd behavior affecting a number of countries simultaneously. Nonetheless, the experience of emerging-market economies over the last three decades, in conjunction with the much longer historical experience we have with financial markets more generally, strongly suggests the need for stabilizing public policy guidance and regulation, as well as orderly work-out mechanisms that can help countries in crisis. Even the most sophisticated financial markets have always needed both a regulator and a lender of last resort. Moreover, the domain of the market has to be the same as the domain of the regulator. If financial markets have become thoroughly global, there is the need for a global regulator as well as something like a global lender of last resort or, at least, a mechanism to play that role. If we want to have global financial markets, we must recognize the need for global public policy to stabilize these markets.

This should be the essential and recognized global policy role for the IMF. When market fundamentalists who still believe that markets somehow function perfectly with little or no institutional and regulatory framework want to abolish the IMF they are not being inconsistent. But progressive critics who otherwise believe in the need for public policy, and yet want to dispense with the IMF or something like the IMF, make no sense unless they take the extreme view that we should go back to tight capital controls and that countries should pursue autarchic development strategies. Some critics argue that while there is a need for a global regulator, the history of the IMF is such that it cannot qualify for that role and that a brand-new institution is needed. Others stress that it may be desirable to separate the purely regulatory and supervisory function of the IMF from its role as a lender. There is a precedent for this debate at the national level. In some countries the central bank has been both a supervisor and a lender, whereas in other countries these functions have been separated. If one started from scratch, it would probably be better to separate the lending and the regulatory role of the IMF. It is doubtful, however, that it would be feasible or even desirable and cost-effective to create a brand-new International Financial Authority–type institution.

If one believes in the need for public policy and regulation in the financial sphere, one needs a regulator and an agent of public policy, be it a renewed IMF or a combination of the IMF and an international supervisory agency. At the global level, it may be warranted to criticize the actions or the general approach of the existing institution, but one cannot dispense with it or ignore the role it is supposed to play.

The Debt Trap and the Systemic Failure of Current Arrangements

There is another related systemic feature of the current international economy that, interacting with the nature of capital markets, has led to a major systemic challenge that must be addressed. Before the 1980s, most developing country debt was foreign debt owed to official institutions or to banks. With the liberalization and development of capital markets, governments and public entities began to issue bonds in international capital markets as well as at home, discovering a new type of resource to fund public spending. Moreover, financial sector liberalization brought with it, unfortunately, frequent banking sector crises in which governments had to assume the contingent liabilities that had accumulated in the banks. The September 2003 issue of *World Economic Outlook* (WEO) prepared by the IMF contains an excellent analysis of public debt in emerging economies.[7] Total public debt levels in a group of emerging-market economies rose from about 30 percent of GDP at the end of the 1960s to about 60 percent at the end of the 1980s and to about 70 percent at the end of the 1990s. These debt levels are very high and have created a qualitatively new and very constraining economic environment in these countries. The problem addressed is, broadly speaking, debt sustainability. The report explores the question of when do public debt levels become "too high," leading to crisis. The WEO explains why these debt levels should be considered too high. Defining a benchmark level of public debt as a debt level that would equate the stock of debt to the present discounted value of future expected primary surpluses in the budget, the WEO arrives at the tough conclusion that the median of such "warranted" public debt-to-GDP ratios would be only 25 percent, compared to the 70 percent actual ratio in the sample of emerging-market countries

7. The IMF study defines emerging-market countries as the 27 countries in the Emerging Market Bond Index (EMBI) at the beginning of 2002, plus Costa Rica, Indonesia, Israel, and Jordan.

studied! This compares to a benchmark ratio of 75 percent for the sample of fully industrialized countries.

Why is there such a huge difference between these two benchmark ratios? Why should the advanced economies be able to carry so much more debt as a ratio of their GDP than the middle-income countries? As explained in detail in the WEO, the difference is due to the combination of shorter maturities, much lower fiscal revenue-to-GDP ratios, higher variability of that revenue, higher real interest rates, and a track record of lower primary surpluses in emerging-market economies. Because of all of these factors, many emerging-market economies have ended up in what must be called a "debt trap." Many have debt-to-GDP ratios that are not really sustainable, making them vulnerable to repeated crises of confidence. There are, of course, important differences among emerging-market economies, with many Asian countries in much better shape than countries in Latin America or in the Middle East and North Africa. Nonetheless, it is possible to tell the following "stylized" story for a large number of emerging-market economies.

With debt ratios well above 50 percent of GDP and short maturities leading to the need for substantial rollover of debt every month, there is a constant underlying fear in financial markets that a combination of unfavorable developments could lead to what is called a "debt event," meaning a sudden inability to service debt on time, with ensuing market panic, surge in interest rates, and pressure on the exchange rate. This kind of event could be triggered by a terms of trade shock, sudden political turmoil, or a serious problem in the banking sector. A confidence crisis could also be caused by "contagion" from a debt event in a different country. To protect against such an event, the "typical" high-debt, emerging-market economy has to run substantial primary budget surpluses and continuously pay a high risk premium on outstanding and new debt. Countries with public debt-to-GDP ratios in the 50 to 80 percent range, paying real interest rates in the 10 to 20 percent range on their domestic currency–denominated debt and in the 5 to 12 percent range on their foreign currency–denominated debt, are likely to need surpluses that are large and politically difficult to sustain.[8] The high real interest rates exert downward pressure on the growth of GDP, which in turn makes it *more* difficult to reduce the debt-to-GDP ratio. Figure 5.1, taken from the

---

8. Statistical annexes of IMF Staff Reports collect detailed data on market fundamentals, and these reports are available for a good number of emerging-market countries.

Figure 5.1 *Yields on developing versus developed country debt*

Percent

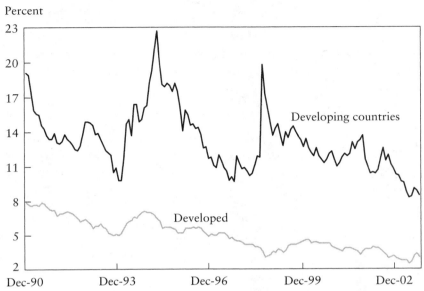

Notes: Developing country yields refer to yields on benchmark emerging-market bond indexes, and developed country yields refer to the average of long-term (10–year) benchmark government yields for the United States, Europe, and Japan.

Source: World Bank *2004 Global Development Finance Report*. GDF sources for this graph are Bloomberg, J.P. Morgan Chase, and World Bank staff calculations.

World Bank's Global Development Finance (GDF) Report of 2004, shows how large and persistent the difference in interest rates on foreign debt has been between developed and emerging-market economies.[9] Data on domestic real interest rates are more difficult to assemble in a consistent fashion, but the difference in such rates between emerging and advanced economies is even larger, reflecting the greater exchange rate risk in the former.

In the group of high-debt, emerging-market economies, fiscal policy tends to be procyclical rather than anticyclical, as it is in the mature industrial countries. When there is a recession in an economy that does not have to worry about a debt event, fiscal policy can be expansionary

9. Thanks are due to Himmat Kalsi, one of the authors of the GDF 2004 Report, for sharing this figure and the data behind it.

and attempt to stimulate domestic demand. In industrial countries, government expenditures increase by *more* than national income in a downturn—as should be the case to counteract cyclical recession—and they increase by *less* than national income in an upturn. The same does not take place in a "typical" emerging-market economy because the income decline in a downturn tends to worsen the debt-to-GDP ratio, creating debt event fears that tend to lead to a need to tighten rather than temporarily relax fiscal policy. On the contrary, in an upturn, debt-event fears diminish and governments tend to want to catch up in their expenditures! This makes fiscal policy procyclical rather than anticyclical, a point often emphasized by critics of IMF-backed stabilization programs.[10] While this situation is unfortunate, it is really not possible to avoid it in countries where public debt-to-GDP ratios are high, because relaxing fiscal policy at a time of crisis is likely to lead to fear of default and deepen the crisis. When a crisis strikes, involuntary debt restructuring accompanied by capital controls seems to be the only other option for such high-debt countries, with disruption and costs that are likely in most cases to outweigh the costs of procyclical fiscal policies!

The combination of volatile capital markets and economies that are on a tightrope because of high debt-to-GDP ratios has created an important systemic problem for emerging-market economies and the world economy as a whole. The high interest rates prevalent in these economies create an attractive short-term investment opportunity for mobile and liquid international capital. It is hard for short-term investors to resist opportunities that offer very high real returns in the bond market.[11] The returns can of course be even higher during upturns in equity markets. When things seem relatively stable politically and the debt-to-GDP ratio has gone down a little, thanks to good growth and/or strong fiscal policy performance, short-term capital flows into the typical emerging-market economy, often in the form of surges that can exceed 5 percent of GDP. For a while this sets off a "virtuous" cycle. The exchange rate appreciates, leading to a decline in debt-to-GDP ratios, as a significant part of total debt is denominated in foreign currency. Real interest rates decline in domestic currency terms as the demand for bonds goes up. Real returns

10. See, for example, Stiglitz (2001), who focuses on fiscal policy and the Asian economies, most of which did not have high debt-to-GDP ratios when the crisis struck in 1997. A more countercyclical fiscal policy is possible and desirable in such circumstances.

11. Of course, by definition, these high returns reflect the currency and sovereign default risk premia.

to foreign investors remain very high, however, because of the exchange rate appreciation. This leads to further capital inflows, leading to a further appreciation of the exchange rate and so on.

At some point the cycle reverses itself, however. Real exchange rate appreciation will tend to lower real growth. The current account deficit will widen and the external debt will grow due to the capital inflows. During the capital surge episodes, interest rates decline, but not to a degree that would really remove the underlying debt worries. As soon as the exchange rate starts to depreciate instead of appreciate, domestic interest rates rise again and so does the debt-to-GDP ratio. If, in addition, the capital surge episode has led to a decline in fiscal austerity, as governments take advantage of the good times to fulfill some electoral promises or prepare for the next elections, the rise in the debt-to-GDP ratio might be quite sharp, leading to an acceleration of exchange rate depreciation and a sharper rise in the debt burden indicators. If that is the case, a precrisis or crisis situation develops, bringing with it calls for an even larger primary surplus to restore market confidence. During the crisis "management phase," IMF money will tend to replace private capital, in a sense bailing out both the country and private creditors and lengthening the maturity of the debt without reducing it. If the stabilization effort is relatively successful, the exchange rate depreciation will stop, the country will again appear as a good short-term investment opportunity to foreign investors, and the whole cycle is likely to start all over again.

Several things must be stressed about this kind of situation, which affects many middle-income and some low-income countries. First, while domestic real interest rates fluctuate over the cycle described above, they consistently remain very high, usually above 10 percent on average over a period of years. This leads to chronic, persistent debt worries. The only way to reduce the debt-to-GDP level for this class of countries to the 25 percent benchmark ratio, or even to something less ambitious in the 30 to 40 percent range, would be to run primary surpluses in the 6 to 8 percent range for an extended period of time and at the same time maintain relatively high growth rates, at least in the 4 to 6 percent range.[12] This is, of course, extremely difficult. It is much more likely that the domestic political cycle will contain episodes of "adjustment fatigue" where the primary surplus falls to much lower levels.

12. The change in a country's debt-to-GDP ratio depends on the combination of initial conditions (the initial ratio), the primary surplus, GDP growth, and the real interest rate adjusted for changes in the real rate of exchange.

It is also quite likely that primary surpluses are achieved at the expense of long-run investment expenditures in the budgets of the countries concerned. It is politically easier to cut investment expenditures in basic infrastructure and education than it is to cut wages and salaries or public employment levels, because the political costs of investment cuts are less immediate. Tight fiscal policy is often accompanied by a decline in the long-term quality of public expenditures. While the aggregate demand-restraining effect of tight fiscal policy can have a short-term, Keynesian depressing effect on growth, very low public investment levels maintained over time have a more damaging negative impact on the long-term growth rate. The combination of adjustment fatigue episodes, during which primary surpluses fall, and mediocre growth performance, partly due to the "anti-investment" nature of fiscal policy, makes it is very difficult to achieve significant and sustained declines in the debt-to-GDP ratios. Many emerging-market economies have remained caught in this kind of debt trap for decades.

The costs of the types of financial crisis experienced by East Asian and Latin American countries, as well as Russia, and Turkey, are massive. Stephany Griffith-Jones (2004) has recently estimated the forgone output for the group of countries consisting of Argentina, Brazil, Indonesia, Korea, Malaysia, Mexico, Thailand, and Turkey. In her research with Ricardo Gottschalk, she estimates output loss for those countries in the 1995–2002 period as $1.250 trillion, or an annual average of $150 billion! Such figures are huge when compared, for example, to total worldwide foreign aid flows (not more than about $40 billion a year measured in terms of grant equivalent value of these flows).[13]

An important factor that magnifies the financial crises experienced by emerging-market economies has been referred to as "original sin" and is due to the severe impact these crises invariably have on the balance sheets of the financial and corporate sectors. In 1999–2000, developing countries accounted for 8 percent of world debt, but less than 1 percent of currency denomination. Eichengreen, Hausman, and Panizza (2002) have coined the systemic problem of not being able to borrow in one's own currency as "original sin." This problem affects almost all countries except the issuers of the five major currencies: the dollar, the euro, the yen, the pound sterling, and the Swiss franc. A country that suffers from original

---

13. Griffith-Jones estimates output loss by measuring the difference between projected potential output and actual output over the years, where potential output is taken to be a country's output trend over the years preceding a major crisis.

Table 5.1 *Impact of the financial crisis on poverty in four East Asian countries, 1997 and 1998*

Percent

Country	Poverty headcount index	
	1997	*1998*
Indonesia	11.0	19.9
Korea	2.6	7.3
Malaysia	8.2	10.4
Thailand	9.8	12.9

Source: World Bank, *Global Monitoring Report* (2004, 62) adapted from Fallon and Lucas (2002).

sin will accumulate debt that will be heavily denominated in foreign currency and will have an aggregate currency mismatch on its balance sheet. A reversal of capital flows therefore will have serious balance sheet effects as the value of domestic assets declines and the value of debt goes up. Eichengreen, Hausman, and Panizza propose putting together a diversified basket of emerging-market and developing-country currencies (EM Index) in which each currency in the basket is indexed to that country's inflation rate as a disincentive for borrowers to debase their own currency. This proposal led to a big debate on the role of the Bretton Woods institutions, and whether they should issue debt in an EM index, as their AAA ratings would be helpful in creating some market for these bonds.

Another important dimension of the problem relates to the distribution of income. The pressure of capital markets combined with periodic crisis situations has an unequalizing effect on the distribution of income. Sustained high real interest rates act as a mechanism constantly redistributing income to the rich, both across borders to foreign fund owners and, domestically, to the owners of liquid wealth. Moreover, when there is an actual crisis necessitating further fiscal tightening measures, the burden inevitably falls on the poor and middle-income groups rather than on the rich. Overcoming a crisis necessitates reestablishing confidence in financial markets. Financial capital is highly mobile and the capital account liberalizations that were implemented throughout emerging-market economies in the 1980s and 1990s mean that capital can flee very quickly if it wants to. Table 5.1, adapted from Fallon and Lucas (2002) and quoted in the World Bank's *Global Monitoring Report* (2004), describes the impact of financial crisis on the number of people living in poverty in four East Asian countries during the 1997–98 crisis.

Many policymakers have contemplated imposing higher taxes on wealth or high incomes when confronted with the need to "find" another 1 or 2 percent of GDP to meet a "strengthened" primary surplus target at the onset of a macroeconomic crisis triggered by debt event fears. I lived through a typical example of this in Turkey at the peak of the 2001 crisis. We had agreed with the IMF in March 2001 on a new and more ambitious primary surplus target of 5.5 percent of GDP and were trying to put together a revised budget that would meet this target. The distribution of income in Turkey is highly unequal, and the pending decline in GDP and employment due to the crisis was going to hurt the poor and threaten many jobs. It would have been very desirable, for equity and social cohesion, to derive greater tax revenue from the rich. The problem is that, in a crisis situation, one needs revenue quickly and cannot wait for the results of a comprehensive tax reform. We considered an income tax surcharge, a tax on liquid wealth, and a windfall gains tax, because many investors that had held foreign exchange before the onset of the crisis had made spectacular gains due to the collapse of the Turkish currency.[14] In the end, we decided reluctantly, however, that any significant measure of that type would accelerate capital flight and increase the degree of panic that was already our biggest problem. We did try, using an amendment added to a bill in Parliament around midnight, to increase the deposit insurance "tax" received on deposits in the banking system, but we failed even at that because of the defection of a group of government deputies during the midnight vote. In the end, there was an increase in the value added tax, increases in taxes on tobacco, alcohol and fuel, and many increases in administered prices. The budget targets had to be met, as usual, by increasing the effective tax burden on the middle- and lower-income groups. We tried to compensate this by direct income support programs to the poorest sections of the population. The 2002 data published by the State Institute of Statistics suggest that we had some success. But we could not impose new taxes on the rich at the height of the crisis. It would have led to a further acceleration of capital flight and would have ended up hurting the country and the poor through a deepening of the crisis.[15]

---

14. In general, changes in tax laws with retroactive effects should, of course, be avoided. But in special circumstances, when large numbers of citizens are asked to accept severe belt-tightening measures, some contribution by the lucky few who benefited from the crisis can promote social cohesion and help prevent deepening of the crisis.

15. See Miller (2004) and Derviş (2004) for an analysis of the Turkish crisis.

To summarize the situation with respect to income distribution, the "structurally" high real interest rates due to sovereign default risk and currency risk, combined with fiscal difficulties during a crisis, impart an *unequalizing* bias to the process of economic development in the typical emerging-market economy. There may, of course, be countervailing forces, such as good education policies, the nature of internal migration, or the particular effects of foreign trade, which could lead to an improvement in income distribution. It will be difficult, however, for such potentially equalizing factors to overcome the unequalizing bias due to the debt trap and the tendency to run into macroeconomic crisis.

The combination of volatile capital markets, often driven by herd behavior and high debt burdens inherited from the past, have created a long-term structural problem for a group of emerging-market, middle-income countries facing chronic debt event fears, chronic high real interest rates, an inability to run countercyclical fiscal policies, and a tendency toward worsening distribution of income. Some countries, particularly in Asia, which never let their debt ratios become excessive, have been able to avoid this trap and insure themselves against future crises by accumulating very large amounts of foreign exchange reserves.[16] Other countries, however, particularly in Latin America but also in Asia and the Mediterranean area, find themselves in this structural debt trap. A concerted effort is needed to help them out of this trap so that their own growth and poverty reduction efforts can succeed and the danger of recurrent financial crises of the type experienced in the 1990s, affecting the world economy as a whole, can be avoided.

Helping Emerging-market Economies Overcome the Debt Trap

The analysis presented above, drawing on the 2003 *World Economic Outlook* as well as many other publications on the topic, suggests that there is a group of middle-income, emerging-market economies that have accumulated a debt burden that will be very difficult to sustain given the cost of that debt, their growth performance, and their capacity to generate primary surpluses. These economies seem condemned to recurring crises.[17]

16. Note that the accumulation of massive foreign exchange reserves with low yields itself carries welfare costs. If these resources could be invested at normal yields, the countries in question would gain, provided, of course, they continued to avoid crisis.

17. See Zahler (2004) for an excellent recent overview of capital flow reversals and excessive volatility affecting emerging markets, including a review of various proposals on what to do about it.

They also have to struggle with a chronic tendency for income distribution to worsen due to high real interest rates and the effects of crises on distribution. This group of countries also contributes to systemic risk in the global economy because of the danger of contagion. A crisis in Argentina alone may not pose systemic risk. A crisis that erupts in, say, Argentina and Brazil at the same time could lead to worldwide contagion infecting emerging markets and affecting the global economy as a whole.

It has been easier to manage existing debt burdens in recent years because dollar and euro interest rates have been at historic lows. This has made it possible to carry foreign-denominated debt and has led to a dangerous degree of complacency, despite interest rates remaining high on domestically denominated debt in many emerging-market economies. Given the US twin deficits, there is a fair chance that US interest rates will have to rise again; we may be entering a period where the cost of carrying and rolling over large debt burdens will increase because of the higher cost of large amounts of dollar-denominated debt. This would make an already difficult situation even worse.

For the countries concerned, there are only two ways out of this debt trap. The first is to *grow out* of the trap by a combination of rapid GDP growth and strong fiscal policy with the help of moderate real interest rates, all the while avoiding a crisis that would constitute a major setback on the path to debt sustainability. The other way out would be to be able to negotiate an across-the-board *reduction* in the debt burden with a whole class of creditors.

The past three decades do not offer many examples of countries that have reached very high debt burdens and then successfully grown out of the debt trap.[18] For most of the high-debt emerging-market economies it has been more a touch-and-go story of periods of improvement alternating with periods of deterioration, including years of crisis where progress made over a number of years can be lost in a few months. It is time for the Bretton Woods institutions to focus on this systemic problem and thereby both strengthen the stability of the world economy and help the

18. One important exception is Chile. When the debt crisis erupted in 1982, the total debt-to-GDP ratio was almost 72 percent. Through the aggressive use of a variety of debt conversion plans between 1985 and 1991, Chile retired an estimated $10.5 billion of debt, most of which was converted into equity in Chilean companies. Chile rescheduled the principal of its debt, but otherwise met its obligations. Chile did not enter into interest arrears, nor did it seek debt reduction under the Brady Plan. It is today one of the few Latin American countries that seems to have escaped the recurrent debt-related crisis syndrome.

hundreds of millions of poor people in the emerging-market, middle-income economies escape poverty.

The financial facilities and program support offered by the Bretton Woods institutions to emerging-market economies should reflect the need to overcome the chronic high debt problem as well as help countries address specific acute crisis situations. It would therefore make sense to offer two types of facilities to emerging markets. The first type of facility would be designed to help overcome the systemic debt trap issue highlighted in the 2003 WEO. The second type of facility would deal with problems arising in specific cases, as is the case for current stand-by programs. The following discussion will focus on the IMF and its lending because the Fund is the lead institution when it comes to debt and balance of payments problems, and because it has larger resources to address these issues. Nonetheless, the World Bank's lending program has always played an important complementary role to IMF resources and should continue to do so. Moreover, the World Bank does have the potential to increase its lending volume to emerging-market economies significantly, even in the absence of an increase in its capital. A more radical reorganization of the division of labor between the two Bretton Woods sisters is also conceivable, giving the World Bank a clear mandate to expand its medium-term lending program in support of more stable growth in emerging-market economies. The discussion below essentially refers to the IMF. But the proposals outlined could also be formulated with the World Bank as the lead agency, although this would require a fairly radical "reweighting" of the two institutions.

What is clearly desirable is an IMF facility in the form of financial support for a medium-term economic program that would help a large number of emerging-market countries grow out of the debt trap and help protect them from contagion and financial crisis. To a certain degree this was the objective of the contingent credit line (CCL) introduced by the IMF Executive Board in 1999. The CCL was designed as a response to the rapid spread of turmoil through global financial markets during the Asian crisis. Favored by the US Treasury during the Clinton administration, the facility would have provided foreign exchange reserves to draw upon in order to bolster investor confidence in healthy emerging markets that are threatened by volatile capital flows and possible contagion.

Member countries not at risk of an external payments crisis of their own making, but vulnerable to contagion effects from capital account crises in other countries, would have been eligible if they met the following IMF criteria: no expected need for IMF resources except because of contagion; positive assessment of policies and progress toward adherence to internationally accepted standards; appropriate indicators relating to fiscal balance, economic growth, inflation, capital flows, international reserves, the current account balance and soundness of the financial system; constructive relations with private creditors; progress toward limiting external vulnerability; and a satisfactory medium-term macroeconomic and financial program with a commitment to adjust policies. Access to the contingent credit line required endorsement by the Executive Board of a quantitative quarterly macroeconomic program and structural reform policies, together with a commitment to adjust policies as needed.

A key problem with the contingent credit line was that many countries with sound economies were afraid to give the wrong signal to the markets. They feared that conditions for entry to the CCL were too low; therefore they risked being lumped in the same category with weaker economies. Other countries, on the contrary, feared that after expressing interest they might fail to qualify. In 2000, the IMF introduced several important changes aimed at making use of the facility more attractive. First, the interest rate charges on the contingent credit line were reduced; they were still above lower-tranche stand-by rates, but were lower than rates on the IMF's Supplemental Reserve Facility (SRF), which makes relatively large short-term loans to countries experiencing capital account crises. Second, the disbursement of the first portion of the facility would be more automatic. Yet, no IMF member country used the facility even once and the facility was left to expire in late 2003. The reason for this failure, despite high hopes when the facility was launched, was that it ended up being neither a "lender of last resort facility" that could quickly be drawn on at time of crisis, nor a "protection facility" that would ensure a country against the risk of crisis. Countries that viewed themselves at low risk of crisis did not find it desirable to go through the required prequalification process. Moreover, for these countries, the contingent credit line did not offer financial terms that were significantly more favorable than what they could obtain from financial markets. Countries at higher risk had, or would have had, trouble meeting the prequalification criteria. Some countries also feared the possibility that the potential loss of qualifying status due to a disagreement with the IMF on policy, or a temporary slippage in policy implementation, would send a very negative message to markets that would make things much worse. These problems are real. On the other hand, making access to such a facility almost automatic for a large number of countries could lead to irresponsible macro policies, as politicians would have a virtual bailout guarantee, causing serious moral hazard problems. Keeping countries qualified to access the facility even if policies deteriorate would lead to the same kinds of problems and would make the IMF co-responsible for the development of a crisis. On the other hand, withdrawing qualification could trigger the crisis itself. These "entry" and "exit" problems could not be overcome, and the contingent credit line was discontinued with instructions to IMF staff to come up with a reformed proposal that could work.

The underlying problem with the CCL was that it was a short-term approach to a long-term problem and focused too much on preventing contagion, whereas the bigger problem is the excessive indebtedness of an important group of emerging-market economies that have to function within an environment of highly volatile international financial markets. This volatility actually tends to be procyclical, and it raises the risk premia on emerging-market debt. What is really needed is a systematic effort to help middle-income countries overcome the debt trap that many of them have not been able to escape.

Stability and Growth Facility

An approach addressing this long-term debt problem could be developed along the following lines. The IMF, in close cooperation with the World Bank, would offer middle-income, emerging-market economies a Stability and Growth Facility (SGF) with the explicit aim of reducing their chronic vulnerability to debt-related problems over a period of time. A participating emerging-market country would agree with the Bretton Woods institutions on a medium-term growth and debt reduction program, the centerpiece of which would be a time path for the growth of real income and the reduction of a set of indicators of indebtedness. The typical qualifying country would be one where there is no current crisis, but where there is a high debt burden and therefore chronic vulnerability. Countries such as Brazil, Uruguay, Ecuador, Turkey, the Philippines, and Indonesia would be among possible candidates. To qualify and to remain qualified, the participating country would have to be certified as having acceptable policies in place, as was the case for the contingent credit line, and also have a medium-term growth program with a path for the primary surplus and structural policies in support of growth that would lead to a substantial reduction in the debt indicators. To overcome the difficulties faced by the CCL, this approach would have three elements that, taken together, would make it more attractive and more relevant than the contingent credit line.

First, conditionality, i.e., the conditions attached to lending from the Bretton Woods institutions, would be *phased* in such a way that, *given the initial conditions,* the likelihood of upfront disqualification would be low. Take the concrete case of a country such as Turkey. If 2003 is the base, there was no crisis, the realized primary surplus was above 6 percent of GDP, growth was 6 percent, and the consolidated public debt-to-GDP ratio stood at about 70 percent, with an average maturity of less than four years. Let us assume that the target debt-to-GDP ratio for 2010 would be set at 50 percent of GDP and the average maturity would be targeted to extend to eight years. Turkey's medium-term program would have to present a credible scenario, including specific policies that could lead to such a reduction in the debt burden and lengthening of maturities. The starting point would be existing policies, which would then be modified gradually to further strengthen the program. Fiscal policy, for example, would become more growth oriented, with a gradual change in the *structure* of revenues and expenditures, while the *aggregate* primary surplus would be determined every year as a function of the progress towards the desired debt indicators.

Second, once a robust program was agreed upon, the amount of available Stability and Growth Facility financing would be *phased* over the program period. There would *not* need to be a large *upfront* disbursement, and moral hazard would thus be limited. On the other hand, a participating country could count on *a stable source of medium-term financing* that would not be impacted by the ebbs and flows affecting private finance to emerging markets.[19]

Third, and this too is important for the scheme to work, Stability and Growth Facility resources would have to be extended *at a price low enough* and in amounts *sufficient* for the debt reduction dynamic to work while the pursuit of social policies aimed at poverty reduction and broad-based growth would not be stalled by lack of fiscal resources. This could be achieved in various ways, all of which, however, would require some resources to allow the IMF to extend the loans at relatively low cost. The cost to the borrower should be close to LIBOR itself, or even slightly

19. The overall supply of private debt capital to middle-income countries often depends on advanced country market conditions, which have little to do with domestic policies in a specific emerging-market economy.

below, as opposed to including a 150 to 500 basis point spread proposed in the various versions of the contingent credit line and available in other IMF facilities, and maturities should be in the 8- to 10-year range. A yearly aggregate volume of lending in the $20 billion to $40 billion range would be needed over a decade or so to make a significant contribution to debt reduction and growth for the group of emerging-market economies concerned. The time path for the volume of lending would depend on participation rates and could be structured to first increase and then decrease.

A detailed quantitative model would be needed to analyze precise resource needs and the trade-offs involved between the speed of achieving robust debt sustainability, the primary surpluses and growth rates involved, and the volume of Stability and Growth Facility lending, as well as the pricing of these resources. The cost of the funds would need to be brought down by about 150 to 250 basis points compared to what was foreseen for the contingent credit line. Volumes in the range proposed above would require a significant but not unreasonable amount of resources that would allow for some "blending" between concessional funds and the "normal" resources of the IMF and the World Bank. A reduced interest cost of 200 basis points on an initial flow of $20 billion would amount to a modest $400 million the first year. The annual "cost" of allowing "blending" in this form would of course go up as the stock of Stability and Growth Facility debt increases, and could peak in the $3 billion to $4 billion range before declining again. A sunset clause should be built into the SGF because it is a program needed to correct a malfunctioning in the way international capital markets have worked over the last three decades. During the decade or so the SGF would be in effect, reforms such as enhancing IMF surveillance with special attention to debt buildups and contingent liabilities, the generalized practice of including collective action clauses in debt contracts and strengthening and widening the use of standards and codes, including codes of conduct for debtors and creditors, should get us to an international environment where the Stability and Growth Facility would no longer be needed or appropriate.

One might ask whether it is worth it to try to introduce blending in the form of an interest cost reduction element into the Stability and Growth Facility. The volume of resources proposed for the cost reduction amounts (cumulatively) to only a few percentage points of total emerging-market debt. While the proposed enhancement does complicate the proposal, it would have a crucial catalytic role in allowing the "package" to work. SGF resources would be the most desirable resources available to highly indebted emerging-market economies, not only in terms of being reliable and coming with reasonably long maturities, but also in terms of interest costs. This desirability would be helpful in facilitating the internal reform processes. It would also demonstrate the willingness of the international community as a whole to shoulder some part of the burden accumulated in the past and to help accelerate growth and fight poverty in the economies concerned. It is the *combination* of continued internal reforms, within a framework that is considered helpful and legitimate by domestic citizens, and a steady long-term source of finance at moderate cost that would be the key to success.

One attractive way to raise the additional resources required for an effective Stability and Growth Facility would be to use special allocations of special drawing rights. The use of SDRs for developmental purposes and to finance global public goods has been considered in the past and most recently proposed by George Soros (2002). The Soros proposal is different in its primary objective in that it aims at providing grants for specific global public goods or poverty reduction programs rather than country loans. [20] The logic of using special drawing rights, which is to *raise resources* and achieve an *equitable burden sharing* that avoids the free rider problem among donor countries, is the same, however.

When discussing the pros and cons of the creation of special drawing rights in the context of the Soros proposal or as a means to lower the interest cost of a Stability and Growth Facility as discussed above, it is worth stressing that given the orders of magnitude involved, there is no danger that SDR creation would have any significant impact on world inflation. Total world GDP and total world reserves amount to about $40 trillion and $2.5 trillion, respectively. If the world economy were to grow at about 3 percent per annum, a relatively modest projection, total reserves could grow by about $75 billion a year without increasing the total reserve-to-income ratio. The creation of several billion dollars worth of special drawing rights a year, which is all that would be needed for an SGF that lends at a cost close to LIBOR, would not, therefore, have any noticeable inflationary impact on the world. There could of course be other means to finance some blending for emerging-market economies. Various forms of international taxation have been proposed. The pros

---

20. The Soros proposal could of course be implemented separately and in addition to what is proposed here. See the discussion below on least-developed countries.

and cons of various international resource mobilization mechanisms to support development objectives will be discussed in greater detail in chapter 6, as the discussion on how best to raise these resources should look at overall needs, and resources are needed in much greater amounts for the least-developed countries and then for emerging-market economies.

Building a more robust international financial system by helping a whole group of emerging-market economies out of their debt trap is a global public good. The Stability and Growth Facility would also allow for more effective poverty reduction in the emerging-market economies and reduce the somewhat arbitrary "all-or-nothing" approach of providing highly concessional aid or grants to the poorest countries, while middle-income countries, where most of the poor actually reside, can only access funds at close to commercial cost. Finally, if implemented gradually and within growth-oriented macroeconomic frameworks, it would not be disruptive of existing global financial markets. On the contrary, in the long run, by contributing to more rapid and stable growth worldwide, everyone would benefit.

In some ways, the Stability and Growth Facility would be the middle-income country companion to the Poverty Reduction and Growth Facility (PRGF) that exists for poor countries.[21] The degree of concessionality would be much lower and the focus would be explicitly on much more robust debt sustainability in the medium term. To qualify, countries would have to have already achieved at least short-term stability and not be in immediate danger of a debt-related crisis. Conditionality would be needed, but it would be geared to growth and indebtedness *outcomes* along the medium-term growth path and would not have to be as intrusive and comprehensive as in crisis situations or in the case of countries with much weaker governance structures.

The IMF would retain its "normal" stand-by program option, although a country could not simultaneously be in a stand-by and a Stability and Growth Facility program. The stand-by option would be available for countries that need immediate assistance in the face of a financial

---

21. The PRGF is the IMF's low-interest lending facility for poor countries. The annual interest rate on loans is 0.5 percent, and repayments begin 5 ½ years after the first disbursement and end 10 years after the disbursement. Repayments are made semiannually. The targets and policy conditions in a PRGF-supported program are drawn directly from the country's Poverty Reduction Strategy Papers. Eligibility is based principally on the IMF's assessment of a country's per capita income, drawing on the cutoff point for eligibility to World Bank concessional lending, which at the time of this writing was 2001 gross national income per capita of $875.

crisis. In stand-by programs, conditionality will have to remain more comprehensive, reflecting the needs arising in crisis situations and the danger of moral hazard. The stand-by programs would be targeted at helping overcome an actual or imminent crisis in individual countries, whereas the Stability and Growth Facility program would have the objective of reducing the chronic vulnerability to crisis that characterizes a whole category of middle-income countries that carry debt burdens that are too heavy.

As mentioned above, the World Bank rather than the IMF could be chosen as the lead institution offering and managing an SGF type program. This would require, however, a major strengthening of the World Bank's capability to deal with macroeconomic and growth issues in an integrated and programmatic manner. If one were to go that route, the IMF would hand over the area of long-term macroeconomics to the World Bank, restricting itself to a strictly short-term focus. All things considered, and given the current functioning of the institutions, it may be easier to work within a model where the IMF takes the lead on the SGF, working closely with the World Bank on the policy issues, and with the World Bank complementing the overall SGF lending with operations at the sectoral level that would form an integral part of the SGF-supported, long-term debt reduction and poverty eradication strategy.

Crisis Management and Sovereign Debt Restructuring

A program through the Stability and Growth Facility would not include support for upfront debt reduction, and the countries qualifying for SGF support would be those that could through their own efforts and with some modest help, in the form of a small amount of interest cost reduction or blending conveyed through the IMF facility, attain robust long-term debt sustainability. There may be a group of countries or "country situations," however, where growing out of the debt trap even with SGF type support will not be a realistic option. Such extreme situations are usually due to relatively sudden and very large surges in debt due to a banking crisis or a massive devaluation, or both. A recent example has been Argentina, where by 2001 the nation's public debt had clearly become unsustainable. In such cases, there is a need for orderly debt reduction within the framework of something that resembles a Chapter 11 bankruptcy proceeding, which exists for similar situations in the case of enterprise debt within a nation-state.[22] With these considerations in mind, and in response to the issues raised by Argentina's collapse in 2001 and 2002, IMF first deputy managing director Anne Krueger proposed a Sovereign Debt Restructuring Mechanism (SDRM) to deal with the serious collective action problems that arise in such crisis situations.[23] The potential benefits of moving quickly to restructure debt before a crisis hits with full force, destroying an economy and its remaining capacity to generate debt service capacity because of massive dislocation, should be clear also to creditors. In the short run, bringing into existence a type of Stability and Growth Facility would not diminish the need for a Sovereign Debt Restructuring Mechanism for countries outside the scope of the SGF and threatened by massive disruption. In the long run, however, a successful Stability and Growth Facility program would of course reduce the likelihood of debt situations requiring statutory or indeed voluntary restructuring from arising.

After a lively debate, during which the IMF refined the original proposal, the "Krueger approach," which would have provided for a *statutory* mechanism for orderly debt reduction to be achieved by an amendment to the IMF's Articles of Agreement, was shelved by the IMF governors at the 2003 Bretton Woods annual meetings in Dubai. Opposition to the approach came from the US Treasury, major private creditors (expressing themselves through the International Institute of Finance), some other rich country governors, and some emerging-market governments that feared that embarking on a Sovereign Debt Restructuring Mechanism would raise the cost of their access to international markets.

22. Chapter 11 is the part of the US Bankruptcy Code that contains the provisions for court-supervised reorganization of debtor companies. Under Chapter 11, debtors are permitted to postpone all payments on debts in order to reorganize their businesses. While other bankruptcy proceedings seek to have the debtor's assets sold and have all the creditors paid as much as possible, Chapter 11 seeks to give debtors some room in order to allow their businesses to recover and all creditors to be fully compensated. Most member countries of the Organization for Economic Cooperation and Development (OECD) are slowly moving towards a Chapter 11–type system, replacing more informal procedures.

23. Anne Krueger's first public announcement of the Sovereign Debt Reduction Mechanism proposal was in November 2001 at the National Economists' Club. After Krueger made a few more public speeches on the SDRM mechanism, the IMF published a pamphlet entitled "A New Approach to Sovereign Debt Restructuring" in April 2002. The IMF Executive Board published a paper later in 2002 further discussing the design of possible sovereign debt restructuring mechanisms. Related proposals have been made before by academic economists.

What has been agreed upon instead is to encourage the use of collective action clauses in new emerging-market debt. This decentralized, market-oriented approach championed by the US Treasury would have sovereign borrowers and their creditors put a set of collective action clauses into their debt contracts. The clauses would describe in advance and as precisely as possible what would happen in the event of a restructuring, including majority action clauses that would allow a supermajority of creditors to agree on terms binding for all.

It is possible that over time—where "time" may mean six to eight years—widening the use of collective action clauses may qualitatively change the environment in which debt restructuring for crisis countries takes place. Once a substantial proportion of debt instruments carry these collective action clauses, work-outs may become more orderly and sovereign debt restructurings may begin to look more like their domestic corporate counterparts. In this context, and as a further contribution to measures reducing the risk of crisis, it may also be very useful to consider the EM Index proposal by Eichengreen, Hausman, and Panizza, and have the World Bank and the regional development banks support the creation of emerging-market debt denominated in a basket of emerging-market currencies rather than dollars, euros, or yen, so as to mitigate the currency mismatches on the balance sheets of the public or private sectors of emerging-market economies. All these steps taken together, and implemented over a number of years, could create a much healthier and robust environment for emerging-market economies at the beginning of the next decade. As recently stressed by Roubini and Setser (2004) quoting Truman (2002), however, the international bonds of sovereign governments are only one component, and often not even the major component, of a country's public debt. Short-term bank loans and domestic debt are often larger than international bonded debt.

In the near-term future, it is almost certain that some emerging-market countries will suffer from serious financial crisis. For such countries, old-style stand-by arrangements with strong conditionality and substantial IMF resources, supplemented in some cases with debt restructuring and debt reduction, remain unavoidable, despite the high economic, social, and political costs involved. The hope should be that decisive implementation of a Stability and Growth Facility type approach, outlined above, incorporating a small part of interest cost reduction, could gradually reduce the number of countries that remain vulnerable to financial crisis and could eliminate the frequency of crisis management–oriented stand-bys. The early functioning of a Sovereign Debt Restructuring Mechanism would hasten the process by allowing middle-income countries with very large debt burdens and close to a crisis situation to reduce their debt and gain access to a sustainable growth path. After a certain amount of debt reduction, they could thereby qualify for the Stability and Growth Facility, instead of having to go through much more disorderly work-outs involving huge resource and welfare losses that end up being partly borne by the world economy as a whole because of contagion effects and a degree of disruption in growth and trade that could be avoided if a more orderly process was possible.

It may be of interest to contrast the proposals made here with those of former IMF research director Kenneth Rogoff in a recent article in *The Economist* at the onset of the Bretton Woods sisters' 60th anniversary.[24] Rogoff essentially argues, very much along the lines of Meltzer, that private capital markets are today sufficiently developed to make lending by the Bretton Woods sisters redundant. Development *grants* by the World Bank are okay—but neither institution should make *commercial* loans. It is quite true that if all that the sisters do in their lending is exactly what commercial banks do or what can be obtained in the bond market, there is no need for them. But neither "crisis lending" nor the type of lending through a Stability and Growth Facility proposed here can be provided by private lenders. And such lending is needed—it can improve welfare both in the countries concerned and in the world as a whole—provided of course that it is carried out appropriately and with the right kind of political support. Moreover, the all-or-nothing approach to concessionality prevalent in much of the official discussions is strange. Countries with incomes below a rather arbitrary cutoff point get outright grants or highly concessional loans. If average income had been a few hundred dollars higher, there would have been no grant element at all, even though the country may contain large numbers of very poor people. Would it not be more logical to graduate concessionality and introduce some blending for the lower-middle-income, emerging-market economies, which must also contribute to meeting the Millennium Development Goals?

24. See Kenneth Rogoff, "The Sisters at 60," *The Economist*, July 24, 2004. Incidentally, I do fully agree with parts of Rogoff's analysis: "If Brazil had been given only an additional $15 billion in August 2002 instead of $30 billion, I believe its program would have collapsed. What good is it to throw a man ten feet of rope if he is drowning in 20 feet of water?" True. But why suggest that there should be no rope at all? Would it have been better to let Brazil drown? And having kept it afloat, would it not be smart to actually try to cure the chronic illness and forestall future crisis with a Stability and Growth Facility?

To summarize, it would make sense to group IMF facilities under two broad headings: (i) resources designed to help emerging-market economies that are not in crisis and pursue reasonable policies, but that are vulnerable because of a high debt burden accumulated in the past, grow out of the debt trap that constrains their development and worsens their income distribution; and (ii) resources deployed in countries where there is a crisis and policymakers are willing to undertake tough adjustment measures. Some of the countries in the latter category are likely to need actual debt reduction complementing the IMF-backed program. (Both types of countries could continue to have access to the Compensatory Financing Facility to help cushion external shocks due to sharp terms of trade changes or natural disasters.) The Stability and Growth Facility would deal with the first category of countries and, in contrast with the contingent credit line, would not just be an insurance program against contagion, but a program to address the fundamental vulnerability of a whole category of emerging-market economies so well documented in the IMF's own 2003 *World Economic Outlook*. It would be a long-term program dealing with a long-term issue. Programs coming under the second heading and taking the form of stand-bys would address actual or near crisis situations that, unfortunately, will continue to arise in the coming years. I do not believe that it is desirable to make a distinction within the second category between large countries, which could trigger systemic risk, and smaller countries, which cannot have systemic impact.[25] It is very difficult to define and measure systemic risk. Moreover, it is not always clear whether those who have proposed such a distinction have in mind purely financial risk or also wider geopolitical considerations. Finally, it does not appear equitable at all to allow extraordinary access to IMF resources for some countries in crisis and not for others. Such a distinction would undermine legitimacy. It would be better to have clear rules and policies applicable to all irrespective of size or purely political considerations. Risk arising from individual country situations would be addressed within a fair and transparent framework equal for all. The long-term systemic risk coming from the excessive indebtedness of a whole group of middle-income countries would be

25. The distinction between systemic risk countries and others has often been made, including by Larry Summers when he was still secretary of the treasury, during an important speech at the London Business School (December 1999) in the aftermath of the Asian and Russian crises. Systemic risk has never been defined, however. The implicit assumption seems to have been that the G-7 (or the United States all by itself!) will define it case by case.

addressed by the Stability and Growth Facility. It is worth stressing one more time that the high indebtedness of this group of countries constitutes a serious obstacle not only to macroeconomic stability and growth, but also to any attempt at improving very unequal distributions of income.

Alongside the management of its lending facilities, the IMF would continue to carry out its surveillance, monitoring, and data dissemination functions for all countries. It is true that the development of private markets and institutions worldwide, as well as the "learning" that has taken place, including in the private sectors of many emerging-market economies, has led to a situation where part of the surveillance and monitoring is now carried out by the markets and private institutions. This does not, however, obviate the need for IMF surveillance, which provides a comprehensive and longer-term global perspective and remains less prone to passing fads and moods that often affect private markets. In addition to pure surveillance, it may be worthwhile to encourage the IMF to develop financial insurance mechanisms that would be available to all members in good standing. Insurance works, however, only if preexisting debilitating conditions do not exist! It is likely, therefore, that an insurance-like system would only become generally workable once the "illness" of excessive indebtedness has been cured by a Stability and Growth Facility type approach and once mechanisms are in place that would greatly diminish the chances of the illness recurring.

6 | The Special Challenge of the Poorest Countries

The threat that terrorism and weapons of mass destruction pose to international security has received growing attention in recent years.

What has not been sufficiently emphasized is that poverty and exclusion also foster violence; and that peace is the outcome of greater development and social justice.

As I recently stated in Geneva, hunger in itself is a weapon of mass destruction. It kills 24,000 people a day and 11 children every minute.

The international community has certainly moved forward, and took on specific commitments, within clearly defined time frames, at Monterrey and Johannesburg.

Those commitments must now be put into practice. The Millennium Development Goals must be achieved—this opportunity to truly advance in fostering international development must not be lost.

PRESIDENT LUIZ INACIO "LULA" DA SILVA OF BRAZIL
Speech before the conference "Making Globalization Work for All"
February 16, 2004

The discussion in chapter 5 on financial markets and the debt trap referred to emerging-market countries integrated into global capital markets that have built up a significant burden of public debt to private creditors. The situation in the poorer countries of Africa and parts of Asia and Latin America is quite different. There is no absolute and clear dividing line between the middle-income countries—whose long-term problems could be addressed by equitable growth-oriented domestic policies and a combination of some form of Stability and Growth type medium-term financing facilities, and a more proactive approach to restructuring unsustainable debt—and the least-developed countries, which do not yet have significant access to capital markets and some of which cannot even repay the very concessional debt they have accumulated over the past decades. Nonetheless, a distinction has been made for a long time and continues to exist between the poorer countries that qualify for highly concessional debt and middle-income countries that largely borrow at commercial terms. While this distinction is somewhat arbitrary and there are clearly borderline cases, the situation of the poorest countries is very different, and much worse, than that of the emerging-market, middle-income economies.

Continued Exclusion and Growth Failures in the Poorest Countries

Over the last three decades a whole category of countries that are both poor and often small has been essentially excluded from global growth.[1] Most of these countries are in Africa, but some are in Latin America and the Caribbean and some are in Asia. There is still a lot of extreme poverty in the emerging-market economies discussed above, but these economies are now linked to the global growth process and have a chance of benefiting from it if they can overcome some of their key structural problems. China and India, the two largest low-income economies that were not much richer than most of Africa two decades ago, have also been able to grow rapidly for a long period and have now reached average income levels well above those of the least-developed countries.

While more than two billion people in China and India are improving their living standards, be it at unequal speeds within these giant countries, hundreds of millions of people in the poor countries of Africa, but also in parts of Latin America and Asia, remain trapped in extreme poverty. The Heavily Indebted Poor Countries (HIPC)/Poverty Reduction Strategy Papers (PRSP) initiative, even after various "enhancements," has not been able to break the vicious cycle of poverty, low savings rates, and considerable debt burden in these countries, despite genuine efforts. These efforts have also been unable to forestall tendencies towards violent domestic strife and "state failure" in a large number of the poorest countries.[2] More of the same is simply not going to be enough to help the one

1. From 1980 to 1990, the least-developed countries had real GDP per capita growth of −0.2 percent, developing countries, 1.9 percent, and developed countries, 2.5 percent. From 1990 to 1999, respective growth rates were 1.1, 3, and 1.6 percent.

2. A team of World Bank experts led by Paul Collier concluded in *Breaking the Conflict Trap: Civil War and Development Policy* (2003) that economic forces such as entrenched poverty and heavy dependence on natural resource exports are more often the primary cause of civil wars than ethnic tensions and ancient political feuds. Their report asks for three sets of actions to prevent civil wars: more and better-targeted aid for countries at risk, increased transparency of the revenue derived from natural resources, and better-timed post-conflict peacekeeping and aid.

billion or so people trapped in this vicious cycle and excluded from normal life on our planet.

The poorest countries are not integrated into global capital markets because of the small size of their financial systems, their lack of institutional development, and their still very weak infrastructure. They did accumulate a large burden of debt, but it is mostly to bilateral or public donors, including the Bretton Woods institutions themselves. In terms of GDP growth, the performance of the least-developed countries has been much worse than that of the emerging-market economies. It is true that their total population is only a fraction of the total developing country population because of the weight of giants such as India and China. Looking at poverty worldwide, the remarkable progress of India and China leads to optimistic assessments of the global fight against poverty. It must be remembered, however, that if we take India and China "out" of the numbers, progress in poverty reduction appears much less impressive. Indeed, if we look at the least-developed countries alone there has been almost no progress at all.[3]

Past Efforts

During the 2000 meeting of the United Nations General Assembly in New York, world leaders, spurred by concern over the situation in the poorest countries but also in an effort to target poverty reduction worldwide, solemnly adopted a set of global social objectives called the "Millennium Development Goals" (MDGs) that have provided a new political impetus to the global fight against poverty and underdevelopment.[4] Adoption of the MDGs was followed in early 2002 by the Monterrey Conference on Development, resulting in the Monterrey Consensus, largely based on the work of a Special Commission on Financing Development led by the former president of Mexico, Ernesto Zedillo, referring to an agreement of major donors to double the amount of concessional development assistance to support the achievement of the MDGs by 2015.[5]

3. See, for example, UNCTAD's *The Least-developed Countries Report 2002: Escaping the Poverty Trap;* a short overview of globalization from the IMF staff in 2000 entitled "Globalization: Threat or Opportunity?"; and the World Bank's *World Development Report 2000/2001: Attacking Poverty.*

4. There are MDGs ranging from eradicating extreme poverty and hunger to promoting gender equality and empowering women. The eight MDGs and related country-by-country indicators can be found at the UN MDGs website at www.un.org/millenniumgoals/.

5. The Zedillo Report is available at www.un.org/reports/financing/.

In fact, the situation of the very poor and heavily indebted countries had been perceived as so bad that the World Bank and the International Monetary Fund (IMF) launched the HIPC initiative in the late 1990s. The HIPC initiative was not the first debt relief effort targeting very poor countries, but without a doubt it is the most comprehensive one. Debt relief efforts can be traced back to 1977–79, when, in an UNCTAD meeting, official creditors wrote off $6 billion in debt to 45 poor countries by eliminating interest payments, rescheduling debt service, untying compensatory aid, and offering new grants to reimburse old debts (Easterly 2002, 1678–79). In 1987, the Special Program of Assistance for Africa provided bilateral debt relief, International Development Association (IDA) credits for World Bank debt service relief, and funding for commercial buybacks to 21 African IDA-only borrowers that had debt service-to-exports ratios above 30 percent. Debt relief efforts continued with initiatives such as the Paris Club Toronto Terms (1988), Brady Plan (1989), IDA Debt Reduction Facility (1989), Paris Club Houston Terms (1990), Paris Club London Terms (1991), and Paris Club Naples Terms (1995).[6] By the mid-1990s, however, it was quite clear that traditional debt relief measures through the Paris Club or the other existing schemes were inadequate to alleviate the unsustainable debt burden of very poor countries.

The first HIPC program was negotiated in 1996. The HIPC initiative, for the first time in the history of development assistance, emphasized comprehensive reduction of debt-stock—not as a goal in itself, but as a tool to remove the disincentive effects of "debt overhang" on private investment and to achieve "debt sustainability." It was also novel because for the first time a debt relief initiative included the reduction of debt owed to the multilaterals such as the World Bank, the IMF, and the regional development banks. In 1999, the HIPC initiative was enhanced in order to provide a permanent exit from debt rescheduling and to target freed-up funds for social spending. The enhanced HIPC initiative also aimed to give more weight to social and poverty-related reforms during performance assessments.

By the beginning of 2004, 42 countries were HIPC eligible: 34 in Africa, 4 in Latin America, 3 in Asia, and 1 in the Middle East. To qualify for debt relief under the HIPC initiative, a country must satisfy three

---

6. See Birdsall and Williamson (2002, 23, box 2.2). The Paris Club Lyon Terms (1996) and Paris Club Cologne Terms (1999), the two most recent Paris Club initiatives, are debt relief agreements that are designed within the HIPC framework.

criteria: it must be eligible for highly concessional IDA assistance from the World Bank[7] or from the IMF's Poverty Reduction and Growth Facility (formerly called the Enhanced Structural Adjustment Facility); its debt burden must be deemed unsustainable even after the country has exhausted all other debt relief options; and it must have established a track record of "good policies."

The HIPC is a two-staged initiative. The first stage is normally a three-year period during which the country works in coordination with the Bretton Woods institutions to establish a record of implementing economic reforms and poverty reduction policies. At the Bretton Woods annual meetings in 1999 it was agreed that nationally owned, participatory poverty reduction strategies should provide the basis for all World Bank and IMF concessional lending and for the HIPC initiative. The HIPC countries need to submit Poverty Reduction Strategy Papers to the Bretton Woods institutions that are prepared after consultation with civil society representatives and in which they describe their proposed economic and social policies and programs to reduce poverty. At the end of this initial stage is a decision point when it must be determined whether the country's debt level is sustainable. For those countries whose debt burden remains unsustainable, a debt relief package is prepared and committed to by creditors to be irrevocably implemented at the time of the completion point. While interim debt relief is provided by the Paris Club and multilaterals such as the World Bank between the decision and completion points, countries receive their full package of debt relief once they have implemented a set of key and predefined structural reforms. The country is entitled to debt relief of at least 90 percent from official bilateral creditors. In addition, multilateral creditors reduce the present value of their claims so as to achieve debt sustainability for the country in question.

The PRSP/HIPC initiative taken by the Bretton Woods institutions in the late 1990s, with prodding and encouragement from civil society, constituted an important and much needed effort to bring the poorest and most highly indebted countries into the world economy and to try to prevent their exclusion from the global growth process. Actual debt levels have been reduced very substantially.[8] While there has been progress in

7. The Gross National Income per capita threshold for IDA eligibility as of date is US$ 865.

8. The HIPC initiative will provide nominal debt service relief of about $41 billion ($25 billion in net present value terms). Taken together with other traditional debt relief mechanisms and additional voluntary bilateral debt forgiveness, 26 HIPC countries will see their

some countries, the overall situation has unfortunately not really changed in terms of sustainable development and strong inclusion in the world economy. The majority of the poorest countries, most of them in Africa, are still essentially excluded from global growth.[9] The assessment in the spring of 2004 was that the majority of HIPC/PRSP countries will not attain the Millennium Development Goals by 2015, or even a decade later, unless they have access to much more foreign resources to complement their domestic savings. If these foreign resources are provided as debt, however, even concessional debt "à la IDA," most of these countries will again not be able to service that debt, even though their old debts have been reduced.

The obstacles facing the poorest countries are deeper and more intractable than the problems in the emerging-market economies. The latter do have functioning social and governance structures, and while they suffer from widespread poverty, weaknesses in governance, and market failures, as well as the excessive debt burden described in chapter 5, many of the emerging-market economies are making progress and are participating in global growth. Many of the poorest countries are in a much worse position and face the danger of almost complete exclusion from the world economy. Some positive energy was gathered thanks to the adoption of the Millennium Development Goals, the Monterrey Conference, and the PRSP initiative. When one looks at the results, however, it is very clear that as far as many of the poorest countries are concerned, progress has been minimal. Deep-seated structural and political problems persist, and if they are not addressed much more decisively, progress will be elusive.

State Failure

The really central problem is that too many of the countries in this category are either *failed states* or in *imminent danger of becoming failed*

debts fall on average, in net present value terms, by about two-thirds. Data for 26 HIPC countries that have reached "decision points" show substantial improvement. For example, from 1999 to 2003, debt service/exports decreased from 15 percent to 9 percent; debt service/fiscal revenue decreased from 21 percent to 13 percent; and social expenditure/debt service increased from 187 percent to 406 percent.

9. The average yearly GDP per capita (in constant prices) growth rate of 46 sub-Saharan African countries in 1996–2003 was 1.6 percent. However, when the two sub-Saharan countries with the highest growth rate during this period, Equatorial Guinea (22.5 percent) and Mozambique (6.4 percent), are excluded, the average rate drops to 0.5 percent. The GDP per capita data is taken from the World Economic Outlook database of the IMF.

states. "Failure" here refers to failure of a government to provide security, prevent internal conflict, and provide even the most basic public services to its population. Over the last decade we have witnessed such failure or situations close to failure in countries such as Afghanistan, Tajikistan, Myanmar, Angola, Burundi, Rwanda, the Democratic Republic of Congo, Haiti, Liberia, Sierra Leone, Somalia, and Sudan. Countries as diverse as Georgia, Sri Lanka, Côte d'Ivoire, and Chad have come dangerously close to becoming failed states, while others in the Balkans such as Serbia, Bosnia, Albania, and Macedonia are still recovering from war and/or internal turmoil. As expressed in the report of the Commission on Weak States and US National Security (2004):

> In dozens of developing countries, the term state is simply a misnomer. Governments are unable to do the things that their own citizens and the international community expect from them: offer protection from internal and external threats, deliver basic health services and education, and provide institutions that respond to the legitimate demands and needs of the population.

The failed states or those close to failure constitute a tremendous challenge for a better globalization. Even in a relatively advanced region such as the Balkans, countries experiencing state failure have been unable to overcome their problems without outside intervention. In many parts of Africa the situation is of course much worse than in the Balkans. State failure is also an imminent threat in parts of Central Asia, the Caucasus, Southeast Asia, and the Middle East. In some ways, globalization and the end of the Cold War seem to have exacerbated the problem of potential state failure. Globalization has brought with it the vivid contrast between local poverty and images of what exists elsewhere, leading to bigger gaps between expectations and reality and, in that sense, making government more difficult. Moreover, with the end of the Cold War, the superpowers stopped offering unconditional support to various dictatorships in exchange for their alignment in the great ideological struggle that was taking place. This, in itself, is of course a good thing. But the neglect that ensued often led to the disintegration of the shaky power structures that had survived only with outside support, leaving a power vacuum and political chaos.

Afghanistan is a telling example. In the post–World War II period, the superpowers competed for Afghanistan. For a long period, the West dominated, and pro-Western regimes backed by the United States and Pakistan as a local ally were able to rule Afghanistan. Then came a Soviet-backed communist coup that installed a pro-Soviet regime. The West and Pakistan reacted by arming anti-Soviet forces, including extreme fundamentalists. Once the Soviets withdrew, however, and ceased to be a danger as the Soviet Union itself collapsed, the big powers basically ignored Afghanistan, which descended into lawlessness and state failure. This allowed the fundamentalist Taliban regime to take over in alliance with those who ended up causing September 11. Situations that are not very different are numerous in Africa, as dictators propped up by the Soviets or the Western powers collapsed without workable political alternatives emerging.

This phenomenon of state failure spreading in the poorest parts of the world must be stopped for the sake of the people of those countries and for the sake of a safer and better world. State failure and fundamental weaknesses in governance are the root causes explaining why a whole group of poor countries not only shows no signs of even slow convergence to world income averages, but actually experiences declines in per capita income. What is required is a "big push" in terms of resource deployment to support investment in these countries. Such an effort can only succeed, however, if it is accompanied by drastic improvements in governance and the arrest of the phenomenon of state failure.

The "Big Push" to Fight Exclusion and State Failure

In a *Financial Times* commentary on the World Commission on the Social Dimension of Globalization report entitled "A Fair Globalization: Creating Opportunities for All," and sponsored by the International Labor Organization (ILO), Martin Wolf expressed more openly than most the frustration felt by many:

> The world's 20 poorest countries are just about as poor today as they were 40 years ago. That can be changed only if they start to function quite differently from before, which will take a great deal of outside help. But it will also require radical domestic transformation. If the sovereignty of such dysfunctional states is protected, their peoples will remain impoverished. If their people are to be helped, the sovereignty of their states must be challenged.[10]

10. Martin Wolf, *Financial Times* (London), March 3, 2004, 19.

Frustration led to bluntness in this paragraph, but honesty requires that one acknowledge the real problems. As hard as it is to achieve, the world urgently needs a *combination* of substantial foreign aid in the form of grants, perhaps at least twice the amount that is currently available, with a mechanism that ensures that these resources are actually put to good use.[11] There is really nothing that automatically leads to the inclusion in the world economy of countries that have been marginalized by history, geography, civil war, governance failures, and/or foreign power struggles on their soil. Globalization does not "work" for these countries. The linkages that exist between them and the growing parts of the world economy are insufficient. Some optimists seem to think that global growth will eventually "reach" these countries as it will reach the poorest parts of India and China. Unfortunately there is nothing inevitable about this. To make an extreme comparison: there is no reason for the growth of the world economy to benefit the moon! Where there are insufficient linkages, nothing happens. China and India can use the apparatus of the nation-state to "create" linkages between their own prosperous regions and their poor regions. Somalia or Sierra Leone can do very little on their own to create equivalent linkages between themselves and the dynamic parts of the world economy.

This exclusion poses a tremendous ethical challenge because there are hundreds of millions of human beings trapped in extreme poverty. Exclusion and state failure also pose a huge security challenge for the entire world, as has been demonstrated in the case of Afghanistan. The absence of significant economic linkages does not mean that terror networks cannot use failed states as bases—or that viruses carrying disease cannot reach the rest of the world.

What we need during the next 10 years that separates us from the target date set for the Millennium Development Goals is a really *big push* to help the people trapped in the poorest countries escape exclusion and join the world. These countries are in a vicious circle from which they cannot escape without substantial outside help. They are extremely poor, so it is

---

11. See the Zedillo Report (2001). Former Mexican president Ernesto Zedillo led the high-level panel that prepared the report in the context of the UN-sponsored International Conference on Financing for Development, which took place in Monterrey, Mexico, in 2002. There has been much analysis of the link between foreign aid and development. For a recent update with new evidence see Clemens, Radelet, and Bhavnani (2004), which also includes a list of the most important references.

very hard for them to save. Private economic activity needs to be supported by much better infrastructure—but low savings means low investment and therefore the inability to create that infrastructure. Investment rates vary in the 15 to 25 percent range. The upper end of this range does not constitute a low investment rate given world averages, but more is required given the immense needs of these very poor countries. Physical investment alone is not enough, of course. Overall productivity growth requires an increase in skills, but there are insufficient resources for education. Poor health aggravates the productivity problem and continued poverty prevents improvements in health. Many of these countries are too small to create regions or poles of growth from which development could spread over time, as happened, for example, in China and India. On top of all this and partly because of extreme poverty and lack of education, many of these countries have horrendous governance problems. Many of them have borders that were rather arbitrarily drawn by the ex-colonial powers. As a result, there is little feeling of national identity; tribal, ethnic, or religious loyalties dominate and when combined with extreme poverty, lead to civil war and even genocidal violence of the kind recently experienced in Eastern Africa.

An important dimension of the problem relates to conditionality—the rules and conditions under which the resources are transferred. For a "big push" backed by substantial resources to succeed, there will have to be *more* conditionality rather than less, including sufficiently high standards in the areas of domestic governance, education, health, government budget composition, and political institutions. Of course, these conditions attached to aid must support local reform efforts and must reflect local conditions and priorities. But history demonstrates quite clearly that there is no point pouring resources into countries where a small group in power is able to waste these resources or where there is not a minimum of effective institutions. But who will monitor the reform process and enforce the conditionality? For the comprehensive conditionality required to be at all acceptable, the governance of the Bretton Woods institutions and of the whole international process with regard to the poorer countries will have to be perceived as much more legitimate. The central thesis of this book is that a better globalization requires more legitimate global governance. This is true also in the context of the poorest countries. Poverty reduction as well as success with policy reforms and with aid effectiveness depends on improved global governance and greater legitimacy.

Global Resource Mobilization

The economic takeoff of these very poor countries will have to be designed in a global context with substantial grant aid resources so that sufficient investments in human and physical infrastructure can trigger a qualitative change in the growth process and unleash new hope and confidence. Linkages between the least-developed countries and the growing parts of the world economy will have to be encouraged and subsidized— both as regards human capital formation (training, education, temporary migration) and with respect to transport and communication. The existing *framework* created by the Heavily Indebted Poor Country/Poverty Reduction Strategy Papers initiative is appropriate as an *approach,* but it is insufficient in its *degree of ambition* and in the *amount of resources available* to make it work. As already argued in detail in the Zedillo Report, resources deployed worldwide in the fight against extreme poverty must be doubled, with most of these resources going to the poorest countries, if the MDGs are to be met.

A big push strategy to launch growth in the poorest countries will require substantial additional resources that must somehow be mobilized. The orders of magnitude involved here are much larger than the several billion dollars a year that would be required to finance the modest interest cost reduction for a group of highly indebted, emerging-market economies discussed in the preceding chapter. A resource mobilization target should be at least in the order of $30 billion a year in addition to existing programs. If this is added to, say, $5 billion a year for "blending" resources for middle-income countries, including the interest reduction cost of a Stability and Growth Facility (SGF), one arrives at a need to find an *additional* $35 billion a year for development aid.[12]

When discussing the alternative methods that could be used to raise these resources, one notices that most of the revenue sources proposed are tied to other, complementary objectives. The most "neutral" proposal is that of some form of income tax surcharge. Proposals such as a tax on armaments or a carbon tax are viewed as potentially useful not only for raising development funds, but also for discouraging global "bads," the

---

12. In 2002, the Zedillo Report provided the estimate that total development aid (including concessional aid to lower-middle-income countries) would need to double, rising by about $50 billion a year, for the Millennium Development Goals to be attained. A modest increase in existing official development assistance (ODA) programs has so far delivered perhaps $15 billion of the required $50 billion in the form of future commitments.

arms race, and global warming. The regular creation of special drawing rights (SDRs) would allow "a more balanced distribution of seignorage power," to use the words of Griffith-Jones and Ocampo (2004). "In a world characterized by the use of the national currencies of major industrial countries as international monies, the accumulation of international reserves generates, in fact, a redistribution of income from developing countries to the major industrial countries."[13] As noted before in the context of the discussion on emerging markets, assuming 3 percent growth in the world economy and a constant ratio of global reserves to world GDP implies that reserves could grow by about $75 billion a year. If the world economy were to grow by 4 percent, reserves could increase by $100 billion a year. It is true that reserve accumulation by many Asian countries has been extremely rapid, and one could argue that in a world of more flexible exchange rates reserves should grow by less than GDP. Be that as it may, a partial funding of additional development resources through special drawing rights creation, while large in the context of aid programs, would still remain small in terms of creation of world liquidity and would not present an inflationary danger, although if the *entire* additional aid resources would have to be funded by SDR creation the overall macroeconomic impact would no longer be insignificant. Regular SDR allocations could have an additional benefit of allowing an expansion of world reserves not tied to the accumulation of assets denominated in one or two particular currencies, a process which is likely to be tied to global macroeconomic imbalances.

Another approach to raising additional resources that can be deployed for development and for meeting the MDGs is global taxation. Until very recently, proposals for global taxation were considered outlandish. In recent years, however, some world leaders, including some from developed countries, have signaled their willingness to consider such an approach. Generally, the approach taken is one where a global "public bad," such as pollution, financial volatility, or arms sales, would be taxed to raise resources to finance global public goods or the fight against poverty. Note that the revenues derived from taxing global "public bads" need not be earmarked to specific public goods any more than national taxes on cigarettes need to be spent exclusively on lung cancer treatment for the approach to be valid. The most popular proposals are a global tax

---

13. Griffith-Jones and Ocampo (2004, 30). A country that can issue money that others will hold as reserves actually gets "something for nothing."

on carbon emissions, armament sales, and short-term financial transactions (the Tobin tax). A carbon tax would be a very attractive form of international taxation. The tax could be collected relatively easily on the sale of coal, petroleum products, and natural gas. A tax of one and a half cents per gallon of fuel, if collected everywhere, could fund the entire $35 billion of additional resources mentioned above (Reisen 2004). A tax on the sale of armaments would unlikely be a great revenue collector, unless the tax rate was quite high. This in turn could lead to serious incentive problems encouraging illicit arms trafficking, which is already very significant. On the other hand, if the tax could be levied on production rather than cross-border sales, a very low rate could yield significant revenues. The "Tobin tax" is the oldest of the global taxes proposed. Even a very small tax of, say, 0.01 percent would raise substantial resources (close to $20 billion) if diversion of transactions could be prevented by all major money trading centers participating and by the imposition of sanctions on those who do not. It would also be necessary to design the tax in such a way that it could not easily be circumvented by swaps and forward contracts.

Instead of raising revenues by taxing global "public bads," it has also been proposed that resources be collected by modest "global" surcharges to existing taxes such as corporate profit taxes imposed on corporations working globally and having a minimum size. If such an approach were feasible, a very low surcharge could clearly produce the resources needed to raise the additional $35 billion required.

Finally, the government of the United Kingdom has recently proposed the creation of an International Financial Facility (IFF) that would be funded through long-term pledges by donors committing themselves to an annual flow of payments to the IFF. These commitments would be binding and provide the security based upon which investors would lend to the IFF, creating the upfront resources to the MDGs ahead of actual official development assistance (ODA) flows that will become available only over time.

Starting from development-focused special drawing rights allocations, each of these proposals would not by itself solve the resource mobilization problem. It may be difficult to rely on a steady demand for SDR-denominated reserves if the amounts are large. Global taxes may only be feasible or even desirable if the tax rates are very small. The legal systems of some countries do not allow the precommitment of resources required by the IFF, and in countries where such commitments are possible, the amounts would have to be limited for the commitments to be credible and politically feasible. That is why it would be best to consider a *package* of these proposals together: some regular issuance of SDRs to be allocated to development ($10 billion to $15 billion annually), some very small global taxes (raising another $10 billion to $15 billion), complemented by the IFF frontloading some of the ODA that will become available over time. The UN Economic and Social Security Council proposed in chapter 4 would be the ideal institutional vehicle to design this package and promote it in the national legislatures and the UN system.

Reform of the Management of the Poorest Countries Programs

Within the overall framework of the United Nations Economic and Social Security Council (UNESC) and the new arrangements proposed in chapter 4, it would also be desirable to revisit the management of the programs designed to support the poorest countries in the international system. At the Bretton Woods institutions, the efforts directed at the poorest countries are currently managed largely as part of these institutions' general operations. Both the Poverty Reduction and Growth Facility (PRGF) at the IMF and the International Development Association (IDA) operations at the World Bank are integral parts of the work of these institutions, although the financial resources raised for these programs have separate governance structures.[14]

14. Whereas the World Bank raises most of its funds on the world's financial markets, the IDA is funded largely by contributions from the governments of the richer member countries. Additional funds come from repayments of earlier IDA credits and from the World Bank's net income. Donors get together every three years to replenish IDA funds. The United States, Japan, Germany, France, the United Kingdom, Italy, and Canada were the major donors to the most recent IDA replenishment. But some middle-income countries that are currently eligible to borrow from the World Bank—namely Argentina, Brazil, the Czech Republic, Hungary, Korea, Mexico, Poland, Russia, the Slovak Republic, South Africa, Turkey, and Venezuela—are also IDA donors. Other contributors to the most recent IDA replenishment were Australia, Austria, Barbados, the Bahamas, Belgium, Denmark, Finland, Greece, Iceland, Ireland, Israel, Kuwait, Luxembourg, the Netherlands, New Zealand, Norway, Portugal, Saudi Arabia, Singapore, Spain, Sweden, and Switzerland. Donor representatives, also called IDA deputies, agreed to commit SDR 18 billion (about $23 billion) to poor IDA members over the next three years, beginning in 2002. For the first time in the IDA's history, these discussions have been opened up to IDA borrowers, whose representatives participated in all meetings. The IMF administers concessional lending under the Poverty Reduction and Growth Facility through the PRGF and PRGF/HIPC trusts. The PRGF trust borrows resources from central banks, governments, and official

This integration of the work on and the management of poorest country programs with the rest of the programs at the Bretton Woods institutions has advantages as well as disadvantages. The most important advantage is that the poorest countries get better access to global knowledge and experience, because management and staff dealing with them have more global experience and responsibilities than would be the case if there was institutional separation between the poorest countries and the rest of the world. There are also disadvantages, however. Particularly at the IMF, the financial "size" of middle-income and emerging-market programs is huge compared to the resources going to the poorest countries. In the case of country programs in Argentina, Brazil, Turkey, or Korea, tens of billions of dollars were at stake compared to the hundreds of millions of dollars at stake in poorest country programs, a ratio of one to one hundred! Moreover, the large emerging-market economies have immediate systemic significance for the world financial system, which the poorest countries lack. It should not come as a surprise, therefore, that it is the emerging markets and the immediate systemic problems that attract the lion's share of top management attention at the IMF. And yet the human significance and the *long-term broader socioeconomic systemic importance* of what happens in the poorest countries are as important as what happens in the middle-income economies.

Finally, as discussed above, sustainable development for the poorest countries requires the availability of resources in greater amounts than in the past and in a form very close to grants, accompanied by very tough conditionality relating to domestic governance and the quality of public expenditures. For such resources to be made available and for such conditionality to be acceptable, a special focus on the poorest countries and special governance and management arrangements may be needed.

The following ideas might contribute to more focused management of poorest country programs and more acceptable governance and conditionality, while preserving the global nature of the Bretton Woods institutions and avoiding building additional walls between the poorest countries and the rest of the world when we are in fact trying to integrate

---

institutions, generally at market-related interest rates, and lends them to PRGF-eligible countries. The difference between the market-related interest rate paid to PRGF trust lenders and the rate of interest of 0.5 percent per year paid by the borrowing members is financed by contributions from bilateral donors and the IMF's own resources (primarily by the investment income on the net proceeds from off-market gold sales in 1999 that were deposited in the IMF's PRGF/HIPC trust).

them more fully into the world economy. The IMF should *retain* its role in these countries with the Poverty Reduction and Growth Facility and normal consultation and surveillance activities, but one of the IMF's three deputy managing directors should be appointed at the same time as the managing director by the UNESC and should have special coordinating responsibility for poorest country programs.[15] Once appointed, she or he would be, of course, fully part of the integrated management structure of the IMF, although the way the various departments are organized may need amendments to strengthen the focus on poorest countries. A similar arrangement is not necessary for the top management at the World Bank, because the nature of the Bank's business and the share of the IDA in total lending more naturally assure top-level senior management attention to the poorest countries. Both institutions, however, should introduce and enforce much more rigorous rotation and promotion procedures requiring and rewarding successful staff for their work on poorest countries programs.[16] This has been talked about for decades but has never been comprehensively implemented.

Another very important feature of reformed arrangements in relation to the poorest countries should be the use of *peer review* and *peer participation*, something already proposed by some poor country governments as well as by the United Kingdom. A significant number of young to mid-career staff recruited directly in the least-developed countries from government agencies and the private sector could be brought to the World Bank and the IMF on a strictly temporary basis (for example, three years not renewable in any way before a five-year period) and deployed both at headquarters and in field offices (excluding their own countries) as part of country teams working on poor country programs. For this to be significant and have a real impact both on the nature of the programs and their perception in the poorest countries, the numbers of such staff would have to be substantial and reach *at least* 20 percent of all staff working on these countries. During their assignment, a special period should be reserved for an intensive study and training program open also to other longer-term young staff members, ending with the awarding of diplomas

---

15. An oversight function for poor country programs was created at the IMF in 1999, but not at the top management level.

16. At the World Bank, for example, the technically more specialized staff who work in the global "networks" such as education, health, finance, etc. should be deployed across the globe in such a way as to work on the least-developed countries a specified percentage of their time over a given period, say at least 30 percent in a five-year period for everyone.

to successful participants. A special budget allocation would be needed and fully justified to fund such a reform, which would have the double benefit of skill formation for young people from these countries, while adding to the effectiveness of Bretton Woods–supported programs.

Finally, the UNESC could create a special PRGF/IDA policy board made up of 20 to 25 senior members, with one-fourth being currently active policymakers in poorest countries, one-fourth eminent personalities from these countries, including representatives from the private sector, one-fourth policymakers from middle- and higher-income countries, and one-fourth coming from international nongovernmental organizations and academia. This board would have the job of preparing an annual review of conditionality and policy advice contained in PRGF/IDA programs, which would include evaluation of the recent past as well as recommendations for the future. This should be ongoing, not a once-and-for-all exercise. These recommendations would not be binding, as they should not interfere with the normal functioning of Bretton Woods management and board decisions, but they would clearly carry a great deal of moral weight and would certainly have an influence on how policy advice and conditionality are designed and implemented. Special prizes could be awarded by this policy board for successful projects and policy programs with real financial rewards and incentives for participants.[17]

Implemented jointly, these proposals or other arrangements close in spirit to those cited above could go a long way toward strengthening the legitimacy of Bretton Woods–supported programs and make more acceptable the unavoidable conditionality that will have to accompany the "big push" needed to free these countries from the debt and poverty trap that currently tends to exclude them from global growth. A judicious balance must be struck between respect for sovereignty of any member country, as well as respect for cultural differences, and the pressing need to enforce decent governance and protect populations from predatory and sometimes criminal behavior of local power holders, sometimes allied with outside financial interests. The effort of the international community toward the least-developed countries must not be sporadic, but systematic and sustained. It is not sufficient to send a few thousand troops to Haiti every five years or so—Haiti must be helped to become a self-sustaining and viable country. This will at times require that for

17. Such prizes are currently awarded inside the World Bank to particularly successful activities. Awards by an outside policy board would complement these internal awards and could become high profile events.

certain periods the international community or regional organizations on behalf of the international community become a *custodian of sovereignty* in some of these failed states. This should not be viewed as some form of neocolonialism but as a reflection of the belief that African or Asian human beings need and deserve protection as much as people in Kosovo or in Bosnia. It is better to be honest about this and recognize reality rather than try to avoid it. Such a process can only work, however, within the framework of the United Nations providing strong legitimacy, and in a setting where citizens of the least-developed countries as a group play an important role themselves. This role should be clear and visible at all levels—inside the UNESC, on the PRGF/IDA policy board, in the management of the Bretton Woods institutions, and among the staff working on the poorest countries.

7 International Trade and the WTO: Old Debates and New Passions

Brazil wins ruling on EU sugar subsidies.

The World Trade Organization increased the pressure on the European Union to make sweeping reforms of its costly sugar regime yesterday by finding that subsidies paid under the policy violated global trade rules.

The preliminary ruling—in a case brought by Brazil, Thailand, and Australia—is expected to strengthen the hand of agricultural exporting countries that want wealthy nations to agree to deep cuts in their farm support spending as part of the Doha global trade round.

The decision by a WTO disputes panel follows a WTO ruling in June in favor of a complaint from Brazil that $12.5 billion of subsidies paid by the United States to its cotton farmers were illegal. Washington plans to appeal.

Financial Times, August 5, 2004

Ernesto Zedillo, former president of Mexico and today a global leader in the debate about growth, development, trade, and economic governance, was giving a lecture in one of the top Turkish universities in front of about 300 students and faculty members in March 2004. The audience, full of idealistic young women and men with the "Porto Alegre spirit," was very interested in hearing about globalization, trade, and the dilemmas facing the world from someone who had led one of the major emerging-market countries.[1] It was close to the time of the Mumbai, India, meeting of the "alterglobalization" movement. President Zedillo surprised and destabilized the audience with the following question:

> How is it that Jose Bove, the French activist who leads a campaign in France with the aim of protecting French agriculture, is celebrated as a hero by the alterglobalizers? Is it not true that agricultural

[1]. Turkey and Mexico are similar in many ways. In both countries, democracy emerged from a revolutionary one-party system. Both countries have strong economic ties to prosperous advanced economies in the North. Both countries have experienced dynamic growth, but both have gone through more than the average number of financial crises.

protectionism and subsidies paid to their farmers by the rich countries undermine poor peasant producers in the developing countries and contribute in a significant way to continuing poverty? By closing their markets and subsidizing their producers in just the way Jose Bove wants to perpetuate, the rich countries make it impossible for millions of poor farmers in Asia, Africa, and Latin America to produce more and sell more of their products. How can the alter-globalizers claim to care about the poor in this world and have their interests at heart, and, at the same time, applaud Jose Bove?

This example struck a particularly responsive chord in Turkey, as the impact of American cotton subsidies on otherwise quite competitive Turkish cotton farmers had been much in the news. Why indeed would young people interested in development and intent on fighting world poverty be on the side of an agricultural protectionist from a rich country? And on whose side is the World Trade Organization? The quote from the *Financial Times* at the beginning of the chapter refers to two rulings against the United States and the European Union. Is the world changing more rapidly than we think?

Passions about Trade

The Jose Bove example illustrates the complex nature of the passions unleashed in the debate about trade and the WTO. These passions, of course, are not just about trade, but also about the many dimensions of globalization, and they go well beyond international trade itself. Jose Bove's attack of a McDonalds outlet in France reflected not only agricultural protectionism, but was also perceived as a protest against the American superpower, an expression of cultural nationalism and rejection of global standardization, and as the "small guy" standing up to the huge multinational corporations. The debate about trade and the WTO, even more than the debate about global finance and the Bretton Woods institutions, is a debate about globalization itself with all the economic, political, and cultural dimensions.

On one side of this debate are the arguments of the economics profession, which, to a large extent, stress the potential benefits of more and freer trade. There are, of course, exceptions to the beneficial role of trade recognized by professional economists, and this chapter will provide a review of the purely economic aspects of the debate. But, by and large, economists support more and freer trade—even those, such as Paul Krugman, who have developed approaches that go beyond the basic comparative advantage models with competitive markets and diminishing or constant returns to scale, and who stress that, under certain conditions, managed trade could be superior to free trade.[2] Professional economists tend to believe that, both for comparative advantage reasons and for reasons linked to the exploitation of economies of scale and the benefits coming from enhanced competition, trade is most likely to have overall beneficial effects in the medium and long run, although there may be transition costs and distributional effects that should be taken into account when designing optimal policies. Looking at the empirical evidence, it is not easy to substantiate strongly a simple link leading from open trade policies to more rapid growth. It does seem clear, however, that countries that have been good *export performers*—particularly countries that have been able to conquer important shares in the world market for *industrial* products—have also been the better overall performers in terms of long-run growth and living standards.[3]

On the other side of the debate is a wide and diverse coalition that uses not only economic but also many noneconomic arguments to contest the benefits of international trade and criticize the WTO.[4] There is a wide spectrum of opinion represented in this coalition, with positions ranging from those wanting to reform the WTO-centered system to those wanting

2. See, for example, Krugman (1986); Krugman and Smith (1994); Brander (1995); and Krugman (1999).

3. The link between trade, openness, and economic growth has received ample attention from economists. Edwards (1993) provides a comprehensive survey of the literature on openness and growth through the late 1980s. Dollar (1992), Sachs and Warner (1995), Ben-David (1993), Edwards (1998), Frankel and Romer (1999) are among the most cited papers of the literature in the 1990s, all of which find a positive relationship between trade openness and economic growth. Rodríguez and Rodrik (2000), however, provide a critical analysis of these papers and cast doubt on the empirical evidence, although their criticism concerns methodologies of these researchers rather than an argument in favor of trade protection. The more recent paper by Dollar and Kraay (2001) again presented arguments relating protrade policies to growth, but Birdsall and Hammoudi (2002) show convincingly that if one controls for primary commodity dependence, the Dollar and Kraay conclusions no longer hold. Cline (2004) provides a comprehensive survey of all the empirical work and concludes that the weight of the evidence suggests a substantial link going from trade openness to more rapid growth, although a link between open trade *policies* and growth is harder to substantiate.

4. The WTO is criticized as the symbol of the protrade and globalization-is-good-for-you worldview, although, as discussed later in this chapter, it has very little institutional power itself, certainly much less than the Bretton Woods institutions.

to abolish the WTO and drastically reduce international trade. The quote below is taken from *A Better World Is Possible,* a report by the International Forum on Globalization, which is not a marginal group but a nongovernmental organization referred to as one of the more significant civil society critics by prominent mainstream and free trade advocate economists such as Jagdish Bhagwati. This example shows how far some of the critics want to go:

> The goal of societies should not be to find cheaper prices for products but to find the means to ensure that all the needs of all people are met and that a satisfactory and stable life is perpetuated within a system that does not collapse from being part of the volatile global market. If people grow their own food, produce their own necessities and control the conditions of their lives, the issue of price becomes irrelevant (International Forum on Globalization 2002, 20).

Passions run high on both sides of the trade debate. Those who see international trade as the key engine of world growth do not disguise their antagonism towards the "protectionists" who back narrow special interests against the common good, or their contempt for those who, while perhaps well intentioned, fail to understand that trade is a vehicle to spread knowledge, improve productivity, exploit both comparative advantage and economies of scale and thereby reduce poverty. Some sentences from Bhagwati's *In Defense of Globalization* give a good flavor of the strong feelings among the free traders:

> As for the charges of hypocrisy, double standards, and unfair trade that are passionately leveled today at these (IMF, World Bank, WTO) international institutions and also at the rich nations—in particular that they maintain protection for themselves while they force others into free trade. . . . these beliefs and allegations are often little more than rubbish (Bhagwati 2004, 6).

And a few paragraphs further in the same book, Bhagwati criticizes Oxfam, one of the largest, most serious, and active development-oriented nongovernmental organizations, with very strong language:

> Causing harm to the poor cannot have been the intention of Oxfam, yet the road to hell is paved with good intentions. Oxfam knows a little, but not enough about trade policy, I am afraid, and I have been moved to remark, not just in this instance, that mission creep,

even by noncreeps, is often not a good idea. Their overreach sub-
tracts from the great good that they have done when they concentrate on what they do best (Bhagwati 2004, 6).

As an official international institution, the World Bank is more measured in its style. Nonetheless, reading *Global Economic Prospects 2002:
Making Trade Work for the World's Poor,* for instance, one still feels the
passion with which the authors believe that trade is one of humanity's
great instruments in the fight against poverty. Simultaneously, the World
Bank team working on the Global Economic Prospects series is well
aware of the various theoretical and practical qualifications relevant in
this context and of the need for complementary policies and efforts that
should be implemented for protrade policies to yield the desired results.[5]

Passions also run high in the opposing camp, where there is a broad
coalition made up of disparate groups that can mobilize important segments of public opinion against more and freer trade in both the rich and
poor countries. In this coalition one finds, of course, the old-fashioned
and well-known protectionists representing their various sectoral interests: American steel producers, European dairy farmers, the Indian car
industry, or Turkish sugar manufacturers simply want measures to protect their sector from more efficient foreign producers. Protectionism as
such does not have much ideological appeal, although many are under-
standably concerned about the transition costs associated with sudden
and rapid liberalization. There are deeper fears and less self-serving
forces, however, that explain the appeal of the antitrade component of the
alterglobalization movement beyond sectoral interests.

Trade is part of the process of increasing international integration that
makes the world a more cosmopolitan place by leading to a dazzling
increase in the diversity of products consumed and encouraging shifts in
tastes and habits, while allowing successful producers or brands to
exploit large economies of scale, make huge profits, and threaten old
habits or entrenched positions. An extreme and telling example of what
an opening to trade can do not only to individual sectors, but also to

5. Since 2001 the World Bank's Global Economic Prospects studies, published once a year
ahead of the annual meetings, have formed a series that provides one of the best presenta-
tions of international trade issues as they have been discussed in key trade meetings and
grounded in empirical analysis of global trends. The fundamental message is one that
strongly believes in the benefits of more and freer international trade. See World Bank (2002,
2004). For another recent eloquent defense of more and freer trade, see Cline (2004).

whole economies and lifestyles, is the fate of the ex-Soviet style economies in the 1990s. Countries that *appeared* to be upper-middle-income countries in terms of their per capita income suddenly became much lower-income countries, as the capital stock they had accumulated in their industries became practically worthless. My point here is not to argue about whether or not this collapse was inevitable in the long run (it was), but to show how opening to trade forces standards and transformations on societies that can be very threatening in the short run, although they may bring great benefits over time. Another example of such dramatic transformation is found in the impact modern shopping malls have on small scale shops and the whole lifestyle associated with traditional retailing, including personal contacts, informal credit, and neighborhood solidarity. Multinationals such as Carrefour, Wal-Mart, and Ahold, as well as smaller global chains such as Macro, Metro, and Casino, have been at the forefront of such transformations.[6] Globalization often triggers a sense of upheaval of identity, linked to rapidly changing production and distribution structures, which leads to insecurity and fear about the future. The truth is that when one carefully considers these factors, trade is only one rather small component of a multifaceted process that is creating this new type of insecurity. What is perceived as threatening is not *just* the economic insecurity linked to the loss of protected income or employment, but also the loss triggered by a change in lifestyle. It is difficult in this context to disentangle the purely economic factors, such as the fear of unemployment, from these identity and "sense of belonging" related insecurities. The latter exist and magnify the impact of the former, particularly when large segments of a population are affected in a short period of time. Moreover, in the rich countries, trade, outsourcing, and immigration often get linked in the minds of those affected and give rise to an overall "conservative" reaction against *cosmopolitan globalization*, despite the fact that trade is in fact an economic substitute for immigration! Given its shrinking labor force, a result of its demographic structure, Germany, for example, will either have to "outsource" an increasing part of it production or encourage immigration. As unreasonable as it may

6. Peter Timmer and others are doing work on the impact of the rise of supermarkets in developing countries on local food supply chains. They argue that small local suppliers and distributors may be squeezed out of the market because they cannot meet (or verify) that their produce meets the required standards and quality of the supermarkets, and that it is necessary to redesign development policy to enable small local suppliers to meet these challenges. See, for example, Reardon et al. (2003).

seem to pragmatic economists or to cosmopolitan elites, the trade debate is not unrelated to the cultural insecurities and even to the religious confrontations that, unfortunately, we are witnessing at the beginning of this new century. The famous Arab-French novelist Amin Maalouf has written an important, somewhat autobiographical book on the cultural-religious tensions that the world faces at the turn of the century. In part 2 of this book, which has the theme "when modernity comes from elsewhere," he writes:

> For the Chinese, the Africans, the Japanese, the Indians, the American-Indians and also for the Greeks and the Russians as well as for the Iranians, the Arabs, the Jews or the Turks, modernization has always implied a certain "giving-up" of part of oneself. Even if at times modernization generated enthusiasm, the process never took place without a certain feeling of bitterness, including some humiliation and self-denial. It never took place without a profound crisis of identity (Maalouf 1998).

A second dimension of antitrade sentiment is linked to negative feelings about the power and functioning of large multinational corporations. These corporations are perceived as "organizing" an increasing part of economic and social life worldwide by influencing or even determining decisions thanks to their lobbying at the level of national governments or international institutions. It is feared that the multinationals are encouraging an "international race to the bottom" in environmental standards and social policies. Their capital and know-how, and the cosmopolitan skilled labor they employ, are believed to allow them to move production to wherever environmental and social standards are lowest, forcing governments to compete for investment by lowering these standards and thus contributing to environmental degradation, lower taxes, and diminished social benefits. Critics of the current international economic system perceive as both important and deeply objectionable the following aspects of what they call "corporate globalization:"

- Erosion of the tax base of the welfare states that were developed after much social and political struggle in the 20th century. First, corporations can use the complex system of transfer pricing to shift their profits to whatever jurisdiction has the lowest corporate income taxes. This can be done without actually moving the location of production. Second, corporations can actually move their production facilities to the lowest tax host countries. In an attempt to attract footloose capital, countries will compete with each other in lowering taxes and thereby erode the basis for a social welfare state that can redistribute income and provide generous social services. A free and open trading system facilitates this type of behavior by multinational corporations.

- A similar race to the bottom with regard to environmental standards. Production facilities can be installed wherever environmental standards are lowest, potentially leading countries to compete with each other by lowering their environmental standards in a fashion very similar to the presumed race toward lower tax rates.
- The same race to the bottom with regard to labor standards. Production facilities can be moved to wherever the right to strike is the most circumscribed, wherever it is easiest to fire workers, wherever hours are longest, and wherever unit labor costs are lowest. They could even be moved to locations where child labor can be exploited.
- By freeing production from the necessity of being located close to consumption, international trade allows capital and highly skilled labor to move to wherever the most advantageous conditions exist. In today's world, capital and highly skilled labor is mobile, facing few effective barriers at borders, whereas unskilled labor is immobile. This mobility of capital and skilled labor is seen to change the very nature of the political process and of the conditions determining the bargaining strengths of social actors. If the representatives of unskilled labor become politically too powerful in a particular country, or if they bargain too aggressively, the mobile factors can just leave instead of having to face their opponents and agree to a compromise within a given geographical location. This is believed to undermine the very core of democracy.

Taken together, all of these *possible* consequences of the liberal globalization process facilitated by free trade *could* indeed amount to a massive downside; unless there are compensating measures, they could overshadow the benefits the world can obtain by taking advantage of comparative advantage and economies of scale through more and freer international trade. The key set of questions that arises in this context is *how important* these negative aspects have been and are likely to be in practice and to what extent public policy can counteract them while still allowing the world to realize the benefits from trade. The answer is that, so far at least, there is not much evidence that a strong race to the bottom is actually taking place.[7] On the tax front, for example, there is no evidence that total taxes are declining in economies of member countries of the Organization for Economic Cooperation and Development (OECD), although there are some shifts away from direct income and profit taxation with possible consequences on income distribution. Taxes on footloose capital have declined in many countries, often compensated for by taxation of purchases of goods and services. On the environment, there is even less evidence of a race to the bottom actually taking place. It is not hard to understand, however, that these potential negative aspects are perceived as dangers and that fear of these dangers has the potential to trigger a passionate rejection of the whole trade-driven globalization process.[8] The fact that there has not been so far a race to the bottom does not prove that it cannot take place in the future.

Finally, there is a third dimension in the broad alterglobalization or antiglobalization movement related to, but distinct from, the cultural fears and opposition to corporate domination referred to above. Particularly among intellectuals (writers, artists, academics), there has long been a "revolt" against *possessive individualism* as a philosophy of life that seems to come with and be imposed by the global marketplace. According to this critique, human beings are being pushed to become single-minded profit maximizers, pursuing *economic* objectives at the expense of *all* other objectives in life. The more the world integrates economically, the more difficult it becomes for countries, communities, or individuals to balance purely economic objectives against other pursuits in life. Consider the difficult trade-off between leisure and work, where leisure can stand for time spent with family and friends, time spent on artistic and aesthetic pursuits, or time spent pursuing culinary and other pleasures. Is it sustainable in today's world economy for a community to decide as a collective choice to restrict work time in favor of more leisure, as in the case of France's experiment with the 35-hour week? Can individuals and

7. See Wolf (2004) for an accessible and well-presented review of the evidence. On issues related to investment rules, foreign direct investment, and multinationals, see also Graham (2000).

8. Note that these fears are not at all confined to less well-educated electorates in poor or middle-income countries—witness the emphasis on the dangers of outsourcing in the 2004 US electoral campaign or recent warnings by the West European leaders against the low corporate taxes their new East European partners are planning to offer.

communities opt for less work and less consumption to make space for more leisure and greater happiness derived in nonmaterial ways without the risk of increasingly losing ground to individuals and communities that opt for more material production and more competition? In a world where dynamic effects are very important and where one has to innovate and constantly "learn by doing" in order to remain competitive, can those who want to move a little less rapidly and "smell the roses" survive? Is it still possible to make marginal choices in these fundamental matters, or does the international economic "system" now have such "winner takes all" characteristics that it imposes a lifestyle? Additionally, solidarity and a sense of community are desirable features of life in themselves, and there may be a trade-off between achieving solidarity, on the one hand, and competition in the market place, on the other.

These thoughts express real questions and real fears. Such dilemmas may not mean much to those who struggle to simply survive; for the poorest there is no doubt that access to food, shelter, basic health care, and basic education overshadows all other aspirations. It would be a mistake, however, to think that it is only the very rich who need more than material goods and services. One can sometimes sense a certain amount of elitist contempt for the poor, mostly unconscious, in a way of thinking that argues that leisure and quality of life are irrelevant for the vast majority of humanity. To sum up, there is fear that a global culture with excessive focus on economic competition and material consumption would bring with it tremendous dangers of alienation and despair. This fear has been expressed forcefully by authors such as Pierre Bourdieu, whose views have a substantial following.[9]

It is good to keep all of these broader dimensions of the debate in mind when evaluating the current difficulties faced by the WTO framework and the attempts to move toward further trade liberalization. Nowhere else are the arguments about institutions, policies, special interests, and broader philosophical viewpoints so intertwined. Nowhere does one find stranger bedfellows, as illustrated in the quote from Zedillo above. And yet, good trade policies and improved institutions have real potential to advance the welfare of many and reduce global poverty very significantly.

9. See Pierre Bourdieu's many publications. Bourdieu argues that US-led corporate capitalism is trying to impose a specific narrow set of values on the entire world that are not the outcome of some kind of natural universal evolution but the product of one geographically and historically limited social structure.

Institutional Framework

From GATT to WTO

The World Trade Organization was established in 1995 as the successor to the General Agreement on Tariffs and Trade (GATT). As discussed in chapter 2, GATT was created in 1947, a product of the Bretton Woods Conference but quite different in structure from the International Monetary Fund and the World Bank. GATT was essentially a "facilitator" for rounds of intergovernmental conferences and negotiations rather than a large international organization wielding some degree of bureaucratic power. Indeed, the original idea for the third pillar of the international economic and financial architecture was much more ambitious in scope than GATT, as John Maynard Keynes had envisioned what would have been called the International Trade Organization (ITO) with a mandate to stabilize primary commodity prices and address a very wide range of trade issues.

Most participants at the Bretton Woods Conference were convinced that a third pillar dealing with trade was necessary, and initially they strongly supported the ITO proposal. However, disagreement between the United States and the United Kingdom, with the latter supported by European and developing countries, over fundamental aspects of the proposed trade policy paradigm made concrete agreement difficult. Most notably, the UK insisted on "escape clauses" that would enable temporary protection when a domestic economy was in trouble and wanted to maintain imperial preferences in its colonies.

This disagreement regarding the limits to free trade was not a surprise given the structural difference between the European and US economies in the postwar period. In Europe, governments played much more active and substantial roles in domestic economies, largely because European nations had to be reconstructed after a war that took place in Europe and because, philosophically and politically, Europe was much more strongly influenced by socialist thought than the United States.

By 1946, 23 of the 50 countries that were negotiating the creation of the ITO had nevertheless decided to reduce and bind customs tariffs. This first round of negotiations resulted in 45,000 tariff concessions, affecting almost one-fifth of the world's total trade. The 23 countries, which are known as GATT's founding members, meanwhile agreed to accept some of the trade rules of the draft ITO charter in order to protect the value of the tariff concessions they had negotiated. The end result was a combined package of trade rules and tariff concessions called the General Agreement on Tariffs and Trade. It entered into force in January 1948, while the ITO charter was still being negotiated. The ITO charter was presented and finally accepted at the UN Conference on Trade and Employment in Havana, Cuba, the same year.[10] Unlike GATT, however, the ITO charter aimed beyond tariff reductions: it included rules on employment, commodity agreements, restrictive business practices, international investment, and services.

The charter needed ratification, however, and that proved impossible to achieve in the United States. US president Harry Truman did not even try to seek congressional approval for the ITO charter. There was growing skepticism in the US Congress concerning the UN and international institutions, and also strong opposition to the ITO charter. Without the ratification of the treaty by a sufficient number of national legislatures, it was impossible for the ITO to become an international organization. Even if countries signed the ITO charter, without the United States on board it would amount to an exercise in futility. Because of the premature death of the ITO, GATT remained the only agreement governing international trade until 1995.

The pillars of GATT were nondiscrimination, tariff bindings, and elimination of quantitative restrictions. Nondiscrimination rested on two basic principles: most favored nation rule (MFN), by which member nations would generally agree to accord no special trade status to any one member that was not accorded to all; and the national treatment rule, which required that foreign products be treated no less favorably than competing domestic products (for example, agreement not to impose higher domestic sale taxes on foreign products than on competing domestically produced ones). Tariff bindings simply mean that a member, after agreeing to tariff concessions, cannot raise the tariffs above bound levels. Finally, to ensure that nontariff measures do not impair the value of tariff concessions once tariffs had been bound, GATT prohibited quantitative restrictions on exports and imports. Agricultural products were an exception, with qualitative restrictions and subsidies still allowed in many cases. Tariffs on agricultural products were in many cases not bound until the Uruguay Round. The Multi Fiber Arrangement (MFA) also made an exception to this rule by allowing textile and apparel quotas in the form of "voluntary" export restrictions.

10. Information in this section is based on World Trade Organization (2003).

Trade Rounds Held under the Auspices of GATT

GATT was a provisional legal agreement, not an international organization with permanent arrangements, although a small secretariat was established in Geneva.[11] As the initial agreement was limited in scope, eight rounds of multilateral negotiations have been carried out since to increase GATT coverage. The first five rounds of multilateral trade negotiations held under GATT auspices dealt with tariff reductions only. These rounds were the Geneva Round (1947) with the participation of 23 countries, the Annecy Round (1949) with 13 countries, the Torquay Round (1951) with 38 countries, the Geneva Round (1956) with 26 countries, and the Dillon Round (1960–61) with 26 countries.

For the first time in GATT's history, the Kennedy Round (1964–67), with the participation of 62 countries, went beyond tariff reductions and included a GATT antidumping agreement and addressed several other trade-related issues. One hundred and two countries participated in the seventh multilateral trade negotiations held under GATT, the Tokyo Round (1973–79). Tariff reduction negotiations led to an average one-third cut in customs duties in the world's nine major industrial markets, bringing the average tariff on industrial products down to 4.7 percent. The tariff reductions, phased in over a period of eight years, were designed to ensure proportionally larger cuts on higher tariffs. The Tokyo Round covered a wide range of issues, from agriculture and subsidies to safeguards (emergency measures to limit imports temporarily in order to protect domestic markets), and from technical barriers to trade to public procurement. Yet success with dealing with these issues was limited, and the resulting agreements were not accepted by the whole GATT membership. These agreements and rules were accepted only by some members (mostly industrialized countries) and for that reason were referred to as "codes." The result was a "plurilateral" system instead of a comprehensive multilateral one.

Thus, GATT was initially limited to negotiating tariff reductions, but as tariff levels were reduced drastically and as international trade evolved into a much more complex system, the expectations for further rounds and for the secretariat as a *de facto* world trade organization grew. However, having bound tariffs at low levels, governments responded

11. For a comprehensive background on GATT and the WTO, see World Trade Organization (2003), upon which this section is based.

to the series of economic recessions in the 1970s and early 1980s, which resulted in a period of stagflation during which a slowdown in growth was accompanied by rising prices, by devising other forms of protection for sectors facing increased foreign competition. With the 1973 OPEC (Organization of Petroleum Exporting Countries) oil embargo, the price of oil increased almost 10 times, hundreds of thousands of workers were laid off, factory closures became everyday business, and unemployment rates jumped to disturbingly high levels across Western Europe and the United States. Governments in Western Europe and North America tried to soften the hardship by negotiating market-sharing arrangements with competitors (for example, in the automotive sector) and provided farm subsidies to maintain their global market share in agriculture. These neoprotectionist trends undermined GATT's credibility and effectiveness.

In addition, the expansion of trade in services and international investment posed new challenges. GATT's institutional structure and its dispute settlement system were also causing concern. The efforts to deal with all these issues resulted in the Uruguay Round and finally the creation of the WTO.

The Uruguay Round was a long and difficult process. GATT members took four years to reach agreement on launching a new round of negotiations after a failed ministerial meeting due to conflicts on agriculture in Geneva in 1982. By the time the round was launched in 1986 in Punta del Este, Uruguay, the negotiating agenda covered almost every outstanding trade policy issue. This included the most contentious areas of international trade such as trade in services, intellectual property, and reform of trade practices in the most sensitive sectors, namely agriculture and textiles and apparel, in which industrialized countries refused to open their domestic markets to imports from developing nations. Member countries also decided that in this round all of the original GATT articles would be put on the table for review. The Uruguay Round was the single largest negotiation ever undertaken, and not surprisingly it took four years to draft it and an additional four years to get all members to sign a final agreement.

The GATT ministers met again in Montreal, Canada, in 1988 to clarify the agenda for the remaining two years. Although no comprehensive agreement was in the end reached on the agenda, they agreed on some concessions on market access for tropical products, aimed at assisting developing countries, a streamlined dispute settlement system, and the

Trade Policy Review Mechanism, which provided for the first comprehensive, systematic, and regular reviews of the national trade policies and practices of GATT members. The Uruguay Round was to be concluded in 1990 with a final ministerial meeting in Brussels, but sharp disagreements on agricultural trade reform led to the extension of the talks.

Despite the hopeless environment, GATT director-general Arthur Dunkel compiled a first draft of a final legal agreement, the "Final Act," and it was put on the table in Geneva in 1991. The text fulfilled every part of the Punta del Este mandate except that it did not contain the participating countries' lists of commitments for cutting import duties and opening their services markets. The draft became the basis for the final agreement.

Over the next two years new areas of conflict emerged besides agriculture, including disputes over services, market access, antidumping rules, and the proposed creation of a new institution, the WTO. A large part of the problem was solved in 1992, when the United States and the EU settled most of their differences on agriculture in a deal known informally as the "Blair House accord." By July 1993, the Quad countries (the United States, the EU, Japan, and Canada) announced significant progress in negotiations on tariffs and related subjects such as market access. It took until December 15, 1993, for every issue to be finally resolved and for negotiations on market access for goods and services to be concluded. On April 15, 1994, the deal was signed by ministers from most of the 123 participating governments at a grand meeting in Marrakesh, Morocco. The Uruguay Round agreements contained timetables for new negotiations on a number of topics, and the Marrakesh agreement included commitments, now incorporated into the Doha Development Agenda, to reopen negotiations on agriculture and services at the turn of the century.

The major institutional result of the Uruguay Round was the creation of the WTO, which replaced the GATT secretariat as an international organization. The General Agreement, though updated as a result of the Uruguay Round negotiations, still exists as the WTO's umbrella treaty for trade in goods.

Organization of the WTO

The WTO secretariat is located in Geneva and has a staff of around 550, headed by a director-general who has to be appointed by consensus of all the WTO members.[12] In 2003, the annual WTO budget amounted to 155 million Swiss francs ($116 million), with individual contributions calculated on the basis of shares in the total trade conducted by WTO members. This was less than just the travel budget of the IMF. Part of the WTO budget also goes to the International Trade Centre (ITC), which is the technical cooperation agency of the WTO, and the United Nations Conference on Trade and Development (UNCTAD) for operational, business-oriented aspects of trade development.

As of April 2004, the WTO had 147 members. Most WTO decisions require the *consensus* of all its members, either at ministerial conferences held at least once every two years or by members' delegates who regularly meet in Geneva. Thus the WTO significantly differs from the Bretton Woods institutions, where decision making is delegated to a board that represents countries or groupings of countries through a weighted voting scheme. Moreover, the rules are enforced by *the members themselves* through the use of trade sanctions. If reaching a consensus is not possible on certain issues, the WTO agreement allows for voting based on a one country, one vote principle. There are four cases for which the WTO agreement allows for voting. First, a majority of three-quarters of WTO members can vote to adopt an interpretation of any of the multilateral trade agreements. Second, a majority of three-quarters of members may decide to waive an obligation imposed on a particular member by a multilateral agreement during the ministerial conference. Third, decisions to amend provisions of the multilateral agreements can be adopted through approval either by all members or by a two-thirds majority depending on the nature of the provision concerned. However, such amendments only take effect for those WTO members that accept them. And lastly, according to the WTO agreement, a decision to admit a new member is taken by at least a two-thirds majority in the ministerial conference. While the WTO agreement states these exceptions to the consensus requirement, in practice the pursuit of consensus dominates WTO decision making.

12. It took months to solve a deadlock over who would become the next head of the WTO in 1999. Two candidates were the former New Zealand premier, Mike Moore, who was supported by the United States and most of the EU, and the deputy prime minister of Thailand, Supachai Panitchpakdi, who was supported by the Asian bloc and the UK. Overall, the support of the WTO member countries was almost equally divided between both candidates. After months of negotiations, member governments came up with an unprecedented time-sharing arrangement and decided to divide a regular term into two, allowing Moore to serve for the first three years and Panitchpakdi the last three years of the presidency.

The ministerial conference, which has to meet at least once every two years, is a venue for all decisions on any matter under any of the multilateral trade agreements. Day-to-day work in between the ministerial conferences is managed and performed by the general council, the dispute settlement body, and the trade policy review body, which all include all members of the WTO. The general council acts on behalf of the ministerial conference on all WTO affairs, and also meets as the dispute settlement body and the trade policy review body to oversee procedures for settling disputes between members and to analyze members' trade policies. Three subcouncils report to the general council, each handling a different broad area of trade: goods, services, and trade-related aspects of intellectual property rights (TRIPS). Each of these councils also has its own subsidiary bodies: for example, under the goods subcouncil, there are individual committees dealing with agriculture, market access, antidumping measures, etc.

In addition to the formal meetings, informal meetings are held that still include the full membership, such as those of the heads of delegations. Most of the difficult issues, however, are negotiated in smaller groups. A common practice is for the director-general or the chairperson of a negotiating group to hold consultations with delegations individually, with a few delegations, or in groups of 20–30 of the most interested delegations in order to achieve a compromise. This is what has come to be known as the "green room" process, a phrase taken from the informal name of the director-general's conference room. For a long time, most developing countries were practically excluded from the process; during Tokyo Round years, for example, participants in this process usually numbered less than eight parties. At present, up to 25 to 30 delegations may meet in the green room, with the countries that participate generally including the Quad countries, Australia, New Zealand, Switzerland, Norway, possibly one or two transition economies, and some developing countries.[13] As participation and the number of issues covered in the green room process have grown over time, so have criticisms of this procedure. Several nongovernmental organizations and some delegations in the WTO argue that the green room process excludes most developing countries from decision making and results in deals that are struck behind their backs.[14]

13. Schott and Watal (2000, 285)
14. Perhaps the most official expression of frustration with this process was the open letter (November 6, 1999) to WTO chairman of Ambassador Ali Mchumo of Tanzania from

Like the informal "green room" decision-making process, the WTO's formal decision making by consensus rule has also received much criticism. Jeffrey J. Schott, for example, a prominent expert on trade policy, argues that "the WTO will likely suffer from slow and cumbersome policy-making and management—an organization with more than 120 member countries cannot be run by a 'committee of the whole.' Mass management simply does not lend itself to operational efficiency or serious policy discussion. Both the IMF and the World Bank have an executive board to direct the executive officers of the organization, with permanent participation by the major industrial countries and weighted voting. The WTO will require a comparable structure to operate efficiently. . . . [But] the political orientation of smaller . . . members remains strongly opposed."[15]

As mentioned above, the decision to admit a new member to the WTO is made either by a two-thirds majority in the ministerial conference or the general council in between conferences. The WTO allows, in principle, any state or customs territory having full control over its trade policies to join the WTO, but accession negotiations can be quite complex and difficult. The applicant submits detailed documentation of its trade and economic policies that have a bearing on WTO agreements in a memorandum. The memorandum is evaluated by a working party formed to work on this specific accession case (working parties are open to all WTO members, so any member can volunteer to be in), and the working party reviews the applicant's trade regime in detail. The next step is parallel bilateral talks between the applicant and individual countries on tariff rates, specific market access commitments, and other policies with regard to trade in goods and services. The new member's commitments have to apply equally to all WTO members under normal nondiscrimination rules, even though they are negotiated bilaterally. Once the working party has completed its examination of the applicant's trade regime, and the parallel bilateral market access negotiations are complete, the working party finalizes the terms of accession. These appear in a report, a draft membership treaty, "protocol of accession," and lists, "schedules," of the

11 developing countries (Bolivia, Honduras, Cuba, Mauritius, the Dominican Republic, El Salvador, Guatemala, Uganda, Paraguay, Panama, Djibouti) stating their concern over the lack of transparency, i.e., the "green room" process in the WTO in the context of the preparations for Seattle.

15. Schott quoted in World Trade Organization (2003, 101). To read more about his proposal to remedy the WTO decision-making process, see Schott and Watal (2000).

172 A Better Globalization

applicant's commitments. The final package, consisting of the report, protocol, and lists of commitments, is presented to the WTO General Council or the ministerial conference. If a two-thirds majority of WTO members vote in favor, the applicant is free to sign the protocol and to accede to the organization. In many cases, the country's own parliament or legislature has to ratify the agreement before membership is complete.

The WTO Rounds

The first WTO ministerial conference (or round, as conferences are sometimes called) held in Singapore in December 1996 launched exploratory work on four new areas: investment, competition, transparency in government procurement, and trade facilitation. These are now simply referred as "Singapore issues." The second conference in Geneva in May 1998 took place at a particularly significant time, during commemoration of the 50th anniversary of the establishment of the multilateral trading system.

The third conference in Seattle in December 1999 was a watershed event for any number of wrong reasons. Approximately 50,000 protesters crammed into downtown Seattle, shutting down WTO sessions as overwhelmed police fired tear gas and rubber bullets. Some 600 people were arrested and there was $3 million in property damage. While the street protests certainly did not help produce an atmosphere conducive to productive negotiations, the Seattle conference was a failure mainly due to a growing rift between the industrialized and developing countries, and because of strong differences within the Quad nations. The United States, the European Union, Japan, and Canada were unable to reach agreement on such substantial issues as agriculture, antidumping, investment and competition policy, trade and the environment, and labor issues. Despite 36 straight hours of negotiations by trade ministers, they were unable to set the agenda for a new round of global trade talks.

Labor issues in particular became a contentious area of disagreement in Seattle between the developed and developing nations.

"The scenes at Seattle . . . gave a sharper edge and clarity than ever before to the poor countries' growing concerns," writes Bhagwati (2004). "After all, at the close of the Uruguay Round, they had already been bamboozled into accepting intellectual property protection into the WTO even though it was clearly not a trade issue and it was equally obvious that it was a dagger aimed at the poor countries. Now, labor issues, framed deliberately so as to aim at them, were sought to be imposed on the WTO: a bone thrown to the unions in the rich countries but down the gullets of the poor countries."

The fourth ministerial conference in Doha, Qatar, in November 2001 was the starting point for what came to be called the Doha Round of new trade negotiations. The Doha talks tried to make many issues of specific concern to developing countries central to future trade negotiations. These issues included access of agricultural goods to developed world markets, access for poor countries to pharmaceuticals at affordable prices, and possible financing to help poor nations cover the cost of implementing trade policies. These aims were only expressed in general terms, however, leaving much work to be done at subsequent meetings.

The fifth conference in Cancún, Mexico, in September 2003 started with the aim of reviewing the state of the Doha Round, although in the period between Doha and Cancún there had been little reason for optimism regarding progress with the new negotiations. None of the self-imposed deadlines had been met, and developing countries were more vocal and discontent than ever about the concessions that the developed nations had offered. The EU-US compromise agreement reached just before Cancún exacerbated the dissatisfaction of the developing nations. A last-minute agreement prior to the conference allowing poor countries without manufacturing capacity to import cheap medicines briefly raised hopes for a compromise, but it was not enough.

The failure in Cancún was different from that in Seattle because it was due not to confusion and chaos, but rather to a new and more unified front among major developing countries that denied consensus to the European Union and the United States. Cancún also illustrated the inherent difficulties of decision making by consensus when negotiation involves close to 150 participants.

Finally, in July 2004, WTO members reached agreement (the "Geneva compromise") that marked progress in the trade negotiations under the heading of a development-oriented Doha Round. However, both the aims of the round and the institutional framework in which it is to take place remain controversial. It is only after the new US administration and the new EU Commission are in place that it will be possible to move forward. Overcoming the difficulties and finding common ground are among the major challenges to better global governance facing the international community.

The sections that follow review the economic arguments and counter-arguments of protagonists on both sides of the trade debate—arguments that underlie not only the acrimony in recent WTO negotiations, but also the passionate and distinctly different positions on trade and globalization issues.

Economics and the Trade Debate

Theoretical and Empirical Considerations and National Policy Choices

The economics profession in general strongly supports free trade. The classical Ricardian comparative advantage model and the neoclassical Heckscher-Ohlin factor–endowments model laid the foundation for the basic proposition that trade allows a country to augment the utility of the amount of goods it can consume: countries import goods that they can produce with relatively more difficulty in exchange for exporting goods that they can produce more easily. To take an extreme example, if there are two countries, one of which is only able to produce cheese and the other only bread, they would both clearly be better off if they traded with one other and enabled the citizens of both countries to enjoy both bread and cheese. Even if the first country were able to produce some bread, though with difficulty, in addition to easily producing cheese, and the second country could produce some cheese, with difficulty, alongside its easily produced bread, both countries would still be better off importing the more difficultly produced commodity in exchange for exporting the more easily produced one. Moreover, if these two countries constituted the entire world, allowing free trade between them would lead to the best possible global allocation of resources in terms of maximizing the benefits derived by consumers from world production.

Both of these propositions are quite robust in the sense of holding true given a wide range of circumstances, although the "free trade is best" proposition is not as obviously true as the "some trade is good" proposition.

Theoretical complications arise quickly when one asks, for example, whether a country can influence to its own advantage the relative world prices of cheese and bread, i.e., the rate at which cheese is exchanged for bread, with taxes and subsidies. The simple answer is yes, if the country is a big supplier in the world market. But countries must also worry about the reaction of other countries to their attempts to favorably influence prices: if every nation tried to influence prices to its own advantage the end result for all countries might be much worse than if prices were not manipulated at all. Moreover, most (though not all) countries worldwide are too small to influence global prices.

Questions of income distribution also arise even in the simplest models of distribution effects. It can easily be understood, for example, that if labor is used intensively in the production of cheese in the country that produces cheese with difficulty (perhaps because it has very little labor), allowing importation of cheese from the country that easily produces cheese may reduce the income of labor in the first country because labor will become less valuable in the production process, although the same labor may gain by being able to consume a better combination of bread and cheese. If the first effect outweighs the second, labor in the first country will be worse off.

On the other hand, the owners of land used intensively in the production of bread, the commodity which can be exported and for which there is greater overall demand, will be better off on both counts: their land becomes more valuable in production and they benefit from a more balanced (and more desirable) consumption bundle thanks to international trade. Furthermore, using reasonable assumptions about technology and tastes, it can be shown that the landowners could compensate labor and still accrue a net gain. Thus it is possible for the country in question to gain in the broadest overall sense from opening to trade. Of course, this theoretical ability of landowners to compensate labor means nothing to those who could lose from trade unless the compensation actually occurs. This point is important and quite basic to welfare economics. It is perfectly rational for a group of people who will lose because of a particular policy to oppose that policy, even though the country as a whole may benefit. Using US steel producers as an example, if losses are so concentrated that this group cares very strongly about the issue, while the gains are distributed over a wide number of consumers and other steel-using industries, democratic politics may allow a small minority to block a policy that would ultimately benefit a larger number of people.

Other theoretical considerations have been discussed by economists who analyze the possible benefits and costs of trade, such as arguments having to do with risk. More open trade tends to transfer risk from consumers to producers. As an economy opens to trade and increases specialization in production, producers become more vulnerable to changes in world market conditions. Consumers, on the other hand, face reduced risk because increased imports can compensate for domestic production shortfalls. As in other aspects of life, there is a cost of insurance against risk. World market conditions may be such, for example, that it would be best for a coffee-producing country to simply produce coffee and not much else. But if for some reason there were to be a dramatic fall in the price of coffee, the country in question would suffer greatly. If it had insured itself by protecting the production of some other items instead of importing everything but coffee, it would be less affected by the coffee collapse. Insurance can take other forms, of course, which may be preferable, such as nations accumulating large reserves while times are good. However, the basic worry about overspecialization due to trade remains, particularly for small economies.

Another set of arguments relates to macroeconomics and unemployment. If for macroeconomic reasons a country does not have the full employment assumed in most trade models, the removal of protectionist policies may lead to greater unemployment rather than to the beneficial reallocation of employment foreseen in trade models, and therefore to welfare losses rather than gains. In other words, in the short run, protection can play the role of a Keynesian effective demand policy that channels demand to domestic producers. It is not a first-best effective demand policy because it has negative side effects, not least indirectly hurting exports by making the imports needed as factors of production for exports more expensive. An exchange rate devaluation would usually have better effective demand stimulating effects. Essentially, then, trade liberalization can in the short run lead to an increase in unemployment.

Economists get quite passionate about the basic proposition that trade is beneficial because the basic economic theorems are quite robust and because antitrade propaganda is so often driven by narrow and purely protectionist interests. Take cotton subsidies in the United States, for example. When a University of California economist documented the harm they did to producers in developing countries, as well as to American taxpayers, the protectionist lobby went so far as to accuse him of treason and argued that if this professor had been in the army he would have been court-martialed (Edward Alden, "Cotton Report Frays the Tempers of US Farmers," *Financial Times*, May 21, 2004, 8).

While it is the blatantly misleading propaganda of the protectionist lobbies that triggers emotional protrade reactions by economists, there also are intellectually valid and honest arguments for some policy interventions that may sometimes restrict trade. Though this book is not a comprehensive survey of the economic literature on trade, it may be useful to briefly review some key points that should be kept in mind when discussing the problems faced by progressive international governance in the context of trade. [16] The first point to consider is that what happens over time is much more important than what happens in a short period, or, to use more technical economic language, dynamic effects matter more for the welfare of the people concerned than comparative static effects. The famous "welfare triangles" of basic comparative static welfare economics are invariably quite small, except where protection is high initially. These welfare triangles refer to the real income that can be gained thanks to a reallocation of existing factors of production and adjustments in consumption following the removal of policy distortions resulting from trade protection, holding constant technology and the physical productivity of labor and capital. For example, if a country has a comparative advantage in agriculture but a high protective tariff for industry, removal of that tariff will shift resources into agriculture and allow higher real income thanks to the "better" allocation of resources. Through the use of computable general equilibrium models, this underlying analysis has been extended to multisector models that are closer to reality than simple agriculture-industry models, and the results can be quantified. [17] Such static welfare analysis, given plausible values for some key variables—like the degree of substitutability of various factors in production and of goods and services in consumption and the initial degree of protection—invariably comes up with results showing gains of around 1 to 2 percentage points of GDP. As levels of protection have declined over the last three decades, the static gains from moving to free trade have, naturally, also declined, and current estimates are closer to gains of 1 percent of GDP rather than the 2 percent that could have been attained starting from the much more distorted environment of the 1960s and 1970s.

Such static effects, however, are only part of the story in a world where markets do not extend perfectly into the future. If factors of production can only move between sectors gradually, and if some sectors are inherently more conducive to various forms of technical progress than others, it may be advantageous to attract factors into such sectors

16. See Corden (1985, 1992, 1997), Cline (1994, chapter 3), and Stiglitz (2003) for analyses and surveys on international trade that are accessible to the nontechnical reader.

17. For a comprehensive discussion of computable general equilibrium models, see Derviş, de Melo, and Robinson (1982) and also Brown, Deardorff, and Stern (2001). For a recent general equilibrium analysis of trade liberalization and its impact on global welfare, see World Bank (2002), Organization for Economic Cooperation and Development (2003), and Cline (2004).

by policy interventions, even if such interventions distort optimal resource allocation at a given point in time. If technical progress depends on what the economic literature refers to as "learning by doing," such dynamic effects gain an added dimension if labor acquires skills more rapidly by working in high-tech industries. It may make sense to attract labor (and capital to work with labor) into such sectors by policy interventions, even though, again, these interventions may have real economic costs at any point in time. Finally, a case exists for policy interventions if there are secular trends in the world economy leading to relative price declines for a category of products, such as primary commodities,[18] and if the absence of highly developed, long-term future markets prevents market-based decision making from taking these trends adequately into account in production and investment decisions.

This is the essence of the well-known "infant industry" argument for protection. The cumulative welfare benefits of dynamic effects can be large compared to the invariably modest static welfare effects referred to above, since the latter are "once and for all" effects, whereas dynamic effects can cumulate exponentially. Suppose, for example, that free trade were to lead to a resource allocation that increases GDP by 2 percent. Suppose, on the other hand, that if a particular trade policy intervention remained in effect it would lead to an increase in the average growth of the economy of 0.5 percent per year. After four years, GDP would be larger with "protection" than without, although it should be remembered that in each of the first four years of the period under consideration, citizens would have lost approximately 2 percent of income because of the distortion, and they would continue to miss that 2 percent as long as the distortion remained in place.[19] Nonetheless, as the additional half a percent accumulates exponentially, the dynamic effect ends up more than compensating for the static loss and, as times goes on, the dynamic effect completely dominates the static effect.

18. Primary commodity prices, excluding oil, have declined by 20 to 50 percent relative to the price of manufactures over the last three decades (World Bank 2001a). Some predict that this decline will reverse at least temporarily due to a massive increase in demand for many of these commodities, particularly from the rapidly growing Chinese economy. A similar terms-of-trade loss currently affects producers of low-skilled and labor-intensive manufactured goods.

19. The "once and for all" higher income obtained through free trade will also have a small dynamic effect, as more income leads to more saving and investment. If the marginal savings rate is 20 percent, 2 percent more income could lead to an increase in investment of 0.04 percent of GDP, which would have a small growth effect that must be subtracted from the infant industry effect to obtain the net growth benefit of infant industry protection.

Much needs to be added to this discussion. First, a direct subsidy to the infant industry, if financed by nondistorting taxes, could induce the same dynamic effects without the static costs caused by trade protection. Second, the state might pick losers rather than winners, and if it turns out that the wrong industry is protected, dynamic costs could result rather than benefits. This is a variant of the usual point: while markets do not efficiently extend into the future, there may be public choice failure that is as bad or even worse than market failure. Third, while there may be an initial period with dynamic technology and learning-by-doing benefits, this period could be short, and protection, once established, might be politically difficult to remove. Finally, the entire argument can be and has been turned on its head by those who argue that it is exposure to harsh competition, rather than subsidization or protection, that spurs technical progress, and thus that there is no trade-off between static and dynamic welfare analysis. In fact, increasing evidence shows that openness to trade stimulates total factor productivity growth. Few take the extreme view that the development of a new activity would not be assisted by initial help, but many argue that as soon as the infant becomes a child, protection actually harms development, whereas competition leads to more rapid learning.[20] In the end, theory alone cannot settle all of these questions. As Rodrik (2002a) maintains, "The answer (on the link between trade and growth) varies depending on whether the forces of comparative advantage push the economy's resources in the direction of activities that generate long-run growth (via externalities in research and development, expanding product variety, upgrading, product quality, and so on) or divert from such activities."

The extent to which trade brings these benefits and the type and degree of policy intervention that maximizes these benefits are empirical questions. It is quite clear from the evidence and stands to reason on *a priori* grounds that autarchy or near autarchy is bad for growth. However, Birdsall and Hammoudi (2002) have shown in their critique of the Dollar and Kraay (2001) paper on trade, growth, and poverty that some of the sweeping generalizations about the link between increasing openness

20. See Cline (2004) for an up-to-date review of recent evidence on the dynamic effects of trade openness and trade policy. The balance of evidence does not seem to favor the traditional infant industry argument when it is applied to subsectors within industry and services. Nonetheless, it is significant that a free trader such as Martin Wolf (2004, 206) concludes that "commodities seem to be a bad place for countries to be" and urges nations to encourage diversification. While the world may have entered a new cycle of higher commodity prices in 2003–04, Wolf's recommendation is likely to remain valid in the long run.

per se and growth are misleading. Dollar and Kraay's category of slow globalizers that failed to grow after 1980 "because they had policies leading to a decline in the trade-to-GDP ratio" essentially was a group of countries dependent on primary commodity exports that faced a steep decline in the terms of trade. The successful globalizers specialized in manufactures and were successful at exporting them. On balance, the evidence suggests that trade policies that have successfully sustained rapid export growth—climbing up the ladder of comparative advantage over time, reaching production of more sophisticated products, and avoiding terms-of-trade losses—have stimulated more investment and greater productivity growth, and in turn more rapid development.

This overall conclusion favorable to protrade policies should not lead one to forget the dimension of the debate that relates to income distribution effects. There may be net gains from trade liberalization for a country as a whole, but not only will there be some who gain much more than others, but some may actually lose while others gain. The Stolper-Samuelson (1941) theorem postulates that trade liberalization will increase the income of the abundant factor. Simply put, the theory suggests that trade liberalization will increase the real wages of unskilled labor in developing countries, where it is the abundant factor, but decrease the real wages of unskilled labor in industrialized countries.

Another important theorem, resulting from the Heckscher-Ohlin model, is factor-price equalization. The implication of this theorem is that, as the prices of goods equalize with free trade, and assuming the same technology is available everywhere, the wages of unskilled workers will converge to a common international level. Thus, in an otherwise static world an absolute decrease would occur in the wages of unskilled workers in industrialized countries. Numerous rigorous theoretical and empirical studies emphasize the restrictive conditions required for the strict validity of this theorem and therefore challenge its practical relevance, but economists agree that trade liberalization one way or another is likely to create some losers, not only because of the broad Stolper-Samuelson factor-price equalization effect, but also simply because capital and labor in formerly protected sectors and subsectors will lose their relative positions with liberalization and may have trouble relocating for a long time.[21]

21. Many factors apart from trade, of course, affect distribution of income, most notably the nature of technical change, but also demography, immigration, and education policies. See Cline (1997) for a review of the literature on trade and income distribution.

Theoretical and Empirical Considerations in a Multicountry Setting

The discussion above examined the advantages and disadvantages of alternative trade policies for a single country, but trade, of course, is a multicountry endeavor where the actions of one country often immediately affect other countries. Moreover, the policies adopted by one country may affect the policies adopted by others.

The first important multicountry issue relates to the potential ability of one nation's policies to affect world prices, i.e., the prices at which they import and export. A country may be a large enough importer of a particular commodity that importing less of it will lower the price of that commodity, leading to a welfare benefit for the importing country. Very large consumers such as the United States, the European Union, or China may be in such a position. Or, as happens more often, a country may be a large enough exporter of a commodity that exporting less will increase the world price and generate a welfare benefit for that country (Saudi Arabia and oil, Turkey and hazelnuts). More generally, while a single country often is too small to have much of an impact on world market conditions, the combined behavior of many small and medium-sized countries will affect world prices.

In its global setting, the trade debate analyzes the reactions of countries to each others' policies and the movement of prices (terms of trade) in response to these different policies, taking into account the effects of these various interactions. Such global general equilibrium analysis is useful for clarifying the issues at stake for the WTO-sponsored multilateral trade negotiations. Reliable quantification is not easy, of course, because it involves estimating degrees of substitutability between all kinds of inputs in the production process and between a multitude of commodities and services in consumption. Moreover, as is the case in a single country setting, the short- and medium-term effects of various policies will have different magnitudes.

Fortunately, there is now a large amount of literature on the quantitative effects of trade policy that uses various partial and general equilibrium models supplemented by econometric analysis of key relationships and substitution elasticities.[22] While there is still considerable uncertainty

22. This section draws on several sources. A study by Cline (2004) cosponsored by the Center for Global Development and the Institute for International Economics—and conducted just in time for the beginning of the new Doha Round—provides a comprehensive

about the empirical relationships, some agreement has emerged on the broad orders of magnitude.

To start, it is important to consider the base or initial conditions from which the Doha Round negotiations begin. Industrial country protection against imports of manufactures from other industrial as well as developing countries has been considerably reduced over the past few decades, with the exception of textiles and apparel and selective antidumping measures, mostly in the steel sector. While industrial countries apply only modest average tariffs to manufactures from developing countries (the poorest countries enjoy special privileges), those tariffs are still significantly higher than tariffs on imports from other industrial countries. Estimates are 3.84 percent and 2.25 percent, respectively, for bound tariffs in the United States. The difference is due overwhelmingly to the composition of imports, not to different tariffs applied to different countries, which is not possible under most favored nation practice. The situation is broadly similar in other OECD countries, although Europe and Japan started the Uruguay Round with much higher protection levels. Tariff protection in the European Union remains a little higher than in the United States, while in Japan it is slightly lower. It must be added that average nominal protection is not a reliable indicator of the real protection given to capital and labor in a particular sector of production. What is called effective protection also depends on the structure of tariffs on inputs and outputs. For example, a high input duty on cotton fabric combined with a low tariff on shirts would not really protect the shirt producers. On the contrary, a high duty on imported cotton shirts combined with a low duty on fabric could be highly protective.

Industrial country protection remains substantial in agriculture, services, and the textile and apparel sectors. For textiles and apparel, tariffs are in the 10 to 20 percent range and quotas remain in effect despite the fact that it was agreed at the Uruguay Round that these quotas would be phased out by 2005. The industrial countries have moved very slowly toward eliminating quotas, and there are now worries that they will violate the spirit of the Uruguay agreement by replacing quotas with contingent protection measures (such as safeguards against import surges and

---

survey of the various estimates and presents the results of the study's own general equilibrium analysis. The World Bank (2002) also provides up-to-date information on the quantitative work conducted over recent years. A report by Stiglitz, Charlton, and the Initiative for Policy Dialogue (2004) prepared for the Commonwealth Secretariat also contains quantitative estimates of the results of various trade policies.

antidumping duties) after 2005. In the United States and the European Union, as of one year prior to the supposed phaseout, the practical importance of quotas remains comparable (and additional) to that of existing tariff protection.

In agriculture, the combination of import tariffs and export and production subsidies amounts to substantial support for advanced country farmers. Tariff protection averages about 9 percent for the United States, 30 percent for the European Union and Canada, and an amazing 76 percent for Japan (Cline 2004, 118, table 3.7). In addition, industrial countries use a multitude of farm subsidies (export, input, and production subsidies, direct income support to farmers, and rural infrastructure subsidies) to protect agriculture. The WTO framework attempts to distinguish between subsidies that directly distort trade, such as export subsidies and direct support to production, and subsidies that do not directly affect amounts produced, such as support for agricultural research or payments delinked from production. The total support for agriculture in the advanced economies, including the effect of tariffs, is in the $300 billion to $350 billion range, although only part of that support is directly linked to trade and considered by the WTO to distort trade. The distinction between that which is trade distorting and that which is not is somewhat tenuous, however, because any support for activities that benefit agriculture ultimately leads to a cost advantage for some farmers, although it is true that the chain of causation is much more indirect for infrastructure support and crop research than for export subsidies or price support programs. The upshot is that directly production-oriented subsidies amount to a tariff equivalent of 10 percent for the United States and the European Union, 16 percent for Canada, and only 3 percent for Japan, which relies much more on very high tariff protection as mentioned above.[23] Finally, as is the case in industry, calculating effective protection to producers would have to take into account not just average subsidy and protection rates, but also the dispersion and structure of the agricultural tariffs and other support measures.

To date, services have not been significantly subject to trade liberalization negotiations, so much less empirical work on them is available. Preliminary discussions in the Uruguay Round distinguished between cross-border services (back-office and software services, call centers, etc.),

23. Tariff-equivalent estimates depend on the share of imports in total demand. Subsidies are higher in the European Union than in the United States, but the share of imports is also much higher, so the subsidies apply to a larger base, yielding lower tariff-equivalent figures.

consumption abroad (tourism, medical treatment received abroad), commercial presence (direct establishment of firms abroad), and temporary movement of workers (as opposed to long-term immigration). It is increasingly clear that liberalization of trade in services by the advanced countries, particularly if one includes even modest liberalization in temporary immigration, has the potential for welfare gains perhaps even two to three times larger than gains from liberalization of all the other sectors (Rodrik 2002b).

It should also be noted that their protectionist policies notwithstanding, advanced economies have provided special access to some of the poorest nations. In 2001, the European Union added the "Everything but Arms" initiative to the duty-free access regime that already applied to a large number of products, mainly from African countries. The United States supports the least-developed nations through its Caribbean Basin Initiative, Andean Trade Preference Act, and African Growth and Opportunity Act. Japan also has special access programs for very poor countries.

As beneficial as these programs may be, however, they do not account for a significant proportion of advanced country imports. Even if the programs were broadened to include essentially all imports from a group of 64 very poor countries, they would account for just 4 to 9 percent of wealthy country imports (Cline 2004, 100). Nonetheless, from the point of view of these poor countries, the trade preferences of advanced economies are significant. If there were an immediate move worldwide toward a global free trade regime under which these poorest nations would have to compete with all other countries on equal terms, the least-developed nations could suffer noticeable trade losses.

The extent of protection by developing countries is another dimension of the prevailing conditions at the start of the Doha Round negotiations. By the late 1990s, most developing countries had reduced their protection levels quite rapidly from the high and differentiated tariffs and widespread quantitative restrictions that prevailed through the mid-1980s. Nonetheless, outside of agriculture, developing country tariff protection remains higher than protection in advanced economies. Though average developing nation tariffs in 1997–98 on agriculture, textiles, and other manufactures were 30, 18 and 11.5 percent, respectively, production subsidies for agriculture were much lower than in advanced economies, and consequently the level of protection accorded to agriculture in poor countries is roughly equivalent to that in rich countries (Cline 2004, 100).

Starting from these initial post–Uruguay Round conditions, many authors have attempted to simulate the results of various Doha Round liberalization packages on total income worldwide and the distribution of income both within and across countries. A key distinction in the estimates is between the static (i.e., short-term) effects, holding the total amount of capital and total factor productivity constant, and the dynamic effects, where the total amount of capital and/or technology and productivity changes. Given the number of assumptions one has to make about the nature of key parameters and behavioral relationships—often without being able to base them on solid econometric evidence—the results of the various simulations should be evaluated with caution. Nonetheless, the simulations are useful in providing orders of magnitude and drawing attention to interaction effects that one might miss in more partial forms of analysis. Some of the key points that have emerged from this work are the following:

- The overall static effects of movement to complete liberalization of trade in agriculture and manufactures are no longer very large, with an order of magnitude slightly below 1 percent of world GDP. Developing countries gain a little more in relative terms, about 1.25 percent of their GDP compared to about 0.80 percent for the advanced economies.
- Close to half of these static effect gains can be attributed to liberalization in agriculture. Moreover, more than half of the developing countries' total short-term gains from liberalization would, in fact, be due to liberalization by advanced countries. What others do matters—welfare gains do not depend primarily on what the developing countries do by themselves. The forming of coalitions to press others to act does have a compelling rationale.
- Close to 30 percent of the total short-term gains would be due to liberalization in the textiles and apparel sector, with about two-thirds of the gains going to the developing countries. Workers in these industries in wealthy countries would lose, while consumers would gain, with the consumer gains outweighing the producer losses.
- Careful analysis of changes in the terms of trade is crucial to understanding the results. Agricultural liberalization, including removal of production subsidies, could raise world agricultural prices by about 10 percent. This would benefit countries with a comparative

advantage in agriculture and hurt countries without such an advantage. However, it is incorrect to simplistically define comparative advantage by whether or not a country is a net importer of agricultural products. If a county has an overall trade deficit in which the deficit in nonagricultural goods is higher than the deficit in agricultural goods, it will still benefit from a rise in the price of agricultural goods because such a rise implies a (relative) fall in the price of other goods (Cline 2004, 134).

- Some countries that currently benefit from preferential access to wealthy country markets could lose from complete liberalization of world trade. Mexico, because of NAFTA, is in such a situation. The group of very poor countries that have preferential access to EU and US markets would also lose that advantage in a global free trade scenario. The various simulations show, however, that on the whole the loss of privileged access status would be offset by free access to other developing country markets, as well as by domestic efficiency gains in the poorest countries themselves. Nonetheless, some individual countries could be net losers because of preference erosion.

- Global trade liberalization would have significantly divergent effects on different income groups within the various regions and countries. Global agricultural liberalization, for example, will hurt wealthy country farmers and poor country urban consumers, while benefiting wealthy country consumers, who would be better off despite the higher prices because they would not have to subsidize their own countries' farmers any more. In some sectors, these consumers would also gain from lower world prices for the most protected products such as sugar. Poor country farmers, of course, would also benefit. Liberalization in the textile and apparel sectors would bring widespread gains for consumers in wealthy countries but concentrated losses for some highly protected producers in the OECD countries, sometimes in the most disadvantaged regions within these countries.

- Most simulations do not include liberalization in services. Those that do, suggest that the gains from a comprehensive opening of the services sector, even excluding the temporary migration category, could be two to three times as large as the effects of liberalization in all the other sectors combined. If one were to include temporary migration, the estimates go through the roof because one would be essentially starting from a very highly protected situation, as evidenced by the very large wage and salary differential between labor of similar quality, as opposed to the much smaller differential that prevails for product prices (Rodrik 2002b).

- When the modelers include dynamic and longer-run effects, the gains from liberalization get multiplied by a factor of two to three. This implies that negative short-term effects on various groups are more than offset by the dynamic gains. The key question concerns the strength of the link between trade liberalization and productivity growth. If one believes that link to be very strong, as implied by the World Bank (2002), trade liberalization would lead to global welfare gains on the order of 2 percent of world GDP over a decade and lift somewhere between 300 million to 400 million people out of poverty. The strength of the empirical link between the pace of productivity increases and trade policies are not based on reliable econometrics, however. There are good reasons to believe that the nature of the link is quite complex and dependent on sector, stage of development, and the overall quality of complementary policies. In some sectors at very early stages of development there might still be a case for infant industry protection. Nonetheless, the weight of existing evidence supports the view that the information sharing, learning, and enhanced competition that comes with greater openness leads to an acceleration of productivity growth, and that if more liberal policies can be sustained politically they will lead to widespread gains, even for groups that might be initial losers in the process of opening.

A Stronger Trade Agenda and the WTO

The *in extremis* agreement reached in Geneva at the end of July 2004 on the broad framework of how to proceed in the Doha Round trade negotiations showed that, despite all the acrimony and doubts during the previous two years, practically all of the official actors recognized that much could be gained from further trade liberalization, and that there are scenarios likely to benefit their principals or constituents. The Geneva agreement is only a broad framework, however, committing the wealthy countries to substantial cuts in support to their agriculture sectors in exchange for commitments by the developing countries to cooperate on efforts to further liberalize trade protection policies across the board.

For the Doha Round to be successful, three main sets of issues deserve particular attention, and a reformed approach is needed to achieve real progress.

First, it must be accepted from the start that most if not all liberalization packages to be discussed and negotiated will lead to winners and losers, both among and within countries. A package might emerge where the world taken as a whole is much better off, but if enough countries perceived as the losers vis-à-vis that particular package try to block the entire deal, they will likely succeed, given the WTO's consensus-based decision rules and the previous successes of such efforts. Similarly, if particular groups within countries stand to lose, they will try to prevent their country delegations from agreeing to proposed deals.

Within the trade negotiations themselves, the deal making essentially aims to compensate those who stand to lose from a particular set of measures by offering other trade measures in return. As mentioned above, the Geneva compromise was based on the developing countries offering the wealthier ones more liberalization in manufactures in exchange for decreased farm subsidies. But the fact that this compensation comes only in the form of trade measures can make compromise difficult. For example, a number of the least-developed countries that already have substantially free access to developed country markets may lose from the combination of reduced agricultural subsidies and manufacturing tariffs. This owes to the fact that they do not have comparative advantage in agriculture, and at the same time already have free access to wealthy country markets for their manufactures. Extending that free access to the middle-income countries is likely to displace some of their exports, and so they may be hurt both as food importers having to buy more expensive food and as exporters of manufactures who would no longer have privileged access to developed country markets.

Similarly, within countries, prospective losers will campaign against an accord, particularly in an environment where employment seems at risk, as reflected in growing concerns over outsourcing in the United States and Europe. As basic welfare economics always stresses, winners actually may have to compensate losers in order to achieve an overall desirable outcome. The question not sufficiently addressed is how to organize this compensation process within a country and across countries.

The second matter critical to success of the Doha Round relates to the interaction between trade and nontrade issues. Some of the policy issues that people care about are intimately and immediately related to trade, such as customs procedures (trade facilitation). Other issues are connected to trade, but not as immediately, such as public procurement rules and regulations regarding competition and investment. Still other issues such as standards on labor (working hours, minimum wages, child labor laws) and the environment (protection of natural resources, emission controls, biodiversity protection) have even less of a direct link to trade, although regulations in these areas will sometimes significantly affect the composition and direction of trade. Finally, there are the even broader issues of human rights, democracy, and individual freedom, which are part of the international agenda and about which people often care deeply. All of these issues have become part of the trade debate and have inspired some of the protests from Seattle to Cancún and beyond. One could argue that each of these sets of issues should be debated and addressed separately, and that many have only a remote connection to trade as such. On the other hand, in a world of sovereign nation-states, trade is often the only way that the international community or a group of nations can influence what happens inside the borders of an individual nation-state. During the period of apartheid in South Africa, the international community through the United Nations imposed a (partial) trade embargo on South Africa, thereby using trade sanctions as a tool to bring about change. On the other hand, most would agree that it would not be reasonable to impose a trade embargo on a country because it does not sufficiently protect biodiversity. Where does one draw the line? Who bears the burden of particular measures? Did not poor and black South African children bear much of the cost of the trade embargo even though it was designed to help them live in a more just society? What part of the overall burden of desirable socioeconomic policies should the WTO framework have to carry?

These issues need to be discussed and clarified in order to better understand what the WTO framework can and cannot be expected to achieve, who bears what costs, and where protests should be directed so that they can be most effective.

Finally, the third set of issues important to Doha relates to the decision-making rules used in WTO negotiations. WTO decision-making rules are quite unique in that they rely mostly on consensus and include a one nation, one vote principle irrespective of the country's size or weight in the world economy. However, with almost 150 WTO members, the process has become extremely cumbersome. Given these difficulties and what one might call anomalies, it is not surprising that informal procedures have taken over, with the biggest countries taking the lead in the "green room" process and with various forms of pressure brought to bear on the smaller countries to conform. Somewhat miraculously, this mixture of a formally democratic but unwieldy structure combined with informal but less democratic arrangements has actually produced results. Nonetheless, it must be asked whether a more effective and streamlined decision mechanism could not produce better and more rapid results. In this context, one should also clarify which issues to address and subject to trade negotiations under the WTO umbrella, and which others to take up through different international negotiations under different auspices. Moreover, the question of who should discuss and decide this allocation of issues must also be addressed.

Winners, Losers, and Compensation

One of the characteristic features of the current globalization process is the accelerating nature of change. A corollary is that rapid change creates winners and losers without the latter having much time to adapt, a phenomenon that has contributed to the increasing anxiety about globalization even in the most prosperous economies. Lifelong employment and careers have become less common, and new skills must be learned constantly as the work-a-day world evolves far more rapidly than was the case just decades ago. International trade intensifies competition and the need to rapidly adapt. Economic activities can relocate with greater ease, choosing new bases from which to serve world markets. The freer trade is, the easier it is to relocate without losing the home market. The upside is that this mobility and flexibility bring with them the potential for worldwide improvements in efficiency, reductions in costs, and increases in productivity, which, if fully exploited, could accelerate the growth of the world economy and greatly enhance the potential for poverty reduction.

As regards poverty reduction, however, the emphasis should be on the word "potential," because not all boats get lifted together. Worse, in the short to medium run, some people may lose significantly from change. According to estimates by Cline (2004) and Stiglitz, Charlton, and the Initiative for Policy Dialogue (2004), poverty in a number of countries would actually increase as a result of the global agricultural liberalization package, at least in the short run. Moreover, in a much larger number of countries, the urban poor would lose because of agricultural trade liberalization. In the longer run, the benefits will trickle down from the winners, and as productivity increases everybody may become better off. The long run may amount to decades, however. Moreover, if the losers organize, they could well prevent the policy changes from being implemented in the first place. Reforms that could in the long run make everyone better off are often blocked both at the national and international levels. US and European dairy farmers and steel workers have successfully slowed liberalization that would increase overall welfare in their own countries and the world. African cotton producers joined by other constituencies in Cancún in 2003 contributed to blocking the Doha Round, which undoubtedly could increase overall world welfare, because they felt their needs were not met, and indeed that they might suffer negative consequences because of the erosion of preferences that a multilateral liberalization process might entail.

Thus, a basic problem that must be addressed to realize the potential benefits from trade liberalization is to find ways to compensate potential losers. The problem has several dimensions, one of which relates to who those losers actually are. The richer they are, the less attractive it is to have to essentially buy them off. Most cotton and dairy farmers in the developed countries are actually quite well off compared to poor urban slum dwellers in developing countries. It would certainly not be possible to mobilize international resources to buy off these cotton and dairy farmers, so that problem has to be solved at the national level. On the other hand, who should pay out compensation to poor urban slum dwellers in developing countries if they lose out as part of a global agricultural liberalization package that benefits developing country farmers and rich country consumers? Or if the least-developed countries lose out as a result of the erosion of the special preferences they enjoy because of multilateral trade liberalization?

All this suggests that globalization, liberalization, and the speed of technical change greatly augment the need for public resources to finance change. While US presidential candidate John Kerry may have been right in 2004 to express concern about the impact of outsourcing on US workers and job security, what is the reality and what is the solution? Some surveys show that the outsourcing of US jobs has accounted for less than 2 percent of the nation's job losses to date, but many corporate executives share the view that outsourcing may increase and have a far larger impact in the future.

Is the solution to try to slow change that appears inevitable, in turn harming US corporations vis-à-vis those in other nations that might be able to outsource without incurring fiscal penalties, as well as harming US workers in other industries whose expansion is slowed by protection provided to the older industries? Or is the solution to provide proactive retraining and reinsertion assistance to US workers in sectors that are no longer competitive? Even subsidizing early retirement for workers over a certain age, say 50, may make more sense than protecting jobs that will be dysfunctional in the long run and whose transfer to countries where labor is more abundant fully conforms to principles of comparative advantage.

What criteria should be chosen, however, to determine who gets and who does not get support? How can one ensure that the support provided does not create disincentives for retraining, active job search, and personal effort to adapt to change, particularly as regards young workers? At the national level, the question is how to adapt the proactive, caring welfare state to the needs of the 21st century. This certainly cannot be done by minimizing public resources or the role of the state. As has been noted by Rodrik (1998), globalization actually requires a larger government that can help manage the increases in risk and vulnerability and compensate the losers. At the same time, public policy must not just protect and conserve the old but also facilitate and promote change. The welfare state must be progressive, intelligent in its targeting, selective in its support, and realistic in its ambition. The modern progressive state needs fiscal resources, however. Change does not finance itself.

The problem is greatly complicated by the fact that some of the compensation—and therefore some of the resource deployment required—would be international in nature. Exactly the same principles that apply at the national level apply internationally. To head off a coalition of potential losers from blocking necessary reforms, some resources need to be available to help this coalition overcome its short- to medium-term losses. Sometimes the give-and-take within the trade negotiations themselves may be sufficient to generate an overall balanced compromise. Often, however, trade measures alone may not be enough to bring about a solution where everyone gains. Similarly, a solution restricted to trade measures may constrain potential total welfare gains. A key question, therefore, is how to generate the resources for compensation and how to deploy them in support of a global trade liberalization package. The WTO is not equipped to answer the question or finance the answer. It has neither the authority nor the means to raise these resources, nor would it be equipped to use them. How to address this issue will be revisited later in this chapter in the discussion of governance and decision-making issues that relate to the trade agenda.

Trade and Nontrade Issues and the WTO

In his book entitled *One World*, Peter Singer uses the "tuna-dolphin" dispute as an example of the interaction between trade and other issues in the GATT-WTO framework (Singer 2004, 58–64). As do many other countries, the United States has domestic environmental and animal protection laws and standards. In addition, however, the United States often prohibits the import of goods produced in other countries with processes that would be in violation of US laws and regulations. The US Marine Mammal Protection Act sets standards that apply to tuna fishing boats in areas of the Pacific Ocean where schools of dolphin swim over schools of tuna. If a country cannot prove that it meets these standards, the US government embargos all imports of fish from that country. A dispute erupted with Mexico when the United States tried to ban US imports of Mexican tuna because Mexico violated US dolphin protection regulations. But the GATT panel arbitrating the dispute found that the United States had no right to use trade sanctions to enforce a production process outside its area of jurisdiction.

The WTO has continued to make the distinction between process—i.e., the way something is produced—and product, i.e., the nature of a good itself. A country cannot apply differential trade policies on identical products just because different processes produce them. The basic principle underlying the distinction relating to environmental issues is that the WTO framework should ensure a level playing field for products of equal quality, but should not be used to further other social or political objectives. If every country were to use trade sanctions to enforce standards that it has adopted by itself for itself, there could be no free and open system of international trade. Environmentalists would like to see the WTO help enforce environmental or animal protection standards by authorizing trade sanctions, not only for offenses related to trade policy, but also for failure to practice certain environmental or animal protection standards that a particular country has decided to adopt.

The same kind of dilemma arises in other domains, with one of the most hotly contested issues relating to labor standards. On one side of this debate are those who argue that the WTO should enforce certain labor standards, including limits on hours worked and the age of workers, as well as guarantees ensuring adequate working conditions and worker rights, by allowing trade sanctions against countries that do not implement these standards. On the other side are those who argue that countries may differ, sometimes greatly, with respect to labor market situations, and that labor standards, however desirable, should not be a subject of trade negotiations. Many on this side of the debate suspect those who want to enforce labor standards of purely protectionist aims, while those who want to enforce these standards within the WTO framework suspect the others of wanting to further corporate interests and sponsor a worldwide "race to the bottom" to maximize the return to capital without any regard for social concerns.[24]

Another dimension of the debate on what should and should not be subject to trade negotiations relates to the "Singapore issues" of trade facilitation, public procurement, investment incentives, and regulations and competition policies. It had been agreed at the Singapore ministerial conference in 1996 to put the negotiations on these four issues on the agenda of the next round of trade negotiations. At the end of the Uruguay Round negotiations, many European and American analysts again were calling for broadening and deepening the trade agenda by including the Singapore issues in the next round of negotiations. Frank (1994) summarized the philosophical underpinnings of their position: "What globalization implies, therefore, is the need to extend the horizon of international negotiations from the liberalization of strictly border measures, such as tariffs and quotas, to the coordination of various areas of *domestic* policy that substantially affect the *ability of firms* to conduct their operations worldwide" [emphasis added].

The basic argument for including the Singapore issues is that globalization implies much more integrated production chains, with an increasing role of intrafirm trade, global investment, and production strategies of multinationals. In this new environment, it may not always be easy to distinguish trade from competition policy or public procurement rules, just to cite one example. For the advanced countries, encouraged by the corporate sector, one of the key objectives of the new round was deeper liberalization—a worldwide policy environment supportive of global integration of production chains and favorable to the operations of multinational corporations. Indeed, large corporations were active in influencing the content of the policy agenda. Their first big success was attained by the pharmaceutical industry when the trade-related intellectual property rights (TRIPS) agreement became part of the "single undertaking" agreed upon at the Uruguay Round. Bhagwati (2004, 182) argues that "pharmaceutical and software companies muscled their way into the

24. Elliott and Freeman (2003) examine labor issues and globalization.

WTO and turned it into a royalty-collection agency simply because the WTO can apply trade sanctions." The advanced countries have since stepped back on the Singapore issues in the face of more organized and coordinated opposition from major developing countries wanting to retain greater flexibility for their industrial and competition policies.

Finally, broader democracy and human rights issues are periodically raised in the context of the WTO. Trade sanctions have been a traditional tool for both national policies (i.e., US trade sanctions against Cuba and Iran) and international policies implemented under a UN umbrella (South Africa, Iraq). Moreover, many civil society organizations and advocacy groups would like the WTO-sponsored negotiations to include human rights and democracy issues in the Doha Round. They argue, for example, that there should be prohibitions against importing natural resources exported by countries ruled by dictatorial elites who appropriate the proceeds for themselves or squander them on arms to keep themselves in power. The argument is similar to that against allowing such countries to acquire burdensome debt, which then needs to be serviced by taxes on the poor and by subsequent generations.

Reviewing these arguments, it becomes quite clear that if all were to become part of the WTO agenda, trade negotiations would have to solve almost every problem in the world. Many of these issues deserve priority attention by the international community, but if they all must be solved as part of the Doha Round, the negotiations will never be completed and the significant gains within reach if a balanced and prodevelopment package can be agreed upon will not be achieved. That said, rules clearly are needed to determine what should and should not be part of multilateral trade negotiations. How to reach agreement on these rules is part of the question as to what would be the most appropriate and legitimate governance mechanisms for trade and the WTO.

Overall Governance of the WTO and Trade

Chapter 4 proposed a new UN Economic and Social Security Council that could decide on the overall allocation of functions in the international economic system. The council should not manage the WTO secretariat or the multilateral trade negotiations any more than it should run the IMF, World Bank, or the United Nations Development Program (UNDP), but it could be entrusted to decide which issues are best handled where. For example, the council could agree to a plan whereby the International Labor Organization (ILO) negotiates a progressive worldwide strengthening of labor standards, reasonably differentiated according to country circumstances and initial conditions, and with specific targets to be revised every five years.

Few would insist that labor standards be exactly the same in Sweden and in Bangladesh, because imposing Swedish standards on Bangladesh would hurt Bengali workers and their families by creating much higher unemployment. And yet, most would agree that there should be some universal labor standards, graduated by income and labor market conditions and evolving over time. The UN Economic and Social Security Council, working with the ILO and other relevant organizations, would provide the negotiators of the Doha and subsequent rounds of trade negotiations with a basic framework for labor issues. This framework would be given to the trade negotiators, relieving them of the additional burden of having to deal with the labor standards issue while they are negotiating trade measures. A similar logic would apply to environmental or health problems. The UN Economic and Social Security Council, working with such organizations as the World Bank and the World Health Organization as well as NGOs and various global networks, would try to arrive at a sensible framework of rules within which the trade negotiations could proceed.[25]

The advantage of giving the UN Economic and Social Security Council this role would be twofold. First, the council would have a global, comprehensive, and at the same time bureaucratically impartial perspective, which would help it to fill gaps, organize possible synergies, and promote efficiency. The WTO could concentrate on trade, just as the WHO could concentrate on health, and the ILO on labor issues, while the UN Economic and Social Security Council would deal with the interactions that arise and help streamline the whole process of policy reform.

The UN Economic and Social Security Council could also address the difficult issue of marshaling resources to compensate some of the most deserving losers in any trade agreement. Working with the World Bank, the regional development banks, and the UNDP, the council could help mobilize and support the deployment of resources to facilitate acceptance of compromise solutions to critical trade issues.

---

25. Issues that are narrowly political or security related—such as the oppression of minorities, gross violations of human rights, or failure to cooperate with efforts to combat international terrorism—would best be handled by the UN Security Council rather than the UN Economic and Social Security Council. Such is the case today for the existing UN Security Council, which handles trade sanctions as applied to such issues.

The second advantage of assigning the UN Economic and Social Security Council overall allocation of functions in the international economic system is that its universal participation by weighted voting governance, as described in chapter 4, would give its proposals and decisions the legitimacy needed for the new system to enjoy broader-based support. Of particular relevance to trade matters, the council would not be a forum where individual countries could easily block compromises acceptable to a great majority of nations. At the same time, the weighted votes would reflect the relative importance of countries and country groupings and could be expected to lead to realistic proposals that take into account the interests and concerns of those with economic power and resources.

By providing the basic terms of reference at the start of trade negotiations—including a framework for debate and a definition of the trade issues to be negotiated—the UN Economic and Social Security Council could protect the negotiations from being captured by various special interest groups and single-issue networks. The WTO process would then take over and deal with the actual negotiations. In some ways, this already happens: the Doha, Cancún, and Geneva meetings attempted over a period of more than two years to define the broad framework for the next round of trade talks. It is not clear whether the Geneva compromise finally succeeded in providing a workable framework, however, and reaching it was time consuming. Moreover, both the coverage and the legitimacy of the proposed framework will inevitably be challenged in various ways. It is quite likely that had a UN Economic and Social Security Council existed, it could have provided a more comprehensive framework more rapidly and with greater support from public opinion and civil society.

Turning to the WTO process itself, decision making has become difficult because of the size, complexity, and all-encompassing nature of the "single undertaking" approach employed during negotiations. With the exception of the "special and differentiated treatment applicable" to a group of developing countries, the "single undertaking" approach requires everyone involved in a comprehensive round of multilateral negotiations to subscribe to and implement policies agreed to in their entirety. This does not preclude the formation of customs unions or free trade agreements among willing coalitions, provided that they do not result in increased protection against imports from third countries compared to the situation before these regional trade agreements were formed. There is scope for enhanced cooperation, to borrow a term from the European Union, among subgroups of WTO members. But these groups must nevertheless conform to the "single undertaking," although they are free to go further in terms of freer trade among themselves.

Even within a framework supported by a UN Economic and Social Security Council, the world's trade system would still involve complex and technical negotiations conducted among some 150 countries, each impacted differently by any particular issue. Even with such a complex negotiating process, however, the essentially consensus-based nature of the WTO rules should be preserved. In practice, the consensus rule does not really allow any one country or small group of countries to block progress in a totally capricious way. There would be too much peer pressure on such an outlier or outliers, and the majority could impose serious costs on countries if they were to play a purely obstructionist role. At the same time, the single undertaking rule and nonplurilateral nature of WTO negotiations give developing countries leverage to negotiate with much more powerful counterparts such as the United States or the European Union—as they have shown over the past two years. This has allowed for the formation of developing-country coalitions that have been effective in forcing the developed countries to revise their positions and shift to a more development friendly stance in negotiations.

Without giving up the consensus rule for actual decision making, it would be beneficial to introduce more transparency and formality into the "green room" process by which countries currently reach informal agreements. This could be accomplished by requiring some objective criteria to determine participation in green room sessions based on comprehensive geographic representation, volume of trade, and the relevance of a particular issue under discussion to a specific group of countries.

Schott and Watal (2000) propose that the WTO "establish a small, informal steering committee (20 or so in number) that can be delegated responsibility for developing consensus on trade issues among the member countries. Such a group would not undercut existing WTO rights and obligations or the rule of decision making by consensus." Schott and Watal do not advocate proportional or weighted voting. "Each member would maintain the ultimate decision to accept or reject such pacts. Participation should be representative of the broader membership, and be based on clear, simple, and objective criteria: absolute value of foreign trade (exports and imports of goods and services), ranked by country or common customs region; and global geographic representation, with at least two participants from all major regions."

In conclusion, a package of reforms including the following would go a long way toward building much greater support for further trade liberalization of a kind that benefits the greatest number:

- a high-level oversight role for the UN Economic and Social Security Council,
- appointment of the WTO director by that council according to transparent criteria,
- assigning of important nontrade environmental and social issues during trade negotiations to other agencies in consultation with global civil society and stakeholders (with time-bound follow-up),
- greater priority to liberalization in the service sector including facilitation of temporary migration,
- mobilization of resources to compensate relatively low-income groups that stand to lose from liberalization or that face substantial adjustment costs, and
- streamlining and increased transparency in the WTO processes themselves.

Such reforms would channel the energies unleashed by the passion for greater justice and equity into efforts that can produce real results for the billions of people who stand to benefit from progress toward more and freer trade worldwide.

8 | Regional Integration and Globalization

Have I said clearly enough that the community we have created is not an end in itself? The community itself is only a stage on the way to the organized world of tomorrow.

JEAN MONNET
Statesman regarded by many as the architect of European unity
Mémoires, 1976

Modern communications technology interdependence and economies of scale throughout the private and public sectors make it increasingly necessary to go beyond the limits of the nation-state in organizing significant aspects of economic, social, and political activity. The preceding chapters have discussed the process of globalization and some of the global governance challenges posed by it. The search for supranational problem solving and international cooperation is not always global in nature, however.

Alongside globalization, the post–World War II period also has seen numerous attempts at regional integration, more pronounced in some parts of the world than in others and with varying degrees of success. Moreover, the publication of Samuel Huntington's *The Clash of Civilizations and the Remaking of World Order* in 1996 has popularized a worldview that sees the future not so much as one of an increasingly harmonious international community functioning with more global governance, but rather as one of a world of more or less antagonistic regional blocs made up of countries with geographical proximity and people coming together based on history, culture, and religion.

Thus, when discussing "better" globalization, it is necessary to discuss also regionalization and how it relates to, competes with, or complements globalization. Is the world moving toward regional "superstates" that will gradually replace the old, smaller nation-states? Must global governance be developed within a framework in which Huntingtonian and regional superstate blocs will become the new emerging constituent units of the international system? Is better global governance possible in a world of competing megaregions? What kinds of regional cooperation are really being developed? How do regional organizations, such as the regional development banks, fit in with the global organizations discussed in the preceding chapters? Are regional blocs of the type foreseen by Huntington in the making? How are local, regional, and global dynamics likely to interact in transforming the international system?

The European Union is to date the most ambitious and successful of the regional integration processes undertaken in recent years. The second half of this chapter will focus on the EU as an extraordinary historical process that has resulted in a significant amount of supranational governance. How much further along the European integration process will proceed is the subject of considerable debate. Regardless, much can be learned from the European experience, and much of the debate is not only about the future of the EU, but about future forms of supranational governance worldwide.

Europe has not been the only part of world that has pursued some form of regional integration, nor is it alone in debating its future and its borders. Well over a hundred regional cooperation arrangements now exist, most in the form of regional trade agreements with various degrees of additional features relating to investment, travel, and economic cooperation. Some of these arrangements include attempts at political cooperation, but most are purely economic in nature and basically focus on trade.[1]

Despite their great diversity, the East Asian countries have been trying to move toward regional cooperation at least since the 1970s. Latin America, where countries share a common history and language, has long

---

1. See Ethier (1998) for an overview and theoretical analysis of what has been called the "new regionalism." There are five general types of regional economic integration. A *free trade area* includes a group of nations that have reduced or fully dismantled internal barriers to trade in goods and services but have not adopted common external tariffs (i.e., the countries maintain individual tariffs with regard to outside countries). A *customs union* is a group of nations that have established a free trade area and a common external tariff regime (i.e., trade policy is consistent throughout the member countries). A *common market* involves a group of nations that have established a customs union and, in addition, free mobility of capital and labor across borders, which typically implies harmonization of rules, regulations, standards, specifications, and other commercial policies between member countries. An *economic community* is a group of nations that have established a common market and, in addition, work to coordinate and harmonize fiscal and monetary policies. Finally, an *economic union* is a group of nations that have established an economic community and, in addition, have unified social, fiscal, and monetary policies and a common currency.

sought some degree of integration. As part of the Americas, Latin America also has been part of efforts to better integrate North and South America. Within Latin America and the Caribbean are subregional organizations and groupings that reflect cooperation and integration initiatives. The North American Free Trade Agreement (NAFTA) has brought together the United States, Canada, and Mexico in a free trade zone. The Arab countries, which also share a common language and much common history, have talked about regional integration since they gained independence. In the 1950s, the United Arab Republic briefly brought together several Arab countries under Egyptian leadership. Greater regional integration has also been an objective for African countries.

But what is the current state of the world in terms of regionalization? The brief summaries that follow about integration efforts in the different world regions serve not only as a backdrop for the subsequent, more detailed discussion about the European Union, but also as background as to how regional and global integration dynamics interact. Are globalization and regional integration competing trends, with more regionalization leading to less globalization and vice versa? Or do they complement one another?

East Asia

East Asia includes one giant (China), another giant in terms of economic size (Japan), and other economically important nations ranging from Australia to South Korea. In all, East Asia totals 31 countries, with other major players including Indonesia, Thailand, Malaysia, the Philippines, Vietnam, and New Zealand. The region is also home to numerous smaller nations, including several tiny island economies.

East Asia is ethnically and religiously diverse and has no common language. Two countries, Australia and New Zealand, have populations of largely non-Asian origin. Until the 1990s, the region was also divided ideologically between the communists and their adversaries allied to the United States. After the collapse of the Soviet Union and the liberalizing reforms in China, this sharp ideological divide gradually disappeared.

The degree of integration through trade has been increasing very rapidly in East Asia. The share of intraregional trade in total trade has risen from about one-third to over one-half since 1980.[2] The expansion

2. As a comparison, the share of intraregional trade is about 60 percent in the European Union and 46 percent in North America. The rate of increase, however, is fastest in East Asia. See Kawai (2004) for an analysis of Asian economic integration and interdependence.

of trade has been closely linked to foreign direct investment, with Japanese firms as major players increasingly locating production in Southeast Asian countries. Much trade has taken the form of intrafirm shipments within the framework of increasingly integrated production circuits. Over the last decade, this deep regional integration has also extended to China, although given the size of the Chinese economy, the segments of industry that are part of this integrated East Asian economy are smaller than in the other countries. The degree of East Asian interdependence is also reflected in the high degree of cross-county correlation of macroeconomic variables such as GDP growth, investment, consumption, and inflation.

The 1997–98 financial crisis spurred Asia to enhance cooperation in the financial and macroeconomic domain.[3] The sudden nature of the crisis and the speed with which it spread were a deep psychological blow to a region accustomed to uninterrupted growth, and one which had been so much admired for its economic "miracle" to be emulated by other regions of the world. The regional nature of the crisis clearly reflected the degree of interdependence. Early on, Japan wanted to launch a regional monetary fund and rescue package to help stem contagion and limit the macroeconomic downturn. The US Treasury and the International Monetary Fund (IMF) strongly resisted this initiative on the grounds that it would undercut the IMF during the critical phase of negotiating conditions that would accompany Fund lending, thus reinforcing moral hazard. While Japan's original plan to set up a kind of regional IMF did not materialize, it did pledge $30 billion to a regional recovery fund and continue to push for regional integration and cooperation. This early commitment helped turn around expectations and stabilize the East Asian economies. Japan also joined the United States, the Asian Development Bank (ADB), and the World Bank in promoting needed corporate restructuring in the region. Two years after Japan's initial efforts, the Association of Southeast Asian Nations (ASEAN) met with Japan, Korea, and China (ASEAN + 3) in Chiang Mai to establish a regional network of swap arrangements to help manage currency attacks and contagion. Members requesting liquidity support can immediately obtain short-term financial assistance for the first 10 percent of the Chiang Mai facility. The remaining 90 percent becomes available as part of an IMF-supported program. This constitutes an example of a regional initiative with a clear global link, reconciling regional solidarity with global governance.

---

3. This section is based on information provided in Kawai (2004).

In the fall of 1998, one year after the Asian crisis erupted, ASEAN also established a regional economic surveillance mechanism, which included measures to monitor economic and financial variables as well as a regional peer review process. This was followed in May 2003 by the ASEAN + 3 Economic Review and Policy Dialogue conducted by the regional finance ministers to focus on macroeconomic trends, risk management, capital flows, and the financial sector. The dialogue arrangement has no formal secretariat, but the ADB provides information to the meetings. Headquartered in Manila, the ADB has a membership of 63 countries, with total lending volume of $6.1 billion in 2003 (Asian Development Bank 2004).

East Asia faces a number of rather unique "border" issues. Australia and New Zealand, which are culturally and ethnically more European than Asian, nevertheless are geographically part of Asia. Moreover, the Pacific Ocean creates economic and transportation links with many Pacific island states as well as the western rim of the Americas looking toward Asia. These Pacific links have led to some loose forms of cooperation. The Asia-Pacific Economic Cooperation (APEC) forum was established in 1989 to promote trade and investment links, facilitate business, and augment economic and technical cooperation in the region (Asia-Pacific Economic Cooperation Secretariat 2003). In addition to the major East Asian countries, APEC includes American countries such as the United States, Mexico, Chile, and Canada. Its vision is articulated in what are known as the "Bogor goals" adopted in 1994: establishment of free trade and open investment in the Asia-Pacific region by 2010 for the advanced economies and by 2020 for the developing economies. To achieve these goals, APEC has outlined a strategic framework called the Osaka Action Agenda that delineates general principles, including nondiscrimination, transparency, flexibility, and consistency with the World Trade Organization (WTO). Member economies prepare individual action plans and periodically submit them to peer review. Several policy and cooperation initiatives have ranged from training financial sector supervisors and regulators to submitting corporate governance reforms to peer review and examining economic and institutional factors affecting remittances of expatriate workers.

Developments in East Asia over 1998–2004 demonstrate that in many ways the Asian miracle continues. In many countries, growth has returned to close to precrisis levels, and the huge amounts of accumulated foreign exchange reserves provide a formidable cushion against possible economic shocks. While the Japanese economy is no longer the growth engine it was from the 1960s to the early 1990s—Japanese growth averaged less than 1 percent in the post–Asian crisis period—the increasing weight of China and its phenomenal growth performance have ensured high regional growth averages. Other medium-sized countries such as Korea, Thailand, Taiwan (Republic of China), Singapore, and Malaysia have also overcome the crisis and are growing in the 5 to 7 percent average range. The Philippines and Indonesia have to carry heavier debt burdens and seem more vulnerable. Finally, Australia and New Zealand, with their more mature economies, have a much lower growth rate. Overall, however, the economic performance of East Asia continues to be impressive. China is already attracting more direct foreign investment than any other country, including the United States. In less than two decades, China will likely rival the United States and the European Union in economic size, although the per capita income gap will remain large for a long time.

How much is regional cooperation in East Asia likely to develop over the next two decades? The experience of the last few years suggests that quite advanced forms of regional economic cooperation will contribute to stabilizing the East Asian growth process. The interdependence of the East Asian economies has created a powerful interest in regional stability, and the memory of the 1997–98 crisis encourages cooperation. It is unlikely, however, that East Asia will turn inward or move toward some form of political union. The East Asian economies trade a lot with each other but are also oriented toward the global market, with their growth driven by integration into global production and consumption circuits. There are no strong signs of resurgent regional protectionism, and the East Asian countries are likely to engage in and support further multilateral trade liberalization. Economic links to the United States are strong, complemented by growing links to Latin American economies. Links to Europe also remain important, augmented more recently by ties with India, the Russian Federation, and Central Asia.

The picture that is emerging for East Asia is one of a powerful and dynamic region developing effective and diverse internal economic cooperation mechanisms, while at the same time staying open to the world and very much part of both the global economy and international system. The East Asian nations will seek recognition of their increasing weight, but provided that such a legitimate demand is satisfied, there is little reason to expect that East Asia will develop in ways antagonistic to other regions or to global cooperation.

South Asia

South Asia includes the giant nation that is India with more than 1 billion citizens, as well as Pakistan, Bangladesh, Sri Lanka, and the small Himalayan states of Bhutan and Nepal. South Asia has long been one of the poorest regions of the world. Over the past decade, however, it has also become one of the fastest growing regions, due in large part to a remarkable transformation in India that has gradually moved the country to an annual average rate of per capita growth close to 5 percent. India by itself, like China, is emerging as one of the world's largest economies.

The decades-old rivalry between Pakistan and India has limited cooperation in South Asia, although India now has strong links with its other neighbors. Ties also are likely to increase between India and East Asia, as India may join some of the East Asian cooperation organizations.

For its part, Pakistan has developed strong economic links with many Middle Eastern countries, particularly Saudi Arabia. The tension between Pakistan and India has declined recently, and if political problems between the two nations over Kashmir can be resolved, greater economic cooperation may become possible within South Asia. That said, the emergence of a South Asian cooperation zone or some kind of a regional bloc is unlikely in the near future.

Latin America

Latin America has a long history of efforts to forge regional cooperation. The Organization of American States (OAS) traces its origins to Simón Bolívar's proposal for a League of American Republics at the 1826 Congress of Panama. The modern OAS is a post–World War II organization conceived in 1948. All 35 independent countries of the Americas have ratified the OAS charter and belong to the organization, although the Cuban government, despite Cuba being a member, has been excluded from OAS participation since 1962. The OAS promotes cooperation in the Americas and in 1994 adopted the goal of establishing a Free Trade Area of the Americas (FTAA) by 2005, a goal that will not be reached by its target date.

The Americas are home to a number of subregional customs unions. The Caribbean Community and Common Market (CARICOM), established in 1973, brings together such countries as Jamaica, Barbados, Guyana, and many other small economies. Inspired by the European

Union, CARICOM has ambitions to evolve toward a strongly integrated regional single market and economic zone. Its revised treaty provides for joint sectoral policies, fiscal harmonization, a single currency in the future, and a Caribbean Court of Justice to apply the treaty. To date, however, there has been little progress beyond the common market arrangement.

Mercosur, the Southern Cone Common Market, is a regional economic cooperation agreement set up between Argentina, Brazil, Paraguay, and Uruguay in 1991. In 1998, Mercosur created a mechanism for political consultations, and the process of institutionalizing that mechanism has been furthered by the recent establishment of a Committee of Permanent Representatives and a Dispute Settlement Court. Several Latin American countries have become associate members of Mercosur with access to preferential trade terms.

The Andean Community is a subregional organization comprised of Bolivia, Colombia, Ecuador, Peru, and Venezuela. It began operating in 1997 as the successor to the Andean Pact, which had been formed in 1969. The Andean Community is an economic and social integration organization that promotes liberalization of subregional trade, implementation of a common external tariff, harmonization of foreign trade policies, and coordination of economic policies, all of which are encompassed in the community's common foreign policy. Furthermore, a free trade area was established in 1993 and a common market is to be formed by 2005. The institutional reforms that created the Andean Community have attempted to extend integration into the political sphere by forming an institutional framework known as the Andean Integration System, which includes a presidential council, council of foreign ministers, commission, general secretariat, court of justice, parliament, development corporation, reserve fund, and social, education, business, and labor institutions. However, integration beyond the economic sphere has stagnated due to the reluctance of the member states to part with any national sovereignty (Martínez 2002).

NAFTA, the largest and best known of the American regional trade agreements, followed the Canada-US Free Trade Agreement of 1989 and was established in 1994 as a comprehensive agreement linking Canada, the United States, and Mexico. The agreement immediately ended tariffs on a wide range of goods and stipulated more gradual elimination of other tariffs. While NAFTA has provisions that go beyond trade as such, reaching into areas such as intellectual property rights and investment regulations, it does not include longer-term political integration objectives, nor does it create supranational bodies or a body of law that would take precedence over national law, as is the case for the European Union.

The Inter-American Development Bank (IDB), the regional development bank for Latin America and the Caribbean, had annual lending of $6.8 billion in 2003. The IDB was founded in 1959 as a partnership between 19 Latin American countries and the United States, with European countries and Japan joining later. In Latin America today, the IDB is probably as important as the World Bank in terms of deployment of financial and staff resources. Of course, the IMF is still the most important institution in terms of macroeconomic crisis management and lending to overcome financial crisis.

Neither the Americas nor Latin America as such is emerging as a regionally integrated political or economic bloc. As in Asia, diverse forms of regional and subregional cooperation are progressing, particularly in trade and development banking, but there is no process of political integration comparable to that of Europe. Moreover, regional integration has been running parallel to participation in WTO-sponsored multilateral trade liberalization, and Latin America has also participated in the global UN system and the Bretton Woods institutions. The major Latin American nations such as Brazil, Mexico, and Argentina have been proactive leaders in attempts to form intercontinental alliances with other major developing countries, such as India, China, and South Africa, on various global issues, particularly trade.

Arab Countries

The Arab world[4] from Iraq to Morocco, and from Yemen to Syria, shares a written language, a great deal of common history, and a broad identification with Islam, although not all Arabs are Moslems.[5] Despite these bonds, which should create the conditions for strong regional cooperation, there is little effective cohesion in the Arab world. The functions of the Arab League in bringing together all Arab countries have been largely ceremonial. Some progress has been made with the Arab Free Trade

4. The members of the Arab League are Algeria, Bahrain, Comoros, Djibouti, Egypt, Iraq, Jordan, Kuwait, Lebanon, Libya, Mauritania, Morocco, Oman, Palestine, Qatar, Saudi Arabia, Somalia, Sudan, Syria, Tunisia, United Arab Emirates, and Yemen.
5. A significant number of Egyptians, Lebanese, Syrians, and Palestinians are Christian. Other Arab nations have smaller numbers of Christians and other minorities.

Agreement, decided on within the Arab League framework in 1997 with the aim of achieving free trade among Arab countries by 2008. Nonetheless, intraregional trade barriers in the form of tariffs and nontariff restrictions remain high and inter-Arab trade represents only 8 percent of the Arab countries' foreign trade.

Regional development banks and development organizations, such as the Arab Fund for Economic and Social Development, the Kuwait Fund, and the Islamic Development Bank (IsDB), have played a considerable role in financing projects throughout the Middle East and Africa. They represent the most successful aspect of regional cooperation in this part of the world. To some extent, the activities of these development banks reflect the huge income and wealth differentials in the Arab world, which make resource transfers from the rich to the poorer countries both feasible and a political necessity. The Arab Monetary Fund, with its headquarters in the United Arab Emirates, has attempted to develop some regional monitoring and a macroeconomic consultation process with a certain degree of success. Overall, however, the Arab countries have not developed cooperation mechanisms that are as extensive as what has emerged in East Asia or even in Latin America.

Organization of the Islamic Conference

Islam, more than any other religion, still links the temporal and spiritual sphere. The Islamic *Oumma* or "community of faith" has a meaning and a political-emotional connotation for most Moslems for which there is no modern equivalent among other religions, except perhaps the Jewish faith in the context of Israel, where religious and temporal identity are also interlinked. There is an Organization of the Islamic Conference (OIC), whereas there is no similar organization grouping countries in which the majority of citizens are from the other big world religions. The OIC, established in 1969, is composed of 56 member states that "decided to pool their resources together, combine efforts and speak with one voice to safeguard the interest and ensure the progress and well-being of their peoples and those of other Muslims in the world over."[6] The Islamic Conference is made up of three main bodies: the Conference of Kings and Heads of State and Government, the Conference of Foreign Ministers, and the General Secretariat. In addition, it has four specialized institutions: the Islamic Development Bank, Islamic Educational, Scientific and Cultural

6. See the OIC website at www.oic-oci.org/.

Organization, Islamic States Broadcasting Organization, and International Islamic News Agency, as well as numerous ministerial committees. In the economic sphere, the OIC strives to strengthen intra-OIC economic cooperation through a General Agreement on Economic, Technical and Commercial Cooperation, an Agreement on Promotion, Protection and Guarantee of Investments, and a Framework Agreement on Trade Preferential System.

The OIC's permanent General Secretariat was established in 1970 and the organization's charter was adopted in 1972. The charter enumerates the fundamental principles of the OIC, including nonintervention in the domestic affairs of member states, the unmitigated sovereignty of each nation, peaceful settlement of disputes among member states, and, similarly, a pledge to refrain from using force against another OIC country. Unfortunately, the bloody war between Iraq and Iran, which cost well over a million lives in the 1980s, is just the most obvious example of how these resolutions have failed to translate into reality.

Africa

In many ways, Africa is the most fragmented of the large regions of the world—aggressed and exploited by colonialism for many centuries, its inhabitants enslaved at home or kidnapped for slavery in the Americas and the Middle East, and its natural resources plundered by colonizers. Only after the Second World War, and initially with the support of the Soviet Union,[7] were Africans able to reach for self-rule and independence. Unfortunately, with their borders having been arbitrarily drawn by the colonial powers, the African nation-states that emerged had little of the sense of common national identity that was an ingredient in the emergence of nation-states in Europe and, to a lesser extent, elsewhere. The national borders that emerged in the postcolonial period were mostly inconsistent with tribal identities or geographical realities.

Moreover, while the African Union encompasses the whole of the African continent, North African Arab countries such as Egypt and Tunisia have a stronger emotional attachment to Arabism and the Middle East than to sub-Saharan Africa. Further, many sub-Saharan African

---

7. While the Soviets were by no means pursuing altruistic aims in Afica or elsewhwere, the communist ideological challenge and the assistance provided by the Soviet Bloc to various independence movements contributed to ending the empires of the colonial powers.

countries can be grouped as Francophone or Anglophone, reflecting their cultural and linguistic heritage from the colonial period.[8]

Nonetheless, regional integration emerged as a prominent issue in Africa in the 1960s as a correlate to inward-looking development. At the time, regional integration was conceived as entailing free trade within Africa and a unified protectionist stance toward the rest of the world (Hoff 1999). Subregional cooperation schemes proliferated, viewed as building blocks of a pan-African economic union, and consequently African nations established over 200 regional groupings and agreements, largely between 1970 and 1985, though without many concrete results. Inspired by the development of the European Union, interest in regional integration resurged in Africa during the 1990s based on a new paradigm of a multi-lateral liberal trading system in accord with the dynamics of globalization. Modern African regionalism thus buttresses the characterization by Schiff and Winters (2003) of regional integration over the past 10 years as based on a more outward-oriented model, in line with the worldwide shift away from import substitution as the preferred model of development.

After coordinated industrial development in southern Africa proved largely unsuccessful due to the lack of supranational institutions to enforce regional decisions, the Southern African Development Community (SADC) charted a different course in the 1990s by evolving into a regional economic integration organization to facilitate the pooling of its member countries' resources. The SADC has proposed establishing a free trade area by 2008, and member nations have reduced all external tariffs and pursued trade agreements with the United States, the European Union, Mercosur, and ASEAN. Similarly, pursuant to the 1981 treaty that established the Preferential Trade Area (PTA) for Eastern and Southern Africa, the PTA was transformed in 1993 into the Common Market for Eastern and Southern Africa (COMESA). COMESA encompasses 20 eastern and southern African countries, 385 million people, and a combined GDP of over $180 billion. It became a free trade area in 2000 and is designed to develop into a customs union in 2004 and, eventually, an economic community.

The West African Economic and Monetary Union (WAEMU), composed of Benin, Burkina Faso, Côte d'Ivoire, Guinea-Bissau, Mali, Niger, Senegal, and Togo, might actually be the most advanced regional organization in Africa in terms of level of integration attained, having made

8. Angola, São-Tome, and Mozambique have kept linguistic ties with Portugal.

concrete progress in establishing a common market. In addition, the Southern African Customs Union (SACU), established in 1969 by South Africa, Botswana, Lesotho, Namibia, and Swaziland, is the oldest customs union in the world. In 1993, the 16 West African member states of the Economic Community of West African States (ECOWAS) revised the organization's treaty to accelerate economic integration and augment political cooperation. Similarly, the Intergovernmental Authority for Development (IGAD), originally formed in 1986 to address drought and desertification in its seven member nations, was revitalized in the mid-1990s as a political, economic, development, trade, and security entity.

As for pan-African integration, the Organization of African Unity (OAU) was succeeded in 2002 by the African Union (AU), which includes 53 nations and promotes the political and economic integration of Africa and the integration of the continent into the global economy. The AU defines itself as "Africa's premier institution and principal organization for the promotion of accelerated socioeconomic integration of the continent . . . based on the common vision of a unified and strong Africa and on the need to build a partnership between governments and all segments of civil society . . . in order to strengthen solidarity and cohesion amongst the peoples of Africa." The structure of the AU includes an assembly, the main legislative body, an advisory Executive Council made up of the foreign ministers of the member nations, a pan-African parliament, an administrative commission, an advisory Economic, Social and Cultural Council, and a Peace and Security Council with mandates to intervene to prevent genocide and crimes against humanity and to engage in peacekeeping missions.

Functionally, the AU has introduced a voluntary peer review scheme whereby member states are expected to monitor one another's adherence to democratic practices and prudent economic policy. Plans also are in place to establish a central bank, a monetary fund, an investment bank, a human rights court, a rapid reaction force for the Peace and Security Council by 2010, and an African Economic Community with a single currency by 2023. However, many question the financial capacity of the AU, with its $43 million annual budget, to carry out its ambitious schemes, and in 2004 the AU asserted that it needed a Marshall Plan. The AU also oversees the New Partnership for Africa's Development (NEPAD), a strategic socioeconomic development framework adopted by the OAU in 2001 that centers on the Capital Flows Initiative, under which African heads of state have pledged commitment to democracy and good governance, protection of human rights, regional and continental integration, peace and security, capacity-building, and the African Peer Review Mechanism in return for increased overseas development assistance (New Partnership for Africa's Development 2001).

The African Development Bank Group, now headquartered in Tunis, has also played a significant role in African regional integration, though it disburses less financing annually to sub-Saharan Africa than do the World Bank and the primary bilateral donors. All 53 African nations and 24 nonregional countries are members of the Bank Group. The nonregional countries primarily fund the group's activities and hence have considerable voting power. The Bank Group is made up of three institutions. First, the African Development Bank (AfDB), established in 1964, makes nonconcessional loans to creditworthy borrowers, including governments and, increasingly, the private sector. In 2003, the AfDB had total lending of $1.1 billion, but stricter lending policies introduced in the late 1990s have meant that the 38 poorest African nations are ineligible to borrow from the Bank (African Development Bank Group 2003). Instead, most sub-Saharan African countries rely on the two soft loan institutions of the Bank Group: the African Development Fund (AfDF) and the Nigerian Trust Fund (NTF). Established in 1972, the AfDF makes highly concessional loans for poverty alleviation, health, education, and good governance to African nations that cannot access commerical credit. Total AfDF lending in 2003 was $1.4 billion. The NTF was established in 1976 by the Nigerian government to assist the poorest AfDB group members. Its total lending in 2003 was $32 million.

While African nations aim to overcome constraints to development faced by individual countries by aggregating into larger economic and trading units, the effectiveness of regional integration in Africa has been limited by insufficient infrastructure and transport links as well as weak institutions. As a result, intraregional and intra-African trade have not significantly increased in recent years, and economic convergence and policy harmonization have been halting.

However, while regional integration schemes have produced only marginal benefits with regard to intraregional trade and economies of scale, they have facilitated trade agreements, such as the SACU-US Free Trade Agreement, that transaction costs likely would have precluded if not for the aggregation of a number of African nations. For some, even many

Africans, the ultimate objective of African integration schemes remains amalgamation into an African economic community. The emergence of such a community would strengthen Africa's self-confidence and allow Africans to increase their influence in international affairs. It is not likely, however, that Africa will emerge as a regional bloc with well-defined borders and strong political cohesion. The more likely scenario is one of increased cooperation among the subregions and, hopefully, stronger links to the world as a whole. North Africa will continue to have a dual allegiance to the Arab world and the African continent, while also developing increasingly strong links with the European Union.

Commonwealth of Independent States

The Soviet Union broke up in surprisingly peaceful fashion in 1990–91, giving birth to 15 new nation-states, all ex-Soviet Republics.[9] There were, of course, extensive economic and infrastructure ties between these ex-Soviet republics, and regional cooperation was immediately on the agenda. Russia, Belarus, and Ukraine initially formed the Commonwealth of Independent States (CIS) in 1991 to replace the Union of Soviet Socialist Republics. By the time of formal inception of the CIS in January 1992, Moldova, Tajikistan, Armenia, Azerbaijan, Turkmenistan, Kazakhstan, Kyrgyzstan, and Uzbekistan had also joined, and Georgia joined in 1993. The CIS is thus comprised of both Slav and non-Slav former Soviet republics. The CIS has a Council of Heads of States, Council of Heads of Government, Council of Foreign Ministers, Defense Ministers, and Border Troop Commanders, Inter-Parliamentary Assembly, Executive Committee, Interstate Economic Committee, and Collective Security Council, which arranges joint exercises under the Collective Security Treaty.

The primary impetus behind establishment of the CIS was to avert a collapse of interrepublican trade by maintaining economic, financial, and monetary cooperation between the former Soviet republics; facilitate market reform and liberalization; promote coordination in internal and external policies (the Alma-Ata Declaration); and prevent interrepublican conflicts through clear recognition of borders. However, the CIS does not

9. The Soviet break-up was not entirely peaceful, as the Caucasus and Tadjikistan saw their share of armed conflict and there has been the fighting in Chechnya inside the Russian Federation. Nonetheless, compared to what could have been, the post-Soviet order emerged with a minimum of bloodshed. The contrast with the bloody breakup of Yugoslavia is striking.

have any supranational powers—though obligations established under agreements are binding on member states—and consequently its exact role is uncertain.

As for the economic realm, the heads of state signed an agreement in 1993 establishing an economic union based on free trade, harmonized monetary and foreign economic policies, and the fostering of direct production links. The Economic Union Treaty called for reduced internal tariffs, common external tariffs, and a system for payments and settlements. The CIS Free Trade Zone Treaty was signed in 1994, and in 1999 a protocol replaced the existing bilateral free trade zone with a multilateral one, a step toward the creation of an economic union. However, CIS cooperation initiatives were hampered throughout the 1990s, especially by the lack of effective enforcement powers. Intra-CIS trade actually declined, whereas trade with the outside world, especially the European Union, increased.

In response, Belarus, Kazakhstan, Kyrgyzstan, Russia, and Tajikistan formed the CIS Customs Union in 1996, and in 2000 they signed the Eurasian Economic Community (EEC) integration treaty to augment the customs union with sanction and enforcement capability. The EEC is modeled in part on the European Union, North American Free Trade Agreement, and Mercosur, and it includes its own court, the power to dismiss noncooperative member states, and negotiating responsibilities with organizations such as the WTO. It seeks recognition by the United Nations as a regional international organization. It is not clear whether the EEC will be more successful than prior CIS economic cooperation efforts.

Diversity and Cooperation versus Regional Blocs

This brief survey of the world's regions, regional organizations, and efforts at cooperation depicts an extraordinarily diverse scenario worldwide. Trade and economic interests drive the most advanced types of cooperation, which take the form of common markets or free trade zones. Regional development banks play a significant role and provide certain regional public goods in terms of the environment, infrastructure, and regional knowledge. Latin America may be the most well-defined region geographically and culturally, although it is ethnically diverse. The other regions face more difficult border problems. Many countries belong to more than one region—Algeria, for example, is an Arab, African, and Moslem country. Australia is Asian up to a point. Armenia and Azerbaijan are hard to classify. Mexico is very much a Latin American nation but is now part of a North American Free Trade Area and deeply integrated with the US economy. The Ukraine is the second largest country in the CIS but has its sights set on the European Union. Spain is clearly part of the European Union but is also a leading Latin country with strong economic and emotional ties to Latin America.

Attempts to initiate and strengthen regional cooperation have been substantial and widespread. However, in most regions, cooperation outside of the sphere of trade and development banking remains rudimentary. Most nation-states big and small still face the world as well as the globalization process essentially as individual nation-states. Many, particularly in Africa, have barely been able to become nation-states. Across the world are countries of vastly different sizes (consider China and Malta), degrees of development, military and economic capabilities, and regional affinities.

With such glaring differences across the world, the formation of regional trade blocs could indeed have a detrimental effect on the progress of global trade and economic integration, especially if the WTO system breaks down. On the whole, however, regional cooperation has promoted economic opening and improved growth performance. Regionalism is not, however, an alternative to an overarching framework of political and economic governance. Moreover, Huntington's cohesive civilizational blocs have not, so far at least, materialized. Regional cooperation has slowly progressed in all of the world's regions, particularly in Asia, but nowhere has it taken, or is it taking, the form of real regional political integration.

Nowhere, that is, except in Europe. The exceptional postwar story of Europe is worth discussing separately in any analysis directed toward "better" globalization. Even with its successes, however, Europe entered a new phase of turmoil with the enlargement to the east in 2004. In sum, the extraordinary story of Europe, postwar to date, has a significance beyond the continent that is profoundly linked to the debate over the nature of globalization and the forms that global governance might take in the future.

The European Adventure

The keynote speech to the Annual Congress of Young European Entrepreneurs in Istanbul in June 2002 focused on the upcoming European

Constitutional Convention. The audience of some 800 strong included young people from all over the world. Suddenly during the speech, two young women in the second row of the conference hall stood up together, and one raised her hand and shouted: "I am French and she is German. We are together and we will never again be at war!"

The audience erupted in applause, and as the speaker I was happy to have been interrupted in this way. Resuming my speech, I said that many young men and women from Greece and Turkey—two countries also mired historically in disputes but one now a member of the European Union and the other a candidate for membership—shared just such contemporary European values and also were ready to raise their hands in the same way.[10]

Two years later, a draft constitution was indeed approved at the European Summit, but the atmosphere was far less encouraging. Michael Howard, leader of the British Conservative Party, flatly declared: "I don't want to live in a country called Europe." Turnout for elections for the European Parliament in early June 2004 declined to 45.7 percent of eligible voters from nearly 50 percent in 1999, and eurosceptic populist-nationalist parties increased their share in some countries by as much as 15 to 20 percent.[11]

Clearly, Europe arrived at a crossroads in 2004–05 that lay somewhere between the idealism of the two enthusiastic young women in the conference hall and the array of feelings—ranging from apathy to defiance—that at any moment could block or undermine the momentum toward greater European integration that has been moving forward since the 1950s.

Today three different visions of Europe are competing to shape the future. First is the vision of a Europe consisting of a large customs union, with the old nation-states retaining most of their sovereignty. For those sharing that vision—let us call them the "sovereignists"—some of the power that has gradually moved to the European institutions in Brussels should be handed back to the nation-states. The European Union would

10. At the time of writing in July 2004, Greece won the European soccer championship in Lisbon. Polls taken by the media in the days before the final game reported that the public was rooting for Greece—in Turkey!

11. For more on the European elections, see www.elections2004.eu.int/ep-election/sites/en/results1306/index.html. On the European Union draft agreement, see http://europa.eu.int/futurum/documents/other/oth250604_2_en.pdf. Appendix C provides a summary of the proposed European Constitution.

continue as a loose association of nations with minimal pooling of sovereignty. The sovereignists do not foresee a common fiscal policy, see little
merit in the euro, do not support a European defense and security policy,
and see no point in having a European constitution. They want to mini-
mize whatever can be decided by majority or qualified majority voting in
the European Council, which is the highest decision-making body of the
European Union. They oppose more power for the European Parliament
and want to curb existing powers of the European Commission. The sovereignists strongly emphasize national governments as the constituent
units and see all European institutions as deriving their legitimacy solely
from decisions taken by the national governments.

Sovereignists can be found on both the right and left end of the political spectrum. The more extreme sovereignists on the right are militant
nationalists who do not regard global governance any more favorably
than European governance. The more moderate majority sovereignists
do not espouse old-style militant nationalism and are sometimes favorably disposed to limited global governance within the framework of
global institutions such as the United Nations, the Bretton Woods institutions, or the WTO. Many heads of government, particularly in the
United Kingdom and Eastern Europe, could be classified as such moderate sovereignists. The moderate sovereignists in many European countries are generally favorable to a strong alliance with the United States.
They basically accept an international system led by the US superpower
and view this acceptance as a requirement of realism. They are not particularly obsessed with *defining* Europe, culturally or otherwise, nor are
they keen to draw Europe's *borders*. The moderate sovereignists have
been favorable to enlargement in general, and they have no fundamental
objection to Turkey joining the union, although some of them have
catered to popular fears of immigration and diversity. The moderate sovereignists would not be averse to having other countries join the EU in the
long term, such as the Ukraine and the nations of the Caucasus, even
though these countries have not been officially accepted as candidates.

A second vision of Europe is diametrically opposed to the vision of the
sovereignists. I shall call those who share the second vision "superstate
Europeans." The superstate Europeans essentially want to see Europe
evolve into a new 21st century integrated superstate, reproducing the
characteristics of the old nation-states with what would amount to a federal government, an army, a common currency, and common economic
policies. It is important to emphasize that many of the superstate Europeans do not explicitly formulate their goal to be a federal superstate. It

is, rather, that they cannot help but conceptualize the future of Europe in terms of a superstate. Many, if asked, will deny that they want a superstate, but they nonetheless argue about Europe as if it was to become one.

Some of the superstate Europeans, numerous in Germany, for example, have a basically pacifist world view and are not keen on trying to make Europe a military superpower. Others, more numerous in France, would like to see a United Europe emerge explicitly as a political-military counterweight to the United States. The superstate Europeans are concerned about Europe's borders: they would like to have final clarity on where Europe ends, or where it begins. Thinking of Europe essentially as a nation-state, it is very important for them, therefore, to describe the territory as well as the nature of this superstate. Because they know that a nation-state has always been in need of national identity, they are quite concerned with describing "European identity." Given that there is no European language and given Europe's ethnic diversity, the search for a European identity tends to emphasize history and religion. In many ways the superstate Europeans think of European integration *as if* it were a modern version of the unification by Bismarck of the German states in the mid-19th century, which is to say as the creation of a larger new state from a number of smaller existing states. Since old-style national identity based on language and some idea of joint ethnicity cannot work to define Europe, there are attempts to rely on Christianity and on historical images and emotions. Often these are historical images of enemies and wars fought for the "nation" or for the "faith." The superstate Europeans rightly sense that any successful political project must be backed by some emotional energy. Thankfully, in 21st century Europe it should not be necessary to ask people to die for a "cause" anymore, but purely economic considerations or the building of common bureaucratic institutions are not sufficient to create a strong sense of community and common purpose.[12] The problem is that the superstate Europeans search for the required emotional energy almost exclusively *in the past*. A politician in France recently declared that to be European it was not sufficient to be Christian, but one had to have been Christian for at least 15 centuries![13] The superstate Europeans tend to want to define Europe in opposition to the "other," just as old-style nationalists did with respect to the nation.

12. There is a worrisome recent tendency to imply that that "something" is Christianity, and that Europe should be "emotionally Christian." This goes beyond practicing a certain faith, and acceptance of such a view would destroy the secular nature of European democracy.

13. Jean-Louis Bourlanges quoted in *Le Monde*, March 25, 2004.

There is emerging a third, forward-looking vision of Europe. Such a vision is much more difficult to define precisely because it is trying to invent something new that cannot be easily described by an analogy with something that exists or has existed in the past. It is most appropriate to describe those who are attempting to formulate this third vision as the "21st century Europeans." These Europeans understand that it is neither possible nor desirable to reenact the history of the 18th and 19th centuries in the 21st century. The feeling of "belonging" that a European citizen of today must experience cannot have an adequate source in ethnicity and/or religion, but must derive primarily from shared values and a shared project for the future. The 21st century Europeans are inspired by *constitutional patriotism* championed by Jürgen Habermas, Germany's premier philosopher. Among European statesmen, the most articulate proponent of constitutional patriotism is German foreign minister Joschka Fischer. Fischer's association with Habermas dates back to the 1980s, when they ran seminars together in the back room of "Dionysus," a Greek restaurant in Frankfurt (Jan-Werner Müller, 2004). This kind of patriotism is closer to the liberal version of American patriotism than classical German patriotism based on race and language. American patriotism has been mostly "modern" in that it has not been based on race or religion. The new European patriotism referred to here is different from American patriotism, however, in that it does not need to go as far as the latter in identifying a clear territory with the "nation," and it needs to go further than American patriotism in associating emotions with an ongoing project of "governance building" as Europe both integrates and expands.[14] The 21st century Europeans believe that Europe must be negotiated and built continuously. Their vision is dynamic and oriented toward the future; while learning from the past, Europe should not try to re-create a real or imagined past. Their vision of 21st century Europe is also not at all directed *against* the "other" or the enemy. On the contrary, these Europeans are keenly aware of the fact that the European project was needed precisely because Europe wanted to *overcome* the images of

---

14. Note that there are elements of a nonterritorial patriotism also in America despite the fact that the United States has a well-defined geographical territory. American patriots often appeal to "liberty" enshrined in the constitution as a universal value to believe in and fight for. A strong belief in individual freedom is a source of American patriotism not linked to ethnicity, territory, or religion. Americans often conceptualize their going to war as a defense of universal "freedom" without there being a clear territorial threat to the American nation-state.

the past, the fear of the "other," and the emotions that had, again and again, led to war and even genocide. The 21st century Europeans feel part of the world[15] and are inspired by the Kantian tradition of searching for universal and perpetual peace. Europe is not only a project of peace among Europeans, but also a project of peace for the world, with Europe as a power standing for peace. Many of the great statesmen who laid the foundations of Europe 60 years ago were in fact 21st century Europeans, as illustrated by the quote from Jean Monnet at the beginning of this chapter.

It is useful to distinguish between these three visions for the sake of clarifying the arguments and structuring the debate, although when one analyzes the views of any one particular political leader in Europe, it is often possible to find a mixture of these visions rather than just one vision in its pure form. The three visions have different implications for the many practical policy decisions that the European Union has to make in the 2005–06 period, when the new constitution will be debated and voted on, with the vote taking the form of a referendum in many countries.

The sovereignists could do without a constitution. They generally support the long since agreed-upon common trade policy and agree, therefore, to the existing pooling of trade policy authority in Brussels with one European trade commissioner negotiating for the union. They fought hard at the Constitutional Convention in Brussels to preserve the prerogatives of the national governments and national parliaments and to prevent what they see as "creeping federalism." They tend to think in terms of traditional national interest as emphasized in the realist school of international relations theory. Thus, British sovereignists believe that British national interest requires a continuing special and privileged relationship with the United States and strong links with the Commonwealth. French sovereignists in the tradition of de Gaulle emphasize the need for independence from the United States and strong links to francophone Africa. They have been more "European" than their British counterparts, mainly because postwar circumstances allowed France to have a very strong influence on the European institutions and they saw Europe as a source of French power and influence. There are sovereignists in all European countries, and as just illustrated with reference to Britain and France, they do not necessarily pursue the same foreign or economic policy goals.

---

15. Timothy Garten Ash (2004, 91–93) recently drew attention to this contract between what he calls the "world nation" Europeans and the "patriots of transnational Europeanism."

They do share a common reluctance, however, to devolve greater authority to Brussels, and they jointly and largely successfully fought to restrain federalist tendencies during the constitutional discussions at the European Convention. They do not support any move toward single European representation in international organizations such as the United Nations.

The moderate sovereignist leaders will support a yes vote on the European Constitution at the occasion of the referenda and national parliamentary votes planned in 2005 and 2006. The moderates are generally strong enough in their parties, and their views will carry the parliamentary groups. They will be in conflict, however, with the more extreme sovereignist and populist groups, and the behavior of voters in the case of referenda is harder to predict. The moderate sovereignists have a problem. They cannot put much enthusiasm into a campaign for Europe. They do not really have a vision that can capture the imagination. What they have to offer is "practicality:" it is difficult to carry on with the day-to-day business of government in Europe without some of the unifying and simplifying elements of the new constitution. It is impractical to rotate the chair of the European Council every six months between 25 or more members, it is unwieldy to carry on with a commission of 25 or more members, and it is unreasonable to have a single country block an otherwise widely supported council decision. But there is little emotion or enthusiasm behind the moderate sovereignist stance, and this may lead to major problems with moderate voters who may simply abstain as many did during the elections for the European Parliament. The more extreme sovereignists, on the contrary, will be able to put emotion (negative emotion!) into their "no" campaign and draw their supporters to the polls.

The superstate Europeans did not achieve the stronger federal structures that they had hoped for in the draft European Constitution, but they still see the existing draft as a step forward and will, by and large, call for a yes vote. They are favorable to developing a common security and defense policy and would like to have Europe speak with one voice in international affairs. They would support a powerful single European seat in the United Nations Security Council as proposed in chapter 3. They are also favorable to merging the European seats on the boards of the Bretton Woods institutions. They are strongest in "core" Europe, i.e., France, Germany, the Benelux countries, and the Mediterranean countries, although they have been losing ground as the economies of most of these countries have slowed down and the European project has not been able to deliver economic growth and full employment in the last decade. They are also facing resurgent nationalism and a negative reaction to what is perceived as bureaucratic and excessively centralized decisions in Brussels. The superstate Europeans correctly perceive the huge gains Europe has made in terms of creating an area of peace and political stability, and they rightly stress that while Europe may be experiencing some economic difficulties, it is still a very prosperous region with social services and a standard of living largely unrivaled elsewhere in the world. They sense, also correctly, that Europe needs an emotional push, a renewed political energy to consolidate the gains of the past, to absorb the 10 countries that joined in 2004, and to achieve a new sense of purpose and cohesion in and around the European institutions.

The problem is that the vision of the superstate Europeans is increasingly inspired by the past. Their appeals to religion, culture, and nostalgia are unable to capture the spirit of our times. There is no European nation in the sense that there are French, Spanish, German, or Polish nations, and it will not be possible to create one in the traditional sense. Moreover, in their effort to encourage a European identity based on past allegiances and religious feelings, they stress differences with the "other." That "other" is sometimes the United States, but more often Islam. The superstate Europeans sometimes begin to share dangerous common ground with the populist nationalists. By doing so, they run the danger of giving credence and respectability to racism and xenophobia and actually facilitating the propaganda of the extreme sovereignists who appeal to some of the same emotions, although with very different aims.

The 21st century Europeans, or the patriots of transnational Europeanism, to use Timothy Garten Ash's term, have the task of building a renewed allegiance and enthusiasm for the European project in a different way. They share both a sense of achievement and European purpose with the superstate Europeans. They know that to progress, Europe needs a new constitution with a greater role for qualified majority voting, a smaller and more effective commission, and greater support for and legitimacy of the European institutions. They also know that a political project cannot be successful without an emotional commitment and an appeal that can mobilize and succeed in ensuring participation. Practical rules and directives are not enough to generate such mobilization. The challenge for the 21st century Europeans is to define the European project, following Jean Monnet, in a truly progressive and dynamic way as *Europe's contribution to building the 21st century.*

The new progressive Europe cannot be built on old identities or old ways of thinking. Europe must contribute to global governance, not undermine it by seeking to build a regional bloc based on some form of cultural or religious nationalism and exclusion. Europe should not be built "against" other regions, other cultures, or imagined enemies. Europe should not try to exclude, but include. Europe should celebrate diversity, not encourage the building of new psychological walls.

For Europe to be able to function within and play that supportive role for global governance, it does need something like the new draft constitution, however imperfect the compromise draft that emerged from the convention may be. The constitutional draft was, of course, an imperfect compromise. It would have been desirable to produce a simpler text. It would also have been desirable to give the European Parliament the right to actually nominate the president of the commission in a somewhat more open and "Eurodemocratic" process than having the council decide who should be nominated. The parliament today has little choice but to accept the council's choice, which is another factor reducing the democratic visibility and effectiveness of the European Parliament.[16] Nonetheless, the constitution would be a major step forward. Europe does need more qualified majority voting in the highest decision-making bodies. It does need greater cohesion in foreign and defense policies. The existing draft can be the basis for progressively greater integration in the medium term. As proposed in chapter 3, the European Union should speak and vote with one voice on the UN Security Council. It should do the same on the proposed United Nations Economic and Social Security Council. The European Union should also increasingly pool its foreign assistance. In the economic domain, greater Europe-wide coordination of fiscal policy is highly desirable, and a rethinking of the stability pact allowing stronger Eurozone-wide, procyclical fiscal policy is necessary. European budgetary arrangements should eventually be revised to allow some part of the European budget to be financed by a Europe-wide tax. On all these issues, the superstate or federalist Europeans are right. On other matters, it is quite possible, however, that judicious use of the principle of subsidiarity would lead to some competences being given back to national and regional authorities. The drive to create the single European market

16. With Valdo Spini, an Italian socialist, I proposed an amendment to the constitutional draft that would have required that 10 percent of all eurodeputies coming from at least a third of the member countries nominate a candidate for the presidency of the commission. The proposal was not accepted by the convention.

has led to some excessive regulation and standardization. Was it really necessary, for example, to exactly define what is "chocolate" at the European level? Are such European standards really necessary? Could one not let countries set some of the rules and standards in line with local traditions and tastes, without doing serious harm to the dynamism and integration of the European economy?

Europe and Global Governance

The most important characteristic of 21st-century Europe is that it should be built as part of rather than in opposition to efforts to support better and more effective global governance. The building of a strong Europe is not an attempt to build a new empire, but an endeavor to end, once and for all, the age of empires.

Were Europe to have a common seat and thus a stronger voice in the United Nations, for example, the European voice could call for strengthening international institutions and the application of international law. Europe should encourage and support similar moves toward improved cooperation in and among Asia, Latin America, and Africa, promoting a vision of a world integrated for the common good, rather than one divided into antagonistic geopolitical blocs. The borders of either Europe or of the European Union cannot be defined forever, just as the borders of many other areas of cooperation will remain fluid. Moreover, cultural, economic, and political borders may not neatly coincide. Spain can have strong ties to Latin America and be fully European, Turkey can have strong ties to Central Asia and the Middle East and be European, and the United Kingdom can be European but with strong ties to North America. More cooperation in Asia, Latin America, Africa, and other regions would facilitate more effective global governance. The belief that should drive forward Europe's political progress is the possibility of "better" globalization, the pride of being an example of multilevel governance for the world to see, the extension of democracy, and the pooling of sovereignty that can make the years ahead an age of peace and shared prosperity.

*National Politics
and Global Choices*

Human progress is neither automatic nor inevitable. We are now faced with the
fact that tomorrow is today. We are confronted with the fierce urgency of now. In
this unfolding conundrum of life and history, there is such a thing as being too
late. Procrastination is still the thief of time. Life often leaves us standing bare,
naked and dejected with a lost opportunity. The "tide in the affairs of men" does
not remain at the flood; it ebbs. We may cry out desperately for time to pause in
her passage, but time is deaf to every plea and rushes on. Over the bleached bones
and jumbled residues of numerous civilizations are written the pathetic words:
Too late.

MARTIN LUTHER KING JR.
Where Do We Go from Here: Chaos or Community? 1967

During the days Martin Luther King spoke the words above, American society faced the challenge of integrating African Americans
into the mainstream of American life. Serious socioeconomic problems
still affect the African American community, but America succeeded to a
great extent in meeting the challenge—an African American is about to
succeed another as secretary of state of the United States. Had America not
taken up the challenge, it is likely that it would have been greatly weakened by internal strife. Today the challenge is better global governance.

The global order that will emerge in the world of the 21st century—the
nature of the United Nations, the rules or lack of them governing intervention, the future of our environment, the evolution of international
financial institutions, and the World Trade Organization—will be decided
on by national policymakers, acting first and foremost as politicians
mindful of the expectations of their electorates. That is still a fact of life
and will remain so for a long time. Even in the European Union, which
has traveled much further than others toward supranational decision
making—politics remains a very local affair.

How, then, could national politics interact with global trends in a way

226

that promotes acceptance of the reforms proposed throughout this book? The proposals are concrete and go beyond generalities, although it is their fundamental nature rather than their exact form that matters. The United Nations Security Council could consist of 16 rather than 14 members and include Brazil and Nigeria or South Africa as permanent members. There could be five rather than four variables determining voting strengths, with the fifth being contributions to a standing UN peacekeeping force in addition to general military capability. What is essential is to go beyond just adding new members to the Security Council and build a voting system that reflects the world at the beginning of the 21st century and is legitimately perceived as such. No matter how one gets there, only a change that sweeping will stop the political paralysis that so often constrains the United Nations in the face of pressing challenges.

The security challenges are immediate. Environmental challenges are longer term but just as real. Neglect of global warming over the next two decades could create huge social and economic costs later in this century. Much of the environmental problems are distributional: we have or will have enough knowledge and technology to deal with most resource shortages and can even improve the quality of the environment, but we have to agree on the policies to achieve specific objectives and compromise on the sharing of the costs and benefits.

What I have referred to throughout this book as "better" globalization also depends on a truly development-oriented round of trade talks to unleash new dynamics of growth and start encompassing services, an area with huge potential for large global efficiency gains. This implies winning the battle for the hearts and minds of people the world over on trade issues by clarifying what is at stake and covering the costs of short-term adjustment. Only then can the long-term benefits be realized.

Chapter 5 proposed a Stability and Growth Facility under the auspices of the International Monetary Fund (IMF), although a strengthened World Bank might be even better suited to manage such a facility, with the IMF working in cooperation by focusing on surveillance and acute crisis management. Whatever shape and under whoever's umbrella the facility functions, what is essential is to recognize that a significant number of emerging-market economies desperately need to escape the debt trap that has constrained their development for so many years, both due to their own past imprudence and because capital markets have exacerbated volatility and surges in the cost of carrying debt.

The obstacles confronting the world's poorest countries are so daunting that a gradual approach to solving them simply will not work. Only a concerted "big push" strategy, as described in chapter 6, will enable these nations to become part of a growing world economy. Meeting or even getting close to the United Nations' Millennium Development Goals requires a substantial increase in resources targeted to development. Some version of a small international development tax in the form of a surcharge on profits or an environmental tax could provide some of the additional resources required both to keep the cost of borrowing from the Stability and Growth Facility close to the LIBOR rate, and to finance the "big push" strategy to help the poorest of the poor with only concessional resources.

The "frontloading" of development assistance required for the "big push" strategy would clearly benefit from the idea put forward by Gordon Brown, British chancellor of the Exchequer, to authorize borrowing guaranteed by future aid allocations in rich country budgets, which would increase the resources that can be quickly deployed in support of more rapid and equitable development. Regular development-oriented allocations of special drawing rights (SDRs), as proposed by financier Georges Soros and others, represent another potential approach to raising resources.

These are all important details—and in global affairs as much as anywhere, one must remember that sometimes the devil can be in the detail. But the foundation upon which those details can be negotiated must be an unwavering willingness to reform the international system in such a way that (i) the security sphere is governed by international rules based on explicit consent and measured by methods that are inclusive and reflect democratic values, and (ii) economic globalization is embedded in institutions and policies that stabilize market forces, foster greater equity and fairness, and incorporate the poor, the disadvantaged, and the excluded into the global development process.

More effective, functional, and representative governance of the international system is critically important to the reform process. A renewed United Nations with top governance councils that are both effective in action and perceived as legitimate the world over must provide the integrating framework, but without adding on layers of bureaucracy that slow the ability of individual agencies to act decisively on a day-to-day basis. Table 9.1 compares the framework of governance—voting strengths—on the current UN Security Council with what would be the voting strengths on a renewed UN Security Council and a new UN Economic and Social Security Council as proposed in chapters 3 and 4.

Table 9.1 *Current UN Security Council versus proposed*
UN system voting strengths

| | *Voting strength under renewed UN system* | | |
Current Arrangements *UN Security Council*	*Permanent* *members* *(6 seats)*	*Transition* *UN Security* *Council*	*UN* *Economic* *and* *Social* *Security* *Council*
Permanent five with veto power			
United Kingdom	European Union	27.43	25.74
France			
United States	United States	22.91	17.78
	Japan	9.83	12.76
China	China	8.76	8.75
	India	4.65	6.28
Russian Federation	Russian Federation	3.44	1.53
Regional allocation (10 seats)	*Constituencies (8 seats)*		
Asia (2)	Other Asia (2)	8.10	9.87
Latin America, Caribbean, and Canada (2)	Latin America, Caribbean, and Canada (2)	6.67	8.47
	Arab League (1)	3.07	3.96
Africa (3)	Africa (2)	2.86	2.62
Western Europe and Other (2)			
Eastern Europe (1)	Other Europe (1)	2.29	2.24

Two key determining factors of the likelihood and the speed with which fundamental reform in the international system will take place in the years ahead are the direction taken by the United States following the November 2004 elections and the debate unfolding in Europe over the new constitution that must be ratified by referendum or parliamentary vote. The sections that follow examine how the choices that the United States and Europe make might interact with the behavior of other major regional players and with global political dynamics.

The Choice for the United States

The Iraq war and the events surrounding it have unleashed a strong, often passionate debate on global governance and national sovereignty in the

United States, a debate that one wishes could have taken place in the early 1990s when the Cold War ended.

As to what is at stake when the United States is involved, Zbigniew Brzezinski (2004, vii) might have put it best: "American power and American social dynamics, working together, could promote the gradual emergence of a global community of shared interest. Misused and in collision, they could push the world into chaos while leaving America beleaguered."

In an October 2003 lecture delivered at Chatham House in London, Brookings Institution president Strobe Talbott presented the key question as "whether the US recommits itself to the utility of collaborative institutions and consensual arrangements—not just as a participant, but as a leader."

Will the United States try to dominate the world relying primarily on unrivaled military might, and regard global institutions as potentially useful but nonessential tools to supplement its power as a nation-state? Or will Americans try to lead the world into building a 21st century order where nation-states will abide by rules under a reformed international system that reflects the current realities of relative power and democratic values?

US policy over the past decade has not been encouraging for those who hope that America will opt for leadership rather than domination. As discussed in chapter 3, the United States has tended to oppose proposals that imply some degree of shared sovereignty, whether it has been the Kyoto Protocol, the International Court of Justice, the Treaty to Ban Landmines, or the necessity to wait for UN Security Council authorization before invading Iraq.

Sometimes the United States has tried to justify its unwillingness to use the international cooperative framework by arguing that the existing system is ineffective. It is true, for example, that the intervention in Kosovo—which most would agree was desirable and successful—had to be carried out without UN Security Council authorization because a single veto would have stopped it. It could also be argued, although with less evidence and conviction, that any intervention in Iraq, regardless of the degree of international support, would have been blocked by one veto or another. That is precisely why comprehensive reform of the UN Security Council is so necessary—to prevent gridlock and facilitate a functional decision-making structure. A simple enlargement of the Security Council preserving current veto rights would not be sufficient—no UN-backed intervention in Kosovo would have been feasible even if Germany, Japan,

India, and some other nations had been permanent members. For the UN Security Council to truly become a useful tool of international governance, the most critical reform must be to restrict the ability of countries to use veto power, and to adopt a voting system that allows for strong and worldwide supermajorities to use the UN to act in a timely and decisive manner.

But instead of actively seeking reasonable reform, US policies over the past decade have been directed toward downplaying the potential role of international institutions and instead emphasizing reliance on sheer US power. For example, in her oft-quoted article "Promoting the National Interest," Condoleezza Rice (2000) argued against "the appeal . . . to notions of international law and norms, and the belief that the support of many states—or even better of institutions like the United Nations—is essential to the legitimate exercise of power." One might agree with her if the exercise of power is truly self-defense, or to prevent massive loss of life in ethnic cleansing or genocide. But who has the legitimacy to judge in a particular situation?

Despite the unprecedented military might of the United States, there is growing evidence that unilateralism is not working. The most telling paradox is that at a time when US military capability is unrivaled, Americans feel less safe than they have felt in decades. This domestic insecurity has become so strong that it is creating a new and difficult-to-manage trade-off between homeland security and civil rights.

It will become increasingly apparent that economic realities also will constrain unilateralism. Material progress has continued in the United States, but serious problems are looming ahead. The budget surpluses of the late 1990s have turned into record budget deficits, with the large financial burden the United States is shouldering for military operations in Iraq and elsewhere bearing some of the responsibility. The dollar has lost about 20 percent of its value with respect to other major currencies, and yet the trade and current account deficits are widening, signaling the danger of further declines in the value of the US currency. A steeply declining currency has never been a sign of particularly good economic health or national power. The military operations in Afghanistan and Iraq seem bogged down, despite huge financial expenditures, and there is serious concern that the United States might be overstretched. The emergence of a military challenge elsewhere (North Korea, for instance) would force the United States to take drastic measures to mobilize the human and financial resources necessary to meet such a threat. Further increases in military expenditures would add to the already worrisome fiscal situation. Arguably, all this does not amount to an increase in the security and well being of the United States.

Perhaps even more important than the issues enumerated above is that US policies have earned resentment throughout the world that can only be compared to sentiments that prevailed during the Vietnam War. Various polls conducted in 2003 and 2004 show an almost universal lack of support for US policies, with disapproval ratings often reaching beyond 60 or even 70 percent, even in countries traditionally friendly to the United States.[1] This situation cannot long endure for two fundamental and related reasons, one practical and the other ideological.

The practical reason is based on economic and financial matters, as the United States will have an ongoing need for peacekeeping operations in various parts of the world, not least in Afghanistan and Iraq. If and when a peace accord can finally be reached between Israelis and Palestinians, more peacekeepers will be needed to enforce and secure the agreement. What will happen in the broader Gulf area is anybody's guess, and further needs could well arise in places not easy to predict—peacekeeping and humanitarian intervention in Africa, and potential trouble spots in Central Asia, and perhaps even in parts of Latin America.

Some of these problem areas may be used by terror networks as bases and pose direct challenges to the physical or economic security of the United States. A Report of the Commission on Weak States and US National Security (2004) states, "The inability of many poor countries to effectively control and manage their territories makes them particularly susceptible to incursions by terrorist groups, illicit trafficking, crime, and the spread of disease. . . . Illicit transnational networks, particularly terrorist and criminal groups, exploit weak states for the porous borders and minimal law enforcement that allow the easy movement of money, people, drugs, and weapons. Somalia, for example, suffered the near-total disappearance of centralized authority after the failed UN and US intervention in 1992–93. Al-Qaeda moved in, using the country as a safe haven through the 1990s and as a staging ground and escape route for attacks in Kenya as recently as 2002."

1. The Pew Global Attitudes Project (2004) regularly reports on polls conducted worldwide. In the United Kingdom, France, and Germany, the respective percentages of respondents rating the United States favorably dropped from 75, 63, and 61 percent in the summer of 2002 to 58, 37, and 38 percent in the spring of 2004.

US political leaders will have difficulty asking taxpayers to carry most of the financial burdens of containing violence in the world all by themselves. The danger is that a vicious cycle will develop in which the more the United States attempts to intervene in various spots unilaterally, the greater the resistance to these interventions will become, the more the United States will feel threatened, and the more it will feel it has to intervene. Such a cycle would generate ever-increasing financial costs, weaken the US economy, lower the value of the dollar, and make it more expensive for the United States to have a global reach.

What Americans (and the world) now need and expect are results—a concrete return on the hundreds of billions of dollars spent and the thousands of lives lost or forever impaired: in the security domain alone, a secure new Afghanistan that no longer harbors terrorists, an Iraq that can function as a peaceful, independent state, a price of oil that does not go through the roof because of worries of what will happen in the major oil fields of the Gulf, a significant reduction in the threat of terror at home, a peaceful resolution of the Korean nuclear issues, prevention of genocidal mass killings in Africa, and effective control of the spread of weapons of mass destruction worldwide. Moreover, these "results" should be achieved while the United States is reducing its budget deficit and restoring fiscal balance!

It must be added that security does not just, or even primarily, depend on military operations or peacekeeping. Talbott (2001, 75–76) writes, "We must distinguish between, on the one hand, the assassins and those who mastermind and abet their operations and, on the other hand, their constituencies—those millions who feel so victimized by the modern world that they want us to be victims, too. . . . In the budget crunch ahead, there will be a temptation to squeeze down the very programs that will allow us to move from reactive, defensive warfare against the terrorists to a proactive, prolonged offensive against the ugly, intractable realities that terrorists exploit and from which they derive popular support, foot soldiers, and political cover."

In a medium-term perspective, the fight against global poverty and the effort to make globalization into a more equitable process is inseparable from the effort to achieve more physical security. The results Americans are looking for across the world ultimately depend less on military might or peacekeeping operations than on worldwide success in preventing state failure, promoting inclusive growth, and improving social conditions from which terror often emerges.

Such results are not forthcoming, however, without much greater international cohesion and cooperation, and without the willingness of many other countries to share the financial burden of the many interrelated tasks on which such cooperation depends. The US public is increasingly aware of the constraints of unilateralism and increasingly impatient for the results that, to date, have yet to arrive. Perhaps as the stalemate progresses, Americans will become more receptive to an honest message that explains why sharing the burden in terms of resources also requires a willingness to share decision-making power and responsibilities.

In his now famous commencement address at American University in 1963, quoted in chapter 2 this book, US president John F. Kennedy said that "world peace, like community peace, does not require that each man love his neighbor—it requires only that they live together in mutual tolerance, submitting their disputes to a just and peaceful settlement." Flash to some four decades later, and while the American public will want guarantees that the US homeland is secure, it is also likely to understand that true international cooperation, including submission by all to international law as formulated by a legitimate and realistic process, will actually enhance that security at lower cost to the US taxpayer. The message should be clearly and carefully articulated that the Cold War is over, and for the first time in history, nations and citizens the world over actually share a considerable common ideological ground. The overwhelming majority of people in the world have no basic antagonism to the social-liberal synthesis—the social model combining competitive markets, a caring and enabling state, and liberal democracy—so there is no fundamental or insuperable obstacle to greater international cooperation. For the first time in history, agreement to submit to international rules and law is possible.

However, the process of transforming international cooperation into a functional policy must be based to some degree on sharing sovereignty. The 1990s showed that it is not enough to overcome the deep ideological divisions of the Cold War; it is also necessary to accept and elaborate ways to reach decisions that require compromise. International decision making, always difficult under even the best of circumstances, is often virtually impossible if some form of super-majority voting is not an accepted part of the system. In a new world order, this means that at times the United States will be overruled by a supermajority. The US superpower will have to accept this reality if it wants international burden sharing and cooperation to work. Like other nations, the United States can ask for special safeguards to be built into the system. It can certainly ask that the system recognize US strength and influence, but it cannot ask to be the sole, unconstrained decision maker and at the same time expect the world to share the burden of carrying out these decisions.

The second, more ideological, reason why it is reasonable to believe that the United States would ultimately embrace a more multilateral approach within a reformed international order is that the United States itself is becoming much more global in the sense of being even more diverse and pluralistic than it already was. As Kagan (2004, 151) explains, American nationalism has never been "rooted in blood and soil, but rather is a universalist ideology that binds Americans together." Ever since the war of independence, Americans have thought of themselves as a vanguard of mankind willing to defend and fight for freedom throughout the world. As Kagan again reminds us, Benjamin Franklin declared at the time of the Revolutionary War, "We fight not just for ourselves but for all mankind." Similar messages abound in speeches by Woodrow Wilson, Harry Truman, John F. Kennedy, Jimmy Carter, and Ronald Reagan. American patriotism is not based on race, religion, or even language. It actually comes closer to Habermas' "constitutional patriotism" referred to in chapter 8. It is very hard for ethnic or religious nationalism to accept sharing of sovereignty with "others." It should be easier for Americans, who arguably are an aggregation of the world's diversity.

In 2010, about 40 million Americans of a population of 300 million will speak Spanish as their primary language, with strong attachments to Latin America. Close to another 35 million will be African Americans, whose living links to Africa may not be strong, but who have an emotional attachment to their roots and origin. Perhaps 20 million Americans will have strong attachments to Asia, and millions more American communities have substantial emotional links to virtually every part of the world.

In the economic domain, the share of foreign trade in US GDP has almost doubled over the last four decades, and US corporations produce an increasing share of output not only in Europe but also all over the world.

Taken together, all of these diverse factors will facilitate and necessitate US engagement in the world and make it easier for Americans to embrace multilateralism. With trade and travel has come an increase in globalization of the US lifestyle and culture. While global attention often focused on the export of American pop culture to the rest of the world, Americans themselves increasingly embrace elements of foreign cultures as well, ranging from sushi bars to hummus. A return by America to old-style isolationism, with which it at times flirted in the past, seems unlikely.

Globalization requires America to remain open to and engaged with the world, so it is likely that the combination of cultural-ideological factors and the practical need to share the burden of maintaining security with others will eventually lead the United States to choose leadership rather than unilateral domination.

The Choice for Europe

Europe also faces critical choices in the years ahead. Europe does not have the military power or the global political-military reach to even try to dominate the world. The European Union does not yet even have a common foreign and security policy. Europe may advance and develop its capabilities, but even if progress were much more rapid than expected, it would not rival the United States militarily for decades to come. Moreover, Europe's demography is different from that of the United States. The current EU-25 countries have a slowly declining population, as opposed to population growth of close to 1 percent in the United States.

On the other hand, Europe, as is often said, has tremendous "soft power," which is the ideological power that comes from setting an example that others want to emulate, from having taken steps to abolish war between nations that fought each other for centuries, and from showing how supranational governance mechanisms can work. The problem is that, just when the world most needs European engagement and leadership to help build the global governance architecture of the 21st century, weaknesses in many European economies, combined with complications inherent in enlarging the European Union, have turned much of the European policy debate inward. The preceding chapter contrasted three competing visions of Europe's future, and the debate over them will be particularly intense in 2005–06, when European parliaments and electorates will have to vote on the draft constitution. The outcome is uncertain and a real danger exists that the electorates in some countries will reject the draft constitution, prompting serious governance problems inside the EU. Even if such a constitutional crisis were to occur, the union is very unlikely to unravel—European institutions would try to continue functioning according to current rules, however inadequate they have become for the much larger post-2004 European Union. But such developments would definitely make it more difficult for Europe to play a strong and constructive global role.

In the coming years, Europeans will have to decide on the different visions of the future elaborated upon in chapter 8 of this book. The vision of the superstate Europeans will not be successful because it is based on a totally unrealistic historical analogy. Europe cannot become a new 19th century, super nation-state where the identities of the French, the Germans, the Italians, the Poles, the British, etc. all merge into some type of a new euronationalism based on religion and culture. Such euronationalism simply does not exist, and the chances of it emerging are declining, not increasing. By force of demography, Europe like the United States is becoming more diverse: close to 16 million Muslims live in the 25 European Union nations, and immigration to the continent from all over the world will continue. Because of geography and existing family networks, many of the newcomers will be from the southern Mediterranean. Moreover, the union's enlargement to the east has increased other forms of diversity, brought new languages into the union, and increased links to the great Slav-Orthodox region. To turn these challenges into strength, Europe does need a renewed sense of mission instead of old-style nationalism, be it at a continental scale.

If the more extreme sovereignists are able to capitalize on dissatisfaction with recent European economic performance and anti-immigration fears, they may be able to channel local and national reflexes against globalization into an "anti-Europe" vote, which would arrest the progress Europe has made for decades toward greater cohesion and workable sovereignty-sharing mechanisms. That would leave Europe as a large common market, with some countries also sharing a currency, and perhaps a tendency for some countries to try to form islands of enhanced cooperation, although this would be difficult without a common framework. Without some of the institutional changes foreseen in the draft constitution—such as a stronger and longer-term council presidency, a relatively powerful EU foreign minister, a more sensible rule of qualified majority decision making, and a stronger and more streamlined commission more directly accountable to the EU Parliament—Europe and its expanded union would have less cohesion and decision-making capability than it had when it was a union of 15 countries. Europe's progress toward a flexible, multilevel, and postmodern form of supranational governance would be stalled. The European Union would not cease to function altogether, but it would be weaker than in the preceding two decades. The danger of gridlock would increase both on internal European issues and on global issues. It would be unlikely, for example, that such a Europe could agree to joint representation in the renewed UN Security

Council and the new UN Economic and Social Security Council proposed in chapter 3 of this book. It would be impossible for such a Europe to develop a strong and independent military capability.

For all these reasons, the United States would not be able to find in Europe the strong and capable partner willing and able to share the burdens of global governance and policymaking with which a United States more inclined toward multilateralism would want to work—a weak and indecisive Europe would not be helpful to US multilateralists. On the other hand, the frustrations that would be linked to continued European weakness and inability to act could exacerbate anti-American feelings among Europeans, leading to less cooperation and perhaps low-level confrontation.

If Europeans embrace the third vision appropriate to meet the challenges of the 21st century, they will approve a European Constitution or something close to it. Europe would reorganize itself so that governance of a union of 28-plus countries could actually function. An increasing number of policy decisions at the European Union level would be taken by the qualified majority foreseen in the constitution. Europe would move toward much stronger cohesion in overall fiscal and macroeconomic policies and a more coordinated foreign and defense policy. At the same time, regional and local power could be strengthened on matters where there is really no need for interference or centralist directives from Brussels. This increased cohesion would not be based on 19th century nationalism attempting to define itself as an antagonist of the United States, or "against" the Muslim world or China, but rather as an effort to give public policy the power and instruments with which to address economic and social problems whose solutions lay in the supranational domain. This could be seen as a vanguard effort to build the global governance needed in the 21st century. Talk about Europe as a "Christian fortress" would cease and give way to the celebration of European diversity and tolerance and to the recognition that the continent will be multi-ethnic and multireligious. There would be increasing emphasis on Europe's global responsibilities. This Europe not only of nations but also of people could be more cohesive precisely because it accepts diversity and turns it into strength.

In a strategy paper presented at the June 2003 European Summit in Athens, Javier Solana called on Europe to assume its global responsibilities and help strengthen multilateralism by accepting certain sacrifices leading to a more equitable distribution of power in the international system and a more effective European capability to act. Specifically, he urged the individual European nations to speak with one coordinated voice in such global entities as the United Nations, the Bretton Woods institutions, and the World Trade Organization. By working together, the European nations could play a critical role in building stronger bridges of cooperation to other parts of the world.

Assuming Europeans accept the 21st century vision for their future, European borders would probably expand slowly beyond Romania and Bulgaria (2007) and Croatia and Turkey (2010 and 2014) to include the western Balkans (2015–2017?) and then perhaps the Ukraine, depending both on progress made by the new internal European governance mechanisms and on what happens in the neighboring countries. Such a Europe would also develop advanced forms of cooperation with the southern Mediterranean countries, building on the strong common cultural heritage of the three great monotheistic religions and the Greek-Roman-Arab-Jewish contributions to science and European thought, as well as the huge potential of a Euro-Mediterranean economic cooperation zone as a source of growth and shared prosperity. Such a Europe would continue to be an example for other parts of the world, and would be a strong, credible, and attractive partner to a United States that seeks support for building the governance mechanisms to achieve more secure and equitable globalization. The European Union would also need to develop a close special relationship with the Russian Federation. Such a Europe also would have a sense of purpose that would marginalize the kind of knee-jerk anti-Muslim, anti-American, or anti-immigrant feeling that is prevalent today. Clearly, the 21st century vision is one of a Europe that would be better not only for Europeans, but also for the United States, the Middle East, and the entire world.

The United States, Europe, and the World

The animosity that has emerged over Iraq between old and close allies has focused much attention on the future of transatlantic relations and the need to repair the damage already inflicted. But analyses of the situation diverge considerably. Robert Kagan (2004) writes, "It is time to stop pretending that Europeans and Americans share a common view of the world, or even that they occupy the same world. On the all-important question of power—the efficacy of power, the morality of power, the desirability of power—American and European perspectives are diverging."

Zbigniew Brzezinski (2004, 222), on the other hand, argues that the principal divergence of opinion is within the United States itself between those who want to exercise power to dominate—the majority, according to Kagan, which Brzezinski would dispute—and internationalists who want to lead not by the sheer use of power, but by dwelling on common interests and values. Brzezinski also emphasizes the crucial importance of US-European cooperation: "A genuine US-EU transatlantic alliance, based on a shared global perspective, must be derived from a similarly shared understanding of the nature of our era, of the central threat the world faces, and of the role and mission of the West as a whole."

Having watched the situation evolve in Iraq and the direction of the debate over it in the United States, Kagan, in the afterword he wrote for the second 2004 edition of his book, ends up proposing a renewed US-European alliance centered on the North Atlantic Treaty Organization (NATO) as a way to solve the transatlantic divide and exercise worldwide power more effectively.

"To address today's global threats Americans will need the legitimacy that Europe can provide," Kagan (2004, 158) writes, but "right now many Europeans are betting that the risks from the axis of evil, from terrorism and tyrants, will never be as great as the risk of an American Leviathan unbound."

The first half of 2004 saw renewed emphasis on both sides of the Atlantic on the crucial role of transatlantic cooperation. It became clear to many that the United States and Europe can achieve far more working together than acting alone, with recognition even by the US administration that unilateralism was not delivering results. The danger now is of an unrealistic new expectation that the combination of US and European power can achieve what US power alone could not, when in fact a far more constructive approach would be to examine dynamic and effective ways to build global governance.

An underlying theme of this book is that the victory of liberal democratic values over the totalitarianism that threatened the world in the 20th century has essentially rendered old-style power politics unworkable. It is not possible to have a basic belief in the equal value of human beings and at the same time behave as if this belief is relevant only inside certain national borders or transatlantic regions. In the 21st century, there can be no effective power without legitimacy; in turn, globalization is ensuring that there can be no legitimacy without recognizing the inherently equal value of human beings across the globe. Together, the United States and the European Union account for about 55 percent of world GDP and two-thirds of global military capability. Together, they are also a formidable source of ideas, art, culture, and science. But they can no longer be omnipotent. Their populations together represent less than 14 percent of the world population today and will account for no more than about 10 percent by 2020. This in itself should be sufficient to disqualify any argument that Europeans and Americans can simply rule the world. Legitimacy requires that it is the United Nations, not NATO, which must provide the framework for world security.[2] The same sense of legitimacy requires that international economic institutions such as the IMF, World Bank, and WTO be part of an architecture of global governance that takes into account the resources of the wealthy while providing sufficient weight and decision-making power as well to the large populations of Asia, Africa, and Latin America. The developing countries and their people must perceive international economic institutions as also their own.

The leadership of the United States and Europe is needed to build global governance, and no one is questioning that they will have a determining weight for years to come in any institutional structure that can and will function at the global level. Their joint weight should not be interpreted as total power, however. Moreover, the rules determining voting strengths should foresee periodic revision of the weights as the underlying indicators change with time. The Russian Federation remains a crucial player, and its inclusion in the building of a structure of peace must go beyond ceremonial invitations to G-7 meetings. In particular, Russia should not feel threatened by NATO. China and India are emerging as nations with the size and strategic importance that must be fully recognized in the international system. Incorporating them appropriately into the international architecture would help head off an antagonistic relationship to the West that might sow the seeds for potentially devastating future conflicts.

As made painfully clear by current events, including the Middle East and the Arab world in the structure of global governance is particularly urgent, although this will be much more difficult than including China and India because of the lack of cohesion in the Arab world itself. Still, no effort should be spared to encourage progress toward such cooperation

2. This does not preclude the possibility for NATO to act as an instrument of the UN Security Council, using its capacity for multilateral military action with the endorsement of an explicit Security Council resolution.

and to build the economic, cultural, and religious bridges that would allow the Middle East to become part of progressive globalization. Latin America also must be a strong participant in the new global institutional architecture and, particularly in the economic domain, must receive the support that will allow its nations to reduce excessive debt and start growing more rapidly than in the recent past.

Finally, Africa remains at the heart of the challenge of overcoming exclusion and building a process of all-inclusive globalization. It is a continent that still bears the scars of a history inflicted on it by others for centuries. The possibility of Africa as a peaceful and growing region will only happen if the world community is willing to finance a new and major "big push" that substantially increases investment in the continent over a sustained period of time. Africans will have to be able to work with donors in a framework that is legitimate and combines effective conditionality with local leadership and peer review. Moreover, the United Nations, in cooperation with the African Union, will have to intervene much more quickly and decisively whenever local or national governance breaks down and millions of lives are threatened.

Legitimacy also requires that governments that want to have a say in the international system themselves be able to claim domestic legitimacy. Over the past two decades, democracy and human rights have progressed in Latin America, Eastern Europe, and many parts of Asia and Africa. As argued in chapter 3 when discussing new arrangements for the UN Security Council, it is reasonable to expect and to encourage positive interaction between the global spread of democratic institutions within nation-states and the willingness of the most powerful countries to accept greater power sharing in the international system. The spread of democracy around the world is making global governance more legitimate and acceptable. Conversely, insisting on democratic standards appears more justified if the international system itself becomes more democratic.

Humanity has technological resources and know-how today that are developing with a speed that surpasses the most fantastic dreams. Together with very visible forms of diversity, there is also, more than ever before in history, a greater sense of a shared globe and shared values. Translating the tremendous potential for a safer and better world into reality will require forging a strong alliance between global civil society and progressive national politics that can articulate real choices, explain real costs and benefits attached to global options, and outline the institutional reforms necessary to break out of old straight jackets. What must be overcome is not just the always conservative power of privilege and entrenched positions, but also the old habits of thought and the analytical frameworks that no longer fit our reality. The greatest threat we face is our own fears. Divided we will not be able to overcome these fears. Together, enjoying our diversity and sharing our humanity, we can build the global institutions and global governance appropriate to the new world of the 21st century.

Voting Strengths of a Proposed UN Security Council[a]

Table 1. *Country and constituency voting strengths on proposed UN Security Council*

Countries	Factors determining voting strength				Result
	Contribution to global public goods budget	Population	GDP	Military capacity	Weighted vote
Permanent members					
United States	0.22000	0.04684	0.26662	0.39584	23.233
Japan	0.19468	0.02086	0.16712	0.05411	10.919
China	0.02053	0.20881	0.03306	0.03798	7.509
India	0.00421	0.16949	0.01468	0.01812	5.162
Russian Federation	0.01100	0.02377	0.01117	0.01786	1.595
EU and official					
candidates (28)	**0.36996**	**0.09042**	**0.31173**	**0.26901**	**26.028**
Germany	0.08662	0.01352	0.07994	0.04553	5.640
France	0.06030	0.00972	0.05341	0.05628	4.493
United Kingdom	0.06127	0.00965	0.03949	0.05198	4.060
Italy	0.04885	0.00951	0.03626	0.03479	3.235
Spain	0.02520	0.00675	0.02141	0.01119	1.614
Netherlands	0.01690	0.00263	0.01487	0.01009	1.112
Turkey	0.00372	0.01125	0.00562	0.01250	0.827
Sweden	0.00998	0.00146	0.00832	0.00754	0.683
Belgium	0.01069	0.00169	0.00950	0.00505	0.673
Austria	0.00859	0.00134	0.00798	0.00247	0.510
Greece	0.00530	0.00174	0.00428	0.00925	0.514
Poland	0.00461	0.00634	0.00425	0.00490	0.503
Denmark	0.00718	0.00088	0.00614	0.00397	0.454
Portugal	0.00470	0.00165	0.00389	0.00359	0.346
Finland	0.00533	0.00085	0.00493	0.00229	0.335
Ireland	0.00350	0.00063	0.00334	0.00128	0.219

a. Note that as the weights change over time, the resulting weighted vote could also change.

| Countries | Factors determining voting strength | | | | Result |
	Contribution to global public goods budget	Population	GDP	Military capacity	Weighted vote
Czech Republic	0.00183	0.00168	0.00169	0.00175	0.174
Romania	0.00060	0.00368	0.00102	0.00125	0.164
Hungary	0.00126	0.00167	0.00167	0.00110	0.143
Slovak Republic	0.00051	0.00089	0.00070	0.00055	0.066
Bulgaria	0.00017	0.00130	0.00039	0.00051	0.059
Slovenia	0.00082	0.00033	0.00071	0.00044	0.057
Luxembourg	0.00077	0.00007	0.00074	0.00024	0.045
Lithuania	0.00024	0.00057	0.00026	0.00031	0.035
Cyprus	0.00039	0.00012	0.00033	0.00000	0.021
Latvia	0.00015	0.00039	0.00020	0.00011	0.021
Iceland	0.00034	0.00005	0.00027	0.00000	0.016
Malta	0.00014	0.00006	0.00012	0.00004	0.009
Other Europe (19)	**0.02509**	**0.02031**	**0.02191**	**0.03437**	**2.542**
Switzerland	0.01197	0.00119	0.01007	0.00415	0.684
Israel	0.00467	0.00104	0.00315	0.01281	0.542
Ukraine	0.00039	0.00806	0.00143	0.00772	0.440
Norway	0.00679	0.00074	0.00511	0.00461	0.431
Belarus	0.00018	0.00164	0.00044	0.00194	0.105
Yugoslavia, Federal Republic	0.00019	0.00175	0.00000	0.00158	0.088
Croatia	0.00037	0.00072	0.00068	0.00083	0.065
Azerbaijan	0.00005	0.00133	0.00011	0.00000	0.037
Bosnia and Herzegovina	0.00003	0.00067	0.00020	0.00028	0.029
Georgia	0.00003	0.00086	0.00008	0.00011	0.027
Moldova	0.00001	0.00070	0.00009	0.00005	0.021
Albania	0.00005	0.00052	0.00010	0.00005	0.018
Estonia	0.00012	0.00022	0.00019	0.00014	0.017
Armenia	0.00002	0.00051	0.00012	0.00000	0.016
Macedonia, Former Yugoslav Republic	0.00006	0.00033	0.00015	0.00010	0.016
Liechtenstein	0.00005	0.00000	0.00000	0.00000	0.001
Andorra	0.00005	0.00001	0.00000	0.00000	0.002
Monaco	0.00003	0.00000	0.00000	0.00000	0.001
San Marino	0.00003	0.00000	0.00000	0.00000	0.001
Latin America, Caribbean and Canada (35)	**0.08158**	**0.09046**	**0.08196**	**0.04258**	**7.414**
Brazil	0.01523	0.02830	0.02362	0.01985	2.175
Canada	0.02813	0.00510	0.02123	0.01074	1.630

Countries	Factors determining voting strength				Result
	Contribution to global public goods budget	Population	GDP	Military capacity	Weighted vote
Mexico	0.01883	0.01632	0.01101	0.00339	1.239
Argentina	0.00956	0.00615	0.00829	0.00539	0.735
Colombia	0.00155	0.00707	0.00290	0.00000	0.288
Chile	0.00223	0.00253	0.00245	0.00262	0.246
Ecuador	0.00019	0.00211	0.00642	0.00000	0.218
Peru	0.00092	0.00433	0.00181	0.00000	0.176
Venezuela	0.00171	0.00404	0.00001	0.00000	0.144
Guatemala	0.00030	0.00192	0.00054	0.00024	0.075
Dominican Republic	0.00035	0.00140	0.00052	0.00000	0.057
Cuba	0.00043	0.00184	0.00000	0.00000	0.057
Uruguay	0.00048	0.00055	0.00061	0.00000	0.041
Bolivia	0.00009	0.00140	0.00024	0.00020	0.048
El Salvador	0.00022	0.00105	0.00033	0.00014	0.044
Haiti	0.00003	0.00134	0.00009	0.00000	0.036
Paraguay	0.00012	0.00088	0.00028	0.00000	0.032
Costa Rica	0.00030	0.00064	0.00045	0.00000	0.035
Honduras	0.00005	0.00108	0.00014	0.00000	0.032
Panama	0.00019	0.00048	0.00033	0.00000	0.025
Nicaragua	0.00001	0.00085	0.00000	0.00000	0.022
Jamaica	0.00008	0.00043	0.00017	0.00000	0.017
Trinidad and Tobago	0.00022	0.00022	0.00021	0.00000	0.016
Bahamas	0.00013	0.00005	0.00012	0.00000	0.008
Barbados	0.00010	0.00004	0.00007	0.00000	0.005
Guyana	0.00001	0.00013	0.00002	0.00000	0.004
Suriname	0.00001	0.00007	0.00001	0.00000	0.002
Belize	0.00001	0.00004	0.00002	0.00000	0.002
Saint Lucia	0.00002	0.00003	0.00002	0.00000	0.002
Antigua and Barbuda	0.00003	0.00001	0.00002	0.00000	0.001
Saint Vincent and the Grenadines	0.00001	0.00002	0.00001	0.00000	0.001
Grenada	0.00001	0.00002	0.00001	0.00000	0.001
Dominica	0.00001	0.00001	0.00001	0.00000	0.001
Kiribati	0.00001	0.00002	0.00000	0.00000	0.001
Saint Kitts and Nevis	0.00001	0.00001	0.00001	0.00000	0.001
Other Asia (40)	**0.05035**	**0.17932**	**0.06655**	**0.06391**	**9.003**
Republic of Korea	0.01796	0.00777	0.01894	0.01435	1.475
Indonesia	0.00142	0.03431	0.00641	0.00156	1.092
Australia	0.01592	0.00318	0.01388	0.00965	1.066

Countries	Factors determining voting strength				Result
	Contribution to global public goods budget	Population	GDP	Military capacity	Weighted vote
Iran, Islamic Republic	0.00157	0.01059	0.00328	0.01620	0.791
Pakistan	0.00055	0.02322	0.00216	0.00444	0.760
Bangladesh	0.00010	0.02189	0.00152	0.00094	0.611
Thailand	0.00209	0.01005	0.00517	0.00243	0.494
Philippines	0.00095	0.01286	0.00270	0.00000	0.413
Singapore	0.00388	0.00068	0.00328	0.00639	0.356
Vietnam	0.00021	0.01306	0.00092	0.00000	0.355
Malaysia	0.00203	0.00391	0.00332	0.00250	0.294
Myanmar	0.00010	0.00793	0.00000	0.00000	0.201
New Zealand	0.00221	0.00063	0.00210	0.00082	0.144
Democratic People's Republic of Korea	0.00010	0.00367	0.00000	0.00198	0.144
Sri Lanka	0.00017	0.00308	0.00049	0.00098	0.118
Uzbekistan	0.00014	0.00412	0.00038	0.00000	0.116
Kazakhstan	0.00025	0.00245	0.00076	0.00112	0.114
Afghanistan	0.00002	0.00447	0.00000	0.00000	0.112
Nepal	0.00004	0.00387	0.00017	0.00008	0.104
Cambodia	0.00002	0.00201	0.00012	0.00011	0.056
Kyrgyz Republic	0.00001	0.00081	0.00006	0.00031	0.030
Turkmenistan	0.00005	0.00089	0.00026	0.00000	0.030
Tajikistan	0.00001	0.00103	0.00008	0.00000	0.028
Papua New Guinea	0.00003	0.00086	0.00014	0.00000	0.026
Lao People's Democratic Republic	0.00001	0.00089	0.00007	0.00000	0.024
Brunei Darussalam	0.00034	0.00006	0.00017	0.00000	0.014
Mongolia	0.00001	0.00040	0.00003	0.00003	0.012
Fiji	0.00004	0.00013	0.00007	0.00000	0.006
Bhutan	0.00001	0.00014	0.00001	0.00000	0.004
Timor-Leste	0.00001	0.00012	0.00000	0.00000	0.003
Solomon Islands	0.00001	0.00007	0.00001	0.00000	0.002
Maldives	0.00001	0.00005	0.00002	0.00000	0.002
Vanuatu	0.00001	0.00003	0.00001	0.00000	0.001
Samoa	0.00001	0.00003	0.00001	0.00000	0.001
Micronesia	0.00001	0.00002	0.00001	0.00000	0.001
Tonga	0.00001	0.00002	0.00001	0.00000	0.001
Marshall Islands	0.00001	0.00001	0.00000	0.00000	0.001
Palau	0.00001	0.00000	0.00000	0.00000	0.000
Nauru	0.00001	0.00000	0.00000	0.00000	0.000
Tuvalu	0.00001	0.00000	0.00000	0.00000	0.000

Countries	Factors determining voting strength				Result
	Contribution to global public goods budget	*Population*	*GDP*	*Military capacity*	*Weighted vote*
Africa (43)	**0.00472**	**0.10327**	**0.01090**	**0.00834**	**3.181**
Nigeria	0.00042	0.02132	0.00098	0.00279	0.638
South Africa	0.00292	0.00710	0.00524	0.00332	0.464
Ethiopia	0.00004	0.01081	0.00023	0.00000	0.277
Democratic Republic of Congo	0.00003	0.00860	0.00013	0.00000	0.219
Tanzania	0.00006	0.00566	0.00020	0.00000	0.148
Kenya	0.00009	0.00505	0.00030	0.00037	0.145
Uganda	0.00006	0.00374	0.00024	0.00020	0.106
Ghana	0.00004	0.00324	0.00025	0.00008	0.090
Mozambique	0.00001	0.00297	0.00011	0.00018	0.082
Côte d'Ivoire	0.00010	0.00269	0.00036	0.00000	0.079
Cameroon	0.00008	0.00250	0.00031	0.00000	0.072
Madagascar	0.00003	0.00262	0.00012	0.00000	0.069
Zimbabwe	0.00007	0.00210	0.00021	0.00032	0.068
Angola	0.00001	0.00222	0.00021	0.00000	0.061
Burkina Faso	0.00002	0.00190	0.00009	0.00008	0.052
Senegal	0.00005	0.00160	0.00018	0.00012	0.049
Mali	0.00002	0.00182	0.00010	0.00000	0.048
Niger	0.00001	0.00184	0.00007	0.00000	0.048
Zambia	0.00002	0.00169	0.00012	0.00000	0.046
Malawi	0.00001	0.00173	0.00005	0.00002	0.045
Guinea	0.00003	0.00124	0.00014	0.00010	0.038
Rwanda	0.00001	0.00130	0.00007	0.00011	0.037
Burundi	0.00001	0.00114	0.00003	0.00020	0.034
Chad	0.00001	0.00130	0.00005	0.00000	0.034
Benin	0.00002	0.00106	0.00008	0.00000	0.029
Botswana	0.00012	0.00028	0.00021	0.00031	0.023
Sierra Leone	0.00001	0.00084	0.00002	0.00000	0.022
Togo	0.00001	0.00076	0.00004	0.00000	0.020
Eritrea	0.00001	0.00069	0.00002	0.00000	0.018
Central African Republic	0.00001	0.00062	0.00004	0.00000	0.017
Namibia	0.00006	0.00029	0.00013	0.00014	0.016
Republic of Congo	0.00001	0.00051	0.00007	0.00000	0.015
Liberia	0.00001	0.00053	0.00002	0.00000	0.014
Gabon	0.00009	0.00021	0.00016	0.00000	0.012
Mauritius	0.00011	0.00020	0.00016	0.00001	0.012
Lesotho	0.00001	0.00034	0.00003	0.00000	0.010
Gambia	0.00001	0.00022	0.00002	0.00000	0.006

| | Factors determining voting strength | | | | Result |
Countries	Contribution to global public goods budget	Population	GDP	Military capacity	Weighted vote
Swaziland	0.00002	0.00018	0.00005	0.00000	0.006
Guinea-Bissau	0.00001	0.00020	0.00001	0.00000	0.005
Equatorial Guinea	0.00002	0.00008	0.00002	0.00000	0.003
Cape Verde	0.00001	0.00007	0.00002	0.00000	0.003
Seychelles	0.00002	0.00001	0.00001	0.00000	0.001
São Tome and Principe	0.00001	0.00002	0.00000	0.00000	0.001
Arab League (21)	**0.01788**	**0.04646**	**0.01430**	**0.05790**	**3.414**
Saudi Arabia	0.00713	0.00351	0.00419	0.03748	1.308
Egypt, Arab Republic	0.00120	0.01070	0.00239	0.00333	0.441
Syrian Arab Republic	0.00038	0.00272	0.00039	0.00666	0.254
Morocco	0.00047	0.00479	0.00124	0.00219	0.217
Algeria	0.00076	0.00506	0.00147	0.00000	0.182
United Arab Emirates	0.00235	0.00049	0.00126	0.00223	0.158
Sudan	0.00008	0.00520	0.00031	0.00000	0.140
Oman	0.00070	0.00041	0.00046	0.00378	0.134
Iraq	0.00016	0.00390	0.00000	0.00000	0.101
Yemen	0.00006	0.00296	0.00017	0.00062	0.095
Tunisia	0.00032	0.00159	0.00073	0.00052	0.079
Kuwait	0.00162	0.00034	0.00081	0.00000	0.069
Jordan	0.00011	0.00083	0.00024	0.00108	0.056
Libya	0.00132	0.00089	0.00000	0.00000	0.055
Somalia	0.00001	0.00149	0.00000	0.00000	0.038
Lebanon	0.00024	0.00072	0.00037	0.00000	0.033
Mauritania	0.00001	0.00045	0.00004	0.00000	0.013
Bahrain	0.00030	0.00011	0.00021	0.00000	0.016
Qatar	0.00064	0.00010	0.00000	0.00000	0.018
Djibouti	0.00001	0.00011	0.00001	0.00000	0.003
Comoros	0.00001	0.00009	0.00001	0.00000	0.003

Notes and sources: Contribution to global public goods budget is the member contribution to the UN regular budget for 2004. Population is that of member states in 2001, from the World Bank, *World Development Indicators,* and the CIA Factbook. GDP is in constant 1995 US dollars, from the World Bank, *World Development Indicators.* Military capability is based on military expenditure in constant 1998 US dollars, from the Stockholm International Peace Research Institute (SIPRI).

Table 2. *Country and constituency voting strengths on proposed UN Security Council, adjusted for quality of democracy*

Country	Freedom House index	Weighted vote	Transformed Freedom House index	Weighted vote adjusted for democracy
Permanent members				
United States	1	23.2325	1.5	26.8570
Japan	1	10.9191	1.5	12.6226
China	7	7.5094	0.5	2.8936
India	2	5.1623	1.3	5.3046
Russian Federation	5	1.5951	0.8	1.0244
EU and official candidates (28)		26.0280		29.8550
Germany	1	5.6403	1.5	6.5202
France	1	4.4926	1.5	5.1935
United Kingdom	1	4.0599	1.5	4.6933
Italy	1	3.2352	1.5	3.7399
Spain	1	1.6137	1.5	1.8654
Netherlands	1	1.1123	1.5	1.2858
Turkey	3	0.8273	1.2	0.7439
Sweden	1	0.6825	1.5	0.7890
Belgium	1	0.6733	1.5	0.7784
Austria	1	0.5095	1.5	0.5890
Greece	1	0.5143	1.5	0.5946
Poland	1	0.5026	1.5	0.5810
Denmark	1	0.4543	1.5	0.5252
Portugal	1	0.3456	1.5	0.3995
Finland	1	0.3352	1.5	0.3875
Ireland	1	0.2189	1.5	0.2530
Czech Republic	1	0.1736	1.5	0.2007
Romania	2	0.1637	1.3	0.1683
Hungary	1	0.1425	1.5	0.1648
Slovak Republic	1	0.0664	1.5	0.0767
Bulgaria	1	0.0591	1.5	0.0683
Slovenia	1	0.0573	1.5	0.0662
Luxembourg	1	0.0455	1.5	0.0526
Lithuania	1	0.0345	1.5	0.0399
Cyprus	1	0.0211	1.5	0.0244
Latvia	1	0.0212	1.5	0.0245
Iceland	1	0.0163	1.5	0.0189
Malta	1	0.0091	1.5	0.0106

Country	Freedom House index	Weighted vote	Transformed Freedom House index	Weighted vote adjusted for democracy
Other Europe (19)		2.5420		2.6045
Switzerland	1	0.6845	1.5	0.7912
Israel	1	0.5417	1.5	0.6263
Ukraine	4	0.4401	1.0	0.3391
Norway	1	0.4313	1.5	0.4986
Belarus	6	0.1049	0.7	0.0539
Yugoslavia, Federal Republic	3	0.0879	1.2	0.0791
Croatia	2	0.0649	1.3	0.0667
Azerbaijan	6	0.0373	0.7	0.0192
Bosnia and Herzegovina	4	0.0294	1.0	0.0226
Georgia	4	0.0268	1.0	0.0207
Moldova	3	0.0212	1.2	0.0190
Albania	3	0.0180	1.2	0.0162
Estonia	1	0.0170	1.5	0.0196
Armenia	4	0.0162	1.0	0.0125
Macedonia, Former Yugoslav Republic	3	0.0161	1.2	0.0145
Liechtenstein	1	0.0014	1.5	0.0016
Andorra	1	0.0015	1.5	0.0018
Monaco	2	0.0009	1.3	0.0009
San Marino	1	0.0009	1.5	0.0010
Latin America and Caribbean (35)		7.4144		7.5370
Brazil	2	2.1749	1.3	2.2349
Canada	1	1.6300	1.5	1.8843
Mexico	2	1.2388	1.3	1.2729
Argentina	3	0.7350	1.2	0.6608
Colombia	4	0.2879	1.0	0.2219
Chile	2	0.2458	1.3	0.2526
Ecuador	3	0.2181	1.2	0.1961
Peru	2	0.1763	1.3	0.1812
Venezuela	3	0.1440	1.2	0.1295
Guatemala	4	0.0750	1.0	0.0578
Dominican Republic	2	0.0567	1.3	0.0583
Cuba	7	0.0568	0.5	0.0219
Uruguay	1	0.0411	1.5	0.0475
Bolivia	2	0.0482	1.3	0.0495
El Salvador	2	0.0437	1.3	0.0449
Haiti	6	0.0363	0.7	0.0186
Paraguay	4	0.0322	1.0	0.0248

Country	Freedom House index	Weighted vote	Transformed Freedom House index	Weighted vote adjusted for democracy
Costa Rica	1	0.0345	1.5	0.0399
Honduras	3	0.0318	1.2	0.0286
Panama	1	0.0249	1.5	0.0288
Nicaragua	3	0.0216	1.2	0.0194
Jamaica	2	0.0168	1.3	0.0173
Trinidad and Tobago	3	0.0161	1.2	0.0144
Bahamas	1	0.0076	1.5	0.0088
Barbados	1	0.0053	1.5	0.0061
Guyana	2	0.0039	1.3	0.0040
Suriname	1	0.0023	1.5	0.0027
Belize	1	0.0018	1.5	0.0021
Saint Lucia	1	0.0016	1.5	0.0018
Antigua and Barbuda	4	0.0015	1.0	0.0011
Saint Vincent and the Grenadines	2	0.0009	1.3	0.0010
Grenada	1	0.0009	1.5	0.0011
Dominica	1	0.0007	1.5	0.0008
Kiribati	1	0.0007	1.5	0.0008
Saint Kitts and Nevis	1	0.0007	1.5	0.0008
Other Asia (40)		**9.0029**		**7.2742**
Republic of Korea	2	1.4755	1.3	1.5161
Indonesia	3	1.0925	1.2	0.9822
Australia	1	1.0659	1.5	1.2322
Iran, Islamic Republic	6	0.7911	0.7	0.4065
Pakistan	6	0.7595	0.7	0.3902
Bangladesh	4	0.6113	1.0	0.4711
Thailand	2	0.4936	1.3	0.5072
Philippines	2	0.4128	1.3	0.4242
Singapore	5	0.3558	0.8	0.2285
Vietnam	7	0.3546	0.5	0.1366
Malaysia	5	0.2939	0.8	0.1888
Myanmar	7	0.2008	0.5	0.0774
New Zealand	1	0.1439	1.5	0.1664
Democratic People's Republic of Korea	7	0.1439	0.5	0.0555
Sri Lanka	3	0.1179	1.2	0.1060
Uzbekistan	7	0.1159	0.5	0.0446
Kazakhstan	6	0.1143	0.7	0.0587
Afghanistan	6	0.1123	0.7	0.0577
Nepal	4	0.1041	1.0	0.0802

Country	Freedom House index	Weighted vote	Transformed Freedom House index	Weighted vote adjusted for democracy
Cambodia	6	0.0565	0.7	0.0290
Kyrgyz Republic	6	0.0300	0.7	0.0154
Turkmenistan	7	0.0299	0.5	0.0115
Tajikistan	6	0.0278	0.7	0.0143
Papua New Guinea	2	0.0258	1.3	0.0265
Lao People's Democratic Republic	7	0.0243	0.5	0.0094
Brunei Darussalam	6	0.0142	0.7	0.0073
Mongolia	2	0.0118	1.3	0.0121
Fiji	4	0.0061	1.0	0.0047
Bhutan	6	0.0040	0.7	0.0020
Timor-Leste	3	0.0033	1.2	0.0030
Solomon Islands	3	0.0022	1.2	0.0020
Maldives	6	0.0018	0.7	0.0009
Vanuatu	1	0.0013	1.5	0.0015
Samoa	2	0.0012	1.3	0.0012
Micronesia	1	0.0009	1.5	0.0010
Tonga	5	0.0008	0.8	0.0005
Marshall Islands	1	0.0005	1.5	0.0006
Palau	1	0.0004	1.5	0.0005
Nauru	1	0.0003	1.5	0.0003
Tuvalu	1	0.0003	1.5	0.0003
Africa (43)		**3.1808**		**2.4615**
Nigeria	4	0.6378	1.0	0.4916
South Africa	1	0.4644	1.5	0.5369
Ethiopia	5	0.2770	0.8	0.1779
Democratic Republic of Congo	6	0.2190	0.7	0.1125
Tanzania	4	0.1479	1.0	0.1140
Kenya	4	0.1451	1.0	0.1118
Uganda	6	0.1061	0.7	0.0545
Ghana	2	0.0899	1.3	0.0924
Mozambique	3	0.0817	1.2	0.0734
Côte d'Ivoire	6	0.0787	0.7	0.0405
Cameroon	6	0.0722	0.7	0.0371
Madagascar	3	0.0693	1.2	0.0623
Zimbabwe	6	0.0677	0.7	0.0348
Angola	6	0.0610	0.7	0.0313
Burkina Faso	4	0.0520	1.0	0.0401
Senegal	2	0.0489	1.3	0.0502

Country	Freedom House index	Weighted vote	Transformed Freedom House index	Weighted vote adjusted for democracy
Mali	2	0.0484	1.3	0.0498
Niger	4	0.0479	1.0	0.0369
Zambia	4	0.0458	1.0	0.0353
Malawi	4	0.0452	1.0	0.0348
Guinea	6	0.0377	0.7	0.0194
Rwanda	7	0.0371	0.5	0.0143
Burundi	6	0.0345	0.7	0.0177
Chad	6	0.0341	0.7	0.0175
Benin	3	0.0289	1.2	0.0260
Botswana	2	0.0228	1.3	0.0234
Sierra Leone	4	0.0219	1.0	0.0169
Togo	6	0.0205	0.7	0.0105
Eritrea	7	0.0180	0.5	0.0069
Central African Republic	5	0.0167	0.8	0.0107
Namibia	2	0.0156	1.3	0.0161
Republic of Congo	6	0.0148	0.7	0.0076
Liberia	6	0.0139	0.7	0.0071
Gabon	5	0.0115	0.8	0.0074
Mauritius	1	0.0119	1.5	0.0138
Lesotho	2	0.0096	1.3	0.0098
Gambia	4	0.0061	1.0	0.0047
Swaziland	6	0.0061	0.7	0.0031
Guinea-Bissau	4	0.0055	1.0	0.0042
Equatorial Guinea	7	0.0030	0.5	0.0011
Cape Verde	1	0.0026	1.5	0.0030
Seychelles	3	0.0012	1.2	0.0011
São Tome and Principe	1	0.0009	1.5	0.0011
Arab League (21)		**3.4135**		**1.5655**
Saudi Arabia	7	1.3078	0.5	0.5039
Egypt, Arab Republic	6	0.4405	0.7	0.2263
Syrian Arab Republic	7	0.2539	0.5	0.0979
Morocco	5	0.2171	0.8	0.1394
Algeria	6	0.1824	0.7	0.0937
United Arab Emirates	6	0.1581	0.7	0.0812
Sudan	7	0.1398	0.5	0.0539
Oman	6	0.1338	0.7	0.0687
Iraq	7	0.1015	0.5	0.0391
Yemen	6	0.0953	0.7	0.0490
Tunisia	6	0.0791	0.7	0.0406
Kuwait	4	0.0691	1.0	0.0532

Country	Freedom House index	Weighted vote	Transformed Freedom House index	Weighted vote adjusted for democracy
Jordan	6	0.0565	0.7	0.0290
Libya	7	0.0552	0.5	0.0213
Somalia	6	0.0375	0.7	0.0193
Lebanon	6	0.0333	0.7	0.0171
Mauritania	5	0.0126	0.8	0.0081
Bahrain	5	0.0155	0.8	0.0100
Qatar	6	0.0185	0.7	0.0095
Djibouti	4	0.0033	1.0	0.0025
Comoros	5	0.0028	0.8	0.0018

Notes and sources: Democracy variable is the Political Rights Index from the Freedom House Index, "Freedom in the World 2004," www.freedomhouse.org. For other variables, see sources for appendix table 1.

Table 3. *Country and constituency voting strengths in transition phase of proposed UN Security Council*

| Countries | Factors determining voting strength | | | | Result |
	Contribution to global public goods budget	Population	GDP	Military capacity	Weighted vote
Permanent members					
United States	0.22000	0.04684	0.26662	0.39584	22.909
Japan	0.19468	0.02086	0.16712	0.05411	9.827
China	0.02053	0.20881	0.03306	0.03798	8.758
India	0.00421	0.16949	0.01468	0.01812	4.646
Russian Federation	0.01100	0.02377	0.01117	0.01786	3.436
EU and official candidates (28)	**0.36996**	**0.09042**	**0.31173**	**0.26901**	**27.425**
Germany	0.08662	0.01352	0.07994	0.04553	5.076
France	0.06030	0.00972	0.05341	0.05628	6.043
United Kingdom	0.06127	0.00965	0.03949	0.05198	5.654
Italy	0.04885	0.00951	0.03626	0.03479	2.912
Spain	0.02520	0.00675	0.02141	0.01119	1.452
Netherlands	0.01690	0.00263	0.01487	0.01009	1.001
Turkey	0.00372	0.01125	0.00562	0.01250	0.745
Sweden	0.00998	0.00146	0.00832	0.00754	0.614
Belgium	0.01069	0.00169	0.00950	0.00505	0.606
Austria	0.00859	0.00134	0.00798	0.00247	0.459
Greece	0.00530	0.00174	0.00428	0.00925	0.463
Poland	0.00461	0.00634	0.00425	0.00490	0.452
Denmark	0.00718	0.00088	0.00614	0.00397	0.409
Portugal	0.00470	0.00165	0.00389	0.00359	0.311
Finland	0.00533	0.00085	0.00493	0.00229	0.302
Ireland	0.00350	0.00063	0.00334	0.00128	0.197
Czech Republic	0.00183	0.00168	0.00169	0.00175	0.156
Romania	0.00060	0.00368	0.00102	0.00125	0.147
Hungary	0.00126	0.00167	0.00167	0.00110	0.128
Slovak Republic	0.00051	0.00089	0.00070	0.00055	0.060
Bulgaria	0.00017	0.00130	0.00039	0.00051	0.053
Slovenia	0.00082	0.00033	0.00071	0.00044	0.052
Luxembourg	0.00077	0.00007	0.00074	0.00024	0.041
Lithuania	0.00024	0.00057	0.00026	0.00031	0.031
Cyprus	0.00039	0.00012	0.00033	0.00000	0.019
Latvia	0.00015	0.00039	0.00020	0.00011	0.019
Iceland	0.00034	0.00005	0.00027	0.00000	0.015
Malta	0.00014	0.00006	0.00012	0.00004	0.008

Countries	Factors determining voting strength				Result
	Contribution to global public goods budget	Population	GDP	Military capacity	Weighted vote
Other Europe (19)	**0.02509**	**0.02031**	**0.02191**	**0.03437**	**2.288**
Switzerland	0.01197	0.00119	0.01007	0.00415	0.616
Israel	0.00467	0.00104	0.00315	0.01281	0.488
Ukraine	0.00039	0.00806	0.00143	0.00772	0.396
Norway	0.00679	0.00074	0.00511	0.00461	0.388
Belarus	0.00018	0.00164	0.00044	0.00194	0.094
Yugoslavia, Federal Republic	0.00019	0.00175	0.00000	0.00158	0.079
Croatia	0.00037	0.00072	0.00068	0.00083	0.058
Azerbaijan	0.00005	0.00133	0.00011	0.00000	0.034
Bosnia and Herzegovina	0.00003	0.00067	0.00020	0.00028	0.026
Georgia	0.00003	0.00086	0.00008	0.00011	0.024
Moldova	0.00001	0.00070	0.00009	0.00005	0.019
Albania	0.00005	0.00052	0.00010	0.00005	0.016
Estonia	0.00012	0.00022	0.00019	0.00014	0.015
Armenia	0.00002	0.00051	0.00012	0.00000	0.015
Macedonia, Former Yugoslav Republic	0.00006	0.00033	0.00015	0.00010	0.014
Liechtenstein	0.00005	0.00000	0.00000	0.00000	0.001
Andorra	0.00005	0.00001	0.00000	0.00000	0.001
Monaco	0.00003	0.00000	0.00000	0.00000	0.001
San Marino	0.00003	0.00000	0.00000	0.00000	0.001
Latin America, Caribbean and Canada (35)	**0.08158**	**0.09046**	**0.08196**	**0.04258**	**6.673**
Brazil	0.01523	0.02830	0.02362	0.01985	1.957
Canada	0.02813	0.00510	0.02123	0.01074	1.467
Mexico	0.01883	0.01632	0.01101	0.00339	1.115
Argentina	0.00956	0.00615	0.00829	0.00539	0.661
Colombia	0.00155	0.00707	0.00290	0.00000	0.259
Chile	0.00223	0.00253	0.00245	0.00262	0.221
Ecuador	0.00019	0.00211	0.00642	0.00000	0.196
Peru	0.00092	0.00433	0.00181	0.00000	0.159
Venezuela	0.00171	0.00404	0.00001	0.00000	0.130
Guatemala	0.00030	0.00192	0.00054	0.00024	0.067
Dominican Republic	0.00035	0.00140	0.00052	0.00000	0.051
Cuba	0.00043	0.00184	0.00000	0.00000	0.051
Uruguay	0.00048	0.00055	0.00061	0.00000	0.037

Countries	Factors determining voting strength				Result
	Contribution to global public goods budget	*Population*	*GDP*	*Military capacity*	*Weighted vote*
Bolivia	0.00009	0.00140	0.00024	0.00020	0.043
El Salvador	0.00022	0.00105	0.00033	0.00014	0.039
Haiti	0.00003	0.00134	0.00009	0.00000	0.033
Paraguay	0.00012	0.00088	0.00028	0.00000	0.029
Costa Rica	0.00030	0.00064	0.00045	0.00000	0.031
Honduras	0.00005	0.00108	0.00014	0.00000	0.029
Panama	0.00019	0.00048	0.00033	0.00000	0.022
Nicaragua	0.00001	0.00085	0.00000	0.00000	0.019
Jamaica	0.00008	0.00043	0.00017	0.00000	0.015
Trinidad and Tobago	0.00022	0.00022	0.00021	0.00000	0.014
Bahamas	0.00013	0.00005	0.00012	0.00000	0.007
Barbados	0.00010	0.00004	0.00007	0.00000	0.005
Guyana	0.00001	0.00013	0.00002	0.00000	0.004
Suriname	0.00001	0.00007	0.00001	0.00000	0.002
Belize	0.00001	0.00004	0.00002	0.00000	0.002
Saint Lucia	0.00002	0.00003	0.00002	0.00000	0.001
Antigua and Barbuda	0.00003	0.00001	0.00002	0.00000	0.001
Saint Vincent and the Grenadines	0.00001	0.00002	0.00001	0.00000	0.001
Grenada	0.00001	0.00002	0.00001	0.00000	0.001
Dominica	0.00001	0.00001	0.00001	0.00000	0.001
Kiribati	0.00001	0.00002	0.00000	0.00000	0.001
Saint Kitts and Nevis	0.00001	0.00001	0.00001	0.00000	0.001
Other Asia (40)	**0.05035**	**0.17932**	**0.06655**	**0.06391**	**8.103**
Republic of Korea	0.01796	0.00777	0.01894	0.01435	1.328
Indonesia	0.00142	0.03431	0.00641	0.00156	0.983
Australia	0.01592	0.00318	0.01388	0.00965	0.959
Iran, Islamic Republic	0.00157	0.01059	0.00328	0.01620	0.712
Pakistan	0.00055	0.02322	0.00216	0.00444	0.684
Bangladesh	0.00010	0.02189	0.00152	0.00094	0.550
Thailand	0.00209	0.01005	0.00517	0.00243	0.444
Philippines	0.00095	0.01286	0.00270	0.00000	0.372
Singapore	0.00388	0.00068	0.00328	0.00639	0.320
Vietnam	0.00021	0.01306	0.00092	0.00000	0.319
Malaysia	0.00203	0.00391	0.00332	0.00250	0.265
Myanmar	0.00010	0.00793	0.00000	0.00000	0.181
New Zealand	0.00221	0.00063	0.00210	0.00082	0.130

Countries	Factors determining voting strength				Result
	Contribution to global public goods budget	Population	GDP	Military capacity	Weighted vote
Democratic People's Republic of Korea	0.00010	0.00367	0.00000	0.00198	0.130
Sri Lanka	0.00017	0.00308	0.00049	0.00098	0.106
Uzbekistan	0.00014	0.00412	0.00038	0.00000	0.104
Kazakhstan	0.00025	0.00245	0.00076	0.00112	0.103
Afghanistan	0.00002	0.00447	0.00000	0.00000	0.101
Nepal	0.00004	0.00387	0.00017	0.00008	0.094
Cambodia	0.00002	0.00201	0.00012	0.00011	0.051
Kyrgyz Republic	0.00001	0.00081	0.00006	0.00031	0.027
Turkmenistan	0.00005	0.00089	0.00026	0.00000	0.027
Tajikistan	0.00001	0.00103	0.00008	0.00000	0.025
Papua New Guinea	0.00003	0.00086	0.00014	0.00000	0.023
Lao People's Democratic Republic	0.00001	0.00089	0.00007	0.00000	0.022
Brunei Darussalam	0.00034	0.00006	0.00017	0.00000	0.013
Mongolia	0.00001	0.00040	0.00003	0.00003	0.011
Fiji	0.00004	0.00013	0.00007	0.00000	0.005
Bhutan	0.00001	0.00014	0.00001	0.00000	0.004
Timor-Leste	0.00001	0.00012	0.00000	0.00000	0.003
Solomon Islands	0.00001	0.00007	0.00001	0.00000	0.002
Maldives	0.00001	0.00005	0.00002	0.00000	0.002
Vanuatu	0.00001	0.00003	0.00001	0.00000	0.001
Samoa	0.00001	0.00003	0.00001	0.00000	0.001
Micronesia	0.00001	0.00002	0.00001	0.00000	0.001
Tonga	0.00001	0.00002	0.00001	0.00000	0.001
Marshall Islands	0.00001	0.00001	0.00000	0.00000	0.000
Palau	0.00001	0.00000	0.00000	0.00000	0.000
Nauru	0.00001	0.00000	0.00000	0.00000	0.000
Tuvalu	0.00001	0.00000	0.00000	0.00000	0.000
Africa (43)	**0.00472**	**0.10327**	**0.01090**	**0.00834**	**2.863**
Nigeria	0.00042	0.02132	0.00098	0.00279	0.574
South Africa	0.00292	0.00710	0.00524	0.00332	0.418
Ethiopia	0.00004	0.01081	0.00023	0.00000	0.249
Democratic Republic of Congo	0.00003	0.00860	0.00013	0.00000	0.197
Tanzania	0.00006	0.00566	0.00020	0.00000	0.133
Kenya	0.00009	0.00505	0.00030	0.00037	0.131
Uganda	0.00006	0.00374	0.00024	0.00020	0.095
Ghana	0.00004	0.00324	0.00025	0.00008	0.081

| Countries | Factors determining voting strength | | | | Result |
	Contribution to global public goods budget	Population	GDP	Military capacity	Weighted vote
Mozambique	0.00001	0.00297	0.00011	0.00018	0.073
Côte d'Ivoire	0.00010	0.00269	0.00036	0.00000	0.071
Cameroon	0.00008	0.00250	0.00031	0.00000	0.065
Madagascar	0.00003	0.00262	0.00012	0.00000	0.062
Zimbabwe	0.00007	0.00210	0.00021	0.00032	0.061
Angola	0.00001	0.00222	0.00021	0.00000	0.055
Burkina Faso	0.00002	0.00190	0.00009	0.00008	0.047
Senegal	0.00005	0.00160	0.00018	0.00012	0.044
Mali	0.00002	0.00182	0.00010	0.00000	0.044
Niger	0.00001	0.00184	0.00007	0.00000	0.043
Zambia	0.00002	0.00169	0.00012	0.00000	0.041
Malawi	0.00001	0.00173	0.00005	0.00002	0.041
Guinea	0.00003	0.00124	0.00014	0.00010	0.034
Rwanda	0.00001	0.00130	0.00007	0.00011	0.033
Burundi	0.00001	0.00114	0.00003	0.00020	0.031
Chad	0.00001	0.00130	0.00005	0.00000	0.031
Benin	0.00002	0.00106	0.00008	0.00000	0.026
Botswana	0.00012	0.00028	0.00021	0.00031	0.020
Sierra Leone	0.00001	0.00084	0.00002	0.00000	0.020
Togo	0.00001	0.00076	0.00004	0.00000	0.018
Eritrea	0.00001	0.00069	0.00002	0.00000	0.016
Central African Republic	0.00001	0.00062	0.00004	0.00000	0.015
Namibia	0.00006	0.00029	0.00013	0.00014	0.014
Republic of Congo	0.00001	0.00051	0.00007	0.00000	0.013
Liberia	0.00001	0.00053	0.00002	0.00000	0.013
Gabon	0.00009	0.00021	0.00016	0.00000	0.010
Mauritius	0.00011	0.00020	0.00016	0.00001	0.011
Lesotho	0.00001	0.00034	0.00003	0.00000	0.009
Gambia	0.00001	0.00022	0.00002	0.00000	0.006
Swaziland	0.00002	0.00018	0.00005	0.00000	0.005
Guinea-Bissau	0.00001	0.00020	0.00001	0.00000	0.005
Equatorial Guinea	0.00002	0.00008	0.00002	0.00000	0.003
Cape Verde	0.00001	0.00007	0.00002	0.00000	0.002
Seychelles	0.00002	0.00001	0.00001	0.00000	0.001
São Tome and Principe	0.00001	0.00002	0.00000	0.00000	0.001
Arab League (21)	**0.01788**	**0.04646**	**0.01430**	**0.05790**	**3.072**
Saudi Arabia	0.00713	0.00351	0.00419	0.03748	1.177
Egypt, Arab Republic	0.00120	0.01070	0.00239	0.00333	0.396
Syrian Arab Republic	0.00038	0.00272	0.00039	0.00666	0.229

| Countries | Factors determining voting strength | | | | Result |
	Contribution to global public goods budget	Population	GDP	Military capacity	Weighted vote
Morocco	0.00047	0.00479	0.00124	0.00219	0.195
Algeria	0.00076	0.00506	0.00147	0.00000	0.164
United Arab Emirates	0.00235	0.00049	0.00126	0.00223	0.142
Sudan	0.00008	0.00520	0.00031	0.00000	0.126
Oman	0.00070	0.00041	0.00046	0.00378	0.120
Iraq	0.00016	0.00390	0.00000	0.00000	0.091
Yemen	0.00006	0.00296	0.00017	0.00062	0.086
Tunisia	0.00032	0.00159	0.00073	0.00052	0.071
Kuwait	0.00162	0.00034	0.00081	0.00000	0.062
Jordan	0.00011	0.00083	0.00024	0.00108	0.051
Libya	0.00132	0.00089	0.00000	0.00000	0.050
Somalia	0.00001	0.00149	0.00000	0.00000	0.034
Lebanon	0.00024	0.00072	0.00037	0.00000	0.030
Mauritania	0.00001	0.00045	0.00004	0.00000	0.011
Bahrain	0.00030	0.00011	0.00021	0.00000	0.014
Qatar	0.00064	0.00010	0.00000	0.00000	0.017
Djibouti	0.00001	0.00011	0.00001	0.00000	0.003
Comoros	0.00001	0.00009	0.00001	0.00000	0.003

Notes and sources: See appendix table 1.

Voting Strengths of a Proposed UN Economic and Social Security Council

Table 1. *Country and constituency voting strengths on the proposed UN Economic and Social Security Council*

Countries	Factors determining voting strength (% of total)			Result	Comparison Voting power of World Bank members[a] (% of total)
	Contribution to global public goods	Population	GDP	Weighted vote	
United States	0.22000	0.04684	0.26662	17.78	16.39
Japan	0.19468	0.02086	0.16712	12.76	7.86
China	0.02053	0.20881	0.03306	8.75	2.78
India	0.00421	0.16949	0.01468	6.28	2.78
Russian Federation	0.01100	0.02377	0.01117	1.53	2.78
EU and official candidates (28)	**0.36996**	**0.09042**	**0.31173**	**25.74**	**29.13**
Germany	0.08662	0.01352	0.07994	6.003	4.49
France	0.06030	0.00972	0.05341	4.114	4.30
United Kingdom	0.06127	0.00965	0.03949	3.681	4.30
Italy	0.04885	0.00951	0.03626	3.154	2.78
Spain	0.02520	0.00675	0.02141	1.779	1.75
Netherlands	0.01690	0.00263	0.01487	1.147	2.21
Turkey	0.00372	0.01125	0.00562	0.687	0.53
Sweden	0.00998	0.00146	0.00832	0.659	0.94
Belgium	0.01069	0.00169	0.00950	0.729	1.81
Austria	0.00859	0.00134	0.00798	0.597	0.70
Greece	0.00530	0.00174	0.00428	0.377	0.12
Poland	0.00461	0.00634	0.00425	0.507	0.69
Denmark	0.00718	0.00088	0.00614	0.473	0.85
Portugal	0.00470	0.00165	0.00389	0.341	0.35
Finland	0.00533	0.00085	0.00493	0.370	0.54
Ireland	0.00350	0.00063	0.00334	0.249	0.34
Czech Republic	0.00183	0.00168	0.00169	0.173	0.41

Countries	Factors determining voting strength (% of total)			Result	Comparison Voting power of World Bank members[a] (% of total)
	Contribution to global public goods	Population	GDP	Weighted vote	
Romania	0.00060	0.00368	0.00102	0.177	0.26
Hungary	0.00126	0.00167	0.00167	0.153	0.51
Slovak Republic	0.00051	0.00089	0.00070	0.070	0.21
Bulgaria	0.00017	0.00130	0.00039	0.062	0.34
Slovenia	0.00082	0.00033	0.00071	0.062	0.09
Luxembourg	0.00077	0.00007	0.00074	0.053	0.12
Lithuania	0.00024	0.00057	0.00026	0.036	0.11
Cyprus	0.00039	0.00012	0.00033	0.028	0.11
Latvia	0.00015	0.00039	0.00020	0.025	0.10
Iceland	0.00034	0.00005	0.00027	0.022	0.09
Malta	0.00014	0.00006	0.00012	0.011	0.08
Other Europe (19)	**0.02509**	**0.02031**	**0.02191**	**2.244**	**4.56**
Switzerland	0.01197	0.00119	0.01007	0.774	1.66
Israel	0.00467	0.00104	0.00315	0.295	0.31
Ukraine	0.00039	0.00806	0.00143	0.329	0.69
Norway	0.00679	0.00074	0.00511	0.422	0.63
Belarus	0.00018	0.00164	0.00044	0.075	0.22
Yugoslavia, Federal Republic	0.00019	0.00175	0.00000	0.065	0.19
Croatia	0.00037	0.00072	0.00068	0.059	0.16
Azerbaijan	0.00005	0.00133	0.00011	0.050	0.12
Bosnia and Herzegovina	0.00003	0.00067	0.00020	0.030	0.05
Georgia	0.00003	0.00086	0.00008	0.032	0.11
Moldova	0.00001	0.00070	0.00009	0.027	0.10
Albania	0.00005	0.00052	0.00010	0.022	0.07
Estonia	0.00012	0.00022	0.00019	0.018	0.07
Armenia	0.00002	0.00051	0.00012	0.022	0.09
Macedonia, Former Yugoslav Republic	0.00006	0.00033	0.00015	0.018	0.04
Liechtenstein	0.00005	0.00000	0.00000	0.002	—
Andorra	0.00005	0.00001	0.00000	0.002	—
Monaco	0.00003	0.00000	0.00000	0.001	—
San Marino	0.00003	0.00000	0.00000	0.001	0.05
Latin America, Caribbean and Canada (35)	**0.08158**	**0.09046**	**0.08196**	**8.467**	**11.74**
Brazil	0.01523	0.02830	0.02362	2.238	2.07
Canada	0.02813	0.00510	0.02123	1.815	2.78

| Countries | Factors determining voting strength (% of total) | | | Result | Comparison |
	Contribution to global public goods	Population	GDP	Weighted vote	Voting power of World Bank members[a] (% of total)
Mexico	0.01883	0.01632	0.01101	1.539	1.18
Argentina	0.00956	0.00615	0.00829	0.800	1.12
Colombia	0.00155	0.00707	0.00290	0.384	0.41
Chile	0.00223	0.00253	0.00245	0.240	0.44
Ecuador	0.00019	0.00211	0.00642	0.291	0.19
Peru	0.00092	0.00433	0.00181	0.235	0.34
Venezuela	0.00171	0.00404	0.00001	0.192	1.27
Guatemala	0.00030	0.00192	0.00054	0.092	0.14
Dominican Republic	0.00035	0.00140	0.00052	0.076	0.14
Cuba	0.00043	0.00184	0.00000	0.076	-
Uruguay	0.00048	0.00055	0.00061	0.055	0.19
Bolivia	0.00009	0.00140	0.00024	0.058	0.13
El Salvador	0.00022	0.00105	0.00033	0.053	0.02
Haiti	0.00003	0.00134	0.00009	0.048	0.08
Paraguay	0.00012	0.00088	0.00028	0.043	0.09
Costa Rica	0.00030	0.00064	0.00045	0.046	0.03
Honduras	0.00005	0.00108	0.00014	0.042	0.06
Panama	0.00019	0.00048	0.00033	0.033	0.04
Nicaragua	0.00001	0.00085	0.00000	0.029	0.05
Jamaica	0.00008	0.00043	0.00017	0.022	0.17
Trinidad and Tobago	0.00022	0.00022	0.00021	0.021	0.18
Bahamas	0.00013	0.00005	0.00012	0.010	0.08
Barbados	0.00010	0.00004	0.00007	0.007	0.07
Guyana	0.00001	0.00013	0.00002	0.005	0.08
Suriname	0.00001	0.00007	0.00001	0.003	0.04
Belize	0.00001	0.00004	0.00002	0.002	0.05
Saint Lucia	0.00002	0.00003	0.00002	0.002	0.05
Antigua and Barbuda	0.00003	0.00001	0.00002	0.002	0.05
Saint Vincent and the Grenadines	0.00001	0.00002	0.00001	0.001	0.03
Grenada	0.00001	0.00002	0.00001	0.001	0.05
Dominica	0.00001	0.00001	0.00001	0.001	0.05
Kiribati	0.00001	0.00002	0.00000	0.001	0.04
Saint Kitts and Nevis	0.00001	0.00001	0.00001	0.001	0.03
Other Asia (40)	**0.05035**	**0.17932**	**0.06655**	**9.874**	**9.80**
Republic of Korea	0.01796	0.00777	0.01894	1.489	0.99
Indonesia	0.00142	0.03431	0.00641	1.405	0.94
Australia	0.01592	0.00318	0.01388	1.100	1.53

Countries	Factors determining voting strength (% of total)			Result	Comparison Voting power of World Bank members[a] (% of total)
	Contribution to global public goods	Population	GDP	Weighted vote	
Iran, Islamic Republic	0.00157	0.01059	0.00328	0.515	1.48
Pakistan	0.00055	0.02322	0.00216	0.865	0.59
Bangladesh	0.00010	0.02189	0.00152	0.784	0.32
Thailand	0.00209	0.01005	0.00517	0.577	0.41
Philippines	0.00095	0.01286	0.00270	0.550	0.44
Singapore	0.00388	0.00068	0.00328	0.261	0.04
Vietnam	0.00021	0.01306	0.00092	0.473	0.08
Malaysia	0.00203	0.00391	0.00332	0.309	0.52
Myanmar	0.00010	0.00793	0.00000	0.268	0.17
New Zealand	0.00221	0.00063	0.00210	0.165	0.46
Democratic People's Republic of Korea	0.00010	0.00367	0.00000	0.126	—
Sri Lanka	0.00017	0.00308	0.00049	0.124	0.25
Uzbekistan	0.00014	0.00412	0.00038	0.154	0.17
Kazakhstan	0.00025	0.00245	0.00076	0.115	0.20
Afghanistan	0.00002	0.00447	0.00000	0.150	0.03
Nepal	0.00004	0.00387	0.00017	0.136	0.08
Cambodia	0.00002	0.00201	0.00012	0.072	0.03
Kyrgyz Republic	0.00001	0.00081	0.00006	0.029	0.08
Turkmenistan	0.00005	0.00089	0.00026	0.040	0.05
Tajikistan	0.00001	0.00103	0.00008	0.037	0.08
Papua New Guinea	0.00003	0.00086	0.00014	0.034	0.10
Lao People's Democratic Republic	0.00001	0.00089	0.00007	0.032	0.03
Brunei Darussalam	0.00034	0.00006	0.00017	0.019	0.16
Mongolia	0.00001	0.00040	0.00003	0.015	0.04
Fiji	0.00004	0.00013	0.00007	0.008	0.08
Bhutan	0.00001	0.00014	0.00001	0.005	0.05
Timor-Leste	0.00001	0.00012	0.00000	0.004	0.05
Solomon Islands	0.00001	0.00007	0.00001	0.003	0.05
Maldives	0.00001	0.00005	0.00002	0.002	0.04
Vanuatu	0.00001	0.00003	0.00001	0.002	0.05
Samoa	0.00001	0.00003	0.00001	0.002	0.05
Micronesia	0.00001	0.00002	0.00001	0.001	0.05
Tonga	0.00001	0.00002	0.00001	0.001	0.05
Marshall Islands	0.00001	0.00001	0.00000	0.001	0.04
Palau	0.00001	0.00000	0.00000	0.001	0.02
Nauru	0.00001	0.00000	0.00000	0.000	—
Tuvalu	0.00001	0.00000	0.00000	0.000	—

| Countries | Factors determining voting strength (% of total) | | | Result | Comparison |
	Contribution to global public goods	Population	GDP	Weighted vote	Voting power of World Bank members[a] (% of total)
Africa (43)	**0.00472**	**0.10327**	**0.01090**	**3.963**	**5.30**
Nigeria	0.00042	0.02132	0.00098	0.758	0.80
South Africa	0.00292	0.00710	0.00524	0.509	0.85
Ethiopia	0.00004	0.01081	0.00023	0.369	0.08
Democratic Republic of Congo	0.00003	0.00860	0.00013	0.292	0.18
Tanzania	0.00006	0.00566	0.00020	0.197	0.10
Kenya	0.00009	0.00505	0.00030	0.181	0.17
Uganda	0.00006	0.00374	0.00024	0.135	0.05
Ghana	0.00004	0.00324	0.00025	0.117	0.11
Mozambique	0.00001	0.00297	0.00011	0.103	0.07
Côte d'Ivoire	0.00010	0.00269	0.00036	0.105	0.17
Cameroon	0.00008	0.00250	0.00031	0.096	0.11
Madagascar	0.00003	0.00262	0.00012	0.092	0.10
Zimbabwe	0.00007	0.00210	0.00021	0.080	0.22
Angola	0.00001	0.00222	0.00021	0.081	0.18
Burkina Faso	0.00002	0.00190	0.00009	0.067	0.07
Senegal	0.00005	0.00160	0.00018	0.061	0.14
Mali	0.00002	0.00182	0.00010	0.065	0.09
Niger	0.00001	0.00184	0.00007	0.064	0.07
Zambia	0.00002	0.00169	0.00012	0.061	0.19
Malawi	0.00001	0.00173	0.00005	0.060	0.08
Guinea	0.00003	0.00124	0.00014	0.047	0.10
Rwanda	0.00001	0.00130	0.00007	0.046	0.08
Burundi	0.00001	0.00114	0.00003	0.039	0.06
Chad	0.00001	0.00130	0.00005	0.045	0.07
Benin	0.00002	0.00106	0.00008	0.039	0.07
Botswana	0.00012	0.00028	0.00021	0.020	0.05
Sierra Leone	0.00001	0.00084	0.00002	0.029	0.06
Togo	0.00001	0.00076	0.00004	0.027	0.08
Eritrea	0.00001	0.00069	0.00002	0.024	0.05
Central African Republic	0.00001	0.00062	0.00004	0.022	0.07
Namibia	0.00006	0.00029	0.00013	0.016	0.11
Republic of Congo	0.00001	0.00051	0.00007	0.020	0.07
Liberia	0.00001	0.00053	0.00002	0.019	0.04
Gabon	0.00009	0.00021	0.00016	0.015	0.08
Mauritius	0.00011	0.00020	0.00016	0.015	0.09
Lesotho	0.00001	0.00034	0.00003	0.013	0.06

| Countries | Factors determining voting strength (% of total) | | | Result | Comparison |
	Contribution to global public goods	Population	GDP	Weighted vote	Voting power of World Bank members[a] (% of total)
Gambia	0.00001	0.00022	0.00002	0.008	0.05
Swaziland	0.00002	0.00018	0.00005	0.008	0.04
Guinea-Bissau	0.00001	0.00020	0.00001	0.007	0.05
Equatorial Guinea	0.00002	0.00008	0.00002	0.004	0.06
Cape Verde	0.00001	0.00007	0.00002	0.003	0.05
Seychelles	0.00002	0.00001	0.00001	0.002	0.03
São Tome and Principe	0.00001	0.00002	0.00000	0.001	0.05
Arab League (21)	**0.01788**	**0.04646**	**0.01430**	**2.621**	**6.87**
Saudi Arabia	0.00713	0.00351	0.00419	0.494	2.78
Egypt, Arab Republic	0.00120	0.01070	0.00239	0.476	0.45
Syrian Arab Republic	0.00038	0.00272	0.00039	0.117	0.15
Morocco	0.00047	0.00479	0.00124	0.217	0.32
Algeria	0.00076	0.00506	0.00147	0.243	0.59
United Arab Emirates	0.00235	0.00049	0.00126	0.137	0.16
Sudan	0.00008	0.00520	0.00031	0.186	0.07
Oman	0.00070	0.00041	0.00046	0.052	0.11
Iraq	0.00016	0.00390	0.00000	0.135	0.19
Yemen	0.00006	0.00296	0.00017	0.106	0.15
Tunisia	0.00032	0.00159	0.00073	0.088	0.06
Kuwait	0.00162	0.00034	0.00081	0.092	0.84
Jordan	0.00011	0.00083	0.00024	0.039	0.10
Libya	0.00132	0.00089	0.00000	0.074	0.50
Somalia	0.00001	0.00149	0.00000	0.050	0.05
Lebanon	0.00024	0.00072	0.00037	0.044	0.04
Mauritania	0.00001	0.00045	0.00004	0.017	0.07
Bahrain	0.00030	0.00011	0.00021	0.021	0.08
Qatar	0.00064	0.00010	0.00000	0.025	0.08
Djibouti	0.00001	0.00011	0.00001	0.004	0.05
Comoros	0.00001	0.00009	0.00001	0.004	0.03

a. Regional totals do not represent World Bank member groupings; they are presented here for comparison.

Sources: Contribution to global public goods: members' contribution to the UN regular budget for 2004. Population: population of the member states in 2001, from World Bank, *World Development Indicators,* and the CIA Factbook. GDP in constant 1995 dollars, from World Bank, *World Development Indicators.* World Bank voting shares: members' percentage of total voting power as of June 30, 2004; information issued by the World Bank Corporate Secretariat.

Summary of the Proposed European Union Constitution

I n June 2004, agreement was reached on the text of a European Union constitution to replace the present European Community and European Union with a single European Union, give the union a single foundation for the first time by consolidating the numerous treaties by which it has developed to date, and define the reach of the EU's powers vis-à-vis its member states. The constitution leaves unchanged most of the EU's governing provisions and does not considerably extend the union's competences—indeed, Article 11 states that shared competences may be fully or partially transferred back to member states. But it does simplify decision making and improve the institutional arrangements of the EU. The constitution can only enter into force after it has been ratified by all member states, and its subsequent modification will require unanimous agreement of the member states.

The constitution establishes the principles of "subsidiarity" and "proportionality," meaning that the union's powers are derived from its member states and it can act only in those policy areas where the member states have relinquished their authority under the treaty and when its action is necessary and adds value. The constitution classifies the EU's powers into four categories: (i) exclusive powers, covering areas where the union acts on behalf of the member states, including competition in the internal market or trade with third countries; (ii) shared powers, where the EU's actions add value to those of the member states, covering major policies such as the internal market, common agricultural policy, transport, the environment, asylum and immigration, and judicial and law enforcement cooperation; (iii) supporting powers, for which member states retain authority and the union can only support national policies, such as in the areas of culture, education, sport, and civil protection; and (iv) coordinating powers dealing with areas such as economic and employment policy, for which the EU coordinates national policies and ensures increasing harmonization without passing laws.

Extension of the EU's jurisdiction would essentially only occur in policy areas relevant to freedom, security, and justice, and even the concept for such areas is not new. The constitution calls for creating common policies on asylum and immigration; expanding the union's power to pass laws to ensure a high level of access to justice; eliminating the third pillar system for legislating judicial and law enforcement cooperation on criminal matters (whereby policies were arrived at through the intergovernmental decision-marking arrangement) and instead grouping all policies under the union; establishing common penalties against cross-border offenses; enabling the adoption of framework laws regarding criminal procedure; and making the European Police Office accountable to the European Parliament and national parliaments.

In addition, the constitution contains a Charter of Fundamental Rights that ensures basic "rights, freedoms, and principles" for all EU citizens, though EU citizenship would continue to complement, not replace, national citizenship. The charter specifies rights ranging from civil and political rights to the right to proper administration, workers' rights, the protection of personal data, and bioethics. The charter's exact status will be amorphous until it is tested by the courts, and though all member states must abide by it, the British government, for instance, does not expect the charter to have a pervasive impact on national laws such as those dealing with industrial relations.

The EU institutional framework consists of the European Parliament, European Council, European Commission, Council of Ministers, Court of Justice, European Central Bank, and Court of Auditors. The constitution clarifies the respective roles of the European Council, Parliament, and Commission and also modifies them.

First, the constitution creates the post of an elected president of the European Council, instead of the council presidency rotating between member states every six months. The heads of state or government of EU nations will elect, by qualified majority voting (discussed below), a president for a $2\frac{1}{2}$–year term. The president is allowed to be relected once. The council president will chair the council and possess limited powers.

Second, the number of seats in the European Parliament is increased to 736, to be allocated by what is called "degressive proportionality," and the Parliament is given "codecision" with the Council of Ministers for all policies requiring qualified majority voting. Therefore, under the constitution, the power that the European Parliament gradually accumulated organically is recognized and confirmed, as 95 percent of European laws must be adopted jointly by the Parliament and council, giving the Parliament the ability to block legislation. In this way the constitution augments the directly democratic nature of the union, because, unlike the other EU organs, the members of Parliament are elected by direct universal suffrage.

Finally, the constitution stipulates that the EU Commission, responsible for proposing legislation on which the European Parliament and Council then deliberate, will continue to consist of one representative from each member nation until 2014, at which point the number of commissioners will be reduced to a number corresponding to two-thirds of the member states. Some have strongly criticized this unanimity requirement arguing, rightly, that it will make changes in the constitution very difficult. It should be remembered, however, that this unanimity requirement already exists with reference to the existing treaties that are in force, so that the constitution does not make changes more difficult than they already are. Furthermore, there are provisions in the constitution providing some flexibility. A subgroup of member countries can decide on enhanced cooperation among themselves, such as agreeing to coordinate policies beyond what is already happening at the EU level, provided they constitute at least one-third of the member countries and provided they get approval of the EU Commission and of a qualified majority of the EU Council composed of all heads of government (see below).

Currently, the European Council provides the European Union with political impetus for development and reaches decision by consensus. The principle of co-decision, however, gives the Parliament equal footing with the council, thereby conveying a sense of dual legitimacy, with the Parliament representing the European general public (the people of Europe) and the council the member states themselves. A further significant legislative change is the constitution's introduction of double majority voting, or voting by qualified majority (QMV), within the council. Legislation must have the support of least 55 percent of the member states of the council, comprising at least 65 percent of the EU's population, in order to pass. This replaces the old system in which member states had specified voting weights. The scope of QMV is extensive, but member countries will retain vetoes (i.e., unanimity is required) in the fields of foreign policy, defense, and taxation, as well as partial veto powers on social policy. Guidelines are specified for what share of the total vote can block a decision by the council.

The constitution also specifies that the "Union shall have competence to define and implement a common foreign and security policy, including the progressive framing of a common defense policy." However, every member state maintains the right to veto and go its own way with respect to external policy, and thus the constitution's real aim in this area is simply to achieve as much agreement on foreign policy matters as possible. Moreover, the constitution also creates the post of European Union Minister of Foreign Affairs—to be elected by QMV by the European Council—who will represent the EU internationally. The foreign affairs minister will be the voice of common union foreign and security policies unanimously agreed upon and will be able to speak on behalf of the EU in the UN Security Council, although the voting foreseen in the constitution remains "national." The position combines two existing posts and will serve to raise the EU's prominence in trade and aid negotiations and encourage greater consistency in the EU's external political and economic action. This should facilitate the treatment of the EU as a single entity in international organizations.

The constitution, additionally, explicitly endows the EU for the first time with a "legal personality," enabling it as an organization to enter into international agreements (a right that the European Community had in fact possessed).

Finally, the constitution lays out a formal procedure for withdrawal from the European Union. Member states have always had the right to break from the EU, but by formalizing a mechanism for withdrawal, the constitution emphasizes the voluntary nature of the organization, while at the same time making withdrawal more difficult by requiring that it be agreed to on terms between the departing state and the European Union.

References

Adler, Alexandre. 2002. *J'ai vu finir le monde ancien*. Paris: Grasset.

African Development Bank Group. 2003. Annual Report—2003. Tunis: African Development Bank Group. www.afdb.org/ knowledge/publications/pdf/an_report2003_executive_summary. pdf

Alger, Chadwick F., ed. 1998. *The Future of the United Nations System: Potential for the Twenty-First Century*. New York: United Nations University Press.

Alternative Committee of International Forum on Globalization. 2002. *A Better World Is Possible! Alternatives To Economic Globalization*. International Forum on Globalization. www.ifg. org/alt_eng.pdf

Amin, Samir. 1996. *Capitalism in the Age of Globalization: The Management of Contemporary Society*. New York: St. Martin's Press.

———. 2004. *Obsolescent Capitalism: Contemporary Politics and Global Disorder*. London: Zed Books.

Annan, Kofi A. 2000. Globalization and Governance. In *We the Peoples: The Role of the United Nations in the 21st Century*. New York: United Nations.

Arifovic, Jasmina, and Paul Masson. 2000. Heterogeneity and Evolution of Expectations in a Model of Currency Crisis. www. brook.edu/views/papers/masson/19991208.htm

Ash, Timothy Garten. 2004. *Free World*. London: Allen Lane.

Asian Development Bank (ADB). 2004. *Asian Development Outlook 2004*. New York: Oxford University Press.

Asia-Pacific Economic Cooperation Secretariat. 2003. *APEC at a Glance*. Singapore: Asia-Pacific Economic Cooperation Secretariat. www.apecsec.org.sg/apec/about_apec.downloadlinks.0002.LinkURL.Download.ver5.1.9.

Assetto, Valerie J. 1988. *The Soviet Block in the IMF and the IBRD*. Boulder, CO: Westview Press.

Bacevich, Andrew J. 2002. *American Empire: The Realities and Consequences of U.S. Diplomacy*. Cambridge, MA: Harvard University Press.

Beck, Ulrich. 2002. *Macht und Gegenmacht im globalen Zeitalter*. Frankfurt: Suhrkamp Verlag.

Beigbeder, Yves. 1997. *United Nations Organizations: The Long Quest for Reform*. Houndmills/London: Internal Management of Macmillan Publishers.

Bello, Walden. 2002. Prospects for Good Global Governance: The View from the South. Report prepared for the Bundestag, Federal Republic of Germany. www.attacberlin.de/fileadmin/materialseite/BelloGutachten.pdf

Ben-David, Dan. 1993. Equalizing Exchange: Trade Liberalization and Income Convergence. *Quarterly Journal of Economics* 108, no.3.

Bertrand, Maurice. 1993. The Historical Development of Efforts to Reform the UN. In *United Nations, Divided World. The UN's Roles in International Relations*, eds. Adam Roberts and Benedict Kingsbury. 2nd ed. Oxford: Oxford University Press.

Bhagwati, Jagdish N. 1958. Immiserizing Growth: A Geometrical Note. *The Review of Economic Studies* 25, no. 3 (June).

———. 2004. *In Defense of Globalization*. Oxford: Oxford Press.

Bhalla, Surjit. 2002. *Imagine There's No Country: Poverty, Inequality, and Growth in the Era of Globalization*. Washington, DC: Institute for International Economics.

Bhattacharya, Amar, ed. 2001. *Developing Countries and the Global Financial System*. London: Commonwealth Secretariat.

Berger, Suzanne. 2003. *Notre Premiere Mondialisation, Leçons d'un Echec Oublis*. Paris: Seuil.

Birdsall, Nancy. 2003. *Why It Matters Who Runs the IMF and World Bank*. Center for Global Development Working Paper no. 22, Washington, DC. www.cgdev.org/wp/cgd_wp022.pdf

Birdsall, Nancy, and Amar Hammoudi. 2002. *Commodity Dependence, Trade, and Growth: When Openness is Not Enough*. Center for Global Development Working Paper no. 7, Washington, DC. www.cgdev.org/docs/cgd_wp007.pdf

Birdsall, Nancy, and Augusto de la Torre. 2001. *Washington Contentious: Economic Policies for Social Equity in Latin America*. Washington, DC: Carnegie Endowment for International Peace and Inter-American Dialogue.

Birdsall, Nancy, and John Williamson with Brian Deese. 2002. *Delivering on Debt Relief: From IMF Gold to a New Aid Architecture*. Washington, DC: Center for Global Development and Institute for International Economics.

Borradori, Giovanna. 2003. *Philosophy in a Time of Terror : Dialogues with Jürgen Habermas and Jacques Derrida*. Chicago and London: University of Chicago Press.

Bourdieu, Pierre. 1987. *Distinction: A Social Critique of the Judgement of Taste*. Reprint edition. Cambridge, MA: Harvard University Press.

———. 1999. *Acts of Resistance: Against the Tyranny of the Market*. New York: New Press.

Bourdieu, Pierre, et al. 1999. *The Weight of the World: Social Suffering in Contemporary Societies*. Stanford: Stanford University Press.

Boughton, James M. 2001. *Silent Revolution: The International Monetary Fund 1979–1989*. Washington, DC: International Monetary Fund.

Boutrous-Ghali, Boutrous. 1992. *An Agenda for Peace: Report to the UN Security Council*. New York: United Nations.

Brander, James A. 1995. *Strategic Trade Policy*. NBER Working Paper 5020. Cambridge, MA: National Bureau of Economic Research.

Bretton Woods Commission. 1994. *Bretton Woods: Looking to the Future*. Washington, DC: Bretton Woods Committee.

Brewster, Havelock R. 2003. The Caribbean Single Market and Economy: Is it Realistic without Commitment to Political Unity? Speech in Washington, DC, March 14. www.caricom.org/speeches/csme-politicalunity-brewster.htm

Brown, Drusilla K., Alan V. Deardorff, and Robert M. Stern. 2001. CGE Modeling and Analysis of Multilateral and Regional Negotiating Options. Research Seminar in International Economics, Discussion Paper no. 468. University of Michigan, Ann Arbor. January.

Brzezinski, Zbigniew. 2004. *The Choice: Global Domination or Global Leadership*. New York: Basic Books.

Buchanan, James M., and Gordon Tullock. 1962. *The Calculus of Consent: Legal foundations of Constitutional Democracy*. Ann Arbor: University of Michigan Press.

Buira, Ariel. 2003a. *The Governance of the IMF in a Global Economy*. Intergovernmental Group of Twenty-Four Research Paper. www.g24.org/buiragva.pdf

———. 2003b. *Challenges to the World Bank and IMF: Developing Country Perspectives*. London: Anthem Press.

Cameron, David. 1978. The Expansion of the Public Economy: A Comparative Analysis. *American Political Science Review* no. 72 (December).

Canadian Committee for the 50th Anniversary of the United Nations. 1994. *The Canadian Priorities for UN Reform: Proposals for Policy Changes by the UN and the Government of Canada*. Ottawa: UN Association in Canada/Canada Communications Group.

Canto-Sperber, Monique, with Nadia Urbinati. 2003. *Le Socialisme Liberal, Une Anthologie: Europe-Etats-Unis.* Paris: Editions Esprit.

Cardoso, Fernando Henrique, and Enzo Faletto. 1979. *Dependency and Development in Latin America.* California: University of California Press.

Chari, V.V. 1998. Nobel Laureate Robert E. Lucas, Jr.: Architect of Modern Macroeconomics. *Journal of Economic Perspectives* 12, no. 1: 171–86.

Childers, Erskine. 1997. The United Nations and Global Institutions: Discourse and Reality. *Global Governance* 3, no. 3 (September/December).

Childers, Erskine, and Brian Urquhart. 1994. *Renewing the United Nations System.* Development Dialogue no 1. Uppsala: Dag Hammarskjold Foundation.

Choi, Seok-young. 2004. What Have APEC and Other Organizations Done? Paper presented at the 4th APEC Future Economic Leaders Think Tank. www.axiss.com.au/content/media/events/Choi_Presentation.pdf

Chomsky, Noam. 2003. *Hegemony or Survival: America's Quest for Global Dominance.* New York: Metropolitan Books.

Clemens, Michael, Steven Radelet, and Rikhil Bhavnani. 2004. *Counting Chickens when they Hatch: The Short-term Effect of Aid on Growth.* Center for Global Development Working Paper no. 44, Washington, DC.

Cline, William R. 1994. *International Economic Policy in the 1990s.* Cambridge, MA: MIT Press.

———. 1997. *Trade and Income Distribution.* Washington, DC: Institute of International Economics.

———. 2004. *Trade Policy and Global Poverty.* Washington, DC: Institute of International Economics and Center for Global Development.

Cohen, Daniel. 2004. *La Mondialisation et ses Ennemis.* Paris: Grasset.

Cohen, Samy. 2003. *La Resistance des Etats.* Paris: Seuil.

Collier, Paul, et al. 2003. *Breaking the Conflict Trap: Civil War and Development Policy.* World Bank Policy Research Reports. Washington, DC: World Bank.

Commission on Global Governance. 1995. *Our Global Neighborhood: The Report of the Commission on Global Governance.* Oxford: Oxford University Press.

Commission on Weak States and US National Security. 2004. *On The Brink: Weak States and US National Security.* Washington, DC: Center for Global Development.

Commonwealth of Independent States (CIS). 2003. *Inventory of International Nonproliferation Organizations and Regimes.* Monterey, CA: Center for Nonproliferation Studies. http://cns.miis.edu/pubs/inven/pdfs/cis.pdf

Commonwealth of Independent States. Undated. Belarus: Executive Committee of the Commonwealth of the Independent States. www.cis.minsk.by/ENGLISH/engl_cis.htm

Copson, Raymond W. 2001. *African Development Bank and Fund.* CRS Report for Congress no. RS20329, Congressional Research Service, Washington, DC. www.ncseonline.org/nle/crsreports/03May/RS20329.pdf

Corden, Max. 1985. *Protection, Trade and Growth*. Oxford and New York: B. Blackwell.

———. 1992. *International Trade Theory and Policy*. Aldershot, Hants, UK, and Brookfield, VT: Edward Elgar Publishing.

———. 1997. *Trade Policy and Economic Welfare*. 2nd ed. Oxford: Oxford University Press.

Council on Foreign Relations Independent Task Force. 1996. *American National Interest and the United Nations*. New York: Council on Foreign Relations.

Dahrendorf, Ralf. 2004. *Der Wiederbeginn der Geschichte*. Munich, Germany: Beck.

DeLong, Bradford. 1998. *Neue Zuercher Zeitung*. www.j-bradford-delong. net/Comments/1998.html

Derviş, Kemal. 2004. "Returning from the Brink: Turkey's Efforts at Systemic Change and Structural Reform." In *Development Challenges in the 1990s: Leading Policymakers Speak from Experience,* eds. Tim Besley and N. Roberto Zagha. Washington, DC: World Bank.

Derviş, Kemal, Jim De Melo, and Sherman Robinson. 1982. *General Equilibrium Models for Development Policy*. New York: Cambridge University.

Dixit, Avinash. 1987. "Trade and Insurance with Moral Hazard." *Journal of International Economics* 23: 201–20.

Dollar, David. 1992. Outward-Oriented Developing Economies Really Do Grow More: Evidence from 95 LDC, 1976–85. *Economic Development and Cultural Change* (April): 523–44.

Dollar, David, and Aart Kraay. 2001. *Trade, Growth, and Poverty*. World Bank, Washington, DC. www.worldbank.org/research/growth/pdfiles/Trade5.pdf

Easterly, William. 2002. How Did Heavily Indebted Poor Countries Become Heavily Indebted? Reviewing Two Decades of Debt. *World Development* 30, no. 10: 1677–96.

Eaton, Jonathan, and Gene Grossman. 1985. Tariffs as Insurance: Optimal Commercial Policy When Domestic Markets are Incomplete. *Canadian Journal of Economics* 18, no. 2: 258–72.

Eatwell, John, and Lance Taylor. 2000. *Global Finance at Risk—the Case for International Regulation*. New York: New Press.

Eatwell, John, E. Jelin, A. McGrew, and J. Rosenau. 1998. *Understanding Globalisation: The Nation-State, Democracy and Economic Policies in the New Epoch*. Stockholm: Almqvist & Wiksell.

Edwards, Sebastian. 1993. Openness, Trade Liberalization, and Growth in Developing Countries. *Journal of Economic Literature* 31, no. 3 (September): 1358–93.

———. 1998. Openness, Productivity and Growth: What Do We Really Know? *Economic Journal* 108 (March): 383–98.

Eichengreen, Barry, Ricardo Hausman, and Ugo Panizza. 2002. Original Sin: The Pain, the Mystery, and the Road to Redemption. Paper presented at the seminar entitled Currency and Maturity Matchmaking: Redeeming Debt from

Original Sin, Inter-American Development Bank, Washington, DC (November 21–22).

Elliott, Kimberly Ann, and Richard B. Freeman. 2003. *Can Labor Standards Improve Under Globalization?* Washington, DC: Institute of International Economics.

Ethier, Wilfred J., 1998. The New Regionalism. Royal Economic Society *Economic Journal* 108, no. 449: 1149–61.

Falk, Richard. 1999. *Predatory Globalization: A Critique*. Cambridge, UK: Polity Press.

———. 2002. The United Nations System: Prospect for Renewal. In *Governing Globalization—Issues and Institutions*, ed. Deepak Nayyar. Tokyo: United Nations University.

Falk, Richard, and Andrew Strauss. 2001. Toward Global Parliament. *Foreign Affairs* 80, no. 1 (January/February).

Fallon, Peter, and Robert Lucas. 2002. The Impact of Financial Crises on Labor Markets, Household Incomes and Poverty: A Review of Evidence. *World Bank Research Observer* 17, no.1: 21–45.

Ffrench-Davis, Ricardo. 2001. *Financial Crisis in "Successful" Emerging Economies*. Santiago: McGraw-Hill, and Washington, D.C.: Brookings Institution.

Ffrench-Davis, Ricardo, and Stephany Griffith-Jones. 2003. *From Capital Surges to Drought: Seeking Stability for Emerging Economies*. New York: Palgrave Macmillan.

Fischer, Stanley. 1998. Capital Account Liberalization and the Role of the IMF. *Princeton Essays in International Finance* 207: 1–10.

———. 2001. The International Financial System: Crises and Reform. The Robbins Lectures, London School of Economics.

———. 2002. *Financial Crises and Reform of the International Financial System*. NBER Working Paper 9297. Cambridge, MA: National Bureau of Economic Research.

———. 2003. Globalization and Its Challenges. Lecture at the Institute of International Economics, Washington, DC.

Fitoussi, Jean-Paul. 2002. *La Regle et le Marche*. Paris: Seuil.

———. 2004. *La Democratie et le Marche*. Paris: Grasset.

Frank, Isaiah. 1994. *U.S. Trade Policy Beyond the Uruguay Round*. Washington, DC: Committee for Economic Development.

Frankel, Jeffrey, and David Romer. 1999. Does Trade Cause Growth? *American Economic Review* 89, no. 3 (June): 379–99.

Fukuyama, Francis. 1989. The End of History. *The National Interest* 16: 3–18.

———. 1992. *The End of History and the Last Man*. New York: Free Press.

———. 2002. *Our Posthuman Future: Consequences of the Biotechnology Revolution*. New York: Farrar Straus & Giroux.

————. 2004. *State-Building: Governance and World Order in the 21st Century.* Ithaca, NY: Cornell University Press.

Giddens, Anthony. 1998. *The Third Way: The Renewal of Social Democracy.* Cambridge, UK: Polity Press.

Gilpin, Robert. 2001. *Global Political Economy.* Princeton, NJ: Princeton University Press.

Gleason, Gregory. 2001. Kazakhstan's Nazarbayev Heads New EEC Organization. EurasiaNet Business and Economics, New York, June 18. www.eurasianet.org/departments/business/articles/eav061801.shtml

Goldstein, Morris, and Philip Turner. 2004. *Controlling Currency Mismatches in Emerging Markets.* Washington, DC: Institute for International Economics.

Graham, Edward M. 2000. *Fighting the Wrong Enemy: Antiglobal Activists and Multinational Enterprises.* Washington, DC: Institute for International Economics.

Green, Duncan. 2003. *Silent Revolution: The Rise and Crisis of Market Economics in Latin America.* New York: Monthly Review Press.

Griffith-Jones, Stephany. 2004. Cost of Currency Crises and Benefits of International Financial Reform. Institute of Development Studies, Sussex, UK. Photocopy.

Griffith-Jones, Stephany, and Jose Antonio Ocampo. 2004. What Progress on International Financial Reform? Why so Limited? Document prepared for the Expert Group on Development Issues (IGDI).

Guisan, Catherine. 2003. *Un sens à l'Europe : Gagner la paix, 1950–2003.* Paris: Odile Jacob.

Gupta, Akhil, and James Ferguson, eds. 1997. *Culture, Power, Place: Explorations in Critical Anthropology.* Durham, NC: Duke University Press.

Habermas, Jürgen. 2000. *Après l'État Nation: une Nouvelle Constellation Politique.* Paris: Fayard.

Haq, Mahbub ul. 1998. The Case for an Economic Security Council. In *Between Sovereignty and Global Governance*, eds. Albert Pasolini et al. New York: St. Martin's Press.

Haq, Mahbub ul, Richard Jolly, and Paul Streeten, eds. 1995. *The UN and the Bretton Woods Institutions: New Challenges for the Twenty-First Century.* New York: St. Martin's Press.

Hardt, Michael, and Antonio Negri. 2001. *Empire.* Cambridge, MA: Harvard University Press.

Harvey, David. 2003. *The New Imperialism.* Oxford: Oxford University Press.

Held, David, and Anthony McGrew. 2002a. *Globalization/Anti-Globalization.* Cambridge, UK: Polity Press.

Held, David, and Anthony G. McGrew, eds. 2002b. *Governing Globalization: Power, Authority, and Global Governance.* Cambridge, UK: Polity Press.

———. 2003. *Global Transformations Reader: An Introduction to the Globalization Debate*. 2nd ed. Cambridge, UK: Polity Press.

Held, David, and M. Koenig-Archibugi, eds. 2003. *Taming Globalization: Frontiers of Governance*. Cambridge, UK: Polity Press.

Hobsbawm, Eric. 2000. *On the Edge of the New Century*. New York: New Press.

Hodgson, Geoffrey M. 1999. *Evolution and Institutions: On Evolutionary Economics and the Evolution of Economics*. UK: Edward Elgar Publishing.

Hoff, Peter Oesterdiech. 1999. Regional Integration in Africa: With Particular Reference to the Southern African Development Community. *Economic Focus* 2, no. 4. Ethiopian Economic Association. http://eea.ethiopiaonline.net/Econfoc/ef2-4/hofO2-4.htm

Huntington, Samuel. 1996. *The Clash of Civilizations and the Remaking of World Order*. New York: Simon & Schuster.

Ikenberry, G. John. 2002. *America Unrivaled: The Future of the Balance of Power*. Ithaca, NY: Cornell University Press.

———. 2004. Illusions of Empire: Defining the New American Order. *Foreign Affairs* 83, no. 2 (March/April).

International Forum on Globalization (IFG). 2002. *Alternatives To Economic Globalization [A Better World Is Possible]*. San Francisco: Berrett-Koehler Publishers. www.ifg.org/alt_eng.pdf

Independent Working Group on the Future of the UN System. 1995. *The United Nations in Its Second Half-Century*. New Haven, CT: Yale University Press.

International Monetary Fund (IMF). 2000. *Globalization: Threat or Opportunity?* IMF Issues Brief, April 12, 2000, Corrected January 2002. Washington, DC: Iinternational Monetary Fund. www.imf.org/external/np/exr/ib/2000/041200.htm

———. 2003a. *World Economic Outlook*. Washington, DC: International Monetary Fund. September.

———. 2003b. Special Drawing Rights (SDR). www.imf.org/external/np/exr/facts/sdr.htm

———. 2003c. Country Focus: The Commonwealth of Independent States. *Finance & Development* 40, no. 4: 56.

———. 2004. Heavily Indebted Poor Countries (HIPC) Debt Initiative. www.imf.org/external/np/hipc/index.asp

Jackson, Robert H. 1990. *Quasi-States: Sovereignty, International Relations, and the Third World*. Cambridge: Cambridge University Press.

Johnson, Chalmers A. 2000. *Blowback: The Costs and Consequences of American Empire*. New York: Owl Books.

Kagan, Robert. 2004. *Of Paradise and Power: America and Europe in the New World Order*. New York: Vintage Books.

Kahler, Miles. 2001. *Leadership Selection in the Major Multilaterals*. Washington, DC: Institute for International Economics.

Kaldor, Mary. 2003. Terrorism as Regressive Globalization. *Open Democracy* (September). www.opendemocracy.net/debates/article-3-77-1501.jsp

Kaul, Inge, Isabelle Grunberg, and Marc A. Stern, eds. 1999. *Global Public Goods: International Cooperation in the 21st Century.* New York: Oxford University Press.

Kaul, Inge, Pedro Conceicao, Katell Le Goulven, and Ronald U. Mendoza, eds. 2003. *Providing Global Public Goods: Managing Globalization.* New York: Oxford University Press.

Kawai, Masahiro. 2004. Trade and Investment Integration for Development in East Asia: A Case for the Trade-FDI Nexus. Paper prepared for the East Asia Session at the ABCDE Europe Meeting. http://wbln0018.worldbank.org/eurvp/web.nsf/Pages/Paper+by+Kawai/$File/KAWAI+ABCDE+EUROPE+05-07-2004.PDF

Kenen, Peter B., ed. 1994. *Managing the World Economy: Fifty Years After Bretton Woods.* Washington, DC: Institute for International Economics.

Kenen, Peter B. 2001. *The International Financial Architecture: What's New? What's Missing?* Washington, DC: Institute for International Economics.

Kennedy, Paul. 1993. *Preparing for the Twenty-first Century.* New York: Random House.

Kennedy, Paul, and Bruce Russett. 1995. Reforming the United Nations. *Foreign Affairs* 74, no. 5 (September/October).

Keohane, Robert O. 2002. *Power and Governance in a Partially Globalized World.* London and New York: Routledge.

Keohane, Robert O., and Joseph S. Nye. 2001. *Democracy, Accountability, and Global Governance.* KSG Harvard University Working Papers on International Relations 01-4. www.ksg.harvard.edu/prg/nye/ggajune.pdf

Khor, Martin. 2002. *Rethinking Globalization.* London: Zed Books.

Kindleberger, Charles. 1953. *International Economics.* Homewood, IL: R.D. Irwin.

———. 2001. *Manias, Panics and Crashes: A History of Financial Crises.* 4th ed. New York: John Wiley & Sons.

King, Martin Luther, Jr. 1967. *Where Do We Go from Here: Chaos or Community?* New York: Harper & Row.

Kozlu, Cem. 1999. Türkiye Mucizesi İçin Vizyon Arayışları ve Asya Modelleri. Istanbul: İş Bankası Yayınları.

Krueger, Anne O. 2002. A New Approach To Sovereign Debt Restructuring. International Monetary Fund, Washington, DC. www.imf.org/external/pubs/ft/exrp/sdrm/eng/sdrm.pdf

Krugman, Paul, ed. 1986. *Strategic Trade Policy and the New International Economics.* Cambridge, MA: MIT Press.

———. 1996. Are Currency Crises Self-fulfilling? In *NBER Annual Macroeconomics Report.* Cambridge, MA: MIT Press.

————. 1997. *The Age of Diminished Expectations: U.S. Economic Policy in the 1990s*. Cambridge, MA: MIT Press.

————. 1999. Is Free Trade Passé? In *International Economics and International Economics Policy: A Reader*, ed. Philip King. Boston: McGraw-Hill/Irwin.

Krugman, Paul, and Alasdair Smith, eds. 1994. *Empirical Studies of Strategic Trade Policy*. Chicago: University of Chicago Press.

Kuczynski, Pedro-Pablo, and John Williamson. 2003. *After the Washington Consensus: Restarting Growth and Reform in Latin America*. Washington, DC: Institute for International Economics.

Lange, Oscar. 1967. The Computer and the Market. In *Socialism, Capitalism, and Economic Growth*, ed. C. H. Feinstein. Cambridge: Cambridge University Press.

Maalouf, Amin. 1998. *Les Identites Meurtrieres*. Paris: Grasset.

Maddison, Angus. 2001. *The World Economy: A Millennial Perspective*. Paris: OECD Development Centre.

————. 2003. *The World Economy: Historical Statistics*. Paris: OECD.

Mallaby, Sebastian. 2004. *The World's Banker: A Story of Failed States, Financial Crises, and the Wealth and Poverty of Nations*. New York: Penguin Press.

Martinez C., Alberto. 2002. The European Union and the Andean Community: Two Integration Systems. Speech at the 2002 ISA Annual Convention, Caracas, Venezuela. www.isanet.org/noarchive/martinez.html

Mason, Edward S., and Robert E. Asher. 1973. *The World Bank Since Bretton Woods*. Washington, DC: Brookings Institution.

Meltzer Commission Report. 2000. www.house.gov/jec/imf/meltzer.pdf

McMillan, Margaret, Dani Rodrik, and Karen Horn Welch. 2002. When Economic Reform Goes Wrong: Cashews in Mozambique. NBER Working Paper 9117. Cambridge, MA: National Bureau of Economic Research (August).

Micklethwait, John, and Adrian Wooldridge. 2003. *A Future Perfect: The Challenge and Promise of Globalization*. New York: Random House.

Miller, Calum. 2004. Paper prepared for the Pathways through Financial Crisis Project, Center for Global Economic Governance University College, Oxford University. Photocopy.

Monbiot, George. 2004. *The Age of Consent*. London: Harper Perennial.

Monnet, Jean. 1976. *Mémoires*. Paris: Fayard.

Morishima, M. 1969. *Theory of Economic Growth*. Oxford: Clarendon Press.

Müller, Jan-Werner. 2004. "Is Euro-Patriotism Possible?" *Dissent Magazine* (Spring).

Naím, Moisés. 2000. Washington Consensuses or Washington Confusion? *Foreign Policy* no. 118 (Spring).

New Partnership for Africa's Development (NEPAD). 2001. NEPAD Framework Document. NEPAD, Abuja, Nigeria. www.nepad.org/documents/nepad_english_version.pdf

Newbery, David M., and Joseph E. Stiglitz. 1984. Pareto Inferior Trade. *Review of Economic Studies* 51: 1–12.

Nye, Joseph S. 2004. *Soft Power: The Means to Success in World Politics.* New York: Perseus.

Ocampo, Jose Antonio. 2000. *Financial Globalization & the Emerging Economies.* New York: United Nations.

Ohmae, Kenichi. 1999. *Borderless World: Power and Strategy in the Interlinked Economy.* New York: Harper Business.

Organization for Economic Cooperation and Development (OECD). 2003. *The Doha Development Agenda: Welfare Gains from Further Multilateral Trade Liberalisation with Respect to Tariffs.* Paris: OECD.

Organization of American States. 2004. The OAS and the Inter-American System. Organization of American States, Washington, DC. www.oas.org/main/main. asp?sLang=E&sLink=../../documents/eng/oasinbrief.asp

Organization of the Islamic Conference. OIC in Brief. Jeddah, Saudi Arabia. www.oic-oci.org/ (accessed November 15, 2004).

Persaud, Avinash. 2003. Liquidity Black Holes: Why Modern Financial Regulation in Developed Countries Is Making Short-Term Capital Flows to Developing Countries Even More Volatile. In *From Capital Surges to Drought: Seeking Stability for Emerging Economies,* eds. Ricardo Ffrench-Davis and Stephany Griffith-Jones. New York: Palgrave Macmillian.

Pew Global Attitudes Project. 2004. *A Year After Iraq War: Mistrust of America in Europe Ever Higher, Muslim Anger Persists.* Washington, DC: The Pew Research Center for the People & the Press. http://people-press.org/reports/pdf/206.pdf

Radelet, Steven, and Jeffrey Sachs. 1998. *The East Asian Financial Crisis: Diagnosis, Remedies, Prospects.* Brookings Papers on Economic Activity 1: 1–90.

Rajan, R., and Luigi Zingales. 2003. *Saving Capitalism from the Capitalists.* New York: Random House.

Rasmussen, P.N. 2003. *Europe and a New Global Order: Bridging the Global Divides.* The Party of European Socialists, Brussels. www.eurosocialists.org/upload/publications/74ENPES%20Rasmussen_28_05_2003.pdf

Reardon, Thomas, C. Peter Timmer, Christopher B. Barrett, and Julio A. Berdegue. 2003. The Rise of Supermarkets in Africa, Asia, and Latin America. *American Journal of Agricultural Economics* 85, no. 5 (December): 1140–46.

Reinicke, Wolfgang. 2000. The Other World Wide Web: Global Public Policy Networks. *Foreign Policy* no. 117 (winter): 44–57.

Reisen, Helmut. 2004. "Innovative Approaches to Funding the Millennium Development Goals." OECD Development Centre Policy Brief no. 24. www.oecd.org/dataoecd/61/2/30880682.pdf

Rice, Condoleezza. 2000. Promoting the National Interest. *Foreign Affairs* 79, no. 1 (January/February): 45–62.

Rischard, J.F. 2002. *High Noon: Twenty Global Issues, Twenty Years to Solve Them.* New York: Basic Books.

Rodríguez, Francisco, and Dani Rodrik. 2000. Trade Policy and Economic Growth: A Skeptic's Guide to the Cross-National Evidence. In *NBER Annual Macroeconomics Report 2000.* Cambridge: MIT Press.

Rodrik, Dani. 1997. *Has Globalization Gone Too Far?* Washington, DC: Institute for International Economics.

———. 1998. Why Do More Open Economies Have Bigger Governments? *Journal of Political Economy* 106, no. 5 (October).

———. 2000. Governing the World Economy: Does One Architectural Style Fit All? In *Brookings Trade Forum*, eds. Susan Collins and Robert Lawrence. Washington, DC: Brookings Institution. http://ksghome.harvard.edu/~drodrik/ifa2.pdf

———. 2002a. Trade Policy Reform as Institutional Reform. In *Development, Trade, and the WTO: A Handbook (World Bank Trade and Development Series)*, eds. Bernard M. Hoekman, Aaditya Mattoo, and Philip English. Washington, DC: World Bank. http://ksghome.harvard.edu/~.drodrik.academic.ksg/Reform.PDF

———. 2002b. *Feasible Globalizations.* John F. Kennedy School of Government Working Paper Series RWP02-029 (July). http://ksghome.harvard.edu/~.drodrik.academic.ksg/Feasglob.pdf

Rosamond, Ben. 2000. *Theories of European Integration.* Basingstoke, UK: Palgrave Macmillan and New York: St. Martin's Press.

Rosenau, James N. 1992. *The United Nations in a Turbulent World.* Boulder, CO: Lynne Rienner.

Roubini, Nouriel, and Brad Setser. 2004. *Bailouts or Bail-ins? Responding to Financial Crises in Emerging Economies.* Washington, DC: Institute for International Economics.

Ruggie, John G. 1982. International Regimes, Transactions and Change: Embedded Liberalism in the Postwar Economic Order. *International Organization* 36 (Spring).

———. 2003. Taking Embedded Liberalism Global: the Corporate Connection. In *Taming Globalization: Frontiers of Governance,* eds. David Held and M. Koenig-Archibugi. Cambridge, UK: Polity Press.

Russett, Bruce, ed. 1997. *The Once and Future Security Council.* New York: St. Martin's Press.

Sachs, Jeffrey, and Andrew Warner. 1995. *Economic Reform and the Process of Global Integration.* Brookings Papers on Economic Activity 1: 1–118.

Schiff, Maurice, and L. Alan Winters. 2003. *Regional Integration and Development.* Washington, DC: World Bank and Oxford University Press.

Schott, Jeffrey J., and Jayashree Watal. 2000. Decision Making in the WTO. In *The WTO after Seattle,* ed. Jeffrey J. Schott. Washington, DC: Institute of International Economics. www.iie.com/publications/pb/pb00-2.htm

Schwartzberg, Joseph E. 2003. Entitlement Quotients as a Vehicle for United Nations Reform. *Global Governance* 9: 81–114.

———. 2004. Revitalizing the United Nations: Reform Through Weighted Voting. New York and The Hague: Institute for Global Policy, World Federalist Movement.   www.globalpolicy.org/security/reform/cluster1/2004/ schwartzberg_weighted_voting.pdf

Sen, Amartya. 1999. *Development as Freedom*. New York: Alfred A. Knopf.

Shiller, Robert J. 2000. *Irrational Exuberance*. New York: Broadway.

———. 2003. *The New Financial Order: Risk in the 21st Century*. Princeton, NJ: Princeton University Press.

Singer, H. W. 1995. An Historical Perspective. In *The UN and the Bretton Woods Institutions: New Challenges for the Twenty-First Century,* eds. Mahbub ul Haq, Richard Jolly, and Paul Streeten. New York: St. Martin's Press.

Singer, Peter. 2004. *One World: The Ethics of Globalization*. 2nd ed. New Haven, CT: Yale University Press.

Solana, Javier. 2003. The EU Security Strategy Implications for Europe's Role in a Changing World. EUHR, Berlin. www.foreignpolicy.org.tr/eng/eu/ solana_121103.htm

South Centre. 1996. *For a Strong and Democratic United Nations: a South Perspective on UN Reform*. Geneva: South Centre.

Soros, George. 2002. *On Globalization*. New York: Public Affairs.

Spencer, Christopher. 2004. Global Issues of the Twenty-First Century and United Nations Challenges. www.global-challenges.org/index.html (accessed September 4).

Stern, Jessica. 2003. *Terror in the Name of God*. New York: Harper Collins.

Stern, Nicholas. 2002. *A Strategy for Development*. Washington, DC: World Bank.

Stiglitz, Joseph. 2001. *Globalization and Its Discontents*. New York: W.W. Norton & Company.

———. 2003. *The Roaring Nineties: A New History of the World's Most Prosperous Decade*. New York: W.W. Norton & Company.

Stiglitz, Joseph A., Andrew Charlton, and the Initiative for Policy Dialogue. 2004. The Development Round of Trade Negotiations in the Aftermath of Cancun. Report prepared for the Commonwealth Secretariat. www.thecommonwealth. org/shared_asp_files/uploadedfiles/{F1997C23-BC54-44D0-8E66-7D1166FC 9937}_ StiglitzPaperComsec.pdf

Stockholm Initiative on Global Security and Governance. 1991. *Common Responsibility in the 1990's*. Stockholm Initiative Report. Stockholm: PMO.

Stockholm International Peace Research Institute (SIPRI). 2003. *SIPRI Yearbook 2003: Armaments, Disarmament And International Security*. Oxford: Oxford University Press.

Stolper, Wolfgang, and Paul A. Samuelson. 1941. Protection and Real Wages. *Review of Economic Studies* 9, no. 1 (November): 58–73.

Strauss-Kahn, Dominique. 2000. *La Flamme et la Cendre*. Paris: Grasset.

Straw, Jack. 2004. By Invitation: Charlemagne Steps Aside to Let Britain's Foreign Secretary Reply to Our Leader on the European Union Constitution. *The Economist*, July 10.

Talbott, Strobe. 2001. The Other Evil: The War on Terrorism Won't Succeed without a War on Poverty. *Foreign Policy* no.127 (November/December): 75–76.

———. 2003. War in Iraq, Revolution in America. *International Affairs* 79, no. 7: 1037–44.

Tanzi, Vito, and Ludger Schuknecht. 2000. *Public Spending in the 20th Century: A Global Perspective*. Cambridge: Cambridge University Press.

Thyssen, Fritz. 1941. *I Paid Hitler*. New York and Toronto: Farrar & Rinehart.

Truman, Edwin M. 2002. *Debt Restructuring: Evolution or Revolution?* Brookings Papers on Economic Activity 1: 341–46.

Ulagay, Osman. 2001. *Küreselleşme Korkusu*. Istanbul: Timaş Yayınları.

United Nations Conference on Trade and Development (UNCTAD). 2002. *The Least Developed Countries Report 2002: Escaping the Poverty Trap*. Geneva: UNCTAD. www.unctad.org/en/docs/ldc2002_en.pdf

US Commission on Improving the Effectiveness of the United Nations. 1993. *Defining Purpose: The UN and the Health of Nations*. Washington, DC: US Commission on Improving the Effectiveness of the United Nations.

Van Houten, Leo. 2002. *Governance of the IMF: Decision Making, Institutional Oversight, Transparency, and Accountability*. IMF Pamphlet Series no. 53. Washington, DC: International Monetary Fund.

Viotti, Paul R., and Mark V. Kauppi. 1999. *International Relations Theory: Realism, Pluralism, Globalism, and Beyond*. Boston: Allyn and Bacon.

Von Hayek, Friedrich A. 1994. *The Road to Serfdom*. 50th anniv. ed. Chicago: University of Chicago Press.

Von Mises, Ludwig. 1949. *Human Action: A Treatise on Economics*. New Haven, CT: Yale University Press.

Williamson, John. 1990. What Washington Means by Policy Reform. In *Latin American Adjustment: How Much Has Happened?* ed. John Williamson. Washington, DC: Institute for International Economics.

———. 2000. What Should the World Bank Think About the Washington Consensus? *World Bank Research Observer* 15, no. 2 (August).

Wilson, Peter. 2004. Mercosur Accepts Mexico, Venezuela as Associates. July 9, Reuters. http://quote.bloomberg.com/apps/news?pid=10000086&sid=a1uJs1lmPDjk&refer=latin_america

Wolf, Martin. 2004. *Why Globalization Works*. New Haven, CT: Yale University Press.

Woods, Ngaire, ed. 2000. *The Political Economy of Globalization*. New York: Palgrave Macmillan.

Woods, Ngaire. 2001. International Political Economy in an Age of Globalization. In *The Globalization of World Politics*, eds. John Baylis and Steve Smith. Oxford: Oxford University Press.

———. 2003. The United States and the International Financial Institutions: Power and Influence within the World Bank and the IMF. In *US Hegemony and International Organizations,* eds. Rosemary Foot, Neil MacFarlane, and Michael Mastanduno. Oxford: Oxford University Press.

Woods, Ngaire, and Amrita Narlikar. 2001. Governance and the Limits of Accountability: The WTO, the IMF and the World Bank. *International Social Science Journal* no. 170.

World Bank. 2000. *World Development Report 2000/2001: Attacking Poverty.* Washington, DC: World Bank.

———. 2001a. *Global Economic Prospects and the Developing Countries.* Washington, DC: World Bank.

———. 2001b. Global Development Finance. www.worldbank.org/prospects/gdf2001/

———. 2002. *Global Economic Prospects and the Developing Countries 2002: Making Trade Work for the World's Poor.* Washington, DC: World Bank.

———. 2003. *World Development Indicators (WDI) 2003, CD-ROM.* Washington, DC: World Bank.

———. 2004. *Global Monitoring Report 2004: Policies and Actions for Achieving the Millennium Development Goals and Related Outcomes.* Washington, DC: World Bank

———. 2004. *Global Development Finance 2004: Harnessing Cyclical Gains for Development.* Washington, DC: World Bank.

———. 2004. *Global Economic Prospects 2004: Realizing the Development Promise of the Doha Round.* Washington, DC: World Bank.

———. 2005. *Global Economic Prospects 2005: Trade, Regionalism, and Development.* Washington, DC: World Bank.

World Commission on the Social Dimension of Globalization. 2004. *A Fair Globalization: Creating Opportunities for All.* Geneva: International Labor Organization.

World Trade Organization (WTO). 2003. *Understanding the WTO.* 3rd ed. Geneva: World Trade Organization.

Zahler, Roberto. 2004. How Can Emerging Market Economies Deal with Capital Flows Volatility? An International Perspective. Paper prepared for the 18th APEC Finance Ministers' Technical Working Group Meeting, Arica, Chile (June 23–25, 2004). Photocopy.

Zartman, William. 1995. Introduction: Posing the Problem of State Collapse. In *Collapsed States: The Disintegration and Restoration of Legitimate Authority,* ed. William Zartman. Boulder, CO: Lynne Rienner.

Zedillo Report. 2001. *Report of the High-Level Panel on Financing for Development*. New York: United Nations. www.un.org/reports/financing/.

Ziegler, Jean. 2003. *Die neuen Herrscher der Welt und ihre globalen Widersacher*. München: Bertelsmann.

Index